# HOT PROTESTANTS

# HOT
# PROTESTANTS
## A History of Puritanism
## in England and America

Michael P. Winship

YALE UNIVERSITY PRESS
NEW HAVEN AND LONDON

Published with assistance from the foundation established in memory of Oliver Baty Cunningham of the Class of 1917, Yale College.

For information about this and other Yale University Press publications, please contact:
U.S. Office: sales.press@yale.edu        yalebooks.com
Europe Office: sales@yaleup.co.uk        yalebooks.co.uk

Set in Minion Pro by IDSUK (DataConnection) Ltd
Printed in the United States of America

Library of Congress Control Number: 2018954340

ISBN 978-0-300-12628-0

A catalogue record for this book is available from the British Library.

10 9 8 7 6 5 4 3 2 1

For Peter Lake

# CONTENTS

List of Illustrations                                            ix

Acknowledgments                                                 xii

A Note on the Text                                              xiv

Introduction                                                      1

### PART I RISE AND RETREAT, c. 1540–c. 1630

1   The Seeds of Puritanism                                       9

2   Proto-Puritans in Exile                                      17

3   The Birth Pangs of Puritan England                           26

4   The Elizabethan Puritan Political Movement                   37

5   The Puritan Path to Heaven                                   50

6   Taming Puritanism                                            59

7   The Lure of the Atlantic                                     71

### PART II REFORMATIONS, c. 1630–c. 1660

8   John Cotton Comes to Massachusetts                           85

9   Protestant Reformation and Counter-Reformation in            91
    the 1630s

10  A Miraculous Year Goes Bad                                  114

11  The Wobbly Rise and Precipitous Collapse of Presbyterian    130
    England

12  Shaking out Antichrist in the 1650s                          145
13  Consolidating Reformation in New England                     165
14  Old England's Corruptions Come to New England                178
15  Waban's Reformation                                          193


PART III  TWILIGHT, *c.* 1660–*c.* 1689

16  English Puritanism under Persecution                         203
17  English Puritanism Goes Public Again                         218
18  Religious Pluralism Comes to Puritan New England             233
19  New England's Reformations Come of Age                       241
20  New England's Puritan Autonomy Ends                          251


PART IV  ENDINGS, 1689–1690s

21  Hopes Raised and Dashed                                      265
22  The Final Parting of the Ways for English Puritans           268
23  A Godly Massacre of the Innocents in Post-Puritan            280
    Massachusetts


*Glossary*                                                       293
*Endnotes*                                                       296
*Index*                                                          340

# ILLUSTRATIONS

1. John Hooper being burnt at the stake, illustration from a 16th-century edition of John Foxe, *Actes and Monuments*. © Trustees of the British Museum, MN 1877, 0512.871.

2. Title page detail, John Foxe, *Actes and Monuments* (London, 1563). RB 59840, the Huntington Library, San Marino, California.

3. King Edward VI and the pope, unknown artist, *c*. 1575. National Portrait Gallery, London, NPG 4165.

4. John Dod, unknown artist after engraving, mid-17th century. National Portrait Gallery, London, NPG D2144.

5. Cope funerary monument, St. Peter's Church, Hanwell, Oxfordshire. Photograph by Michael P. Winship.

6. Illustration from Isaac Ambrose, *Prima and Ultima* (London, 1640), p. 1. © Trustees of the British Museum, MN 867, 1012.484.

7. Pulpit, St. Botolph's Church, Boston, Lincolnshire. Photograph by Michael P. Winship.

8. Statue of St. Botolph, St. Botolph's Church, Boston, Lincolnshire. Photograph by Ernest A. Napier.

9. John Winthrop, unknown artist, 17th century. Courtesy of the American Antiquarian Society.

10. Title page, *A True Relation of a Barbarous and most Cruell Murther* (London, 1633). By permission of the Folger Shakespeare Library.

11. Detail from John Vicars, *A Sight of ye Trans-actions of these Latter Yeares* (London, 1646), p. 7. RB 148140, the Huntington Library, San Marino, California.

12. Title page, Thomas Brightman, *The Revelation of St. John* (London, 1644). © Trustees of the British Museum, MN Q5.625.

13. Frontispiece, T. C., *A Glasse for the Times* (London, 1648). RB 633433, the Huntington Library, San Marino, California.

14. An engraving of Christopher Love. National Portrait Gallery, London, NPG D42602.

15. Title page, *The Whole Booke of Psalmes* (Cambridge, MA, 1640). Courtesy of the John Carter Brown Library at Brown University.

16. Signatures or marks of leading Natick Praying Indian men. Guildhall Library MS 7939, fo. 29r, London Metropolitan Archives, with permission of the New England Company. Photograph by Michael P. Winship.

17. Detail from *Divine Examples of God's Severe Judgments upon Sabbath-breakers* (London, 1671). Yale Center for British Art, Rare Books and Manuscripts, Folio B 2011 8, Yale University.

18. Frontispiece, John Bunyan, *The Pilgrim's Progress* (London, 1679). Pictorial Press Ltd / Alamy Stock Photo.

19. Frontispiece detail, Christopher Ness, *The Signs of the Times* (London, 1681). Beinecke Library, Yale University.

20. Frontispiece, J. Nalson, *An Impartial Collection* (London, 1682). © Trustees of the British Museum, MN 1868, 0808.3298.

21. Increase Mather by John van der Spriett, *c.* 1688. Courtesy of the Massachusetts Historical Society.

22. Frontispiece, Richard Baxter, *Reasons of the Christian Religion* (London, 1667). © Trustees of the British Museum, MN 1868, 0328.638.

23. Title page, Cotton Mather, *The Wonders of the Invisible World* (Boston, 1693). RB 18069, the Huntington Library, San Marino, California.

24. Northeastern rear elevation, Old Ship Church, 88 Main Street, Hingham, Plymouth County, MA. HABS MASS, 12-HING, 5–20. Library of Congress Prints and Photographs Division.

# ACKNOWLEDGMENTS

As a Cornell University graduate student, it was my great good fortune to start my academic exploration of puritanism with one of its scholarly masters, Peter Lake, then a visiting professor at Cornell. I could not have found better assistance for that exploration than Peter's steady encouragement, pugnacious enthusiasm, deep knowledge, and boundless intellectual energy, curiosity, and generosity. Thirty years later, I'm still learning from Peter, and it is with heartfelt appreciation that I dedicate this book to him.

Peter read the whole manuscript, as did Frank Bremer, Peter Hoffer, Evan Haefeli, and two anonymous readers for Yale University Press, along with Eleanor Winship and Susan McMichaels, who made heroic efforts to help me see the book through the eyes of general readers. Elliot Vernon and Dan Mandell read sections. I thank them all for their extremely helpful suggestions, comments, and catching of errors. All remaining flaws and mistakes, large and small, are entirely my responsibility.

Ideas for portions of this book that were tried out at Vanderbilt University and Queen's University Belfast evolved into essays in the *Historical Journal* and in *Puritans and Catholics in the Transatlantic World, 1600–1800*, edited by Crawford Gribben and Scott Spurlock. Ideas for the book were also tried out at Columbia University's University Seminar "Religion in America." I thank the Schoff Fund at the University Seminars at Columbia University for assistance in publication of *Hot Protestants*.

I was helped along the way by archivists at the British Library, Dr. Williams's Library, the American Antiquarian Society, the Massachusetts

State Archives, the London Metropolitan Archives, Pilgrim Hall Museum Archives, and the Historical Society of Pennsylvania, as well as by the inter-library loan staff at the University of Georgia.

Ken Fincham and Richard Cust helped with hunting down images. Patrick Curry provided a much appreciated home away from home in London.

A special thanks to Heather McCallum, then publisher and now managing director at Yale University Press, for commissioning *Hot Protestants*, and for her patience as the annual email messages piled up in which I assured her that the manuscript really would get finished. Thanks as well to Yale's efficient Clarissa Sutherland, Marika Lysandrou, and Rachael Lonsdale, along with Jacob Blandy for his sharp-eyed, thoughtful copy-editing.

# A NOTE ON THE TEXT

Early modern spelling and grammar have been modernized. All dates are given according to the Julian calendar, but the year is assumed to start on January 1.

# INTRODUCTION

"The hotter sort of Protestants are called Puritans."

Perceval Wiburn, 1581

*Hot Protestants* is an introduction to puritanism's rich, dense, tumultuous history, beginning in England in the 1540s and ending on both sides of the Atlantic around 1690. During that span of time, puritans executed a king, helped remove another one, founded a short-lived republic in England, and established quasi-republics in New England. Coming from all ranks of society, puritans reshaped England's religious culture, destroyed much of its great medieval artistic legacy, wrote creeds and catechisms with worldwide impact, and created a lasting body of religious literature.

The term "puritan" first emerged in England in the 1560s as an insult thrown at ministers and laypeople who refused to conform to Church of England requirements that fell short of their high Protestant standards. Before long, the insult was being thrown not only at these law-breaking nonconformists, but at people who admired and worked with them and practiced the strict, activist piety they promoted. Anti-puritans who aggressively expanded this insult's range often acted in the fervent belief that puritanism threatened the foundations of church and state and that ripping it out of the Church of England required digging an ever wider, deeper hole around it.

In their own eyes, however, puritans were exemplary Englishmen and women. They were the most faithful, most aggressively intolerant defenders of England's fledgling Protestantism, as well as its most zealous anti-Catholics at a time when Catholic countries were bloodily contesting the boundaries of the emergent Protestant Reformation. They were the most determined seekers of salvation and the most committed activists for the moral and spiritual reformation necessary to keep God's wrath off England for its many sins and for its failure to raise itself to the pristine standards of the Bible. When puritans feared that God's wrath could be held off no longer, some of them crossed the Atlantic to create their own societies.

Puritans met with fierce opposition, which did not surprise them. God had predestined the mass of people to hell, and the ungodly were inevitably implacable enemies of the godly. Opposition only proved the righteousness of the puritans' cause. If puritans' neighbors were not initially hostile, they could easily become so after puritans started trying to force their campaign against sins like drunkenness, dancing, theaters, Christmas, fornication, maypoles, and Sunday recreations upon them. Explained one puritan gentleman bluntly to the archbishop of Canterbury when the latter rebuked puritans for their disruptions, "Christ said that he came not into the world to send peace, but the sword."[1]

"Wheresoever Christ cometh," reiterated the famed puritan preacher Richard Sibbes, "he breedeth division." The conflict Sibbes was speaking of here, however, was not outward and social. It took place on the other great field of struggle against sin for puritans: their own souls. The true path of the soul's salvation had just been mapped out by John Calvin and other continental Protestants, liberating those who followed it from the Catholic Church's deceitful byways that led only to hell. Puritans knew that following this arduous Calvinist path meant a long stormy contest with sin, Satan, and doubt before they could feel assurance that they were among the precious few whom God had predestined for salvation. John Bunyan in the midst of that contest feared that the church towers of Bedfordshire were collapsing on him and heard a voice from heaven warning him of his sins; devils with flaming eyes likes saucers snatched at the despairing future minister John Rogers to drag him to hell; the famously severe minister William Perkins ominously cried out "mercy" repeatedly on his deathbed.[2]

Victory in this soul conflict, although far from guaranteed, could be triumphant. Massachusetts's future governor John Winthrop shed tears of joy as he was flooded with heavenly reassurance that he would spend eternity with Christ in heaven, while the poet Anne Bradstreet wrote of blissfully being called away by Christ the bridegroom in her meditations. An admirer reported that the English housewife Briget Cooke was often so filled with the joy of the spirit that she would cry out "Oh my joy, oh my joy."[3]

The central institution for guidance in these great puritan struggles with outward and inward sin was, or should have been, the Church of England. Each Sunday, all the English were required to gather in its nine thousand parish churches for worship, the sacraments, and sermons. Sometimes they would assemble there for services of prayer and fasting after God inflicted plague, famine, and other disasters on England in response to the country's sins, or for services of thanksgiving after divine aid. Sometimes they might find a sinner before them being disciplined, standing in a white sheet and asking forgiveness for adultery, drunkenness, or a host of other moral offenses after being convicted in a church court.

Puritans supported the Church of England's religious tasks, as well as its religious monopoly. God had only one truth, and England should have only one monarch and one church that governed the country together in their different spheres. The Reformation had been about religious liberty only insofar as that meant the liberty to follow God's law correctly, as outlined in the Bible. For puritans, the problem with the Church of England was that it was following God's law only erratically, which meant, in their eyes, that it did none of its tasks well. It lagged far behind the continental Reformed churches in purging itself of the government, worship, and the inadequate discipline of its Catholic past. Ever-growing hostility toward puritanism from authorities in church and state eventually pushed some puritans to take the drastic step of immigrating to New England.

The self-governing colonies puritans created in New England were largely free of puritanism's enemies and the other obstacles that had defined and hindered puritanism in England. There was no significant mass of ungodly people to ridicule and resent them and to thwart their efforts to repress sin; there were no lordly Church of England bishops to rule over their churches like autocrats and block their reforms; and the kings and queens who saw puritans as a democratic threat to monarchy were a relatively safe 3,000 miles away. In New England, puritans could finish the business of puritanism: fashioning governments and properly reformed Calvinist church establishments that would supervise a unified Christian community and see to it that God's elect were shepherded to heaven (some scholars expand the use of the term "puritanism" further than this[4]).

For the colonists, however, untangling themselves from their English puritan past proved a messy, protracted process. They could not seal themselves off hermetically from the much larger English puritan movement and its ongoing trials and tribulations, nor could they free themselves from the old puritan problem of hostile attention from the English government.

The novel church establishment they created, called Congregationalism, had a great many unresolved puritan conflicts built into it that required slow and painful sorting out.

Congregationalism's conflicts spilled back into England. There, only relatively small numbers of puritans adopted Congregationalism. They did so, however, with the unshakable conviction that it was exactly what God intended for his churches, while other puritans no less intensely opposed it. The wound Congregationalism created in English puritanism would never heal, and it helped ensure that puritan efforts to bring about reformation in England failed.

*Hot Protestants* tells the story of puritanism beginning with the sixteenth- and early seventeenth-century nonconformists, moving to the mid-seventeenth-century puritan reformations in England and New England, followed by the twilight of this badly battered movement during the late seventeenth century, and ending with puritanism's political demise on both sides of the Atlantic after 1688. By design, *Hot Protestants* is relatively short, and it unfolds this story largely through exemplary episodes, individuals, and experiences.

Some of these episodes and experiences were personal, to the limited extent that puritanism could ever be simply personal: a woman, for example, recording God's harsh but, as she finally concluded, merciful interventions in her life and then writing her observations up in a manuscript for the guidance of her family; another woman deciding that her responsibilities to God, to reformation, and to her posterity called on her to break away from her parish church and join a controversial Congregational church, thereby plunging herself into a maelstrom of local and national politics; a Native American realizing, thanks to the arrival of the English, that he had been praying unwittingly to the devil all his life, and with that realization, taking the first step on a journey that would lead to the reformation of his own culture.

Some of those episodes and experiences were collective and widely transformative: an alliance of gentlemen and ministers, for example, implanting and enlivening a controversial puritan subculture in a freshly Protestant English county, against heavy pushback; a fierce struggle in Massachusetts as to whether an effort to slightly roll back the exclusiveness of the colony's churches represented a better understanding of the mind of Christ or a massive plot to impose tyranny on those churches; puritans on both sides of the Atlantic grappling repeatedly with a daunting question throughout this period: how to respond when your monarch or other authorities make a demand of you that you believe violates the laws of England and/or God—with defiance, compliance, subterfuge, martyrdom, or even rebellion? It should be noted that since *Hot Protestants* is a history of puritanism, the many things puritans did outside their particular religious convictions do not fall within its scope.

*Hot Protestants'* twenty-three chapters are divided into four sections. Part I, "Rise and Retreat, *c.* 1540–*c.* 1630," traces puritanism's emergence, expansion, and eventual stalemating in England in the sixteenth and early seventeenth centuries. Chapter 1 covers the first stirrings in the 1540s of the religious discontent that would later be called puritanism, as the Church of England started to shed its old Catholic skin and haltingly take on a Protestant form. Chapter 2 discusses the enduring projects launched by proto-puritans during the brief reign of the Catholic Queen Mary (1553–58) when they chose exile on the continent over burning at the stake. Chapter 3 follows the spread of puritanism and its distinctive, disruptive social practices across England during Protestant Queen Elizabeth's reign (1558–1603). Chapter 4 is about failed national puritan campaigns during that reign, sometimes legal, sometimes not, to change the laws that hindered church reformation. Chapter 5 delves into one of puritanism's most long-lasting religious contributions, its stern, demanding practical divinity that offered guidance about staying on the narrow path to heaven and following the duties God expected of his people while on earth. Chapter 6 is about the different ways puritans coped and adjusted in the early seventeenth century after their drive for church reformation was dead in the water. One way to cope with these changes was to cross the Atlantic, and Chapter 7 discusses the beginning of this movement in the 1620s.

Part II, "Reformations, *c.* 1630–*c.* 1660," covers the middle of the seventeenth century, when puritans on both sides of the Atlantic finally had the opportunity to put their stamp on churches, governments, and societies. Chapter 8 discusses Massachusetts's ambitious, fledgling reformation in the 1630s with its immediately controversial Congregational churches. Chapter 9 is, in part, about the complicated local and transatlantic puritan crosscurrents and tensions triggered by Massachusetts's reformation, and, in part, about the ambitious English effort to entirely purge the Church of England of puritanism. Chapter 10 tells how in the 1640s, in the midst of Parliament's successful puritan-led war against King Charles I, moderate English puritans coalesced around Presbyterianism for the reformed Church of England. As described in Chapter 11, in the late 1640s an uneasy coalition of puritan Congregationalists and emergent Protestant sects supported Parliament's now out-of-control army while it thwarted the Presbyterians, purged Parliament, executed the king, and set up a republic. Chapter 12 is about England's creative, cacophonous 1650s, when this unpopular coalition tried and failed to provide England with a stable government, and Congregationalists and Presbyterians struggled to work out a rapprochement. During those two decades in New England, the puritan colonies were solidifying their reformations and coping with the various local and transatlantic challenges being hurled at them in this turbulent period, as covered in Chapters 13 and 14. The subject of Chapter 15 is reformation among New England Native Americans.

Part III, "Twilight, *c.* 1660–*c.* 1689," follows embattled puritans on both sides of the Atlantic facing a rapidly changing and ever-more religiously pluralistic English world. Chapter 16 is about how in the 1660s vengeful anti-puritans launched an unprecedentedly severe but unsuccessful effort to drive puritanism out of the Church of England and crush the wide varieties of Protestant worship that had recently sprung up outside it, and about how puritans coped with this effort. Chapter 17 is about the dizzying alterations in English puritan fortunes in the 1670s and 1680s, culminating in the possibility that puritans would finally get many of the reforms they had been seeking for over a century. Chapter 18 describes how New England puritans grudgingly groped their way into limited tolerance of religious diversity in the 1660s and 1670s. Chapter 19 is about the catastrophe-driven maturation of New England's Native American and English reformations. Chapter 20 looks at how the English government forcefully turned its hostile attention on Massachusetts in the 1680s, bringing the autonomy of this last bastion of puritanism to an end.

Part IV, "Endings, *c.* 1660–*c.* 1689," brings *Hot Protestants* to a close in three chapters. Chapter 21 is about how with a new, sympathetic king on the throne in 1689, puritan hopes for realizing their earlier ambitions rose on both sides of the Atlantic, and how these hopes came quickly crashing down for good. Chapters 22 and 23 look at two events in the immediate aftermath of this failure, the first, an unsuccessful effort by English Congregationalists and Presbyterians to finally reunite, and the second, the Salem witch trials, a grim consequence of the disintegration of American puritanism.

## Part I

# RISE AND RETREAT, c. 1540–c. 1630

# CHAPTER 1

# THE SEEDS OF PURITANISM

In late 1535, 300-year-old Cleeve Abbey's seventeen Cistercian monks received an emissary of King Henry VIII, the lawyer John Tregonwell. Like the rest of the monks, John Hooper, an Oxford University graduate in his late thirties, must have wondered why Tregonwell was really there. Was it because Tregonwell's master the king was truly concerned about the spiritual health of the monastery? Or did the king have designs on the monastery's wealth? Perhaps the king's emissary had come to sniff out recalcitrant monks who refused to accept that Henry, not Pope Paul III, was now by act of Parliament legally the head of the Church of England. Hooper and the other monks also probably wondered if their visitor was still sound in his ancestral faith. Or had he joined the Protestant heretics who were growing increasingly brazen as Henry flaunted his new independence from the pope? If Tregonwell had gone all the way over to Protestantism, he would be inwardly scoffing at the prayers the monks poured out to shorten the stay of the dead in purgatory, while scorning the pilgrims who flocked to Cleve Abbey's miraculous statue of the Virgin Mary as deluded idol worshipers.[1]

Henry left Cleve Abbey alone, but only for a year. In 1536, a new royal emissary, Thomas Arundell, arrived to close the monastery for good, a doom that would soon befall all of England's monasteries and nunneries. Henry himself had no great religious objections to them (nor, probably, did Arundell), but he wanted their wealth. Cleve Abbey was seized, its church torn down, its abbot pensioned off, and Hooper and the rest of the monks expelled to fend for themselves. Hooper joined Arundell to serve as steward over his household affairs.[2] Hooper could scarcely have imagined that in a few years he himself was to become a committed Protestant, let alone that the conflicts he was to generate in his new-found haste to purge England of its Catholic past would mark the beginning of what would be called puritanism.

John Hooper's conversion to Protestantism came around 1540 when he got hold of two treatises written by Swiss Protestants. Hooper studied them "night and day," he later recalled, with "an almost superstitious diligence." The books' arguments made Hooper realize that by "following the evil ways of my forefathers" he had been guilty of the damnable sins of idolatry and blasphemy. But now, at last, thanks to those books, he "rightly understood what God was."[3]

Protestants were at the time still only a small minority in England, concentrated in London and its surrounding counties. It was not entirely safe to be one, for King Henry remained uncertain how far he wanted to steer his newly liberated Church of England away from Catholicism. He whipsawed back and forth between his Protestant advisors and his religiously traditionalist ones, who clung to their inherited Catholic practices and beliefs. In the early 1540s, traditionalists were in the saddle; Protestants were being burned; and Henry's government was trying futilely to force the Protestant genie of lay Bible reading back into its bottle. Hooper's traditionalist master, Arundell, tipped off Stephen Gardiner, the Protestant-hating bishop of Winchester, about Hooper's conversion to Protestantism. For his own safety, Hooper started periodically retreating to the continent while supporting himself as a cloth merchant. In 1547, he moved to Zurich in Switzerland, a city of about six thousand people where the Swiss Reformation had begun in the early 1520s.[4]

The Reformation had gone through an eventful three decades since Martin Luther in Wittenberg, Germany and Huldrych Zwingli in Zurich had begun it by pushing their criticism of the Catholic Church to the point of breaking away from it. The relationship between the followers of Luther, the Lutherans, and the Swiss Reformed churches like Zwingli's was tense to start with and had grown steadily worse. Lutherans and the Swiss Reformed were starting to disagree about predestination: the Lutherans lacked the Reformed churches' hostility to sacred images and other Catholic survivals; they were less intensely focused on obedience to God's biblical laws; and, unlike the Swiss Reformed, they insisted that Christ was objectively present at celebrations of the Lord's Supper. By the 1540s, Lutheran Protestants and

Reformed Protestants could work themselves into a hatred of each other only slightly less intense than their shared hatred of Catholics.[5]

For Hooper, and for many English Protestants then and later, the Swiss Reformed churches had recovered Christian worship in its true biblical purity and simplicity. The churches of Zurich had been entirely liberated from the idolatrous statues, stained glass, and pictures that still befouled the English parish churches. Ministers wore simple black gowns, not the colorful Catholic vestments still in use in England. Choral polyphony, which buried the sense of its often non-biblical words under glorious clashes of massed melodic lines, was banned. Zurich's plain services of prayer and preaching had no connection to the older, elaborate Catholic liturgies.[6]

In 1547, while Hooper was settling into Zurich, Henry died. His funeral rites remained firmly in the traditional vein: elaborate masses and ceremonies spread over five days to speed the departed king's soul through its otherworldly journey. "Of your charity pray for the soul of the high and most mighty prince, our late sovereign lord and king Henry VIII," cried the king's chief herald at each of these gatherings to the assembled noble and royal household mourners.[7] For English Protestants like Hooper, however, the prayers the kingdom showered upon Henry's soul were pointless. Christ had made complete satisfaction on the cross for the sins of those whom God had predestined for heaven, and Henry had gone immediately to wherever he was going to spend eternity, be it heaven or hell (for Protestants, there was no purgatory). In neither location could he or any other soul, not even the Virgin Mary, respond to or be affected by the prayers of the living.

Henry left behind him a nine-year-old son and successor to the throne, Edward VI. Unlike his father, the precocious boy was serious about his Protestantism. Protestants took control of the Privy Council, the king's advisory and administrative board. Edward's Protestant councilors started to systematically uproot England's remaining Catholic practices. They banned religious processions; stripped priests of their otherworldly nature by allowing them to abandon celibacy and marry; and confiscated the sometimes enormous endowments of the more than four thousand foundations that organized prayers and masses for the dead. They commenced obliterating what they took to be the idolatrous images that crammed the churches. Wall paintings were whitewashed, and often replaced by Bible texts in English; statues were torn down or, if too difficult to be removed, had their heads smashed; and stained-glass windows illustrating biblical stories were destroyed and replaced with clear glass (although much more hesitantly—replacement glass was expensive and the English climate was then, as now, challenging). The enormous crucifixions that conventionally towered on platforms in the middle of churches were torn down and replaced by the Royal Arms; where God had been, the king now was.[8]

In 1549 king and Parliament approved a new directory of worship, the Book of Common Prayer, which substituted English-language Protestant services across the ritual year for the traditional Catholic Latin ones. In the new prayer book, the Latin Mass, the hitherto off-limits heart of Catholic worship, was obliterated and replaced with a communion service for celebrating the Lord's Supper. Now the clergyman faced his congregation rather than keeping his back turned to them, spoke in English, not Latin, and reminded the laity of Christ's crucifixion by offering them bread and wine. What he emphatically did not do, unlike Catholic priests at the Mass, was bring about a repeat of Christ's sacrificial death for humanity's sins, for Christ offered himself as a sacrifice only once, on the cross. To drive that once-and-for-all point home, reformers smashed the stone altars on which priests had claimed to re-enact Christ's death and replaced them with simple wooden communion tables. Advanced Protestant clergymen even refused to call themselves priests because they performed no sacrifice. They accepted only the titles of minister and preacher.[9]

The new communion service made it clear that, unlike in the Mass, Christ was physically absent in the new Lord's Supper. There would be no miraculous transubstantiation of bread and wine into his body and blood. Christ's presence now was a mystical one, intended only for the predestined saved among a congregation, real for them only in a spiritual way and only when they actually consumed the bread and wine. To ram home the point that the old Catholic Mass was finally dead and gone from England, the Book of Common Prayer discarded the Mass's spiritual and even magical highpoint, the priest's gesture of elevating the host (the bread) for all the congregation to see. England's religious traditionalists devoutly believed that merely to gaze upon the elevated host, Christ's real physical body, would wipe away all but the most heinous sins, prevent sudden death and blindness, and ensure a successful childbirth and good digestion.[10] Now when those traditionalists came to their parish churches, they did not even have the fig leaf of the elevation to allow them to pretend that they had not been exiled from their old, comforting religious universe.

The new services drew heavily on medieval Catholic models, and in places those models had not been entirely Protestantized. But these surface

Catholic continuities could not conceal the Book of Common Prayer's momentous changes. The introduction of the new prayer book kicked off a revolt in the southwest in 1549 that left close to five thousand people dead, along with smaller outbreaks elsewhere. The Edwardian Reformation was a work in progress, pushing a country where the majority of bishops, clergy, and laity were foot-dragging religious traditionalists in a radically new Protestant direction as quickly as seemed prudent.[11]

In 1549, Hooper's good friend the internationally famous Zurich theologian Heinrich Bullinger encouraged him to go back to England and assist in its reformation. Hooper returned with a wife, Anna, whose Catholic family had severed all ties with her because of her Protestant convictions, and their infant daughter. He quickly became a fiery, popular preacher in London. It was said that when he preached, the churches were packed to the doors with listeners who looked upon him as a prophet.[12]

In many ways Hooper embodied the spirit of what would soon be called puritanism. He possessed neither the mysterious celibacy nor the quasi-magical sacramental powers of Catholic priests. Hooper's authority as a minister came from his piety and learning, and, above all, from his ability to wrap himself in the divine authority of the Bible. Like later puritans, he saw himself as an heir to the Old Testament prophets, a messenger of the living and unchanging God, whose word and actions were as consistent and applicable in Tudor England as they had been millennia before in the Bible. In emulation of those Old Testament prophets, Hooper, like many continental Protestant ministers, wore a long beard; his countenance was so fierce that a man seeking spiritual consolation once knocked on his door only to go away on Hooper's opening it. Hooper's popularity grew to the point that he was invited to give a series of sermons to King Edward and his court in the winter of 1550. Edward at the age of twelve was already known as a note-taking enthusiast of the sermons of the most extreme Protestant preachers.[13]

Preaching to the court, Hooper denounced the sins of England, from the top of the social ladder to the bottom. He did not spare the sins of the Church of England, especially those that revolved around the incompleteness of its reformation. Hooper singled out two sins that would become staples of puritan criticism. The clergy still had to wear vestments, or Catholic robes and garments; but vestments, Hooper argued, should be returned to the pope and the devil, their rightful owners, along with candles, crosses, and altars. And the laity were still required to kneel like Catholics at the Lord's Supper; kneeling was a show of unbiblical idol worship, Hooper insisted, and it should be abolished.[14]

Hooper's indignation at these Catholic survivals was matched by his indignation at the justification more flexible Protestant clergy and bishops made for them, and would continue to make for well over a hundred years, as long as the puritan struggle for the Church of England continued. Catholic survivals like vestments and kneeling were not mentioned in the Bible, such clergymen acknowledged, but the Bible did not expressly forbid them. As long as the church did not give these requirements a spiritual significance, as the Catholics had done, they were neither good nor bad. They were "indifferent," arbitrary requirements of order—ministers had to wear something; people had to receive the bread and wine in some posture—and just as with other official regulations that the Bible neither commanded nor forbade, people could be compelled to follow them if the authorities saw fit.[15]

For Hooper, that argument for "indifference" was a sacrilegious defense of unacceptably go-slow reformation. Reformation should not "halt in any part," he urgently told Edward's court. Catholic survivals being kept as spiritually indifferent, he warned, would eventually be defended as spiritually necessary (time would thoroughly vindicate Hooper on that claim). By refusing to purge the Church of England of its Catholic practices, Edward's clergy had stolen God's honor and glory from him. They needed to make restitution to God for their theft by completing that purge, "or else doubtless their theft will bring them to damnation."[16]

"Favor Christ," Hooper exhorted his listeners, summarizing his message, rather "than Antichrist." Antichrist was a horrible figure prophesied, it was believed, in various books of the Bible, who tried to lure all Christians to damnation through his false path of salvation. Protestants had no doubt that Antichrist took the form of the pope, leader of the devil's false church that had been martyring the members of Christ's true church ever since Adam's wicked son Cain killed his good son Abel. For advanced Protestants like Hooper, it was a grave sin to keep the slightest remnant of Antichrist and his false church in their true churches.[17]

King Edward and his advisors were so impressed by Hooper's tongue lashing of their reformation that they offered him the bishopric of Gloucester. Hooper declined. The Zurichers had abandoned anything comparable to the English bishops. Where in the simple churches of the New Testament did you find a minister with the pomp and ceremony, multiple palaces, trains of servants and retainers, and sprawling dioceses of the English bishops? English bishops even sat in Parliament's House of Lords. A bishop, Hooper believed, should preside over no more than a single city; he should be a preacher; he should take for his own use only a small portion of his diocesan income and give the remainder to godly causes; and he should have no civil offices at all, for being a minister was a full-time job. The most important English bishop, Thomas Cranmer, archbishop of Canterbury, along with some other bishops, was reaching out to Protestant Switzerland. But Hooper worried that bishops like Cranmer had too much to lose in terms of position and power to transform themselves into the humble bishops of the New Testament and genuinely push for further reformation.[18]

The Privy Council pressed Hooper to accept their offer. Finally, on May 15, 1550, Hooper agreed to accept the bishopric, but only on certain conditions, one of which was that at his consecration ceremony he would not wear the still-required leftovers from Antichrist, the garments of Catholic bishops. The council at first went along with Hooper. Since these garments were "indifferent" and clearly offended a godly man like Hooper, he would not have to wear them if he did not wish to. Scrupulous Protestant ministers had been allowed sometimes to avoid wearing the required garments, but never such a prominent critic as Hooper.[19]

The other bishops, however, including Cranmer, pushed back fiercely against the council's decision. They looked forward to being rid of the Catholic vestments as much as Hooper, they claimed, but there was a legal issue involved. It was not up to them or Hooper to decide whether to obey the law. Legal change, they argued, had to be made with the consent of the whole kingdom through its representatives in Parliament. They undoubtedly had other reasons to resist Hooper. Converting a mostly unwilling nation to Protestantism was a delicate process and the last thing they needed was a new bishop heatedly attacking them for moving too slowly while successfully demonstrating to other impatient advanced Protestants that any religious law they disliked could be ignored. Since the garments were indifferent and the consequences of not wearing them serious, the bishops argued, Hooper should be required to wear them.[20]

The Privy Council was now persuaded by the bishops' arguments and ordered Hooper to obey. Friends in London's "stranger" church, a church for foreigners with much more advanced continental Protestant standards, egged Hooper on to defiance. A brief stint in prison and rumors that the bishops were going to have him executed convinced Hooper to back down. On March 8, 1551, Hooper was consecrated to the office of bishop humiliatingly clothed in Antichrist's livery, the Catholic scarlet-and-white bishop's robes and four-cornered hat. To add insult to injury he was also forced to wear them once while giving a sermon to the king and Privy Council, and he had to endure the disapproval of his continental friends for his cave-in.[21]

Puritans would try unsuccessfully to get rid of the vestments for the next 150 years. Hooper's defeat is often portrayed as the beginning of this failed struggle. But perhaps Hooper, after a cooling-off period, would not have seen his retreat as a defeat for reformation. He went on to embody the puritan ideal of a reforming bishop in the few years of life left to him, weeding out the worst clergymen in his diocese, educating clergy and laity alike in the gospel, appointing superintendents to help him manage the diocese, going on extensive preaching tours, looking after the poor, and, according to one visitor to his household, displaying "very little pomp or nothing at all."[22]

Hooper energetically enforced church discipline in the cumbersome diocesan church courts left over from the days of the Catholic Church, which he personally supervised and invigorated, overriding their often corrupt lay officials. Hooper also banned the practice of accepting money payments for sins; penitents instead were made to stand, bare footed and bare headed, dressed in white robes, in public places and churches confessing their sin: one John Griffith, for example, had to stand in Gloucester market for three Saturdays saying to passersby "I do this penance for my naughty living and for fornication."[23]

Once out in the traditionalist English heartland, where Protestantism had yet to make much impact, Hooper might have started to understand the logic of Archbishop Cranmer's go-gently approach to reform, especially as it became clear that Cranmer did not intend to stop reformation. Cranmer consulted Hooper on the 1552 revision of the Book of Common Prayer; that revision took the book much further in a Protestant direction than the 1549 version, and where it still fell short, more changes were probably in store. Word spread that it was only traditionalist opposition that held Cranmer back on this version, not his own intentions. Cranmer put Hooper on the committee that gently pushed the Catholic laws still governing the Church of England in a more Reformed direction: more social welfare, stricter, parish-based discipline, and the possibility of divorce. The bill failed in Parliament due to extraneous political quarrels, but it was sure to come back again. There was no reason for Hooper to think that England's reformation would not keep moving forward.[24]

No reason, that is, until everything that Hooper and other Protestants had built up during the reign of King Edward came crashing down on their heads.

# CHAPTER 2

# PROTO-PURITANS IN EXILE

In December 1552, King Edward showed the first symptoms of the illness, probably tuberculosis, that would kill him on July 6, 1553. Edward's thirty-seven-year-old half-sister Mary, a devout Catholic, came to the throne, determined to rip out England's shallowly rooted reformation. Her campaign against Protestantism included the public burning of John Hooper for heresy at Gloucester on February 9, 1555. His bungled execution before seven thousand people on a badly prepared, slowly burning pyre took forty-five minutes. Hooper repeated "Lord Jesus have mercy upon me. Lord Jesus receive my spirit" until his mouth was burned away. He beat his hands upon his breast until one of his arms fell off and the other cleaved to the iron chain that bound him to the stake. At least 280 Protestants, of all ranks and stations in life, including fifty-six women, chose the flames above Catholicism.[1]

Most Protestants, though, conformed to Catholicism, at least outwardly; the teenaged Protestant Princess Elizabeth, next in line to the throne, was one of them, as part of the maneuvers by which she managed—barely—to keep her head on her shoulders during Mary's brief reign (Mary would die childless in 1558). A few Protestant ministers continued to hold illegal services for those brave souls willing to attend them, while an underground Protestant church met in London throughout Mary's reign.[2]

Around a thousand Protestant men, women, and children chose to flee abroad. Those going into exile included four bishops, men connected with Oxford and Cambridge universities, over a hundred students, and artisans, including seven printers who would soon be publishing Protestant propaganda. There were many wealthy exiles, along with quiet supporters back in England, who provided charity to the few poor ones. A few women chose the authority of the Bible over the authority of men and took the brave step in this fiercely patriarchal society of leaving without their husbands. Most exiles moved in groups to crammed housing in already overfull Protestant cities in central Europe.[3] In their few years as exiles, they launched projects that would have a long-lasting effect on puritanism and on English Protestantism itself.

Some of these exiles found refuge in the German Lutheran city of Frankfurt. Among them was John Knox, a fiery Scottish reformer who had been active in England and had chafed at the slow pace of its reformation.[4] Knox, like other exiles, brooded over the urgent question of what horrible sin English Protestants could have committed that would provoke God to inflict upon their country a punishment as terrible as Queen Mary. Knox and other exiles in Frankfurt decided that the sin had been their sluggishness in purging English Protestantism of Catholicism and pushing it back to New Testament standards. Frankfurt's government had given the exiles the use of a church building and permission to start their own church. With this church Knox and his circle were determined not to repeat that earlier dreadful sin: their church was going to be a systematic example of what an English church reformed to New Testament purity should look like. This example, they hoped, would inspire other English exile churches and perhaps prompt them to move to Frankfurt and join forces.[5]

A major element of this remodeled church would be strict discipline that taught all its members how to "frame their wills, and doings, according to the law of God," as Knox's committee put it. Heavy doses of edifying sermons were a vital foundation for discipline, but the core disciplinary tool was ongoing supervision of behavior. For Knox's committee, that supervision would be everyone's business. All the members, male and female, were to be godly busy-bodies, continually "admonishing and instructing one another."[6]

When this informal discipline failed, members were to bring their concerns about each other to the church's governing body, a board of clerical and lay elders called the consistory (later called the presbytery in England). The consistory would not be appointed from above by a bishop; its members would be chosen with the consent of the male congregants. This type of government—Presbyterianism—laid out, it was believed, in the New Testament, was already being used with variations by some continental Reformed churches and by the handful of English exile churches.[7]

It would be the consistory's task to maintain constant disciplinary vigilance against anything "that might spot the Christian congregation." The elders would meet on Thursday evenings to examine the sins of members and, especially, their own sins. When other means of discipline had failed, they would excommunicate a sinning member from the church, but the whole church (meaning its male adult members) had to determine that heavy sanction, not just the elders.[8] Excommunication itself was a temporary form of shock treatment, hopefully, and only to be used when nothing else could waken sinners to their wickedness.

Worship for this church was to be strictly biblical, and communal psalm singing was to play a large role in it. Among the Old Testament's 150 psalms were psalms for expressing joy, desolation, repentance, thanksgiving, and praise. If you wanted to call down divine vengeance on your wicked enemies there were psalms for that too. To expand the expressive breadth of their worship, the Frankfurters worked on completing the translation of all the psalms into metrical English. Their Elizabethan offspring, the *Whole Book of Psalmes*, was to be wildly popular, going through 470 editions before the 1640s. Psalm singing became ubiquitous in Elizabethan England, as it did in all the other Reformed countries, spilling out of the churches into the streets, family life, social gatherings, and private devotionals.[9]

The Knox committee's plans for the Frankfurt church, however, came crashing down after the committee crossed a red line for many in the congregation. This it did by insisting that the Book of Common Prayer was entirely useless for true Bible-based worship and had to be abandoned. To take one flashpoint, the Book of Common Prayer's daily morning services closed with the ancient hymn *Te Deum*, a string of praises of God, translated into English. The *Te Deum* postdated the Bible by a few centuries, but the Bible nowhere said that God could never be praised in the future with original hymns. In that way, the hymn was "indifferent," neither specifically allowed nor forbidden by the Bible.

Like many later hardline puritans, Knox's circle did not believe that anything in worship could really be "indifferent." The *Te Deum*, to them, was at best a human creation using up worship time that could have been filled with divinely inspired songs like the psalms. But the hymn in fact had a past that left it spiritually toxic in the eyes of Knox and his fellow committee members. The arrangers of the Book of Common Prayer had lifted it directly from Catholic morning services, and that source alone put it off limits for Protestant use, regardless of its content. Its origins, charged Knox, made it "papistical" and in worship, Knox insisted, all true Christians had the duty to "separate ourselves from that idolatrous Babylon."[10]

Knox's opponents retorted that "indifferent" sections of the Book of Common Prayer like the *Te Deum* were piously uplifting, authorized by king and Parliament, and arranged by holy bishops who were awaiting death in English prisons, while English people were risking their lives by continuing to use them in their worship. What a demoralizing message their rejection in Frankfurt would have sent to England! It would have graphically affirmed what Knox was not ashamed to say in the pulpit: the book for which England's Protestants were willing to go to their deaths at the stake was "superstitious, impure, unclean, and unperfect."[11]

One member of the Frankfurt church, John Bale, an ex-monk and ex-Protestant bishop, vented his spleen against members like Knox and his circle in a two-page, handwritten screed. Those overzealous colleagues "fetche[d] Gods glory from Utopia, or from some other strange land," Bale huffed, and called themselves the "brethren of the purity." Bale riffed with angry contempt on their so-called "purity" throughout his fierce attack, making this Protestant-on-Protestant stream of abuse perhaps the earliest birth pang in the process from which the insult "puritan" would emerge a decade later.[12]

Probably with the connivance of angry church members like Bale, a large contingent of moderate English exiles arrived from Strasbourg in March 1555 and unilaterally reinstated a variation on Book of Common Prayer worship. To get Knox out of the way, they put it in the ears of the Frankfurt magistrates—correctly—that he had made treasonous remarks about the city's overlord, Charles V, the Holy Roman Emperor, whose world-spanning territories included South America, the Philippines, and much of Europe. On March 25, 1555, Knox hastily left the city to avoid execution. With Knox gone, the Frankfurt church settled into more moderate liturgical practices.[13]

Despite their defeat at Frankfurt, the efforts of Knox and these other proto-puritans had hardly been for nothing; they were to have a long, influential life. The committee's church guide was published a year later as *Forme of Prayers*. Knox would take the *Forme of Prayers* to Scotland, where it became the foundation for worship in the reformed Church of Scotland. *Forme of Prayers*, with its Bible-based worship and strict discipline, would be an inspiration to the most advanced English puritans. They would sometimes use it surreptitiously, and they repeatedly lobbied Parliament to replace the Book of Common Prayer with derivatives of it.[14]

Knox left Frankfurt for Geneva, Switzerland, 300 miles up the Rhine, along with most of his committee and other sympathetic church members. An exception was the ex-priest John Foxe. He traveled instead to Basel, Switzerland, to pursue and publish his own project, an account of the true church's martyrs, from the time of the apostles to the present day, who had been cruelly tortured and slain by the devil's false church. It is due to Foxe's assiduous hunting down of documents and witnesses to the English martyr-doms of the 1550s that so much is known about John Hooper's execution, as well as those of many other English Protestant martyrs. Once back in England, with the Protestant Queen Elizabeth now on the throne, Foxe expanded his work on the long history of Christ's church and its martyrs into a vividly illustrated, quietly puritan, and phenomenally influential English-language book longer than the Bible, *Actes and Monuments of these Latter and Perillous Days*. Foxe's often reprinted *Book of Martyrs*, as it was commonly called, became a required purchase for English parish churches, and its stories of heroic English Protestant martyrs and indelibly wicked Catholics flowed into English speaking Protestant culture as it spread across the globe over the next three centuries.[15]

In Geneva, fast becoming one of the leading centers of the Reformation, Knox and his circle were no less productive than Foxe was in Basel. For the past two decades, Geneva had been filling up with French Protestant refu-gees, led by the ex-lawyer, John Calvin, a brilliant, eloquent, extremely self-confident Bible expositor and Presbyterian, who had already had a large influence on the English Frankfurt church experiment. Calvin took for granted that a Christian government like Geneva's would work hand in hand with Presbyterianism's governing consistory, while the consistory would be completely independent from the government; so independent that it could excommunicate the ruler of a country.[16]

Geneva's government had been resisting giving the consistory so much power. The English arrived as Calvin's fourteen-year struggle to establish the independence of the consistory was coming to its bloody conclusion. The 1554 elections gave Calvin's supporters a narrow majority in the city government, and, with Calvin's full cooperation and encouragement, his majority crushed resistance to the consistory's autonomy. They won their victory with the help of trumped-up charges against their opponents, torture, and four beheadings. When God's cause required it in this ruthless century, Calvin could be ruthless.[17]

That victory for the consistory ramped up the power of this already impressive institution, with Calvin its most influential member. Soon up to one in eight of the city's adults was appearing before it each year for sins ranging from loansharking and price gouging to dancing and sexual misbehavior (illegitimate births in Geneva almost vanished). The consistory's muscle was backed up by strict laws; a Jesuit passing through Geneva in 1580 marveled that in three days there, he heard no blasphemy, swearing, or indecent language.[18]

Under Calvin's guidance, Geneva was rapidly becoming the gold standard for the kind of reformation that churches restored to New Testament purity could accomplish while working arm in arm with a sympathetic government. Geneva had started its own university in 1555 and was becoming a hotbed of biblical scholarship, translating, and printing. Calvin's influence rapidly spread beyond Geneva, and with it his model of Reformed Christianity.[19]

"The most perfect school of Christ that ever was in the earth since the days of the apostles," enthused Knox about Geneva in a letter to Anne Locke, the closest of his many female friends.[20] Other exiles in Geneva echoed Knox's praise, as did the settlers of Massachusetts trying to construct their own version of Geneva eighty years later. Knox's descriptions of Geneva were persuasive enough to Locke that she left her husband in London to join his church. Locke's father had seen to it that she received a broad humanist education: while she was in Geneva, she worked on a translation of four sermons by Calvin and on her own related sonnet sequence on Psalm 51. Her works were published in London in 1560.[21]

Locke's was only one of a number of books that the Geneva church sent out into the world. Two were of lasting importance. One was the *Forme of Prayers*, the model of church government and worship that Knox and others developed in Frankfurt. The other was a new English translation of the Bible, finished and published by its editors and translators in 1560, which became famous as the Geneva Bible. The goal of the Geneva Bible was not just to get the laity to read the word of God, important though that task was, but to dig deeply into it and comprehend it. This new Bible followed the recent Genevan innovation of dividing its chapters into numbered verses for easier reference, while summaries, clarifying illustrations, maps, tables, cross-references, and a copious number of marginal notes all helped readers to understand what they were reading.[22]

The marginal notes explained obscurities in the Bible's text and attacked the Catholic Church. Readers would learn from them that the pope was Antichrist and "hath his power out of hell and cometh thence." The notes' most important task, however, was to ensure that unsophisticated lay readers did not get lost in the winding byways of the Bible, possibly to the peril of their immortal souls. This the notes did by their explication of what the editors called the Bible's "hard places," where readers were most likely to go astray. The notes ensured, as the editors explained, that readers would grasp the Bible's "true and simple meaning" and not be led into "errors, sects and heresies," as had already happened to some of the Protestants going up in flames in England. Such confusion among Protestants gave grim satisfaction to Catholics.[23]

But even the learned Reformed Protestants of Switzerland did not always agree with each other about the meaning of the Bible's hard places. One major flashpoint was predestination. The Bible, they all agreed, taught that God had predestined the elect to heaven. However, according to Calvin and the Geneva notes, the Bible also taught that God actively predestined everyone who was going to hell. You might end up in hell because you, like the rest of humanity, were hopelessly sinful by nature and deserved nothing better. But according to Calvin, it was God who decided before time began that you specifically would go there, just as he chose a much, much smaller number of as-yet-unborn but equally vile humans to send to heaven. Why, though, would God predestine people to an eternity of torment before they had even been created? "Chiefly [for] his own glory," as the Geneva notes put it.[24]

That claim produced violent disagreements among the Swiss Protestants. For opponents, double predestination (predestined election for the saved, predestined reprobation for the damned) did not glorify God, it disgraced him. To predestine people for hell made God, they claimed, the author of sin. Some opponents called Calvin's double-predestinating God worse than the devil; one Zurich theologian was so enraged by double predestination that he challenged a proponent to a duel with axes. Puritans, by and large, were to embrace double predestination, and for a while it would become the unofficial doctrine of the Church of England. Calvin's dominating reputation in England as a theologian and Bible expositor at the end of the sixteenth century ensured that "Calvinism" would become the common, oversimplified term for this theology there.[25]

The Geneva Bible achieved enormous popularity. It might have remained the standard English Bible, except that four decades after it was first published, England's King James I decided that some of its Old Testament notes endorsing godly resistance to monarchs were "dangerous and traitorous." In 1604 he commanded the new translation that goes under his name and has almost no notes. The King James Bible, first published in

1611, eventually snuffed out the Geneva Bible, through political and legal means, but not before the latter had gone through at least 140 editions.[26]

Long before the Geneva notes alarmed King James, however, the Geneva church had found an even more effective and direct way to anger monarchs. In the 1550s, as England sank back ever deeper into the mire of Catholicism, the exiles debated among themselves how far a Christian could go to resist a wicked idolatrous monarch like Queen Mary. The standard answer among them had been that these monarchs were God's scourges, sent as punishment for the sins of a people. Since such monarchs came from God, resisting them by force was sinful. Christians could only take up spiritual weapons like fasting and praying. If Mary required you to attend Mass, you would, of course, refuse rather than violate God's law, but you would accept passively whatever punitive consequences followed, including martyrdom. Only governments could use nonspiritual weapons like guns and swords. Leading continental Reformed theologians sometimes hinted that God on occasion might permit more forceful responses, but only gingerly.[27]

Yet as God's church in England headed for extinction under Mary's persecution, some exiles began to have second thoughts. That disappearance of the gospel could not possibly be what God wanted; perhaps he was expecting his church to save itself through violent resistance. Over the winter of 1557–58, the two ministers of the Geneva church, Christopher Goodman and John Knox, published full-throated biblical arguments that God demanded armed resistance against tyrannical and idolatrous rulers like Mary. Goodman's book insisted that resistance was the duty of every Christian, and mentioned in passing that female rulers were an affront to God. Knox built an entire book around Goodman's passing comment, *The First Blast of the Trumpet Against the Monstrous Regiment of Women*. Knox demonstrated at great length that female rule was repugnant to nature, a violation of God's revealed will, and "the subversion of good order, of all equity and justice." The nobility and the people should overthrow female rulers, Knox concluded, just as they should overthrow any other usurpers or tyrants.[28]

Within a year Mary was dead and the Protestant Elizabeth had become queen. Elizabeth was furious equally with the Genevan claim that women could not rule and the claim that monarchs could be overthrown. She barred Knox from England, while Goodman remained in disgrace the rest of his life. Elizabeth held Calvin himself ultimately responsible for their books, and puritanism never shook off its association with disloyalty to monarchy first created by the Genevan exiles.[29]

Knox returned to Scotland to become the clerical force behind a Scottish Protestant national church that would have satisfied almost all puritans. Other Geneva church members returned to England hoping to push the English reformation further along Genevan lines.[30] What neither the Genevan exiles nor those returning from other cities were expecting to find was a Protestant queen, Elizabeth, for whom England's interrupted Protestant reformation had already been, by her standards, too extreme.

# CHAPTER 3

# THE BIRTH PANGS OF PURITAN ENGLAND

May 4, 1566 was an unhappy day in the life of Edmund Grindal, a returned Protestant exile whom Queen Elizabeth had appointed as bishop of London in 1559. Sixty angry, disappointed Protestant women were crowded into his home, wanting Grindal to reinstate a minister under house arrest, John Bartlett. Bartlett had been a lecturer at St. Giles Cripplegate parish church, which meant that he did not conduct church services; his only responsibility was the crucial Protestant one of preaching. Bartlett's offense was that he, like many other London ministers, refused to wear the legally required white surplice in the pulpit, a clerical garment left over from Catholicism. Why wear Antichrist's rags when you were preaching God's word?[1]

Until recently, church authorities had been willing to turn a blind eye to this sort of behavior. But Grindal, under orders from Matthew Parker, the archbishop of Canterbury, had given London's ministers a harsh ultimatum on March 26: wear the surplice or face suspension from the ministry. Thirty-seven ministers had refused. Demonstrations and fistfights broke out in churches, illegal books against the order appeared on the streets, and Bartlett, along with others, had been put under house arrest when he defiantly continued to preach.[2]

Grindal sent word to the women that he would not speak to them, but only to six of their husbands. He did not identify the women in his account of the incident, but some of them might have been ex-Protestant exiles like him. It is possible that Knox's friend Anne Locke was one of the group. Some might also have been among those women who had recently thrown stones at a once-protesting minister after the turncoat appeared at his church in a surplice before pulling him out of his pulpit.[3] Women like these were willing to submit to men's orders, provided those orders did not clash with the word of God. Silencing God's messengers for the sake of the rags of Antichrist was certainly not in line with God's word, and the women refused to leave Grindal's home.

Grindal was on the verge of contacting the London magistrates when John Philpott, another of the suspended ministers, came by. His appearance was probably no coincidence. He had led the clerical protests against Grindal's order, which would have put him in good credit with the women, and he probably knew that they would be there. The women were already used to listening to him attentively, for he was a lecturer at St. Antholin parish church. Its church bells rang at 5 a.m. six days a week to summon pious Protestants from across the city to Swiss-style psalm singing, prayers, and preaching before they went about their daily business. At Philpott's suggestion, the women left, but they continued to harass Grindal when he appeared in public.[4]

Before this controversy broke out, for a few years in a few places like London it might have seemed that the kind of reformation for which the English exiles had hoped and prayed was growing and spreading from the ground up. Now orders were coming from on high, intending to stop it dead in its tracks. But if this Swiss-style reformation could not spread with the support of the higher authorities, it would go on spreading without it.

Why the opposition from above? Bishop Grindal himself had neither wanted to wear the surplice nor take up a bishopric. He and some other returning exiles had accepted their positions from Elizabeth with the conviction that if the Church of England was to be cleansed of the pollution of Antichrist, it would take bishops like them to do it.[5]

Early on, it became clear to these bishops that they were not going to get much royal help. Elizabeth was indeed unashamedly Protestant; in 1559, she had forthrightly told the Spanish ambassador trying to persuade her to marry his Catholic king that she was a heretic. But she was not a heretic in the militant, forward-looking way of her dead half-brother Edward VI. Edward's enthusiasm for preaching was utterly alien to her. Only the determined resistance of her most trusted advisor, William Cecil, pulled her back from insisting that clergymen remain unmarried, like Catholic priests. She was remembered as always speaking of the Virgin Mary and the saints with reverence, just as a Catholic would. Elizabeth created a monumental scandal among her leading churchmen by her idolatrous insistence on keeping a crucifix and lighted candles in her personal chapel. Left entirely to her own wishes, Elizabeth might have restored the Catholic-leaning 1549 Book of Common Prayer. Instead, in the 1559 Act of Uniformity, Parliament reinstated a slightly more conservative version of the 1552 book.[6]

For bishops like Grindal the issue became not how to help Elizabeth push reformation forward, but how to keep her from stifling it. Most of the Catholic parish priests from the reign of Elizabeth's predecessor Mary had chosen to bend with the new Protestant political wind rather than resign. They made the transition from Catholicism to Protestantism with neither much commitment to Protestantism, if any, nor even much understanding of what Protestantism was. If the English people were to be preached into committed Protestants, it would be men like the returning exiles who had the conviction, competence, education, and determination to accomplish that task. But the exiles wished to drive England to what they understood as wholehearted Protestantism, one free of any trace of Antichrist. Initially backed by sympathetic bishops like Grindal, they worked out an understanding that they would not be compelled to adhere to requirements they found odiously redolent of Catholicism, like the surplice.[7]

Just north of London at the village of Hemel Hempstead, one such minister, the returning exile Edward Brocklesby, worked hard to wean his parishioners away from their old Catholic errors. He explained that the Virgin Mary was conceived in sin and was a lump of sin herself, just like other women, and that of course ministers could marry, for was not John the Baptist the son of a priest? But Brocklesby was also conscience-bound to tell his listeners how the Church of England fell short of the pure Protestantism that God expected. He laid out what he saw as the faults of the Book of Common Prayer and refused to wear what he told them was the abominable and stinking surplice. When he was ministering, Brocklesby informed his parishioners, he was above the queen.[8]

Whether these relatively few preachers' push for a pure Protestantism running ahead of England's laws was the most urgent of the problems facing the infant Protestant Church of England was debatable. Elizabeth, however, had no sympathy with the kind of reformation they wanted, and she utterly detested their disregard for her authority. Her attention to the church over which she was, by act of Parliament, the supreme governor, was sporadic, but by the fall of 1564 she had concluded that the nonconforming ministers must be made to obey the law.

She let her concern be known to the most powerful and important of her bishops, Archbishop of Canterbury Matthew Parker, who might have agreed with and even encouraged her. Parker, like everyone else involved in planning the new church settlement, had outwardly conformed to Catholicism in Mary's reign rather than go into exile. If Parker as a Protestant could endure Catholic worship, there was no reason his ministers could not endure a lawful surplice. For Parker, it was a plus that the surplice was a hangover from Catholicism: the garment could help entice Catholics into Protestantism.[9]

Parker's early efforts to cajole the nonconforming ministers into donning the rags of Antichrist failed to budge them, and the queen continued to put pressure on him to act.[10] The result was the 1566 London purge of nonconformist ministers, which has been called the Vestarian Controversy.

One consequence of this noisy controversy was the emergence of the term "puritan" as an insult used against the London nonconformist ministers during the controversy. Soon after it was being thrown at anyone who wanted the English reformation brought more closely in line with Swiss ideas of New Testament church practice, or who displayed the kind of zealous Protestant piety fostered by the nonconformists. Those at the receiving end of the insult preferred to describe themselves with words like the godly, the brethren, the saints, or the church. Their preferences reflected their sense of holy community and common purpose. To their opponents, those preferences exemplified the prideful, holier-than-thou attitude of a self-selected, would-be spiritual elite.[11]

Among those purged by Parker was the minister Perceval Wiburn. Wiburn once described puritans as "the hotter sort of Protestants," as well he might. He himself started out hot, as a member of Knox's Geneva church in the 1550s. During the Vestarian Controversy he was one of the most defiant of the London ministers who lost their pulpits, and the rough treatment he received from the bishops made him even hotter.[12]

Wiburn and a few other puritans returned to Switzerland in 1566 to appeal to its religious leaders to intervene in the English quarrels. They found little sympathy in Zurich: there they were told that the Church of England's ceremonies and centralized, corrupt discipline, although undesirable, were not in flat violation of the Bible, and that in such instances ministers must do as the government commanded. Militant Geneva was much more sympathetic. The Genevan clergy worried that if the English reformation did not pick up speed, God would pour his wrath down on what was the most powerful Protestant country in Europe.[13]

Wiburn returned to England in time to discover that Parker's order against the puritan nonconformists had only slightly hindered the spread of puritanism. Other bishops had refused to enforce it, and the preaching of the ministers Parker had silenced was still needed. Deprived ministers quickly found other positions outside London, while by 1567 some were even back to preaching in London without surplices.[14]

Wiburn spent a few years at Cambridge, where some of the university's colleges were hotbeds of puritan activity. He then headed into the English heartland, summoned to Northamptonshire to plant a Swiss-style reformation in that county by the wealthy landowner George Carleton and other puritans. They were members of the gentry, ten thousand or so interrelated families elevated to their social prominence by a combination of birth, wealth, and education. The gentry shared the governance of England and ownership of half its land with the aristocracy, the seventy-five or so families at the top of society, whose titles passed down from eldest son to eldest son.[15]

Carleton summoned Wiburn not only out of his Christian duty as a high-status puritan but out of his Christian duty as an official of the English government. In 1564, he had received a Crown appointment as a justice of the peace, an unpaid position, like most of those in England's government, but prestigious and coveted by members of the gentry. Officially, Carleton was responsible with fellow justices for investigating crimes, trying small ones, and running the administration of his county—providing poor relief, dealing with the growing problem of vagrancy, licensing taverns, and the like.[16]

For a godly justice of the peace like Carleton, however, the duties of his office soared much higher. The justice of the peace was a magistrate, a ruler, like England's chief magistrate, Queen Elizabeth. A justice's most important task for zealous puritans like Carleton was the same as the monarch's: to promote God's glory and enforce obedience to his law.[17] Even if the queen herself was neglecting that task by dragging her feet about Protestantizing England, her neglect did not relieve a lesser magistrate like Carleton of his Christian duty to do the same on a smaller scale.

This was where Wiburn came in. Carleton and other puritan gentry had invited him to serve as town preacher in Northampton, a large market town and shoe-making center. Carleton and Wiburn's reforming ambitions for this position went far beyond providing a steady supply of edifying sermons for Northampton's residents and all the visitors who came streaming in on market days: Wiburn would reach out to help educate the clergy and laity in the region about true Protestantism, regulate Northampton's worship of God, and foster moral discipline among the incompletely Protestantized population.[18]

To energize Northamptonshire's reformation, Wiburn followed the practice of other evangelizing puritan ministers and set up what was called a prophesying. In one of Northampton's churches, over the course of two hours, three ministers from the region would each preach a sermon in succession on the same scripture text, with a moderator commenting. After they were done, they would retire with other ministers for a private evaluation of their performances and personal faults, followed by a good meal. The prophesying would sharpen their preaching skills and doctrinal understanding, while building professional solidarity. It would also provide an opportunity for Wiburn to hash out with them what truly reformed Protestant churches were like and how the Church of England fell short of those standards. Many of the attendees at the Northampton prophesying later became puritans themselves.[19]

Northamptonshire's bishop, Edward Scambler, was based 45 miles away in Peterborough, and from this blurry distance he initially supported prophesyings, like other bishops. A 1560 survey revealed that only 9 of his 166 parish ministers had the ability to preach. Prophesyings would teach these sorry ministers the basics of Protestantism and of effective preaching. Other bishops praised the prophesyings for keeping ministers from idleness, gambling, drinking, and "from wandering up and down from town to town."[20]

To the laity who had the weekday leisure to attend, the prophesyings were a kind of spectator sport, a chance to see and compare how well professional Protestants interpreted the Bible. It was said that gentlemen and ladies who could otherwise hardly be induced to hear a sermon would travel 6 or 7 miles to attend a prophesying.[21] As the Protestant messages of Northampton's prophesyings began to sink in, more of Northamptonshire's laity would have started to acquire and bring their own Bibles to the prophesyings. They would check the ministers' citations and compare their interpretations with the Geneva notes. Others would have been taking their own notes of the sermons, to study later and to share with people who could not attend.

After the prophesying had ended, the laity's discussions about what they had just heard would spill out from the church into the streets and Northampton's taverns. A Jesuit missionary priest imprisoned under Carleton's supervision in 1588 watched with disdain after a similar gathering, when Bible-armed "men, women, boys, girls, rustics, laborers, and idiots" fell into heated theological and exegetical debates with each other, even to the point of fistfights.[22] What to the Catholic missionary demonstrated the anarchic folly of ignorant Protestants substituting the Bible's unreliable authority for the certain authority of the Catholic Church, would have been to Wiburn part of the healthy, necessary process by which the laity learned what to believe and why to believe it.

Wiburn and his associates formally roped Northampton's government into this religious effort to bring about reformation with a series of reforms outlined in a document called the "Orders and Dealings of the Church of Northampton." The "Orders" were designed to cast a Genevan blanket of piety over the town. Northampton would have twice-weekly hour-long lectures and regular drilling in Calvin's catechism for the young people. There was provision for a sermon to be preached in one of Northampton's four parishes every Sunday, and anyone who during that time chose to take a stroll or "otherwise occupy themselves vainly" could expect a fine. The town's church organs and choirs were to be silenced and replaced by communal psalm singing. The Lord's Supper would be offered regularly, and Catholic practices, like private prayers for the souls of the dead and bell ringing during funerals, were to be repressed.[23]

Many of the "Orders" regulations must already have been instituted in Northampton by the time they were drawn up as a total package. What was new was an ambitious effort to bypass the Church of England's corrupt, cumbersome, and distant centralized ecclesiastical courts. They were to be replaced by a strict, local discipline like that practiced by Geneva's consistory. "Sworn men" in each parish were to write up any drunkards, fornicators, scolders, blasphemers, whores, or other sinners. On Thursday mornings, after Wiburn's edifying lecture, the audience would be further edified by seeing ministers, justices of the peace, and the mayor and town corporation punishing those sinners—the godly governments of church and state cooperating in strict public reformation, as hopefully would soon be happening all over England. The stern spectacle would ensure that "evil life is corrected, God's glory set forth, and the people brought in good obedience."[24]

The strict puritan effort to fashion a new Geneva in Northamptonshire was not universally welcomed. One sin the sworn men were instructed to watch out for was "railing against religion, or the preachers thereof." A woman grumbled, "It was a merry world before there was so much preaching." Local Catholics scattered papers on the streets with nasty rhymes about Wiburn being one of the Genevan knaves who had married all the whores in England and who would soon be burned at the stake. None of the four entrenched ministers of Northampton's four parishes took much, if any, part in Wiburn's prophesying, which mostly attracted the surrounding region's younger ministers.[25]

Bishop Scambler initially approved the "Orders," at least in general form, but through one hostile channel or another, word got back to him that Wiburn and the local puritan magistrates' goals for reformation were considerably more ambitous than his own. Faced with a local quasi-official reformation in church and state that was writing its own rules, Scambler shut it down in 1572, silencing Wiburn as a preacher and having him removed from Northampton. The "Orders" were revoked, although after much pressure from the puritan-friendly earl of Leicester, Scambler permitted the prophesyings to continue.[26]

Scambler's crackdown, however, was too little, too late: activist Protestantism had become entrenched in Northamptonshire. Northampton's governing town corporation continued to select puritan lecturers, as was its right; when the bishop removed them, as was his right, the corporation replaced them with new ones. One of these short-stayed lecturers was Francis Marbury, father of the famous—or infamous—American puritan Anne Hutchinson. "Thou art an overthwart proud puritan knave," the bishop of London exclaimed in 1578 after the imprisoned Marbury had told him that the bishops were soul murderers for silencing preachers like him. Marbury married into the Northamptonshire puritan gentry— intermarriage was another common way by which puritanism was starting to perpetuate itself. After Wiburn was expelled from the Northampton prophesying, ministers just as committed to fundamental change joined. The ordinances the town corporation of Northampton passed to protect Sunday from secular pastimes were so strict that they were later declared illegal. Godly Northampton gentry were choosing puritan clergy for their parishes where they could.[27]

All of this activity in the 1570s was congealing into an intensely social Northamptonshire puritan subculture. "All men do know by experience," as a group of puritan ministers would soon put it, "that sticks of fire scattered can give no such piercing heat as when they are laid together." On Sunday mornings after Wiburn had been removed, these newly lit godly firebrands could be seen together following footpaths and roads out of Northampton to hear preaching in neighboring towns and villages, leaving behind their unenlightened parish ministers; "sermon-gadding" was the term for this lay puritan habit of wandering in search of good preaching. If they headed 2 miles northeast to Carleton's village of Overstone, they could attend services uncontaminated by the Book of Common Prayer. Carleton himself might have organized family, servants, and tenants into a psalm-singing procession to his parish church, with a few servants left at home to watch for robbers.[28]

At the church, the preacher, relying only on the barest notes or his memory, might fiercely pound away on the total sinful depravity of human nature and on God's awful wrath against sin in this world and the next. Having cast his listeners down in despair as they recognized their own sins in the minister's words, he would raise them up by preaching the good news of the gospel. But he would emphasize that those whom God had predestined for salvation could not bask in Christ's precious love. They needed to demonstrate their faith by unceasing obedience to God's stern and demanding law. The sermon might veer off into more topical areas where God's law was being violated, including the impure worship of the Church of England. The preacher would probably have reinforced his points with gestures, the rolling of his eyes, and a sing-song intonation, while the godliest members of his audience would intersperse murmured comments and cries or weeping. At the end of his performance, they would respond with groans, rising to loud cries of "Amen."[29]

On Sunday evenings a puritan like Carleton would see to the vital, pervasive puritan practice of sermon repetition. Family, servants, and neighbors would gather in his great hall with notes of the sermon and Bibles, to discuss the sermon, followed by psalm singing and a prayer. In a family where the wife was better at extempore prayer, she might lead, although this was a controversial practice. Throughout the week, Carlton would lead his household in Bible reading, prayer, and psalm singing, morning and evening, perhaps questioning them on their religious knowledge. He and his friends might meet at other times for prayer and religious discussion. "Conventicle" was the generic, hostile term for this sort of spiritually edifying social gathering, ubiquitous among puritans. Sometimes the groans and sobs of the prayers at conventicles led to complaints by neighbors about the noise.[30]

If for some reason Carleton should stumble in his duties and begin to fear that the wrath of God might fall upon him, he would turn to another major emerging puritan social form, the fast. Fasting, a great ritualized drama of alienation and reconciliation with God, was based on Old Testament practices and given its first puritan instruction manual in 1580. Outwardly, a fast involved physical abasement and what was called humiliation. Lack of food was the main element in this outward humiliation, but it also included the plainest clothes and, the night before, little sleep and no sex. Outward humiliation was only a prop to dramatize and foster inward humiliation, a deep sense of sinfulness and unworthiness leading to a visceral awareness that God would be entirely just if he sent instant destruction. One puritan writer in 1579 compared fasting to a criminal confessing his crimes before a judge and slipping a noose around his own neck.[31] As the puritan instruction manual put it, "When the father frowneth, the gracious son beginneth to quake for fear."[32]

Once fasters had confronted and repented for the depths of their own sinfulness through prayers, exhortations and Bible readings, they would beseech God to avert whatever evil he was sending, or if they were fasting for a blessing, they would now request it. Blessings could range from the successful pursuit of a marriage partner to driving a demon out of a possessed person to acquiring the fortitude to endure punishment for nonconformity. A good fast left the fasters feeling spiritually invigorated and renewed.[33]

Fasting was a public responsibility as well as a private one. It was widely accepted that a Christian country like England was a successor to ancient Israel. Just as Israel had the true church before the Jews rejected Jesus, England had God's true church, thanks to the Reformation. Like Israel, England was in a covenant with God, and like Israel, it would be blessed or punished to the extent that it followed or defied God's law. Therefore, when it strayed, it needed to collectively implore God's forgiveness, just as the ancient Jews had done. The Church of England ordered public fasts when faced with signs of God's wrath—plague, famine, war, and the like.[34]

Church of England fasts, however, were called too infrequently to satisfy puritans, and unless undertaken in a puritan manner, they were too formal and short to generate and express the humiliation and repentance that a jealous God expected. Puritan ministers asserted the dubiously legal right to call public fasts on their own. Zealous Protestants would travel 10 or 20 miles for a puritan fast, which could easily last an entire day between the many long prayers and sermons from the ministers present.[35]

A fast's suspense was heightened by the participants' uncertainty about God's response. Would he respond to them as a loving father or as an angry judge or, worst of all, would he even decide to abandon England altogether for its spurning of the gospel? Numerous Bible texts promised that God would reward his people if they fasted and repented, but others ominously warned that he would reject them if they had repeatedly failed to repent sincerely in the past. Reassuringly, there was ongoing evidence of God responding to fasting by revoking what puritans called his "declaration of war"—evidence like plague and famines abating and earthquakes followed by no further disasters. But no one knew how long God's patience with the stony hearts of the English would last before he decided to withdraw his gospel from the country again, as he had done with such disastrous results in the 1550s.[36]

That dreadful possibility of divine abandonment made the spreading of puritanism all the more urgent. Northamptonshire was not alone in its development of a vibrant puritan subculture in the 1570s. England was slowly being interlaced with small but growing networks of like-minded puritan ministers, magistrates, town corporations, and common laypeople. Just how extended and deep those local networks could become depended on a wide variety of factors: the ambitions and social standing of local puritans, the strength and nature of local opposition, the disposition and energy of the region's bishop, and the ability of all these different groups and people to call on friends in high places in their struggles with each other.[37]

All those emergent regional puritan networks, no matter how vibrant, felt the dead weight of the unreformed government and worship of the Church of England. They might evade that government and worship and even manage to create limited, ad hoc alternatives to them on a local level for limited amounts of time. The government and worship against which they struggled, however, were written into the kingdom's laws, and permanent reformation required that those laws be changed. The great national puritan struggle of Elizabeth's reign was the struggle to do just that.

# CHAPTER 4

# THE ELIZABETHAN PURITAN POLITICAL MOVEMENT

Had you been walking down a village street in Northamptonshire or Essex or any number of English counties in the 1570s or 1580s, you might have heard snatches of a voice coming out of a window, accompanied by loud sighing, humming, and groaning. You might have recognized the sounds as a sign you were approaching a puritan prayer meeting. As you got close enough to make out the words, you might have heard the speaker loudly exclaim, "We beseech thee, God, to work thy people's deliverance from all anti-Christian slavery," accompanied by even louder sighs and groans. The groans and humming would rise to a crescendo as the speaker implored God "for thy glory, to preserve our queen in peace wholly to seek the reformation of thy church."[1] You also might have been well aware that puritans were not leaving the task of spurring Elizabeth to reform the church entirely up to God. The 1570s and 1580s saw an aggressive puritan drive for mostly moderate church reform through the legal channel of Parliament and an even more aggressive drive for extreme reform through various not-so-legal means. None of these efforts came to anything, but the alliances, quarrels, and conspiratorial suspicions they stirred up would last as long as puritanism itself.

Parliament met only when the queen decided to call it, something she preferred not to do. In 1571, Parliament had its first meeting in five years. Over four hundred men were elected to the House of Commons, under a heavily restricted franchise, while over fifty hereditary peers and twenty-six bishops assembled in the House of Lords.[2]

This Parliament met in perilous times for Protestantism. A religious war had recently broken out in France between Catholics and Presbyterians (called Huguenots), while Spain was trying to crush a Protestant rebellion in the Netherlands. Most dangerous of all for English Protestants, Mary, the Catholic queen of Scotland, was a prisoner in England, having fled the wrath of her Protestant subjects. The closest heir to the husbandless, childless Elizabeth, Mary had a dangerous attraction to Catholic plots that might gain her Elizabeth's throne. England's Protestantism hung on the thread of Elizabeth's life, while Pope Pius V had declared Elizabeth a heretic and pronounced any Catholic who obeyed her excommunicated.

Even in this time of general crisis, Queen Elizabeth wanted advice and legislation from Parliament only on topics of her choice, and she regarded the arrangements of the Church of England as none of its business. But for godly members of Parliament (MPs), what could be more of a collective Christian duty than strengthening the Church of England as a strict, preaching, reformed church?

The result in 1571 was a scenario of puritan hope followed by disappointment, which would be repeated again and again in Parliament over the next two decades. Puritan MPs, working with puritan ministers, introduced bills for church reform. A bill to purge the Book of Common Prayer of the ceremonies and garments that puritans opposed enjoyed majority support— puritanism was far from a fringe movement. But the Crown stepped in and barred the MP who introduced it, William Strickland, from attending the House of Commons. Puritan MPs protested against this royal violation of the House's self-claimed rights of free speech and of deciding on the punishment of its members. It was "high treason" to claim that Parliament could not restrict the queen's power, thundered Northampton's puritan MP Christopher Yelverton. Puritan efforts to work for church reform with the bishops sitting in the House of Lords were fraught and unsuccessful. Peter Wentworth, one of the fieriest puritan MPs, lashed out when Archbishop Parker told him that MPs were to leave scriptural interpretation to the bishops. "That were but to make you popes . . . We will make you none."[3]

Elizabeth reluctantly called another Parliament in the spring of 1572, after the imprisoned Mary had become involved in a plot against her. Puritan MPs were among the most vociferous voices in Parliament calling for Mary's death. They were also among the most dismayed when the queen refused Parliament's request to have her cousin executed and then vetoed a bill that would bar Mary from succeeding Elizabeth to the throne. Earlier that spring Elizabeth had sunk a bill that would have allowed ministers to discard the Book of Common Prayer if their bishop approved. She instructed the House of Commons that henceforth all bills on religion must first be considered and approved by the bishops. That was another way of telling it to forget about any church reform.[4]

"We have used gentle words too long," the young minister John Field grimly decided after the debacle of the 1572 Parliament.[5] For puritans like Field, the failed pro-puritan legislation had been half a loaf of church reformation rather than the full loaf they had wanted—the perfection of the New Testament churches, which meant Presbyterianism, at least to Field and like-minded puritans. Since compromise had got them nowhere, why not go the whole way? To that end, Field wrote *An Admonition to Parliament* with another London minister, Thomas Wilcox, and published it illegally in 1572.

"Remove whole Antichrist, both head, body, and branch" was the uncompromising message of *An Admonition*. Gut the Church of England of its glut of unbiblical ceremonies, its time-serving, ignorant clergy, and, most of all, the "tyrannous lordship" of its royally appointed bishops. Replace them with Presbyterianism's simple worship, plentitude of preaching, strict discipline, and stripped-down decentralized government. Let the laity of each parish choose its learned minister and lay elders in elections supervised to ensure godly choices, and let each parish handle its own discipline. The queen herself could potentially be excommunicated from one of these loving but sternly watchful congregations of the faithful.[6]

Three editions of *An Admonition to Parliament* were published in two months, while official demands to hand in copies went unheeded. It was an auspicious time for hot Protestants to call for the purge of Antichrist. On the heels of the last edition, the French monarch Charles IX initiated a slaughter of up to ten thousand French Huguenots in what became known as the St. Bartholomew's Day massacre. This slaughter of Protestants reinforced a fierce conviction held by many English people—including the queen's privy councilors, but not the queen—that Protestant England was engaged in an apocalyptic life-or-death struggle with a savage international Catholic conspiracy.[7]

More uncompromising warriors for that struggle against Catholicism than Presbyterians could not be found, although even many puritans thought their reforming ambitions were unrealistically extreme—all Presbyterians were puritans, and all puritans wanted church reform, but not all puritans were convinced that full-blown Presbyterianism was the way to go. Nonetheless, Presbyterians' usefulness and devotion to the international Protestant cause meant that they had no shortage of friends in high places.

Field and Wilcox landed in prison for *An Admonition*, but wealthy merchants supported them and their admirers flocked to them; "as in popery, they were wont to run on pilgrimage," complained Edwin Sandys, the new bishop of London. Great lords wrote to him, demanding their freedom; they were released, unrepentant, by the end of 1573.[8]

The Presbyterians had made enemies as well as friends, and one of their most determined emerging foes was the minister John Whitgift. His flirtation with puritan nonconformity in the early 1560s was long over, terminated by Whitgift's respect for hierarchical authority and perhaps by his awareness that opposition to puritanism could help him climb the Church of England's career ladder. Whitgift had already quashed the first public call for Presbyterianism, in the form of sermons delivered in 1570 by Thomas Cartwright, the Lady Margaret professor at Cambridge University. Whitgift, at the time a Cambridge University official, had Cartwright stripped of his professorship and prohibited from preaching. Cartwright left for Geneva, for the time being, where he was well received.[9]

To nip this new, much more visible 1572 outbreak of Presbyterian agitation in the bud, Whitgift published a long attack on *An Admonition*. Cartwright sprang to its defense, and they had an extended quarrel via books. Their most dangerously heated arguments came in their debate about whether Presbyterianism or episcopacy—government by bishops— was the real threat to England's monarchy.[10]

For Cartwright, the threat obviously came from episcopacy. The English monarchy, according to Cartwright, worked according to the principle that the queen did not rule her domain alone, which would be tyrannical. She consulted widely, and the people gave their consent to her laws through their elected representatives in Parliament. That mode of governing was like Presbyterianism, where the ruling elders consulted with each other, while the people gave their consent to their decisions. Other Presbyterians stressed that these Presbyterian checks on power were necessary to prevent the rise of church tyranny. Bishops, by contrast, ruled over their dioceses with absolute, unchecked power, which made them, Cartwright stressed, tyrants.[11]

Whitgift himself would soon be a bishop, and he emphatically rejected Cartwright's claims. The queen, Whitgift insisted, was the final source of authority in England, and the concentrated power that Cartwright was calling tyranny was a good thing; the offices that the queen filled herself, like bishoprics, were the ones most likely to have the worthiest incumbents. "All those that are wise and discrete," Whitgift claimed, were realizing that the fewer elections, the better. Cartwright, with his talk of tyranny, elections, and the consent of the people, was worse than wrong, Whitgift charged; he was "savoring of popularity." "Popularity" meant appealing to ordinary people, and that was an insult, not a compliment, in this rigidly hierarchical, top-down society ("art thou officer? Or art thou base, common, and popular?" Shakespeare's Ensign Pistol asks the disguised Henry V).[12]

According to Whitgift, Cartwright and the Presbyterians described the monarchy so falsely because of the sinister, secret, long-term aim of their agitation and "popularity": to make England's government non-monarchical and "popular" like Presbyterianism. No bishops ruling over their dioceses like monarchs had to mean no monarchs in the state, however much puritans professed undying loyalty to Elizabeth.[13]

Whitgift's nightmare vision of treacherous, anti-monarchical, "popular" Presbyterians resonated with conservative Protestants. Only a few months after Whitgift first shared his vision, in February 1574, a con man embellished appeals for money from Archbishop Parker with a terrifying account of a far-reaching and murderous Presbyterian plot. The plot's goal was said to be the assassination of leading bishops and perhaps the queen herself, while the plotters ranged from leading ministers and great lords and ladies to hat-makers and goldsmiths. Parker fell for the con man's story. Its quick exposure as a hoax made him look a fool and broke the momentum of a brief period of intense harassment against nonconformists instigated by the queen. Parker died in May 1575, worn out and bitter that, as he put it, so few besides Elizabeth "were offended with the puritans," who "would undo her."[14]

The queen chose Edmund Grindal, then archbishop of York, to replace Parker as archbishop of Canterbury, the most powerful office in the Church of England. There was widespread hope among puritans that Grindal had not totally lost touch with continental-style New Testament simplicity from his days in exile, despite his episcopal pomp and ceremony—"your train of men waiting on you in the street, your gentleman usher going before you with bare head, your family full of idle serving men," as another former exile reproached him—and that he would begin the reformation that could bring unity to the church.[15]

But all that Grindal's still active reforming convictions brought him was a fatal collision with Elizabeth. Lurid tales had reached her about puritan excesses at some of the multi-sermon prophesyings like the one set up by Wiburn in Northampton (see p. 31). In 1576, she dismissed Grindal's proposals for their better regulation, ordered him to shut them down, and rubbed the order in by telling him in a most un-Protestant manner that "it should be good for the church to have few preachers." Grindal had been prepared to swallow all her previous commands, but this repression of the vital Protestant task of preaching the gospel was an order too far. Grindal informed Elizabeth that he must refuse and that she must heed God's commandments more carefully. Elizabeth, in turn, put him under house arrest, and for the last seven years of Grindal's life there was a vacuum of leadership in the church. The queen shut the prophesyings by her own order (they quietly and widely reemerged in a more sedate form).[16]

During Grindal's archbishopric, Presbyterians continued to make themselves useful to the larger cause of reformation. The earl of Leicester and other Privy Council members helped John Field, writer of the incendiary *Admonition*, get a pulpit again, and Field prepared the government's edition of the 1581 debates at the Tower of London between the imprisoned Jesuit missionary Edmund Campion and a Church of England team ranging from conformists to Presbyterians. Campion had been severely tortured before the debates and afterwards would suffer the gruesome traitor's death of being briefly hanged before being disemboweled while still alive, beheaded, and having his limbs cut off. Campion had avoided overt political meddling, but his Jesuit companion Robert Persons, who escaped to France, had plotted with Spain to return England to Catholicism by force. Most English Catholics wanted nothing to do with plotting, although zealous Protestants had no trust in them. Between 1581 and 1603, Elizabeth's government executed 191 Catholics for alleged treason, above and beyond the crippling fines and possibility of imprisonment that Catholics regularly faced.[17]

As far as Field and other Presbyterians were concerned, the only way to rid England of the Catholic scourge was to set up Presbyterianism, which would root out hidden Catholics with its vigilant local discipline. Field continued his clandestine effort to bring about Presbyterianism, issuing treatises, maintaining a wide puritan correspondence, and keeping an extensive archive of documents about the struggle with the bishops for historical and propaganda purposes.[18]

Field carried on this work with the aid of puritan ministers who had been meeting secretly with him in London since the early 1570s. By the beginning of the 1580s, puritan ministers were increasingly drawn to this sort of hidden, illegal conference, and Field helped them stay in contact with one other. For most puritan ministers, the main attraction of these conferences was professional mutual self-help and shop talk, not the opportunity to plot the overthrow of the bishops.[19]

One such conference was formed in the cloth-manufacturing town of Dedham, Essex, about 60 miles northeast of London, in 1582. Twenty-two ministers from a 30-mile radius agreed to meet once a month in secrecy for fasting, prayers, preaching, and discussions of professional matters. The Dedham conference was run along Presbyterian lines, with no organizational hierarchy and a rotating moderator. In the first year alone, the conference mediated in its members' professional quarrels, advised on suitable jobs for them, discussed pastoral concerns, tried to get the traditional plays held in local villages shut down, thrashed out doctrinal issues, and planned how best to engage with harassment from the bishops.[20]

In that first year, one member raised the question of how much a minister could use the tainted Book of Common Prayer. It was a fraught question. Thomas Cartwright had stirred up a storm in 1576 among his fellow Presbyterians when he said that a minister's first duty was to preach the gospel. If there was no way to do that without performing the prayer book's loathed ceremonies, he should perform them while continuing to work for their removal. John Field's uncompromising nonconformist London conference wrote to Cartwright rejecting his flexibility and asking him to stay silent on that topic rather than "set yourself against . . . the Church and brethren." None of the Dedham brethren responded to the prayer book question, perhaps because they knew that they would strongly disagree with each other.[21]

The Dedham conference pulled together, however, in the face of a new threat to puritanism in 1583. That year, Queen Elizabeth appointed John Whitgift as archbishop of Canterbury; his tireless, tenacious anti-puritanism was a major part of his appeal for her. Whitgift brought to his new office the agenda of crushing not just Presbyterianism but clerical puritanism in its entirety. On October 29, 1583, he unveiled his hammer against puritanism: three articles to which all ministers had to subscribe. The articles required ministers to agree that neither the Book of Common Prayer nor the church's government were against the word of God and that they would follow the prayer book's forms in their services. Those who refused—all ministers who were to the slightest degree puritan nonconformists—would find themselves in a process leading to the loss of their ministry.[22]

The Dedham conference, along with other conferences and many individual puritan laity and ministers, mounted a pressure campaign against Whitgift's drive for subscription to his articles. Whitgift was bombarded with complaints and petitions from aristocrats, privy councilors, members of the gentry, ministers, and common people. By mid-1584, in the face of such heavy criticism, Whitgift made a tactical semi-retreat. He allowed most ministers to give their subscriptions with reservations and qualifications that made them close to meaningless.[23]

But this flexing of muscle did not get puritans wholly out of the woods. Whitgift made that concession only in order to execute a more carefully targeted purge. He continued to pursue particular troublemakers through the hitherto little used ecclesiastical Court of High Commission. This court, unlike ordinary English courts, used the dreaded ex officio oath that compelled suspects to answer all questions, including self-incriminating ones, or face fines and imprisonment. A few members of the Dedham conference were summoned to it.[24]

Puritan lawyers set to work dissecting the legality of the Court of High Commission and soon proved to the general satisfaction of puritans that the court had no right to exist. The ex officio oath violated English liberties, and the court's procedures infringed on the queen's prerogatives (rights and privileges), while the queen did not have the authority to set up the court in the first place. The sinister bishops, to give themselves more power, had fooled her into claiming a power she lacked.[25]

Judges served at the monarch's pleasure, so the lawyers' conclusions had no practical effect. But they served as the capstone of a sinister conspiracy story that puritans had been constructing for two decades, and would go on telling with varying degrees of intensity for a century to come. The lordly office of bishop, as it had come down unreformed from the Catholic Church, was not only a religious menace, it was a secular one. Its occupants were inevitably corrupted into plotting to lead England not only back to popery, but to tyranny, with the assistance of duped monarchs.

In the Parliaments of 1584 and 1586, the struggle for reformation continued. Dedham and the other conferences gave their all to a massive lobbying campaign for religious reform, while keeping their organization secret from hostile eyes; unofficial political pressure groups were considered little short of treasonous in this period.[26]

The main goal of these Parliaments was not religious reformation, however, but persuading Elizabeth to accept that her own life, along with the future of Protestant England, was in peril as long as her continually plotting Catholic cousin Mary was left alive. Mary was finally beheaded on February 8, 1587. Along the way to accomplishing that goal, Presbyterianism bills were introduced in the House of Commons and quickly died. In 1584, the House of Commons took a less extreme, widely approved approach. It rallied behind a petition to the queen asking for puritan church reforms that embodied drastically toned-down versions of Presbyterian goals: more vetting of prospective parish ministers, including giving parishioners some say in the process; better discipline, with selected clergymen authorized to assist their bishops in the task; and tolerance of puritan nonconformity.[27]

The petition, if accepted, would have taken most of the wind out of the sails of puritan protest and left it confined only to a small, manageable number of inflexible Presbyterians. Elizabeth, however, rejected it out of hand as a massive affront to the very idea of monarchy. She warned her bishops in 1584 that puritan preaching "tendeth only to popularity," while to have every man questioning her government was "a danger to kingly rule." Because of puritans expounding scripture and catechizing their serv-ants in their households, Elizabeth complained, she had heard how "some of their maids" had not hesitated to correct learned ministers "and say that such a man taught otherwise in my house." A movement nurturing uppity servants was a movement one step away from rebellion, even if it was not agitating for anything as extreme as Presbyterianism. Elizabeth intended to leave the Church of England, she told the bishops, exactly the way it was at the start of her realm, and she instructed them to crack down more firmly on nonconformists. Elizabeth quickly dashed puritan hopes when they started to revive the petition in the 1586 Parliament.[28]

Lest puritans have any lingering belief that Elizabeth would come around to their side, in 1586 she appointed Whitgift to her Privy Council. Puritan sympathizers on the council were dying off, and in early 1588 the council's last major advocate for their cause, the earl of Leicester, died. Rumors buzzed among desperate puritans that Whitgift himself was part of a Catholic conspiracy.[29]

Gentle words had once again failed to bring about church reform through Parliament, and John Field was once more ready to consider extreme action. He would transform the puritan conferences he had been nurturing into instruments to bring about a peaceful Presbyterian takeover of the Church of England, like activated sleeper cells. On March 6, 1587, the Dedham confer-ence considered a pair of documents sent for their signed approval by Field and his associates. One was an outline for a Presbyterianized Church of England. The other would commit the Dedham conference to start following that outline as much as possible.[30] The members perhaps imagined rope burns around their necks as they read these drastic, illegal proposals. Subscribing to this scheme was "not thought safe in any respect," the confer-ence prudently decided, and the group repeatedly refused even to discuss it.[31]

A few conferences, however, went along with Field and threw them-selves with gusto into the task of subverting their church. They resolved to practice discipline, to shun non-preaching ministers, to avoid contact with the bishops as much as possible, and to instruct the laity in the nature of Presbyterianism. These conferences would serve as seeds for an inexorable, peaceful revolution led by what Field called the "the multitude and people."[32]

Opposition to this long-shot Presbyterian drive for reformation came not only from puritans who worried that it was too extreme, but also from puritans who thought it was not extreme enough. Around the turn of 1588, a worried local schoolmaster paid a call on the Essex Presbyterian minister George Gifford. He was bearing a densely written, incendiary sheet of paper that had been circulating in the meetings of local godly men and women under Gifford's nose. The paper argued that the Church of England was so corrupt and antichristian that it was no real church at all. All faithful Christians needed to separate from it, avoid all contact with it, and create their own illegal, properly reformed churches from scratch.[33] Separation and starting over were the only way to kick-start England's stalled reformation.

Gifford might have known that a few separatist churches had sprung up in London in the late 1560s and had soon fallen apart. A separatist church founded in 1581 in Norwich, around 100 miles northeast of London by the minister Robert Brown, along with some local laypeople, had lasted long enough to get two separatists hanged, make "Brownist" another name for separatist, and leave a small separatist subculture in the region. Gifford would have learned from the schoolmaster who brought this paper, if he did not know already, that the main guiding light of separatism was now the paper's writer, the lawyer Henry Barrow. Barrow was vigorously spreading the word about the urgent need for separatism from his less-than-leakproof cell in London's Fleet prison.[34]

The schoolmaster wanted Gifford to write a reply. Gifford at first brushed off his concerns. Perhaps he gave the schoolmaster the standard puritan anti-separatist response: a church could be filled with corruptions, like the Church of England, and still be a true church. Among other evidence that the Church of England was a true church was that the word of God was preached in it successfully, as witnessed by all the puritans it produced. There was no excuse for the separatists' heinous sin of illegal schism from a true church, especially since the Presbyterians were hard at work reforming it.[35]

If the schoolmaster was under Barrow's sway, he might have replied to Gifford that Christians should flee Presbyterianism's antichristian tyranny as fast as they fled the bishops'. To Queen Elizabeth, Presbyterianism, like puritanism itself, was dangerous because it was too popular, but to the separatists, Presbyterianism was dangerous because it was not popular enough. In the original New Testament churches, Barrow insisted, decisions were made by laymen collectively, not, as in Presbyterianism, by a church's ministers and lay elders. Antichrist's cunning, piece-by-piece theft of the New Testament churches' power began, according to Barrow, when the laity sinfully allowed church elders tyrannically to snatch away from them their Christ-given responsibility to participate in church government. The result of the elders' power grab was Presbyterianism. Barrow also insisted that in the New Testament, each church had the final say about its own affairs. Part of the antichristian fall of those churches came when they sinfully let synods, collective gatherings of churches, give them not just advice, but commands, as in Presbyterianism.[36]

Only by going back to these original pre-Presbyterian New Testament churches, according to Barrow, could England be reformed and avoid God's wrath. Barrow was planting the seed of what was later called Congregationalism. That seed would be taken to New England by the separatist Pilgrims and adopted and modified by puritans for the rest of New England, while being picked up by a relatively small number of English puritans.[37]

The schoolmaster warned Gifford that because of Barrow's writings, many of the godly laity in the area "were troubled, and did hang in suspense" about whether they should separate from the Church of England. It was "for their sakes" that Gifford needed to write a refutation of Barrow. Gifford finally did respond. He did so partly because he knew all too well that the hotter puritans were, the more likely they would be drawn to the extremist purity of separatism, and partly because anti-puritans were quick to blame puritans and their incessant criticisms of the Church of England for creating the separatists. Separatism, for anti-puritans, was one more reason to suppress puritanism.[38]

It was neither separatists nor anti-puritans who finally pulled the Presbyterian movement down. Presbyterians did that themselves. In 1588 while the conferences were building up their hidden Presbyterian church within the Church of England, Job Throkmorton, a Presbyterian MP, along with a few other laypeople and ministers, decided to supercharge another front in the puritan struggle for the hearts and minds of the English people, the battle of books.[39]

Since 1584, Presbyterians and their opponents had been carrying on this renewed battle. The treatises on both sides were long, learned, and intricately argued—precisely the sort of books that your average lord, lady, or country squire would be unlikely to peruse. But that audience would gladly read an upmarket version of the vicious handwritten lampoons and satirical ballads that were part and parcel of local religious brawls. Throkmorton and the plotters decided to write short pamphlets that hammered home the necessity of Presbyterianism and the danger the bishops presented to true religion and to "the common liberty of Her Majesty's subjects." The plotters' stroke of genius was to sweeten up this bitter medicine with a lot of funny satire and mockery, along with irreverent, nasty stories about the bishops' greed and dishonesty.[40]

A brave printer was found and the wealthy puritan Elizabeth Crane set up a secret press in her house outside London. In October 1588, the first of around ten pamphlets under the name of Martin Marprelate appeared. The exact number is unknown because the inventive, animated comic prose that has given them minor landmark status in English literature meant that they were passed from hand to hand, and read and reread until they disintegrated.[41]

Presbyterians, by and large, disapproved of the Marprelate tracts for treating such a serious subject as church reform so flippantly. The queen herself was furious, calling Martin "a dangerous example . . . to subvert all other kinds of government." Her Privy Council marshaled unprecedented resources to find the printer, who had started to move around. The queen's agents pursued him to Northamptonshire and then to points further north. In August 1589, he was finally caught outside Manchester.[42]

But far worse for Presbyterians was yet to come. In the fall of 1589 the all-out government hunt for their unwanted ally Martin Marprelate uncovered their secret organization. The Dedham conference was caught up in the dragnet, and it hastily disbanded, as did almost all other such conferences. Soon Thomas Cartwright and eight other leading ministers joined Throkmorton and other plotters behind the Marprelate pamphlets under arrest. Most of the Marprelate plotters received stiff fines and short sentences. The trials of the ministers slowly petered out, thanks to skillful defense lawyers, lack of rock-solid evidence, and the defendants' connections in high places. Those anti-puritans who wanted to see puritans swing had to content themselves with the hanging in 1593 of Henry Barrow and a couple of other separatists. The separatists' executions had been hastened, rumor had it, by Archbishop Whitgift himself.[43]

With the trials and hangings, the drive for puritan church reformation collapsed and would mostly lie dormant in England for another half-century. Puritanism had embedded itself too deeply in English society, however, to fade away with that disappointment. Now that the intense political efforts to give the Church of England a partial or complete Geneva makeover had ended for the time being, puritans could turn more single-mindedly to building a Geneva in their hearts and souls.

CHAPTER 5

# THE PURITAN PATH TO HEAVEN

In 1585 the MP, militant Presbyterian, and powerful local magnate Anthony Cope needed a minister for his parish church in Hanwell, Oxfordshire. As was often the case with members of the gentry, he possessed the legal right to select the minister himself. Not for a puritan like Cope, however, was the frequent impious use of this right—patronage, as it was called—to place a family member in the pulpit or solicit an under-the-table kick-back from a clerical job hunter. Cope wanted the best puritan preacher he could find, and he knew to whom to turn to locate such a preacher.[1]

England's leading go-to person for patrons seeking godly clergy was Laurence Chaderton, master of Cambridge University's puritan-dominated Emmanuel College, where no one wore the hated white surplice or unbiblically knelt for the Lord's Supper. Chaderton steered Cope in the direction of the recent Cambridge graduate John Dod, whom Chaderton admired enough to have invited him to join his exclusive Cambridge Bible study group. Cope, as a good Presbyterian, voluntarily solicited the consent of Hanwell's parishioners and neighboring puritan clergy before offering Dod the position.[2]

Dod, like Chaderton and Cope, sought a Presbyterian Church of England. More important for his parish pulpit, however, was his soon to be famous persuasiveness as a preacher on matters of eternal life and death. Dod was a practitioner of the puritan "plain style" of preaching: no extraneous rhetorical flourishes, no show-off displays of Latin and Greek, just intense, direct, easily comprehensible preaching that would guide the predestined elect to heaven and keep a lid on sin in this life.[3] The need for such preaching was all the more urgent because with the drive for better

church discipline stalling, puritan preachers would have to rely on persuasion alone to lead their listeners to lives of inner and outer discipline.

Around 1600, Dod preached a long series of sermons on the Ten
Commandments, given to Moses by God on two stone tablets on Mount
Sinai. Buried in the terse Ten Commandments, for those who knew where
and how to look, was the totality of God's law, all the duties to perform and
all the sins to avoid in all spheres of life.[4] Dod's famous and frequently
reprinted sermons lucidly described the strenuous, disciplined, godly,
friction-filled life he and other seventeenth-century puritan ministers set
out before their listeners. Brevity allows only a small sampling from this
pattern book for a puritan way of life.

The Seventh Commandment, "Thou shalt not commit adultery," forbade
not only adultery, but any kind of non-marital sex, including masturbation,
sodomy, and bestiality. Even thinking about illicit sex, Dod warned, was
"hateful to God." The only safe sexual refuge was within the confines of the
right kind of marriage. Marriage itself could not be between a "Christian"
and a Catholic: all Catholics, even those who outwardly seemed to be good
people, Dod warned, were God-hating idolaters and thus unclean. Marriage
between "Christians" was only safe when it was a loving one since "it is not
the having of a wife, but the loving of her that makes a man live chastely,"
and likewise for the woman. Even within a loving marriage, sex had to be
moderate. The medical science of the day had it that women did not
conceive without orgasm, but excessive sexual indulgence, Dod warned,
often resulted in monstrous, stillborn births and mentally crippled or
"ungodly and stubborn" children.[5]

Diving down deeper toward the roots of illicit sex, the Seventh
Commandment implicitly forbade "wantonness," or anything that might
end in forbidden sex. Dancing was out of the question; "all the action is
nothing but a profession of an unchaste heart," Dod warned. So was
attending stage plays, "which serve for nothing but to nourish filthiness."[6]

Plunging deepest of all to nip illicit sex in the bud, the Seventh
Commandment implicitly forbade idleness itself. Idleness, the "mother of
soul lusts," meant the wasting of precious, God-given time in any manner or
fashion, so "that the world . . . shall be no whit the better." The manifestations
of idleness ranged from "lazing in bed" to "vain sports."[7] "Zeal of the Land
Busy" was the apt name of a leading character in an anti-puritan comedy.

God had not entirely forbidden sports and recreation under the Seventh
Commandment, but for puritans recreation was a minefield that had to be

crossed cautiously, lest it explode into wantonness. If the gentry were to hunt, Dod warned elsewhere, they had to commence and end with prayer and they could not hunt with ungodly companions. There must be no delight in the "torture" of the animal being hunted, and horses and hounds must not be overstrained in the chase. It is not a coincidence that the first law criminalizing cruelty to animals was passed in puritan Massachusetts, in 1641. The young gentleman and future governor of Massachusetts John Winthrop abandoned a brief fling at fowling, partly because he always felt guilty doing it, partly because local puritans disapproved, and partly because he rarely shot any birds.[8]

The Third Commandment, "Thou shalt not take the name of the Lord thy God in vain," forbade anything remotely resembling swearing. Even "petty and small" oaths that had nothing to do with God, like "by this light" or "by this fire," Dod warned, "without repentance bring damnation."[9]

But avoiding swearing was only the superficial start of the Third Commandment's prohibitions and demands. If you claimed to be a Christian while failing to show it in the way you led your life, you took God's name in vain just as fatally as you did by swearing. Under the Third Commandment, the godly were positively obligated to make their Christian "light . . . shine forth in the darkness of the world."[10]

Under the Third Commandment, whether puritans wanted to be or not, they were continual sermons to everyone around them, for better and worse. "All the hellhounds in a country" were watching them, Dod warned, and when a single puritan stumbled into "some gross sins" the hellhounds would tar all the godly with that individual's moral failure. "These be they that run to sermons and carry Bibles," the hellhounds would mock puritans; "you may see what godly men they be." But when puritans' light was shining forth successfully, the "furious barking" of the hellhounds would be ignored. Even better, if one of those hellhounds in reality belonged to God's elect, that light might commence their conversion.[11]

Being a shining light required reproving sin wherever it was encountered. Reproving violations of the Third Commandment was particularly onerous because, as Dod acknowledged, swearing was ubiquitous. People who would never let you catch them stealing a neighbor's sheet drying on a hedgerow, he complained, only laughed when you rebuked them for swearing in front of you. But rebuke sinners you must, or the guilt of the sin, whatever it might be, fell on your head. If you found yourself in a situation where rebuking swearing would be too socially awkward, Dod advised, the next best thing was to walk out. And if that was not possible, you should make a conspicuously grimacing face, or at least cover your ears. Dod once attended a feast where some gentlemen were swearing. He stopped them dead in their tracks with a long, clever scriptural exposition showing the wickedness of that sin. The swearing did not resume as long as Dod was present. Some of the swearers might have been shamed by Dod's discourse, while others would have held their tongues, perhaps with difficulty, while Dod went on, to avoid offending their neighbors who esteemed him.[12]

Knowing his puritans well, Dod stressed that reproving sin needed to come from compassion to be effective. He warned that "a sour look and an austere contemptuous gesture ... alienates men's hearts from us." As a contemporary witticism had it, "A puritan is such a one as loves God with all his soul, but hates his neighbor with all his heart."[13]

The Fourth Commandment, "Remember the Sabbath day, to keep it holy," was the commandment on which puritans put their most distinctive and socially divisive stamp. Sunday was the sole day on which most English people might rest. They got up late in the morning, straggled to church, and turned their minds away from God once out of the church door. They frequently spent the rest of the day in dancing, bowling, and other recreation. Hunters keen not to lose any time for sport even brought their hawks and their un-housebroken, barking hounds with them to church. Some people, by necessity or choice, spent part of the day working.[14]

There had always been clergymen and tidy-minded, pious magistrates pushing back against this irreverent Sunday free-for-all. Now, Dod was at the cutting edge of a great puritan drive for the reformation of Sunday that had been initiated by his brother-in-law Nicholas Bownde. Dod argued that Sunday was not just an arbitrary twenty-four-hour period which the church or the magistrates had selected for weekly worship. It was God's divinely appointed Sabbath, and God wanted all twenty-four hours of it devoted to him. The only "rest" on this day was rest from any labor and recreation that interfered with piety. Families should rise early to pray and reflect on their sins, and they should arrive at church on time. After church, they should pray, confer about the sermon, examine their souls further, and engage in acts of mercy like visiting the sick. Even once in bed, thoughts were not to stray back to earthly matters; dreams themselves on this day should have "some taste of religion." God himself enforced the Sabbath with dreadful punishments of its violators. Sabbath-breakers he chose not to punish on earth would be punished even more dreadfully in the afterlife. "Men of account" had a particular responsibility to see that the Sabbath was honored, Dod told his Hanwell parishioners and anyone else present to hear this famous preacher; those men should rebuke and exhort servants, children, and neighbors whom they saw pursuing dancing and other amusements on the Sabbath.[15]

Already in 1589, Dod's patron Anthony Cope stirred up the constable of the neighboring puritan stronghold of Banbury to cut down all maypoles and end all games and dancing on the Sabbath. John Danvers, the fiercely anti-puritan sheriff of Oxfordshire, quickly ordered local justices of the peace to block the constable's initiative, saying that it was illegal. For good measure, Danvers contacted the queen's Privy Council, warning of rumors about large puritan mobs planning to pull down maypoles. The Privy Council proclaimed the Sunday pastimes legal as long as they did not conflict with church services. It was a victory, but one for which Danvers paid a heavy price. He and his family soon had to leave Oxfordshire, hounded by nasty, puritan-spread stories that Danvers committed incest with his daughter, that he and his wife had sex with their servants, and that the family rarely attended church. A joke spread across the country about the Banbury puritan who hanged his cat on a Monday for killing a mouse on Sunday.[16]

Even while Dod unfolded the Ten Commandments in their impossibly heavy rigor to his listeners, he acknowledged that they were set up for failure. No one could obey them in their entirety, yet their slightest violation—one careless, mumbled "by this fire"—led to damnation. Adam and Eve were to blame for that terrifying, doomed-to-defeat situation. For Adam and Eve's salvation, puritans agreed, God had originally made the Covenant of Works. Under its terms, perfect obedience to his law would bring them eternal life. When first created, they could have carried out such obedience, but that possibility ended on the tenth day of the world—November 1, 4004 BC, by one widely accepted calculation. On that dreadful day, Adam and Eve had freely disobeyed God by eating the forbidden fruit, and had fallen into original sin.[17] Now, every person was born with a completely corrupted heart, making it impossible to meet the terms of the Covenant of Works.

Jesus was the exception to this rule. He could and did fulfill the Covenant of Works in his completely sinless life, while he took on the punishment due the elect for their sins on the cross. Under the Covenant of Grace that replaced the Covenant of Works for the elect, God counted Jesus' earthly accomplishments as the elect's, and thereby saved them.[18]

One thing that Dod and other puritan preachers hoped to accomplish by piling the full, bone-breaking weight of God's law on their listeners was to trigger in them a horrified realization of how entirely incapable they were of getting to heaven except through Jesus. Those listeners might believe that they were perfectly good Protestants and had true saving faith in Jesus, and they might be offended, Dod noted, when he bluntly told them that they were wrong.[19] It was only when sinners realized through protracted, anguished self-examination how completely lost they were that they could truly understand how completely they needed Jesus. That realization was the first step to real faith.

In the ordinary course of events, only after the elect had entirely and terrifyingly grasped that they were damned and that Jesus alone saved them, did God justify them (pronounce them saved). Thereafter, Dod told his listeners, they did not have to actually follow the Ten Commandments perfectly, which was still impossible, they just had to make the attempt sincerely, and God, he assured them, would give them the grace to do that.[20]

What was more, the elect could discover for themselves that justification had taken place. When they did, they would have rock-solid assurance that they were, and always had been, among the elect and were going to heaven; God did not change his mind. The quest for assurance of salvation occupied a major place in puritan piety since the stakes could not have been higher—eternity in either heaven or hell.

As Dod explained that quest for assurance, after you had been justified and continued the strict self-examination that was a daily part of puritan spiritual practice, you would start to notice God creating changes in you, changes in your outward behavior, of course, but even more important, changes in your feelings and states of mind: new love for God, a new spirit of prayer, newly heartfelt repentance when you caught yourself breaking one of God's commandments. All these signs and more assured you God was working a true transformation of your heart, meaning that you were unalterably among the saved, even though you kept stumbling into sin because of your still-corrupted nature.[21]

This was the theory of assurance anyway. But Dod was famed as a spiritual counselor, and as troubled puritans came to him and other puritan ministers, their stories contradicted it. They would unburden themselves about how they thought they once were saved but had fallen into "hideous darkness in mind," and how they now feared that any positive feelings they had enjoyed about their salvation had been "delusions and presumptions."[22] For these desperately joyless puritans, the preachers' frightening message of law and damnation was more convincing than their message of the gospel.

To such converts, Dod and other ministers stressed another angle about assurance of salvation. Converts should not expect that the terrors and anguish of conversion would lead to a positive emotional reward, and they must not allow Satan to argue them into despair because of that absence. Feeling one's lack of faith and one's desire for it was in itself "an infallible sign . . . [of] true faith," Dod said, while a steady growth in dread over one's sins was another.[23]

This cautionary message that Dod sent to the villagers and visitors come to hear him preach at Hanwell remained the regular message of puritan ministers throughout the seventeenth century, issued both individually and collectively. The puritan life for most practitioners would be much more likely to involve protracted struggle with fear and doubt than it would a steady sense of God's love. Religious raptures among puritans were not unknown, but these were strictly bounded by a painful awareness of how fallen humans were and how terrifyingly majestic and great was God. Dod cautioned that Christian joy was sound only when it began in godly sorrow, was joined with a "holy fear," and produced shame. A corresponding anti-puritan critique grew steadily over the same period. Puritanism was the manifestation of the mental disease melancholy, and the stern preaching of ministers like Dod, this critique went, drove people to that illness. A puritan was a Protestant scared out of his wits, joked the courtier Sir John Harrington.[24]

Nehemiah Wallington, a puritan London artisan and glutton for sermons, lived out in extreme form this anxiety, both stoked and alleviated by ministers like Dod. During one particularly severe period in late adolescence a toxic brew of doubts about his salvation and frustrated sexual urges pushed Wallington to attempt suicide ten times. He decided not to cut his throat only after reflecting on how such a death would be used to attack puritanism. Wallington went on to become a respected member of London's puritan community. But it was not until he was in his early fifties that Wallington began to accept that he was among the saved, and even savored periods of heavenly joy. Wallington's long refusal to accept defeat in what puritans called "the Christian warfare," the struggle against Satan, the world, and the flesh, was what finally allowed him to dare to hope that God had chosen him for salvation. As Wallington became a more experienced fighter of "the Christian warfare", other people came to him for counseling. It was common for puritan laity like Wallington to share their spiritual experiences and struggles with each other, one-on-one and in larger gatherings.[25]

The Bible was the first book that Wallington turned to for aid in fighting his Christian warfare, but he added to it a swelling flood of books by puritan ministers, including Dod. Some of these books were based on sermons, others freshly written. This puritan practical divinity ranged from detailed instructions on the daily practice of piety, through guidance on the process of conversion and assurance of salvation, to meaty theological discussions in English for those lay readers with no command of Latin, the Europe-wide language of learning. Most of the books, like Dod's, were within the means only of relatively well-off readers, but some were small and inexpensive enough that peddlers sold them from their packs. All of them might be read aloud in household and social gatherings where members of the illiterate majority of the population could learn from them.[26]

Puritan readers actively engaged with these books. Katherine Clarke, a minister's wife, eagerly read books of practical divinity, pen in hand, extracting favorite passages into her own notebooks arranged around different categories—signs of salvation, grounds of spiritual comfort, and the nature of the Covenant of Grace, among other topics. She applied the same editorial extraction to verses of the Bible. Already as a little girl Clarke had taken volumes of notes on sermons in church. She continued that practice as an adult, rereading and meditating on her sermon collections and sharing them with her maids as part of their religious instruction.[27]

For puritans like Clarke, it might be only a short step from activist reader to author. To her husband Samuel, Katherine was a model puritan wife. She abhorred idleness and was pious, an excellent housekeeper, a devoted mother, and, according to Samuel, "very exemplary in that reverence and obedience which she yielded to her husband." Samuel's word was law to her, and she curtsied to him whenever she left the dining table, even when they dined alone.[28] Yet while Katherine carried out her God-appointed office of a meek and deferential housewife to her patriarch of a husband, she saw herself spiritually as a representative human. As such, she had learned valuable spiritual lessons in the course of her life that it was her puritan duty to share, and for that duty, her pen came into play.

After his wife's death, going through her cabinet Samuel discovered a manuscript she had written about "my experiences of God's gracious dealings with me." At the time it was a truism that nothing happened by chance; the hand of God—his providence—purposefully guided all events. Part of the task of being a puritan was to make the abstract concept of providence experiential and personal. To that end, Katherine, like many puritans, probably kept a diary where she noted down events of her life and tried to decipher what God was teaching her through them. Her manuscript, she explained, distilled the lessons she had learned from this exercise for her own edification and that of her relatives.[29]

The focus of the manuscript was on the perennial question of why God regularly caused bad things to happen to people who sought him, and the purpose of that focus was to encourage readers to continue to seek and trust God in and through their troubles. In the most poignant example, Katherine recounted how "it pleased God" for many years to keep her in a "sad and disconsolate" condition without assurance of salvation. Then God took away her youngest son, a minister and her spiritual counselor. In her anguish, she prayed that he would "make up this outward loss with some more durable and spiritual comforts." In response, God manifested "his special love to my soul" and quieted her heart. Katherine's love for God was "much increased, and even enflamed." His grace enabled her to watch herself much more strictly, she reported, and to submit to his will, even in suffering. She still went through periods of doubting her salvation, but never so intensely as before.[30]

Samuel also found in Katherine's cabinet a piece of paper filled with Bible texts. These texts comforted and supported her when she felt deserted by God or when her faith was under temptation. The piece of paper, Samuel noted, was almost worn out from frequent use.[31]

For all her struggles, when Katherine's end came, Samuel reported, she enjoyed peace and serenity, unmolested by Satan. As was customary among puritans, friends and family visited her on her deathbed to talk and pray and receive her admonitions, exhortations, and blessings. Katherine assured Samuel in his grief that she was going to a better husband, Christ.[32]

Dod himself died at the extraordinary age of ninety-six in 1645. On his deathbed he was surrounded by friends and admirers, keen to support him and to hear from him his final reports on the state of his soul before his departure, surely, for heaven. At 2 a.m. on the morning of his death, Dod spoke of how he had been wrestling all night with Satan, who had relentlessly tried and failed to persuade him that all his piety had been false. Dod's final speeches were of his desire to die and be with Christ. Dod's was a properly edifying death to those who saw it or heard or read about it, one that vindicated the severe piety he had preached for seven decades. But it was recognized that even ministers like Dod, "persons of great grace" and "famous in the Church of God," sometimes died in "darkness and distress."[33]

# CHAPTER 6

# TAMING PURITANISM

One day in late 1603, Willem Teellinck, a young Dutch lawyer, was invited by John Dod and other Presbyterians to join them for a day of fasting and prayer. The experience transformed Teellinck: he resolved to devote himself to God's service and stayed on in England for another two years learning from puritans before going back to the Netherlands to become a minister. There he started the Dutch "Second Reformation," a protracted, controversial effort to bring puritan intensity to his Presbyterian homeland. Through the Netherlands's Second Reformation, puritan influence spread to the Calvinist and even Lutheran parts of Germany.[1]

The fast Teellinck attended was particularly well suited to turn him into a reformer. Earlier in 1603 Queen Elizabeth had died. Her successor, her cousin James VI of Scotland, presided in his own kingdom over a mostly Presbyterian church. Puritans had high hopes that he would prove sympathetic to their goals. Teellinck's fast was probably devoted to beseeching God for further reformation in England. Puritans were combining such fasts with a burst of organized agitation for church reform. James, now James I of England, responded by calling a conference with them in January 1604. Momentous changes were indeed in store for puritanism, but those changes would not be at all what Dod and his fellow fasters had hoped for.

What puritans did not know, but would soon discover, was that James had grown thoroughly disillusioned with his insufficiently obedient church in Scotland and wanted nothing like it in England. Only four puritans, hand-picked by James, were allowed to attend the conference, which met in his palace at Hampton Court. Dod and other Presbyterians gathered in the neighborhood and undoubtedly spent most of their time in fasting and prayer.[2]

The puritans invited to Hampton Court were, for James, only bit players at the conference, brought in for one day to debate with two hostile bishops, with James, an amateur theologian, one-sidedly presiding. Any reform, no matter how modest, remotely suggesting Presbyterianism to James was out of bounds for discussion as a threat to monarchy: "No bishop, no king," as James put it to the puritans. James and his churchmen decided to make a few minor ceremonial adjustments, most of which were never carried out, and to commission a more up-to-date translation of the Bible, the famous King James Bible. These crumbs were accompanied with a stern warning that puritans could expect nothing further. "I shall make them conform themselves, or I will harry them out of the land," James warned.[3]

James carried out his threat. He had Convocation, a clerical parliament dominated by the bishops, pass new canons, or laws, for the church. The 141 canons were intended primarily to strengthen the administration of the church, but a strain of anti-puritanism ran through many of them. Most flagrant was canon thirty-six, which revived and strengthened Archbishop Whitgift's anti-puritan subscription for ministers (see p. 43). As with the earlier subscription, ministers would have to swear that the Church of England's government and ceremonies were biblically sound, but now they would have to swear from the bottom of their hearts and with no reservations—no more of the pious puritan crossing of fingers to which Whitgift, under fierce pressure, had reluctantly agreed. A purge drove up to 300 committed nonconformist ministers out of their positions. Parliament's House of Commons struggled in vain to undo the canons, as part of a larger struggle to rein in their monarch's powers. A flurry of illegal puritan pamphlets cheered the House of Commons on while warning of the escalating danger to England's liberties and Protestantism from the sinister bishops and their duped monarch.[4]

Dod was among the puritan ministers who could not stretch their consciences to make this new subscription. He lost his pulpit, but he had no intention of abandoning the cause of saving souls. Dod continued his preaching in print by stepping up the publication of his earlier sermons. With his patron Anthony Cope, he labored hard to fill his position and that of neighboring Banbury with ministers who would become increasingly important in the new regime: conforming puritans. Conforming puritans were strenuous preachers and admired men like Dod, but they were not going to give up their ministries over church ceremonies and government. However unbiblical and undesirable the Church of England's arrangements might or might not be, they were still "indifferent"—the Bible did not specifically forbid them. Ministers should not abandon their pulpits and their work of saving souls and beating down sin because of them.[5]

Dod and Cope's greatest challenge was to get suspicious puritan laity to accept these new conforming puritans as their ministers.[6] Some nonconforming laity would neither listen to nor take the sacraments from a conforming puritan minister; some walked out of a church if the minister appeared dressed in the hated surplice, and some even refused to marry conformists.[7]

Most lay nonconforming puritans, however, ultimately accepted conforming puritan ministers, if reluctantly. Those ministers preached the same kind of strict conversionist piety as nonconforming ministers like Dod, and they did their best not to alienate nonconformist lay puritans. William Whately, the new minister at Banbury, like other conforming puritan ministers, would have had long talks with militant parishioners to persuade them to kneel for the Lord's Supper. Nonetheless, he looked the other way if they still refused. As long as these nonconformists "did indeed show the power of godliness in their lives," remembered another conforming puritan, Whately would "highly esteem them" and "love them." Those militant parishioners, in turn, would have grown to admire Whately's fierce, demanding preaching—not for nothing was he was called the "roaring boy of Banbury."[8]

Both Whately and his puritan parishioners would have appreciated all the opportunities for preaching in the Church of England. Whately took turns with other puritan ministers to deliver a weekly sermon on Banbury's market day. In nearby Stratford-upon-Avon, he preached in another of these "combination lectures," as this common Jacobean institution was called. "Troops of Christians . . . from many miles distant" would flock to hear him, it was reported admiringly. Whately in turn urged his activist godly listeners to help their "neighbors unto grace" with "exhortations and admonitions" and "holy conference." To avoid unnecessary controversy, Whately also urged them to "shun . . . matters of ceremony and disputable points," but doubtless, some listeners paid him no heed. An anti-puritan charged that Whately left "such a foundation of faction in Stratford-upon-Avon as could never be removed."[9]

John Dod, as part of his ongoing work for reformation, met one day in 1606 with other puritan ministers at the home of Lady Isabella Bowes of

Coventry, a religious reformer and generous financial supporter of nonconformist ministers. If you agreed with her zeal, you might find her "very wise,
especially in things of this kind," as her husband put it. If you did not, you
might, like the earl of Shrewsbury, dismiss her religious opinions as the
product of womanly intellectual weakness, while regarding her strong
expression of them as clashing with womanly modesty.[10]

Bowes had summoned the ministers to try to forestall a fresh outbreak
of puritan separation from the Church of England (see p. 46). King James's
canons had stirred up a small puritan hornet's nest in Nottinghamshire,
where the local bishop had excommunicated three defiant nonconforming
ministers in the circle around William Brewster, a minor member of the
gentry and before too long the ruling lay elder of Plymouth Plantation's
church. Brewster's circle had responded to the excommunications with
angry talk about how "the lordly and tyrannous power of the prelates [i.e.,
bishops] ought not to be submitted unto," another member of this circle,
William Bradford, the future governor of Plymouth Plantation, recollected
many years later. The unhappy puritans' anger had led to talk of cutting
their ties with the Church of England.[11]

It was two of these defiant Nottinghamshire ministers, John Smyth and
John Robinson, who had come to Lady Bowes's house, where Dod and
others tried to talk them back from separatism. In this they were unsuccessful, and at the start of 1607, the disaffected group of puritans formally
separated from the Church of England and created their own church,
following what separatists believed was the true biblical Congregational
model—the laity electing their ministers and participating in church
government, while churches cooperated with each other strictly on a voluntary basis. Jail sentences followed, and the congregation, mostly of farmers
and tradespeople, decided to cross the North Sea to take refuge in
Amsterdam. There, tolerant magistrates kept the Netherlands's would-be
persecuting Presbyterian state church on a short leash.[12]

Amsterdam already had an English separatist church, whose members
had come over in the 1590s. For most of the newcomers, that church was
too quarrelsome and too unremitting in its hostility to puritans who had
not separated. In 1609, the new group moved 18 miles from Amsterdam to
the city of Leiden, home to an expanding textile industry desperate for
people willing to work for poverty wages, with Robinson assuming the
ministry of their church and Brewster serving as the ruling lay elder.[13]

A handful of irreconcilable nonconformist puritan ministers also made
their way to the Netherlands. They found positions as chaplains for English

army garrisons with puritan commanders or with churches set up for puritan English merchants. A few got to know Robinson and his church and were impressed by its Congregational form of government, although not by its separation from the Church of England and its blanket condemnation of all England's parish churches as false churches.[14]

One reason why there was only a trickle of exiles to the Netherlands was that the full force of the anti-puritan canons quickly abated. England's government was creaking and inefficient, and James's main concern was only to see that puritan ministers recognized his power over them. A nonconforming puritan minister flexible enough to subscribe and perform a hated ceremony or wear a surplice when the heat was on and who had a bishop who was either lazy or warily sympathetic, and perhaps a frequent preacher himself, often had a fair amount of discretion to pick and choose among the church's ceremonial requirements.[15]

Even an uncompromising nonconformist like Dod was not entirely barred from the pulpit. He found himself another parish by 1606, in neighboring Northamptonshire, courtesy of another powerful patron, Erasmus Dryden, with whom the local bishop would just as soon not cross swords. Dod survived there until 1614, ministering, publishing, and making preaching tours, until enemies got word of his activities to King James, who ordered his suspension.[16]

Dod still had much to keep him busy after his 1614 suspension. Among other things, he was in great demand as a physician of wounded souls. That was why his neighbor Sir John Isham called on him one day. Isham's devout wife Judith had fallen into such despair about her salvation that she would not leave her bedroom. On his very first visit, Dod managed to coax her out through his encouraging exposition of scripture. "All the house rejoiced at it," her deeply pious daughter Elizabeth remembered.[17]

Sir John was scarcely a puritan, if at all, but he was pleased with Dod. He asked him to set up the religious education of his children while continuing his care of Lady Judith. Dod assigned the children to read and try to memorize two chapters of the Bible each day. He would come over in the evening to discuss the chapters and ask them questions. When they were established enough in the routine, he handed over the daily task to Lady Judith. Elizabeth remembered that Dod had a "delightful easy way" with the scriptures that she found very effective. When Elizabeth was courted by a member of the godly Dryden family, Dod served as a go-between in the complicated financial negotiations that such an upper-class marriage always entailed (though the two fathers failed to come to terms).[18] Dod undoubtedly received gifts and other compensation for his labors with the Ishams; then as now, the wealthy had easier access to intensive and sustained soul doctoring than the poor.

One evening Dod arrived to discover the family playing cards. They were playing for pins, not money; nonetheless, Dod rebuked them for engaging in a spiritually unlawful activity. As Sir John perhaps knew, puritan ministers did not speak with one voice on the lawfulness of card playing. Games entirely of chance, like dicing, were out of the question. They left the outcome entirely up to God, and God should only be called on for solemn decisions, as when the apostles drew lots to select a new apostle (Acts 1:26). Games strictly of skill were fine. But card games fell into disputed territory. Did the mere act of shuffling and dealing cards constitute casting lots? Puritan divines disagreed, although they did agree that if money was involved, the card game was sinful. Sir John knew what he was doing when he answered Dod that since they were not playing for money, there was no harm involved. Elizabeth herself later decided that even playing for money was acceptable as long as the sums were no greater than one would willingly lose. On the other hand, Dod once rebuked her for eating fruit during a fast, and that admonition stayed with her.[19] The laity were never blank slates for their ministers' messages, even the messages of ministers as skillful and famous as Dod.

For one kind of soul doctoring, early seventeenth-century puritan ministers had the field pretty much to themselves. Around 1620, a Nottingham man, John Fox, found himself possessed by a devil. The devil within Fox would throw him into violent fits and speak with a voice that could come from Fox's belly, throat, or mouth, while his lips stayed motionless. As was usual with possessions, people flocked to see this fearful spectacle of diabolically driven suffering. In principle, Fox would find no relief for his suffering from the Church of England. Clergy were not permitted to attempt exorcisms without the permission of their bishop, which was almost impossible to obtain. That prohibition was an effort to tamp down on puritan exorcisms, which generated a lot of favorable publicity for puritanism.[20]

Rules or no rules, nearby puritan ministers came to pray and fast for Fox, but to no effect. They decided to call in outside help, having in mind the powerful nonconformist preacher Richard Rothwell, whom Lady Isabella Bowes was paying to preach 15 miles away. As the story was passed down, Rothwell arrived and verbally sparred with the devil possessing Fox until it exclaimed "What stand I talking with thee? All men know thou art bold Rothwell." Rothwell commenced to pray over Fox while the devil howled in protest until it finally grew silent. Fox opened his eyes, the color came back in his body, and at the end of one of Rothwell's long entreaties to God, said "Amen." The entreaties to God turned into his praises, with Fox joining in, and Rothwell took his leave. The fame of "Bold Rothwell," as he was known henceforth, and his triumph over the powers of darkness in this encounter lingered for over a century in the area, precisely the kind of outcome that had caused the bishops to clamp down on puritan exorcisms in the first place.[21]

The life of a nonconformist minister in this period had enough difficulty and uncertainy that Rothwell decided to forgo getting married and starting a family. Such uncertainty might have been on the minds of the governing corporation of the small North Sea port of Boston, Lincolnshire, in 1612 when they were looking for a new minister for their parish church. The last two ministers the corporation had chosen had been nonconformists. But this time, perhaps after some disagreements, they took the safe route and recruited the highly recommended young conforming puritan John Cotton, a fellow at Emmanuel College, the center of Cambridge University's puritanism. The bishop of Lincoln, William Barlow, did not want a puritan minister of any sort in a town that was already tense with divisions between puritans and non-puritans, but bribes overcame his concerns.[22]

That under-the-table money was well spent, for Cotton was an impressive catch. He was widely admired for his holiness, extensive erudition, and mild, non-confrontational temperament, while his gifts as a counselor were to bring him visitors and correspondents from all over Reformed Protestant Europe. In 1614, two agents of the bishop of Lincoln noted that "grave and learned men . . . are willing to submit their judgments to his, in any point of controversy as though he . . . could not err."[23]

A few years later, this outstanding young minister's career was almost derailed by a puritan crisis of conscience. Cotton decided that he had been wrong about the Church of England's ceremonies. Ceremonies had to be purely biblical, which the Church of England's were not, and, in any case, bishops could not command obedience to "indifferent" things. Cotton could therefore no longer perform those ceremonies. He had certainly been supported, and probably encouraged, in his decision to turn nonconformist by some of Boston's laity. They might have been just as offended all along by Cotton's conformity as he finally became himself. After a diocesan court suspended Cotton for his new convictions, one of those laypeople, Thomas Leverett, successfully swayed an ecclesiastical appeals court to reverse the sentence through gifts and the lie-for-a-higher-cause claim that Cotton was now conforming. The town hired another minister to perform the ceremonies to which Cotton objected.[24]

A few years later, zealous Boston puritan laity almost managed to sink Cotton's career again. Some of them, including a future mayor of the town, decided to smash up the last visible remnants of popish idolatry in their parish church. This unauthorized destruction of stained glass and statues drew hostile commentary, but no official reaction (which was not always the case). The Privy Council itself, however, launched an investigation after some zealot in February 1620 recklessly broke off the idolatrous crosses on the ceremonial maces of office that preceded Boston's mayor in his processions through the town. The perpetrator of this felonious defacement of a symbol of the king's authority escaped punishment, for the Council failed to break through Boston's wall of witness coaching, payoffs, and resolutely professed ignorance about the crime.[25] But Cotton ended up suffering for it.

Everyone, including Cotton, agreed, at least when speaking to investigators, that Cotton opposed such vandalism. Nonetheless, in 1621, he found himself once again silenced. Plans were afoot to have him emigrate to the king's realm of Ireland; there the Church of Ireland, in the midst of the island's oppressed and restless Catholic majority, was puritan-tolerant. Before those plans could come to fruition, Boston's diocese obtained a new, sympathetic bishop, John Williams, who successfully appealed to King James on behalf of Cotton. Cotton's occasional assurances then and thereafter that he was thinking about conforming were enough to keep Williams off his back.[26]

Despite Cotton being, by England's church laws, unsuitable for the ministry, he went on to have an impressive career meeting the needs of the local, national, and international godly communities. For Boston zealots seeking more intense communal worship and Christian fellowship, Cotton formed a covenanted group for prayer, fasting, and watchfulness over each other's lives. As with other puritan ministers, Cotton's home served as a finishing seminary for Cambridge graduates and even for students from Germany and the Netherlands. Manuscript copies of Cotton's sermons circulated at a high price, while a letter of recommendation from him was said to be an enormous boost for a young puritan minister seeking a pulpit.[27]

In the meanwhile, Cotton kept up the grueling preaching schedule of a devoted puritan minister—eight or more sermons a week, with the hourglass on his pulpit sometimes turned over twice as his sermon went on. An observer of Cotton's protracted Sunday afternoon service commented "Scarce any man but sometime was forced to wink or nod." Cooped up in his study as he had to be much of the rest of the time, Cotton was fortunate that his wife Elizabeth, sister of a minister and recommended to him by a non-conformist friend from Cambridge University, served as a spiritual counselor to Boston's women and guided him to topics that needed preaching.[28]

Among Cotton's preaching topics were knotty Bible prophecies consisting of elusive references to various series of days, months, and years loosely coordinated with a cornucopia of weird imagery: a beast rising from the sea with seven heads and ten horns; a woman clothed with the sun giving birth to a man-child; a dragon whose tail sweeps a third of the stars out of the sky; and much, much more.[29] The prophecies were exceedingly hard to crack, but the pay-off was enormous, for concealed within them, Protestants generally agreed, were important forecasts about the struggle between Christ's true church and Antichrist's false church down to the end of time.

In the sixteenth century, the general English consensus was that all these heavily veiled prophecies had been fulfilled save for Revelation 20:8's prediction of the soon-approaching final great battle between the forces of good and evil. But there was a rumbling of disagreement. Cotton was particularly attracted to the work of the outspoken Presbyterian minister Thomas Brightman who blew the consensus wide open in a series of Latin manuscripts written between 1600 and 1607 and published posthumously shortly thereafter. Brightman brought the wonderful news that, according to the Bible, there was much more still to come before the end of time. The hope-filled prophecy of a thousand years of peace and prosperity for the true church, the millennium mentioned in Revelation 20:4 and 6, had yet to be fulfilled, along with other prophecies leading up to it.[30]

In sermons preached around 1625, Cotton explained to his Boston audience what this wonderful millennial church was going to be like. All the church's members would be holy, Cotton assured them, all its ministers devoted to preaching, and even mighty kings and queens would bow themselves to its discipline. The church, the bride of Christ, Cotton promised, would wax so lovely during the millennium, "that it were even love itself," and the purified public worship of this radiant beauty, Cotton exclaimed to his listeners, would be "the marriage bed wherein Christ most familiarly solaceth himself with his Church." Millennialism, with its divine promise that Christ's church would finally be properly reformed and that the godly community would finally enjoy rest from its struggles, in spite of all the forces of evil working against it, particularly appealed to puritans.[31]

Brightman calculated that this millennial church was coming as soon as the end of the century.[32] Consoling though that prospect was, it offered little immediate aid for Cotton, who lost his pulpit in 1632. Dod, on the other hand, got a pulpit back for good after the death of King James in 1625. With the hostile king gone, George Abbott, the puritan-friendly archbishop of Canterbury, lifted Dod's suspension. Dod, now seventy-five years old, found a position with another Northamptonshire gentry family, the Knightleys. A false-front ministry in the Knightley's parish church (the Knightley's manor house was the parish's only dwelling), and regular gifts of venison to episcopal officials kept Dod secure there for the rest of his life.[33] Dod had no illusions about how fortunate he was. When puritans came to him to discuss nonconformity, Dod would adjust his answers to his assessment of their capacity to suffer.[34]

Unconflicted conforming puritans might have been the only ones who could sleep entirely securely, and they could have a huge reforming impact. One such minister, John White, arrived in Dorchester, a sleepy town of two thousand people nestled in the Dorset Downs, 5 miles from the English Channel, in 1605. A decade earlier, the only evidence there of the tumult of England's reformation had been the severed head of a Catholic priest, executed in 1594, louring on a pole over one of the town's medieval gates. White threw himself into preaching three lectures a week, on top of his Sunday sermons. To ensure his message was sinking in, White instituted house-to-house visits in his parish, praying with his parishioners and cate-chizing them in the basics of Calvinist theology. White's methods were effective, even unsettlingly so: a wealthy town official grumbled that he would offer £100 to get White out of Dorchester.[35]

Dorchester's reformation took a further leap forward when on August 6, 1613 tallow blazed up in the workshop of a careless candle-maker. Fire roared through Dorchester's thatched roofs and timber house frames and destroyed half the town before it was extinguished. "How are the labors of many a father, grandfather, great-grandfather, suddenly converted into smoke and rubbish, in the space of a day and night?" lamented William Whately when such a fire blazed through Banbury in this age before insur-ance. What clearer sign could there be that God was angry at a town's sins? It was those sins that "cause a tender-hearted father to burn in displeasure against us," as Whately put it.[36]

The divine displeasure behind the Dorchester fire spurred White and a rising group of puritan town leaders to consolidate control of Dorchester's government and embark on an ambitious program of reform. Church attendance was vigorously enforced and Sabbath-breakers punished, while the number of illegitimate children dropped to half the national level. Traveling theater troupes soon found out that Dorchester was off limits, and visiting county gentlemen fumed to discover that high social status gave no protection from fines for drunkenness or oaths. "A fart to you all," sputtered one such gentleman to the puritan justices fining him.[37]

There was one regular Dorchester event that White and his allies were particularly keen to purge of its sin: the Lord's Supper. The bread and wine of that sacrament should have been reserved for God's elect, or at least for those who gave reason to hope they might be among the elect. As the apostle Paul ominously warned would-be participants in the Lord's Supper, "he that eateth and drinketh unworthily, eateth and drinketh damnation" (1 Corinthians 11:29). The most scrupulous puritans hesitated to take the Lord's Supper if they had to do it with their nakedly unworthy neighbors, lest the guilt of those neighbors' participation fall on their heads.[38]

White was among the puritan ministers who tried to work around the legal restraints that left them next to no power to reserve the Lord's Supper for the godly. On Saturday evenings before the sacrament, he and willing parishioners assembled to put themselves in the right preparatory frame of repentance and anticipation. The high point of the evening came when White read out a "covenant unto our Lord" consisting of ten vows, to each of which his parishioners answered "Amen." The vows focused on improving godly behavior: more sermons, more instructing families "in the fear of the Lord," and more admonishing and exhorting each other, among other manifestations of zeal. White lacked the power to make the vows mandatory, but he requested his parishioners who refused to take them to skip the Lord's Supper. A request from a forceful minister well connected to the town's oligarchy undoubtedly carried a lot of persuasiveness.[39]

Besides cracking down on sin, Dorchester's puritan oligarchs pursued the puritan reforming goal of systematic alleviation of suffering. England was struggling with massive population growth, periodic food shortages, and economic depression. Dorchester taxes went up to pay for vastly increased aid to the poor. A surge in charitable giving led to the creation of a school where the children of the poor could learn a trade and an expansion of almshouses for the elderly. Residents gave generously to assist other towns hit by fire, plague, or outbreaks of famine and sent aid to beleaguered Protestants on the continent.[40]

In 1623, White and fellow puritans extended their philanthropic vision across the Atlantic with the foundation of the Dorchester Company. The company's purpose was to provide a permanent New England settlement to make provisions and religious instruction available to the fishermen increasingly leaving West Country ports to fish in that region. Its membership included merchants, ministers, gentlemen, and a few widows (acting on their own behalf since they had no husbands to act for them). The Dorchester Company marked the beginning of the process that led to the founding of Massachusetts, and White was heavily involved in that process as well.[41]

The success of White and his fellow lay puritan oligarchs in reforming Dorchester showed how puritanized England might potentially become, even if still handicapped by bishops and surplices. There would be intelligent, generous charity and ample government intervention for the deserving poor. Although the Church of England lacked adequate disciplinary structures to police sin, the discipline of powerful puritan preaching would reform and convert English people, even to the furthest reaches of the globe. Strict Ten Commandments law and order would reign everywhere— perhaps to the high standard set by the pious Somerset magistrates who had a pair of fornicators whipped in public until they bled, while two fiddlers played before them to remind onlookers that their sin was the consequence of their earlier sin of dancing on the Sabbath.[42]

But of course, such a happy outcome assumed that the rest of the Church of England would gladly welcome conforming puritans who could live with the spiritually "indifferent" government and ceremonies of the church. That unqualified welcome had never been likely, and it was growing less and less so in the early seventeenth century. Back in 1550, John Hooper had warned that nothing could stay spiritually indifferent permanently; leave it in the church and, sooner or later, people would ascribe false spiritual significance to it. Indeed, such significance was starting to adhere to parts of the church that had been free of it in the sixteenth century. Bishops, their supporters were now arguing, were not an indifferent administrative convenience, they were part of God's plan, as in the Catholic Church. The ceremonies were not "indifferent," they were important aids to devotion, as in the Catholic Church. A wing of the Church of England was, from a puritan perspective, retreating from the Reformation, while showing hostility even to conformist puritans—White with his exclusionary Ten Vows faced accusations of fostering a "schism in the church and rebellion in the state," just as Whately had been accused of fomenting faction with his preaching. Even worse was on the horizon, and puritanism's struggles and trials were soon going to sharply increase.[43]

CHAPTER 7

# THE LURE OF THE ATLANTIC

The message preached by Jeremiah Dyke to the members of the House of Commons on April 5, 1628 could not have been blunter or bleaker: "God is departing from us."[1] Puritan ministers had long warned that God was on the verge of abandoning England in anger at its failures to rein in its sinning and complete the reformation of its church. Now, Dyke and other puritans feared that recent changes in the Church of England had driven God past the limits of his patience. When God left, disaster inevitably followed, and some puritans started thinking that they might be better off somewhere else.

John Robinson's separatist Netherlands-based congregation had made the decision to leave England two decades earlier (see p. 62). But by the end of the 1610s, their hopes of fostering reformation in the Netherlands were growing dim. Making a living was hard, and the Dutch did not meet their high standards of piety. They told themselves that these problems were what prevented English people from flocking to them and freeing themselves from the corruptions of the Church of England. If the separatists went to America and prospered, however, their countrymen would be keener to join them there. And so, for the sake of further reformation, the decision was made to cross the Atlantic. In 1620, after receiving unofficial permission from King James to worship as they pleased, they found a group of profit-seeking London artisans and merchants who were willing to fund their venture, and the Virginia Company gave them a patent to create a plantation, a single settlement, on its puritan-tolerant territory.[2]

When the time came to depart from the Netherlands in July 1620, the majority of the congregation got cold feet. They said they would come later and persuaded Robinson to stay with them for the time being. The immigrants would have to leave behind them their beloved pastor and the greater part of their religious community, with no assurance that they would ever see them again. "But they knew they were pilgrims," William Bradford recalled in his history of Plymouth Plantation, "and looked not much on those things, but lift up their eyes to the heavens, their dearest country, and quieted their spirits." Except in the generic sense that every Christian knew that he or she was a pilgrim whose home was in heaven, the immigrants did not call themselves "Pilgrims." The name was applied to them as a specific group at the end of the eighteenth century, and it stuck.[3]

Their boat overshot its destination and ended up off the coast of Massachusetts in December 1620, far north of the territory where they had been given the right to settle. They settled at a site they called Plymouth, an abandoned Native American village devastated by a recent brutal epidemic that left bones and skulls scattered across the region and opened it up for extensive English immigration. Massasoit, the sachem (chief) of the local Wampanoag tribe, had seen his followers plummet from around 3,000 to around 150, and, fortunately for the separatists, he needed any allies he could get against his inland enemies who had not been similarly ravaged. It mattered not how weak those allies were—around half of the hundred or so English passengers died that winter, and only ten households were left by the spring of 1621.[4]

The next few years did not go much better. The London financial backers occasionally sent over more settlers to Plymouth, some separatists, some not. But the plantation was losing money and backers began pulling out. The colonists kept hoping that the Londoners would agree to send Robinson to their church, but he died on March 1, 1625 in Leiden, victim of an outbreak of the plague that killed eight thousand people in the city. In Robinson's absence, the ruling lay elder William Brewster preached twice each Sunday and led the congregation in prayers.[5]

By 1626, the future of the debt-laden, ministerless plantation, its roughly 150 settlers, and the reformation it had hoped to foster appeared grim. Plymouth seemed destined to join the growing scrap heap of failed English North American colonies. "To look humanly on the state of things as they presented themselves at this time, it is a marvel it did not wholly discourage them," Bradford wrote later.[6] That the plantation did survive was because it would shortly acquire a sympathetic, larger, and much better-connected puritan neighbor to the north, as soon as the evidence that God was leaving England became impossible to ignore.

Just as Bradford was losing hope over his plantation, two very worried puritan aristocrats were teetering on the brink of despair over the state of England itself. One was Robert Rich, earl of Warwick, a great landowner, a patron of nonconformist ministers, and a heavy investor in American colonization. The other was William Fiennes, Lord Saye and Sele. His seat of Broughton Castle lay only a few miles from the puritan hotbed of Banbury.[7] Like all puritans, and even many people who were not puritans, the two noblemen feared for England because long-stable religious ground was rapidly shifting under their feet. No matter how much puritans had clashed with the bishops in the past, on the fundamental issue of salvation, they had been in agreement. They were all Calvinists and committed to predestination.

At the end of the sixteenth century, some Church of England ministers and university professors started questioning predestination. They did so gingerly at first since this was a fast way to make powerful enemies. In the early seventeenth century, the varieties of opposition to predestination were often subsumed under the catch-all term of Arminianism, after Jacob Arminius, a Dutch minister who created a scandal in the Netherlands by maintaining that salvation was not entirely predestined: humans genuinely had the ability to choose to cooperate or not with God's grace.[8]

Puritans were horrified by the rise of these anti-Calvinists. For puritans, salvation hinged on discovering through a wrenching, protracted confrontation with your own wicked heart the central saving truth that Arminians denied: you had not the slightest power to save yourself. One puritan long remembered his tutor at Cambridge University laying his hand on his breast and saying, "Every true convert hath something here that will frame an argument against an Arminian."[9] Arminians dethroned God and pulled him down from heaven, as another angry puritan put it, since they were implying that weak, sinful humans were beyond his control to save or damn. John Dod warned that even to question predestination damnably broke the Third Commandment by taking the Lord's name in vain.[10]

King James was stoutly supportive of Calvinism as late as 1618. That year he sent a Church of England delegation to the renowned Synod of Dort in the Netherlands, where they and other representatives of Europe's Reformed churches affirmed their shared Calvinism and condemned Arminianism. But thereafter things went badly wrong for Calvinism and for James's support of it. His son-in-law Frederick V, ruler of the important

German Calvinist territory of the Palatinate, blundered into triggering the horrific Thirty Years' War in 1619. Catholic armies quickly ravaged the Palatinate and other Protestant lands in Germany, with Spain providing much of the military muscle.[11]

James's subjects, puritans and non-puritans alike, took it for granted that James would rally to the aid of Frederick. It was blindingly obvious, at least to devout Calvinists, that the struggle on the continent was part of the great war foreseen in the Bible between the people of God and Catholic princes that would precede Antichrist's overthrow. But James's finances were badly overstretched and he disliked war. To the dismay of most of his subjects, James attempted to pacify Spain by trying to marry his son Charles to a Spanish princess. To sweeten the offer, he loosened up the enforcement of legal restrictions on English Catholics. A barrage of horrified Calvinist alarm sounded all the way from village puritan prayer meetings to the archbishop of Canterbury. Puritans claimed that it was their private fasts and prayers that caused the match to fall through in 1623. Historians are more inclined to stress that the Spaniards never intended it to succeed and were playing James and Charles for fools.[12]

The almost unanimous opposition from his Calvinist subjects produced a drastic religious change of direction for James. While the Calvinists dared to criticize him, one group stayed loyal, the anti-Calvinists. James now listened much more attentively as they expanded upon the old anti-puritan argument that puritanism was inherently "popular" (i.e., of the people) and, therefore, inherently antimonarchical. James already agreed with that old argument, as had Queen Elizabeth. What it missed, however, insisted the anti-Calvinists, was just how wrapped up with puritanism was predestination itself. Untangling the complexity of predestination, they argued, required a time-consuming emphasis on preaching, which led, inevitably, to neglect of ceremonies. This neglect encouraged "popular" puritan rebellion against them. In the wake of that rebellion came demands for popular church government—Presbyterianism—followed by demands for popular government in the state and, finally, rebellion against the king.[13]

The noxious puritan weed that flowered into rebellion had to be torn out by predestinarian roots that ran far deeper and wider than puritanism itself. Preaching needed to be downplayed, ceremonies needed to be played up. The mysteries of divine and earthly kingship should not be probed and analyzed, as James's Calvinist subjects were doing, but accepted with devotional reverence. Catholic subjects needed to be courted, not repulsed, and the pope should not be called Antichrist.

This anti-Calvinist pitch for a drastic change in the Church of England came at a time when the church was working as an all-encompassing national church about as well as could be hoped for, and better than it ever would again. Anti-Calvinists and puritans alike had their discontented places in the church, as did everyone in between, while puritans were putting most of their reforming energies to evangelical purposes that bishops often appreciated.

That precarious, hard-won balancing act amounted to very little against the unhappiness of the supreme governor of the Church of England, King James. In 1622, James banned the preaching of predestination, and in the last years of his reign, he showed increasing favor to anti-Calvinist, ceremonial churchmen. James died in 1625. His son, Charles I, was himself an anti-Calvinist with an intense attachment to bishops and ceremonial religion, who married a Catholic French princess (potential Protestant brides of suitably high rank were few and far between). It was easy enough for puritans and even non-puritan Calvinists to see the anti-Calvinists as sinister secret agents in the larger Catholic plot against God and true religion that was wreaking havoc on the continent.[14]

The advance of the anti-Calvinists was why the earl of Warwick and Lord Saye and Sele were so worried in 1626 about England. Their plan was to coax Charles back to the old Calvinist theological consensus through his favorite courtier, the duke of Buckingham. If the duke could be persuaded of the truth of Calvinism, he could steer Charles correctly. To that end, they set up a conference at Buckingham's London mansion, York House. Buckingham, however, was intensely greedy, had Catholic relatives, and was acutely aware of which way the royal wind was blowing. The tongues of angels could not have persuaded him of Calvinism's truth, let alone the puritan-friendly bishop Thomas Morton and the prominent conforming puritan minister John Preston brought along by the puritan lords. The conference produced neither a condemnation of anti-Calvinism nor an affirmation of Calvinism.[15] Charles would have to be confronted about these undesired religious changes, not persuaded.

The first confrontation took place in the Parliament that was already meeting at the time of the York House conference. Charles wanted it to provide money in preparation for what would be a disastrously conceived and executed war with France. The House of Commons, though, was more interested in impeaching Buckingham, imprisoning leading anti-Calvinists, and providing relief for nonconformist puritan ministers, and Charles quickly dissolved Parliament. Still in need of money for his war, he decided to go around Parliament to raise it, something most English people regarded as illegal. Charles commanded a forced loan from his subjects, with no odds of it ever being repaid.[16]

Resistance to the forced loan was widespread, and sixty-seven gentlemen chose prison over payment. The hottest Protestants were the ones who resisted the loan the most fiercely. For them, a plot was afoot in which religious and secular tyranny marched hand in hand to the destruction of England, its liberties, and its reformation. John Dod traveled to London to buck up the spirits of a prominent imprisoned opponent of the loan, Sir Francis Barrington. He preached a fiery sermon to Barrington based on Revelation 2:10: "Fear none of these things which thou shalt suffer; behold the devil shall cast some of you into prison."[17] The most audacious puritan resisters, including John Cotton and some of his parishioners in Boston, were regularly toing and froing from the earl of Lincoln's estate, while they worked out a propaganda campaign against the loan. In the midst of planning their tax revolt, the earl's godly plotters began discussions about creating Massachusetts, where a number of them would soon end up.

They were probably inspired to turn their attention across the Atlantic by the New England Company, an offshoot of John White's Dorchester Company that was nurturing a tiny settlement at what would become Salem, Massachusetts. As two of this company's settler ships crossed the Atlantic to Salem in 1628, a thoroughly alarmed new Parliament was abuzz with schemes to crush Arminianism, bridle the king's power, and help the nonconforming puritan ministers. The House of Commons managed to persuade the much more deferential House of Lords and Charles himself to agree to a Petition of Right that banned the king's arbitrary imprisonments and taxation. Great bonfires were lit across London in joyous celebration, but it soon became clear that Charles interpreted the petition in a way that made its restraints on him meaningless.[18]

Charles recalled Parliament in January 1629, in vain hopes of getting more money from it. During the death throes of this stormy, defiant Parliament, on March 2, the king signed a charter granting territory around Massachusetts Bay to a new puritan-led company, the Massachusetts Bay Company, which swallowed up the New England Company and its settlement at Salem. Nothing is known about how puritans acquired a charter for a colony from a puritan-loathing king, save that the process, according to the then-governor of the company, Matthew Craddock, required "great cost, favor of personages of note, and much labor."[19]

Eight days later Charles angrily dissolved Parliament. There were widespread, justified fears that he would not call one again for a very long time. A month later, the Massachusetts Bay Company sent another group of two hundred settlers to Salem, accompanied by a few puritan ministers, and started planning for a much larger migration to take place the next year. Charles told the French ambassador that summer, not entirely correctly, that Parliament's leaders were puritans, which meant, according to Charles, that they were enemies to monarchy.[20] You could have kings or you could have puritans, but from Charles's viewpoint, you could not have both.

One of the puritans taking an interest in the Massachusetts Bay Company was John Winthrop, a deeply pious forty-two-year-old lawyer and lord of Groton Manor, about 70 miles northeast of London in the heartland of English puritanism. He had once considered becoming a minister until friends talked him out of it. Winthrop had personal reasons to be dissatisfied with England. He was beset with financial worries as he struggled to provide for his growing family and maintain a way of life appropriate to his social rank—he had surely heard the frightening stories of once-flourishing gentry families reduced to begging and parish poor relief. His own struggles took place as England's chronic problems of severe overpopulation and underemployment were reaching boiling point; "The land grows weary of her inhabitants," as Winthrop put it. Winthrop's formidable leadership capacities had never found an outlet; his one run for Parliament had failed.[21]

Those issues were undoubtedly at the back of Winthrop's mind when he started circulating papers among his godly friends and acquaintances making the case for departure. That case itself was almost entirely religious. A colony would expand the true church. It would strike a blow against the "kingdom of Antichrist" that Jesuit missionaries in the fledgling French colony of Quebec were beginning to create among the Native Americans. More importantly, it would provide shelter from the storm of divine wrath heading to England. The Church of England was corrupt beyond reform and as superstitious as the Catholic Church, while England's other institutions were no less corrupt. Massachusetts, Winthrop wrote, could provide refuge for "God's people." "After the storm," they would return to their English "mother church."[22]

In August 1629 Winthrop and eleven other puritan gentlemen met in Cambridge to write up an agreement about immigrating. They agreed among themselves that the colonization of Massachusetts was a great work "in regard of... God's glory and the Church's good." Moreover, they solemnly bound themselves "in the presence of God" to immigrate. However, they added one audacious condition: the company's whole government and the royal charter itself would have to go with them.[23] If the Massachusetts Bay Company agreed, Massachusetts would be a new kind of chartered colony, a self-governing one, and drastically different from Bermuda, the only American puritan-leaning colony outside New England that survived for any length of time.[24]

Zealous puritans would have found much to like about Bermuda, a twenty-square-mile, tobacco-raising colony in the Atlantic Ocean about 850 miles east of present-day North Carolina, settled in 1612. They would have appreciated that the London-based Bermuda (or Somers Islands) Company sent puritans as governors. They would have been pleased that the ministers the company sent to Bermuda were almost all nonconformists (as far as historians can determine) and that they sat on the governor's council.[25] Puritans would have been glad that Bermuda's civil courts tried to keep the raging sexual lust of fallen humanity within strict legal bounds and preserved the sanctity of the Sabbath firmly enough to impress visitors to the colony. Puritans would also be gratified that plays were banned and that on Bermuda, far away from the inhibiting hand of the bishops, a devil rash enough to possess someone would face a full public puritan spiritual onslaught, a day of fasting, prayers, and sermons called by the governor himself, with most of the island participating.[26]

But zealous puritans would also have been disappointed about the limitations of Bermuda's reformation. Except for permitting ministers to practice nonconformity, the government left the colony's churches barely reformed. There was no church discipline to chasten straying sinners and protect the purity of the sacraments.[27] Ministers were paid erratically and sometimes poorly by the company; they did not, for the most part, remain long to care for their flocks as good shepherds should; and there were almost never enough of them. In the absence of ministers, laymen led church services. But as in the English parish churches, they could do no more than read from the old official Church of England sermon book, the Book of Homilies. A puritan would have been displeased that the churches still observed what puritans took to be the pagan holiday of Christmas and that much of the island's population was not ideal raw material for godliness. Some of them had even been collected from the streets, prisons and almshouses of London. Such people, raised like "heathens," were incapable, one Bermuda minister complained, of raising their own children as Christians. ("Heathens" themselves, in the form of enslaved Africans and Native Americans, started to be brought to Bermuda from the Caribbean as early as 1616.) On Bermuda, according to Richard

Norwood, the colony's schoolteacher, the "truly religious" (i.e., puritans) were outnumbered "by far."[28]

The Bermuda Company had no incentive to push Bermuda's limited reformation any further than it had gone. The company, since it was London-based, might easily find authorities in church and state breathing down its neck if its colony strayed too far from Church of England norms; the company's first concern for the colony, as well as the first responsibility of the governors that it sent there, was that it produce profits, not saints; and, in any case, Bermuda was 3,000 miles distant from where the company's directors lived, prayed, and worshiped. In all those respects, if Winthrop's group had its way, the government of the Massachusetts Bay Company would be completely different.

Winthrop's group was, by rarified English social standards, a fairly unimpressive collection of gentry. The Massachusetts Bay Company itself, however, was deficient in representatives from England's top social tiers and was having a hard time finding anyone to lead the immigration. The freemen of the company approved Winthrop's proposal to take the Massachusetts Bay Company and its charter with them to Massachusetts on October 15. Their consent laid the foundation for what would become Massachusetts's extraordinary experiment in godly self-government. The investors must have been aware that in giving their colony autonomy, they were writing off a large portion of their investment since the colony's government was more likely to be focused on heavenly payoffs than earthly ones. Five days later a new immigrating court of assistants for the Massachusetts Bay Company was elected, with Winthrop as the company's governor.[29]

Winthrop immediately set to work. Suitably godly settlers had to be found, craftsmen needed to be recruited, ministers procured, and supplies assembled. Next spring, thirteen ships with almost a thousand settlers were ready to depart. John Cotton, far more widely known than any of the emigrants, gladly preached a rousing farewell sermon to them, whose numbers included some of his parishioners, as they waited to depart from Southampton harbor. He might have been no less glad to ride back to his influential pulpit in Boston, Lincolnshire instead of sailing off into the unknown. The one safe prediction about the colony, judging by previous efforts, would be that many of the settlers would be dead by the end of the first year. Governor Winthrop prudently left behind his pregnant third wife Margaret and his two-year-old son.[30]

The new governor and assistants of the Massachusetts Bay Company might have been relatively undistinguished in outward accomplishments, but they knew that as God's servants carrying out his will for his church, whatever they did was of utmost intrinsic importance. In a much-later-to-be-famous piece of writing that might have been given as a shipboard exhortation, or might not have been given at all, Governor Winthrop reminded the immigrants of the solemnity of the task facing them. They had asked God's blessing on their venture. In doing so, they had made a covenant with him. If God delivered on his side by bringing them safely across the ocean, they would have to deliver on theirs. In Massachusetts they all must serve each other in love, as befitted true Christians: "We must delight in each other; make other's conditions our own; rejoice together, mourn together, labor and suffer together." If they succeeded, God "would delight to dwell among us as his people." But if they failed, they would break their covenant with God, and then would come disaster: "The Lord will surely break out in wrath against us."[31]

Upon this success or failure hung more than just the immigrants' fates. In their own minds, puritans were always on stage, before their jealous deity and before an earthly audience of whom the greatest, wicked part, as John Dod had warned, was hoping for them to fail. Puritan ministers compared the godly to "a city set upon an hill." They warned that "the men of the world" were watching them closely, not out of admiration, but "out of the hatred of the truth" and that "a little blemish is soon seen in their face."[32]

Winthrop gave the same warning in his speech, "We shall be as a city upon a hill. The eyes of all people are upon us." If the colony failed, as it easily could, that failure would be a huge blow to puritanism, one felt in Europe. "We shall be made a story and a byword through the world . . . We shall open the mouths of enemies to speak evil of the ways of God, and all [puritans] . . . We shall shame the face of many of God's worthy servants." If it succeeded, which most English colonies had yet to do, the effect would be more local; Massachusetts would serve as a model for future colonies, or "plantations" as Winthrop conventionally called them: "Men shall say of succeeding plantations, 'The Lord make it like that of New England.' "[33]

Winthrop's speech, if he ever actually delivered it, was quickly forgotten and lay in obscurity until the early 1950s, when the great scholar of puritanism Perry Miller turned his attention to it. Miller, whose brilliance sometimes outran his scrupulosity, stretched and stretched the meaning of "plantations" long past where it should have snapped until he had, in his own mind, made it synonymous with "countries," which it was not. According to Miller, then, it was not the fledgling, struggling American plantations that Winthrop hoped his prospective colony might prop up, assuming God did not righteously destroy it first; Winthrop was intending to make Massachusetts nothing less than a model for the European Reformation itself.[34]

With that vast claim, Miller invented an ancient puritan explanation for the United States's interventionist, beacon-to-the-world exceptionalism, and Winthrop's speech, along with its evidence-free alleged meaning, finally started attracting attention. By the 1960s politicians were using the phrase "city on a hill" as a rhetorical flourish in their speeches, while critics of America's involvement in Vietnam traced its roots to Winthrop's speech. But it was Ronald Reagan who repeatedly and purposefully deployed "city on a hill" until it and its supposed meaning became the one (incorrect) thing Americans generally know about puritans besides the Salem witch trials. "Americans in 1980 are every bit as committed to [Winthrop's] vision of a shining 'city on a hill,'" Reagan said in his representative final 1980 campaign speech, "as were those long-ago settlers . . . still for [Americans] and for so many other millions in the world a city offering the 'last best hope of man on earth!'" Winthrop, always alert for the afflicting hand of a wrathful God, would have been mortified to be associated with such un-puritan hubris.[35]

In 1630, Winthrop's warning about the watchfulness of God's enemies was especially timely. Those enemies had stopped making any secret of their intention to crush puritanism. William Laud, a leading anti-Calvinist, efficient and determined, had been appointed bishop of London in 1628. He already served on Charles I's Privy Council, and Charles promised that he would become the archbishop of Canterbury upon the death of the incumbent. The next year saw a drive against puritan town preachers and lecturers and a further clampdown on preaching predestination.[36] As Winthrop's fleet finally sailed off toward a reformation free of the escalating compromises puritans had to make in England, Laud and Charles were already at work bringing about their own vision of a godly church and society, both free of puritanism.

# Part II

## REFORMATIONS, c. 1630–c. 1660

# CHAPTER 8

# JOHN COTTON COMES TO MASSACHUSETTS

There must have been extraordinary excitement in Massachusetts on September 3, 1633 as word spread that the famous minister John Cotton had just been rowed ashore from the *Griffin*, moored in Boston's harbor. He and the other minister with him, Thomas Hooker, were the first prominent preachers to come to the 3,000-person, seven-town colony, and the town of Boston had been named in his honor.[1] Cotton quickly joined the Boston church and was elected one of its two ministers. He doubtless did not share with the colonists that he had not immigrated until the problems he saw with Massachusetts were overwhelmed by his lack of alternatives.

The first stumbling block for Cotton back in England in the early 1630s had been that the colony's churches had swerved sharply away from the puritan mainstream. In 1629, two ministers had arrived at the tiny advance settlement of Salem, keen to "gather" (found) a church with the inhabitants. No one had decided in advance what this new church should look like, and Salem's ministers and laity took as their inspiration the only Protestant Reformed church on the continent, the separatist Congregational church down Massachusetts Bay at Plymouth. Much New England and even English history flowed out of that decision.[2]

A foundational principle of Congregationalism was that they insisted that only individual congregations were real churches. Spiritually, there was no such thing as the collective Church of England. Its bishops and their great cathedrals and ecclesiastical courts counted for nothing in the eyes of God; all that existed spiritually of the Church of England were the individual parish churches. And according to the Plymouth separatist

Congregationalists, those parish churches, dens of unpunished sin, ungodliness, and false government and worship were no true churches at all (see p. 46).

What that rejection of the parish churches meant for the puritans aboard the Winthrop fleet in 1630 they discovered when their ships first moored in Salem's harbor. Their hopes of finally celebrating the Lord's Supper in a properly reformed church were dashed. Salem's minister Samuel Skelton bluntly told them that although they might be real Christians, his church only gave visitors' privileges to members of real churches, which their parish churches were not: therefore, no Lord's Supper for them and no baptism for their children.[3]

Cotton learned about this spiritual snub in a letter from Skelton (among those who had been snubbed were ex-parishioners of Cotton's). He fired off an indignant reply objecting to Salem's Plymouth-derived separatist exclusionary excess and circulated the letter in England. Cotton's was the first of what would be many letters in that decade complaining about the extremism of Massachusetts puritanism.[4]

Cotton's opportunity to rethink Congregationalism came shortly thereafter while he was still a parish minister in Boston, England. A loose-living Bostonian found himself hauled before the town's strict puritan magistrates once too often. He struck back by going to London to the Court of High Commission, a church court controlled by the bishop of London, William Laud, and dreaded by nonconformists. The rogue Bostonian informed the court of the Boston magistrates' religious nonconformity, pointed to Cotton as the cause, and soon thereafter, according to puritans, died of the plague in a ditch as an example of God's justice. In early 1632, the court summoned Cotton.[5]

For Cotton, the upcoming end of his ministry shed a new light on Congregationalism. The Congregationalists were right, Cotton decided: the only real churches were autonomous, individual congregations. Therefore, the Congregationalists were also right that there was no legitimate higher ecclesiastical power, such as, for example, the court that was about to end his career. Under God's law, if not the law of the Church of England, Cotton had no obligation to appear for his hearing. Instead, he went into hiding to consider his options, including leaving the country. Seventy-six of England's ten thousand ministers went to New England before 1640, and well over half, like Cotton, only left under direct and immediate pressure.[6]

By now Cotton had probably also learned that the Massachusetts puritans did not consider themselves schismatic separatists. Unlike the separatists, they claimed that some parish churches might be real churches, provided they had enough puritan laity and a puritan minister. But since they could not be sure which parish churches fitted this description at any given time, better safe than sorry: they still would not grant arriving immigrants access to the sacraments. When visiting England, like the Plymouth separatists, they would listen to sermons at the parish churches, but not take the sacraments. Listening to sermons was like listening to a lecture, while taking the sacraments was worship. For many puritans, there was no meaningful difference between the separatism they abhorred and this Massachusetts arm's-length, mostly theoretical affirmation of the Church of England's parish churches, but it worked for Cotton.[7]

By 1632, then, Cotton, still in England, no longer saw Congregationalism as a problem, but Massachusetts itself, remote and raw, still was. After much consultation, he set out in disguise for the Netherlands until a letter from Thomas Hooker, already there for two years, reached him warning that the Dutch neither knew nor wanted to know about "the power of godliness." Hooker had turned down an offer to go to Massachusetts in 1630, but now he was taking up another one from puritans to whom he had ministered in England. Cotton reluctantly decided to go with Hooker, but only because the other alternative, Barbados, was an even sketchier, decidedly ungodly colony. As Cotton wrote in verses he retained until his death, he kept recalling the joys of his old ministry in order that "the grief to be cast out into a wilderness / Doth not so much distress me."[8]

Cotton did not have to face the wilderness alone. After he and Hooker slipped past the government spies watching for them at the ports, they sailed for Massachusetts with family and friends, as was often the case with puritans immigrating to New England. En route, Cotton's wife gave birth to a son they named Seaborn, but Cotton, now a convinced Congregationalist, would not baptize him. He might have been one of the most admired puritan ministers in England, but as a good Congregationalist, he now accepted that he was without the power to administer sacraments. He would remain without that power until a Massachusetts church made him its minister after admitting him as a member, and then only in that particular congregation. This shrunken, congregation-dependent sense of a minister's capacities did not play well with many English puritan ministers.[9]

John Cotton soon discovered that for godliness Massachusetts was indeed a better choice than the Netherlands. Before he arrived, the magistrates had banned smoking in public, ordered households to destroy dice and cards, policed the Sabbath, and instituted the death penalty for adultery, following Old Testament precedent. "We have few that are drunk and here there is no swearing," the Massachusetts minister Thomas Welde wrote to his ex-parishioners in 1632, "for they [that] be drunk or swear . . . are punished."[10]

That much Cotton might have expected from Massachusetts's godly magistrates, but it was their unprecedented political innovations that captured his imagination. Governor Winthrop and his Court of Assistants, Massachusetts's government, were the only members of the Massachusetts Bay Company in the colony. Under the terms of the company's charter that they brought with them, they, as company members, were the only people who could vote. Had they chosen to do so, they could have made themselves a self-perpetuating governing board. But as Charles I had demonstrated, rulers who made themselves unanswerable to their people easily fell into tyranny. In order to avoid such an outcome, they soon created another route to choosing the government, one that ran through the churches.[11]

Massachusetts's churches required would-be members to demonstrate that they were "visible saints." These were people who, to outward visible appearances (only God knew for sure), had been converted and were going to heaven, using the admittedly approximate measuring stick of what was called the judgment of charity. What it measured was the applicants' virtuous lives, their repentance for their sins, and their grasp of religious doctrine.[12]

If a congregation's men approved the applicants as visible saints, they would be allowed to take the church's covenant. This was a solemn vow to join together in fellowship as a church that the founding members had initially taken during a day of sermons, fasting, and prayer. The covenant was what created a church according to Congregationalists. It put a fledgling Massachusetts village church on an entirely equal footing with all the other true churches in the world and under the authority of no higher church body or ruler than King Jesus.[13]

Winthrop and the Court of Assistants decided within a year of their arrival that any adult male who had been admitted to a church would become a freeman of the Massachusetts Bay Company and have the right to vote. Piety, not property—the usual English requirement—would determine who elected the leaders of Massachusetts. Every year the freemen could vote the governor and Court of Assistants in or out of office, along with their own deputies, who met with the assistants four times a year in the General Court, the colony's supreme judicial court and legislative body.[14]

The more Cotton thought about this quasi-republican government for and by the saints, the more he approved of it. Godly rulers, by definition, would rule justly for everyone, saints and non-saints, with the added benefit that they would especially care for Christ's churches, while the godly voters could supervise and rebuke their rulers by voting at the annual elections. Non-church members had every civil right that church members had except the franchise, and a greater percentage of Massachusetts's population could vote than in England.[15]

Cotton did not shrink from the revolutionary political implications of accountable self-rule by the saints. Because of his great prestige, the General Court assigned him the delicate task of answering an offer by two English puritan lords who had accumulated land in southern New England. In 1634 they proposed to Massachusetts that they would immigrate and merge their holdings with Massachusetts, provided that the Massachusetts government add a hereditary upper house like the English House of Lords. Cotton explained to the lords that hereditary rule and godly rule were incompatible since saintliness did not necessarily run in blood lines. True, the Jews in the Old Testament had a monarchy, Cotton acknowledged, but that was only because they were preparing the lineage of the king of kings, Jesus. Where the ungodliness of hereditary rule left the English monarchy, Cotton did not say.[16]

Cotton also approved, and possibly helped to instigate, a major step forward in the exclusivity of Massachusetts's churches. Soon after he arrived, the judgment of charity that was used for the churches' admissions became much less charitable. By 1636, it was not enough to act like a visible saint, you had to explain how God transformed you into one. Applicants now had to tell the church they wished to join a story of how God had awoken them to their sinful natures and how he had lifted them from the depths of their subsequent despair and how they had come to know, however unsteadily, that he had saved them.[17]

A good conversion narrative could reduce a church meeting to tears of sorrow at the depths of human wickedness and raise it to tears of joy at the wonders of God's grace. An unconvincing one could unleash a barrage of questions ranging from the concerned to the hostile: "Are you not one unfruitful tree that should be hewn down?" one Nicholas Wyeth was bluntly asked as he struggled in a Massachusetts meeting house to explain why he thought he was among the saved. Ministers always acknowledged that the procedure was not a completely foolproof test of who was going to heaven; even a highly visible saint was not necessarily a real one. But that acknowledgment could be easily lost in the drama of the moment. One newly accepted woman said the event was for her a foretaste of the saints' meeting in heaven. In the late 1630s, the ordeal helped to keep around 50 percent of the population away from church membership and access to the sacraments.[18]

By the middle of the 1630s, Cotton the reluctant immigrant had grown so pleased with Massachusetts and its churches that he began to see in them a foreshadowing of the glorious millennium that he had predicted back in England (see p. 67). "The order of the churches and of the common-wealth" in Massachusetts, Cotton wrote around 1635, reminded him "of the New Heaven and New Earth" of the millennium. Others in Massachusetts started to share his enthusiasm about Massachusetts's accomplishment. Cotton told his Boston audience around 1640 that as the millennium drew ever closer Congregationalism would spread around the world (1655 was his educated guess as to the crucial date when the Catholic Church would fall).[19]

Cotton would not have been a puritan, however, if he had not also sternly warned New Englanders that standards of holiness would rise sharply during the millennium and that, based on present evidence, New England might not make the cut.[20] God, it turned out, had chosen the New England churches for the glory of being the first to display his millennial church pattern, but at no point did he need them for his will to be accomplished, any more than spring needs the swallows of Capistrano.

# CHAPTER 9

# PROTESTANT REFORMATION AND COUNTER-REFORMATION IN THE 1630s

Reformation was in the air in the 1630s, and not only in New England. In England itself, another, very different reformation, spearheaded by King Charles I and the new, ambitious, anti-Calvinist archbishop of Canterbury William Laud, was making vigorous headway. This was a Protestant counter-reformation intended to insulate the Church of England from puritanism. The success of that counter-reformation was driving even the most conformist of puritans to despair, while ensuring a steady stream of immigrants to New England. It would eventually collapse through its own overreach, thereby opening the door for a puritan reformation in England. But by the time that happened, New England's reformation had laid open the divisions among puritans for all the world to see.

At the start of the 1630s, Charles I was still reeling from what he was convinced had been a puritan-led Parliamentary attempt in 1629 to strip him of his authority and perhaps overthrow him. He was determined to avoid calling Parliament again, even if that meant resorting to measures of dubious legality to raise funds from his subjects. Those subjects must learn not to question him, but to obey him in reverent awe, guided by the magnetic pull of his moral superiority and divine-right authority.

In contrast to his loose-living father, Charles turned his court into an example of virtue for the rest of the country. He practiced the extraordinary restraint, for a king, of denying himself a mistress, and he expected the same from his courtiers. "We all keep our virginities at court still, at least we lose them not so avowedly," as one courtier put it. England's upper classes discovered, none too happily, that under the new regime a gentleman as well as a ploughman might find himself standing penitently in a church in a white sheet for adultery.[1]

Puritans must surely have approved of Charles's enforcement of chastity, but they loathed his and his French Catholic wife's favorite court pastime— staging elaborate plays in which chaos, disorder, and unruly passions faded away at the entrance of the play's most important actors, the king and queen themselves. On May 10, 1634, a blustery puritan lawyer, William Prynne, found himself with his head in a pillory on Cheapside, London's main street, his face wreathed in smoke from burning copies of *Histrio-mastix*, his thousand-page diatribe against plays, and his ears bleeding stumps from the hangman's knife. Prynne, with stunning political tactlessness, if not worse, given the pastimes of the king and queen, had endorsed the assassination of stage-acting Roman emperors and included the index entry "*Women-Actors*, notorious whores" in his diatribe.[2]

To Charles, the proper, lesser luminaries in the governance of England were not the parliamentary representatives of seditious puritan commoners like Prynne but the hereditary aristocracy. They were to be his counselors and strong right arm and were to radiate the beneficent influences of hierarchy and authority over the populace. To that end, Charles forbade them to live in London in order to keep them on their country estates. Bishops, too, had to stay in their dioceses, where they could properly keep hierarchical order.[3]

As for the common people, if they were not to share in ruling, Charles did let them eat cake, figuratively speaking. In 1633, he issued an anti-Sabbath declaration, the Book of Sports. The declaration proclaimed, to the horror of puritans, that games and dancing were entirely legal on Sundays, once church services were over. To drive the anti-puritan nail in, ministers were commanded to read out the declaration, the devil's book, as puritans called it, from the pulpit. While some bishops did not press their ministers to read it, others used the opportunity to sweep puritans from their pulpits. Either way, the Book of Sports tied the hands of godly ministers and magistrates. Now when fiddles, drums, dancing, laughter, and sports polluted the holy stillness of the Sabbath, puritans could do no more than spread stories of dreadful exemplary divine judgments, like that of the man who threw a party on a Sunday to celebrate the Book of Sports, only to be crushed to death the next day by a collapsing woodpile.[4]

In towns with a long history of struggles between puritans and anti-puritans, it was clear that the tide was turning against puritanism. One such place was the market town of Shrewsbury, near the Welsh border in Shropshire. Puritans and anti-puritans in Shrewsbury had long fought over sports, plays, taverns, and the appointment of school teachers, and had traded insults in the streets over their favored ministers. In 1621, the divided town council selected a determined local anti-puritan and anti-Calvinist, Peter Studley, as a parish minister.[5]

Throughout the 1620s, Studley struggled to whip puritans into line. He hauled them before the church courts, often unsuccessfully, for a variety of offenses ranging from abandoning their own parish churches to hear better preaching elsewhere to holding large Sunday evening meetings for repeating sermons, praying, and singing psalms. A particular target of Studley's was the popular nonconformist minister Julines Herring. Herring held a two-sermons-a-week lectureship, endowed by Rowland Heylin, a local man who made good in London, and served as a hub for local puritanism. Spies failed to catch Herring saying anything seditious at the crowded house meetings where he reviewed his sermons, but privately he prayed for Presbyterianism. The local bishop's leniency thwarted Studley's goal of removing Herring from his pulpit.[6]

Herring's patron Rowland Heylin also served as a member of an ambitious London-based puritan group of ministers, wealthy lawyers, and merchants who called themselves the Feoffees for Impropriations. They bought up the rights to choose the ministers of individual parish churches (see p. 50) and to claim the income from tithes, a tax on produce intended to support a church's minister. They then bestowed the pulpits and income on preachers of their own choice. The group was careful only to support conformist puritan ministers, but its idea of conformity was a great deal looser than that of anti-puritans. In 1629, Heylin established another beachhead for puritan influence in Shrewsbury when he purchased those rights for one of the town's churches.[7]

As Charles I's Protestant counter-reformation started to make a substantial impact, Studley could take heart that his side was finally winning. In 1633, after Laud was appointed archbishop of Canterbury, the puritan Feoffees fell under his suspicious eye. What to puritans was a pious vehicle for spreading evangelical preaching was to Laud part of a conspiratorial puritan effort to subvert the established lines of authority in the Church of England. Tipped off by one of Laud's associates, Charles I's attorney general hauled the Feoffees into court and denounced them as being as sinister as the conspiratorial Catholic Jesuits. The court ordered the Feoffees disbanded and confiscated their endowments.[8]

Good news for Studley kept coming in 1633. His diocese received a new bishop that year, Robert Wright. Wright, like other bishops, started cracking down on puritans who only arrived at services in time for the sermons or who left their parishes in search of more satisfying preaching. Studley gloated from his pulpit to his parish's puritans that they now had no choice but to listen to him.[9]

The year 1633 was also when Laud kicked a campaign to make church buildings themselves anti-puritan into high gear. At the center of this anti-sermon, pro-ceremony campaign was a dubiously legal drive to compel parishioners to show the same reverence for communion tables that Catholics showed for altars. This was going to be an uphill battle since Catholic altars were where Christ's sacrifice on the cross was miraculously re-enacted, while communion tables were just surfaces on which to place bread and wine during the Lord's Supper. When not in ritual use, workers rested their tools on them and children used them for school work, while their legs attracted pissing dogs. Laud wanted them treated, from the puritan perspective, like idols: elevated, railed off, and placed away from the congregation at the east wall of the church like altars, and even called altars. Some bishops pursued this campaign more zealously than others, while a handful dragged their feet. In some parishes, puritans ran guerrilla campaigns of resistance to rearranging their communion tables. Studley's new bishop immediately instituted Laud's new policy, and it is hard to imagine Studley resisting.[10]

As part of this campaign of ceremonial beautification, ritual require-ments in worship were much more strictly enforced and new ones invented, all of them—so far as puritans were concerned—reeking of Catholicism and idolatry. Ministers and Laudian laypeople reintroduced once-idolatrous crucifixes, statues, and stained-glass windows into their churches. Studley had his church painted with what one disgusted puritan visitor to the town in 1635 described as "idle, ridiculous, vain, and absurd pictures . . . the like whereunto I never saw in England."[11]

In 1634 Studley seized the opportunity of a bloody scandal to hasten puritanism's downfall. His vehicle was the grisly events at the house of a nearby farmer, Edward ap Evan. The family, Edward, his wife Joan, and their two grown-up sons Enoch and John, prayed together twice a day from the Book of Common Prayer—not for them the pouring out to God of sponta-neous praise and entreaties, as was the puritan norm for prayer. Enoch thirsted for a more intense piety, such as could be found among the godly. Around 1630, he procured a Bible and took it with him everywhere, even reading it while on breaks from ploughing or threshing grain. Enoch developed a puritan thirst for sermons and began attending weekday lectures. Along with a reputation for piety, he acquired a rock-solid conviction that he was among God's elect. In the new circles in which Enoch traveled, he not only found salvation, he learned that there was much that was wrong with the Church of England's government and ceremonies.[12]

That breadth of discovery might be expected for an adventurous layperson moving in godly circles. But, as sometimes happened, the group of godly laypeople with whom Enoch fell in refused to have their spiritual experiences and Bible interpretations held within boundaries set by puritan ministers. This semi-puritan group was exploring widely shunned beliefs reaching back to the murderous, polygamous, revelation-driven Anabaptists who briefly and bloodily seized the German city of Munster in 1535. The Anabaptists' revelations, inspired, they believed, by the Holy Spirit, had in turn inspired a heretical group loathed by orthodox puritans, the Family of Love. Familists, as members of the group were called, believed that Christians under the illumination of the Holy Spirit could eventually enjoy revelations that superseded the Bible, perfect union with God, and freedom both from sin and from suffering God's wrath for it.[13]

The story circulated that Enoch, like the Anabaptists and Familists, had claimed that his soul remained pure after God saved him even while his body sinned. Like those groups, Enoch and others in his circle took the next logical step in separating holiness from the body and denied that Christ had risen to heaven in his physical body. Like them, Enoch had revelations. A rumor spread that he once heard a shrill, invisible voice in church saying "Enoch prepare." One night Enoch saw the Holy Spirit fly into his bed chamber in the form of a dove, "full of brightness," he recalled.[14]

As Enoch's idiosyncratic Familist-cum-puritan piety developed, so did his characteristically puritan appetite for finding fault with the Church of England. When Enoch heard preaching he approved of, it was remembered, he would "be even wrapt up in admiration, and transported with spiritual delight," but when he disagreed, he would scowl and stamp his foot. Enoch's questioning of the Church of England's ceremonies and government led to conflicts with his family, especially on a perennial puritan trigger issue, the mandatory, unbiblical kneeling for the Lord's Supper, which he opposed.[15]

On June 30, 1633, Enoch provoked his mother Joan and his brother John into a heated argument about kneeling. Five days later, John was snoozing head down on the kitchen table during a break from his field chores when Enoch decapitated him with two blows of a hatchet. Joan came into the room and met the same grizzly end. Enoch fled, with their heads wrapped in a cloth. He was quickly captured, tried and hanged, and his corpse was left dangling in chains as a salutary example to others.[16]

Why had he committed this horrendous deed? Rumors spread that the devil had handed Enoch the hatchet, urged him to the crime, and lingered at the scene in the form of a black horse after he had fled. Some people linked the crime to Enoch's dabbling in Anabaptist heresies—of course, a sin-drenched human being who deluded himself about sin's power and placed his own imaginary or satanic revelations above the authority of the Bible would end up, like the Anabaptists, murdering people. Studley agreed that Satan was behind the crime, but for Studely, Satan's vehicle was not Anabaptism, but puritanism and Calvinism itself. It was these that had puffed Enoch full of spiritual pride as one of God's elect and emboldened him, like other puritans, to sinfully question his superiors, immoderately pursue sermons, and defy the law. From Enoch's puritanism, according to Studley, it was only the shortest of steps to massacring people whom he had decided were the enemies of God.[17]

Studley wrote to Archbishop Laud about the murder and the lawless, regional puritan network that, according to Studley, fostered it. For good measure, he published his hostile blame-the-puritans account in 1634. Studley had the satisfaction of seeing a nearby rotating, puritan-dominated lectureship of the kind that Enoch haunted purged of nonconformists and the Presbyterian Julines Herring finally removed from his ministry. "I will pickle up that Herring," Laud insisted to those who pleaded he show leniency toward the minister.[18] Now a marked man, Herring could only resume his preaching by leaving the country.

Herring received invitations to go to Massachusetts, but as he considered his employment options, that colony was slipping off his list of possibilities. Laud had not forgotten Massachusetts in his drive against puritanism. In 1634 he was appointed head of a new royal board called the Commission for Regulating Colonies. Laud's commission could revoke colonial charters, appoint governors, and break up colonies. In 1634, the commission arranged to have the Privy Council order Massachusetts to send its royal charter back, and was having a warship built to bring over a governor-general to rule the colony and enforce religious conformity.[19]

Massachusetts's puritans responded defiantly to this news. The colony's rulers agreed, even if the Privy Council did not, that their charter was irrevocable as long as they abided by its inconsequential terms, giving the

Crown 5 percent of their nonexistent gold and silver ore and making no law repugnant, very loosely defined, to the laws of England. Bolstered by a sharply increasing number of immigrants, the General Court strengthened the colony's forts, built up its militia, and required all males who had yet to join a church to take an oath of loyalty. There was talk that war would soon break out between Massachusetts and England.[20]

Massachusetts's General Court knew, however, that the ultimate source of this danger to the colony was not King Charles, but God, justly angry at the colonists' many sins. To appease God, the General Court engaged in a two-pronged mobilization of state and church. The first prong was to pass a series of laws promoting a crackdown on "new and immodest fashions" and jewelry and a further crackdown on the use of tobacco. The second prong was to call upon the now eight churches of Massachusetts, with eleven ministers, to hold a public fast on September 17, 1634, in order to bewail their sins and implore God's protection.[21]

The immediate threat of English intervention dissolved on its own next year when the warship that was to bring the governor-general sank in an English harbor. But the fast opened the door to a different threat. Mounting the Salem pulpit that day was someone whom most of the magistrates neither expected nor wanted to see there, Roger Williams. Impressively pious and self-denying, Williams had been a minister in England. But at some point, he had taken up decidedly non-puritan, radical convictions that would dissolve the disciplined, unitary Christian commonwealth the puritans were trying to create in Massachusetts.

Williams was, to start with, an extreme separatist: for him, all the parish churches were without exception utterly antichristian, and therefore Massachusetts's halfhearted separation from them was sinfully incomplete. On top of that, and unlike earlier separatists, he believed that there neither could be nor should be a "Christian" state, such as the one the settlers of Massachusetts had crossed the ocean to build. For an earthly government to force Christianity on anyone or protect or supervise it in any way, Williams argued, was "antichristian." Coercive power had no place in true Christianity, whether that power was wielded by the pope, by the king of England, or even by Massachusetts's godly magistrates.[22]

From that principle, it followed, for Williams, that Massachusetts's royal charter, the legal foundation of the colony, was sinful. Since states had nothing to do with real Christianity, it was "blasphemous" for European monarchs to call themselves Christian monarchs and, on that basis, claim the right to give European people land that belonged to Native Americans.

And therefore, Massachusetts's sinful royal charter should be sent back to England.[23]

The magistrates had already called Williams in for a talk at the end of 1633. He agreed to keep his opinions about Massachusetts's sinful government and equally sinful charter to himself and to tone down his blanket denunciations of the English parish churches.[24] But agreement or no agreement, once in the pulpit on a fast day, Williams felt it to be his God-given duty to denounce Massachusetts's sins, and that was what he did.[25]

Having broadcast his concerns about Massachusetts's sins, Williams, like any faithful minister, continued to voice them, undeterred by the increasing indignation of almost all the magistrates and other ministers. As if in answer to Williams, in 1635, the General Court did its coercive duty as a Christian government by mandating fines or prison for anyone who habitually skipped Sunday services.[26]

How to handle Williams himself, though, was a matter for which the Massachusetts theocracy was not well prepared. Following John Calvin, Massachusetts puritans conceived of the churches and the state as cooperating governments with separate spheres of action. Unlike in England, ministers could not serve in public offices, and the churches could not hand out secular punishments like fines and imprisonment. Massachusetts's government was supposed to protect the churches, but it was not supposed to interfere with their internal religious life.[27]

The problem was that in Calvin's original Presbyterian scheme, it was taken as obvious that churches would have higher supervisory boards with the power to discipline straying ministers and churches. Under Congregationalism, however, each church was autonomous, so the most that other churches could do was meet and formally shake their collective finger at Williams, admonish the Salem church for allowing him into its pulpit, and, at worst, withdraw fellowship from it. They could not order the church to do anything. The magistrates thought they had the right to bring the secular charge of contempt of authority against Williams for breaking his promise of silence.[28] Nonetheless, if they acted precipitously, they would alienate the church of the second-largest town in what was a very small, threatened colony.

English godly circles attracted people like Williams who drew sympathizers and even followers because of their impressive piety, yet who promoted various agendas that pushed past puritanism's boundaries. What made the Williams conflict novel was that in Massachusetts, unlike in England, puritans controlled the churches and the government and could bring the conflict to a state-enforced resolution.

The Salem church, however, saw no conflict needing resolution and went on to ordain Williams as its minister. Driving the underlying logic of Congregationalism to an atomistic, every-church-for-itself conclusion, it asserted that a church was free to descend into heresy—even Familism or Catholicism—and to ignore the admonitions of its fellow churches, without it being any business of the government, as long as the church kept the peace.[29] The Salem church's argument would have brought to an end the long quest of puritans for a Christian commonwealth governed by a state and a properly reformed church establishment working hand in hand.

It was Williams himself who inadvertently diverted his church from a major showdown with the General Court. In the summer of 1635, he concluded that the other churches were sinning by allowing their members in the General Court to pressure the Salem church. From his house, Williams wrote a letter to his congregation, telling them that if they did not separate from the Massachusetts churches as antichristian just as they had done from the parish churches—Salem against the world—Williams would separate from them. A majority of the church refused to follow Williams. With Williams's support in Salem eroding, the General Court felt it could safely try him. The magistrates and freemen's deputies, representing ten towns by this time, meeting in the General Court, found Williams guilty of contempt in October 1635 and sentenced him to banishment.[30]

The plan was to ship Williams back to England. When the boat arrived in Salem in January 1636, however, Williams was working his way 65 miles south to Narragansett Bay, beyond the boundaries of Massachusetts's charter, through high snow drifts and bitter cold ("which I feel yet," he wrote thirty-five years later). Native Americans who were his trading partners and friends gave him land that became the nucleus of Rhode Island. Some of Williams's Salem supporters joined him. This new, small colony, religiously tolerant and semi-anarchical, would go on to serve as a thorn in the side of its orthodox neighbors.[31]

Word of the Williams affair reached England while Julines Herring, Laud's victim in Shrewsbury, was still seeking a new pulpit. The fact that Williams had as long a run as he did before being silenced seems to have been the final straw for Herring about Massachusetts. Herring joined John Dod and eleven other prominent, Presbyterian-leaning ministers in 1636 to write an alarmed, angry letter to their ministerial college mates, friends, and colleagues in Massachusetts. These well-connected clergymen, representatives, as it were, of the informally organized puritan network that still saw itself as the evangelical heart of the Church of England, included in their letter ten questions about New England church practices.[32]

The ministers probed various aspects of Congregationalism with their questions. They especially wanted an explanation for their colleagues' rapid, reckless, and dangerous transformation into de facto separatists. That transformation was not only dangerous for the stability of the New England churches, they explained, it was making life hard for ministers in England. Some English puritans were starting to copy them, following on letters from Massachusetts, and separating from the parish church worship led by English puritan ministers. Puritanism's enemies were pointing to Massachusetts to prove that all puritans were latent separatists from the Church of England. Separatism aside, the ministers warned with their questions that Congregationalism was wrong to give the laity so much uncontrolled decision-making power and wrong also to tie ministers and their sacramental powers so tightly to the church that elected them. If, and only if, the New Englanders' answers to their questions were persuasive would the English ministers extend the "right hand of [Christian] fellowship" to the New England churches.

Having put New England Congregationalism on warning, Herring did not wait for a reply, which would not come until 1638. In 1637, he ended his job hunt by accepting an invitation to an English Presbyterian church in Amsterdam. Herring burned his papers and letters before he departed to make sure they did not fall into Laud's hands.[33]

With Herring gone, the times looked grim for the puritans of Shrewsbury. Studley had broadcast his version of their sins to the world, while censorship kept them from publishing their reply. But they could at least circulate their defense of themselves to puritans around the country in manuscript.[34]

Eventually a copy of the manuscript made its way into the hands of an already indignant London minister, Henry Burton. Long before, Burton had been a chaplain to Charles I. His growing rage against Arminianism and then against Laud and his allies had driven him from court favor into nonconformity and, now and then, into prison. On November 5, 1636, that rage provoked Burton to condemn Studley in the midst of a kamikaze pulpit denunciation of all of God's enemies in England. The Arminians were apostates, he preached, the Laudian bishops were "antichristian mushrooms," crushing the people's liberties while encouraging the king to think that he had "unlimited power," and Studley's smear campaign against England's faithful Christians was a part of the plot to drive the country back to Catholicism. Burton subsequently barricaded his house against the officials trying to arrest him while he prepared his sermons for an Amsterdam press. The sermons were ready to smuggle back into England by the time the officers obtained a warrant, smashed his door down with pick-axes, and hauled him off to prison.[35]

Six months later, on June 30, 1637, Burton found himself in one of three pillories set up on Cheapside. Beside him were his acquaintances the lawyer William Prynne (see p. 92) and John Bastwick, a Presbyterian physician. The three men had been convicted of sedition for their vituperative illegal tracts against the bishops, following trials at which they had refused to cooperate with what they regarded as illegal prosecutions. For two hours in their pillories, the convicts harangued the crowd watching them. The onlookers included many puritans who encouraged the three to endure their "martyrdom" with fortitude; perhaps there were present one or two ancient spectators who remembered being in such crowds as little children, while their parents shouted out encouragement to the Protestant martyrs being burned on Queen Mary's orders. The spectacle ended with the hangman slicing off their ears, or, in Prynne's case, what was left of his ears. Prynne's butchering was particularly painful; he had shortsightedly under-tipped the same hangman the last time.[36]

Even non-puritans were uncomfortable seeing stoutly Protestant members of the learned professions subjected to this public degradation and were impressed by the courage with which the trio endured it. Some zealots soaked handkerchiefs in their blood as mementoes, while crowds turned out to cheer and feast them on their separate ways to perpetual imprisonment in remote castles.[37] It was an impressive display of support that alarmed the government and led to further, bitterly resented prosecutions. Archbishop Laud felt the need to publish a speech justifying the legality of his proceedings against puritans.[38]

The archbishop need not have worried. The only institution that could hold him accountable would be a Parliament, and Charles had devised enough ways to raise money without it to avoid feeling any pressure on that front. In 1637, puritans tried to make him call a Parliament by challenging the most legally dubious of his revenue devices, ship money. This had formerly been an occasional levy on coastal areas for defense against piracy, but Charles had turned it into a nationwide annual levy, a tax in all but name, and a very lucrative one at that. Given that judges served at Charles's pleasure, it was unsurprising that the puritan challenge failed.

After the failure of the ship money case, the earl of Warwick and some other puritan lords grew so despondent at what they feared was England's unstoppable slide into tyranny and Catholicism that they commenced serious preparations for emigration. It was not, however, to New England that they intended to go, but to a colony they were building up in the western Caribbean, Providence Island, which combined godliness with privateering against the hated Spanish and the practice of intensive slavery (the English Caribbean's first slave rebellion broke out there in 1638). Providence Island had not a trace of the republican self-rule of New England, which was a hindrance in recruiting settlers. The colony's stormy religious life was marked by micro-management from London, conflicts between godly and ungodly colonists, and the unauthorized creation of a divisive Congregational church. The lords decided in the end to stay put in England in 1638 (the Spanish would wipe their colony out in 1641), but their despondency that year was widely shared. "These proceedings . . .," wrote the wealthy London puritan Isaac Pennington, "make men fly and make many more think of providing for their safety in other places."[39]

Bad news for English puritanism was always good news for New England, the scale of immigration being heavily dependent on regional and national pressure against puritanism in England. After the ascension of Archbishop Laud, the trickle of immigrants swelled dramatically, if erratically, and the grim events of 1637 caused it to peak in 1638, with three thousand arrivals.[40]

Nonetheless, this immigration was a drop in the bucket in a country of perhaps three million people. Other puritans might cheer on New England, and they might even fantasize about it: "The more I have of God, the more I rise after New England," wrote the young minister Samuel Rogers in his diary in 1637. But like Rogers himself, most puritans ultimately shied away from the expense, danger, and uncertainties of traveling to New England. Oliver Cromwell, then an obscure, down-and-out gentleman, might have changed his mind about emigrating after he received a tidy inheritance following the death of an uncle. Many puritans must have concluded, like Susanna Bell, in the face of her husband's importuning, that they lived well enough in England.[41]

For some puritans, though, the reasons to emigrate were compelling. In the summer of 1634, Anne Hutchinson, her merchant husband, eight of their fifteen children, and an unknown number of servants embarked for New England. She was already deeply troubled by the Church of England's corruptions; her brother-in-law, the minister John Wheelwright, had been silenced; she wanted to be under John Cotton's ministry; and God had thrown a scripture verse into her mind that she took as a warning of England's destruction. On the voyage over, Hutchinson voiced opinions about salvation that prompted Massachusetts's governor Thomas Dudley to make inquiries about her and John Cotton to caution her about being too narrow in her judgment before she was admitted to the Boston church.[42]

Concern about Hutchinson subsided, for the time being, because she was, like Roger Williams, a useful person of admirable godliness. Hutchinson found herself much in demand in Boston as a healer, especially at child-births. Women had a 1 percent chance of dying each time they gave birth, and married women could expect to run the odds eight times or more in the course of their lives. In quiet moments during these exclusively female, intense, and, at times, harrowing events, there was frequent occasion for prayer and talk of religion, and Hutchinson was a much admired spiritual counselor. Men, too, came to her for counseling at other times. This kind of informal lay ministry was a puritan vocation open to the talented of both sexes, and Hutchinson was exceptionally good at it (her father and brother were clergymen). According to John Cotton, Hutchinson, "wrought with God, and with the ministers, the work of the Lord . . . [and] found loving and dear respect from both our church elders and brethren, and so from myself."[43]

But in March 1638, nearly four years after her arrival in Massachusetts, this godly woman stood before her congregation on trial for heresy. The colony had barely pulled through what would be the worst religious crisis in its history, thanks in no small part to Hutchinson, and perhaps the fiercest and most potentially self-destructive crisis in puritanism up until then. In November 1637 Hutchinson had been convicted by the General Court of slandering all the colony's ministers except John Cotton, and was ordered to leave the colony by the spring. At that previous civil trial, Hutchinson astounded the court by warning it that she had received a scriptural revelation predicting that it would be destroyed if she were punished.[44]

Among the many ministers and lay visitors who crowded into the Boston meeting house to observe Hutchinson's subsequent church trial was the minister Thomas Shepard of Newtowne (soon to be renamed Cambridge). Shepard listened while Hutchinson defended opinions similar to those of the Familists and Enoch ap Evan, the Shropshire ax murderer (see p. 94)—Christ's human nature was not in heaven, souls were mortal, and there was no resurrection of the body.[45]

Those opinions would lead to the "overthrow of all religion," one minister bluntly told her.[46] Orthodox puritans envisioned conversion slowly healing believers' corrupted human nature through an ongoing struggle with sin.

That healing, Catholics and Protestants alike insisted, culminated in heaven with the saints' glorified physical bodies, resurrected on the Last Day through Christ's power, just as Christ had resurrected in his own physical body and ascended to heaven.[47]

Hutchinson jettisoned the body as a distraction right at the beginning of conversion. Christ did not transform a believer's human nature, he bypassed it. Believers needed only Christ's holiness in them, not any of their own. They would engage in no more transformative struggle with the sins of human nature; that would be fighting on abandoned territory. Stay focused on Christ, and the Holy Spirit's revelations would lead you to endless joy in this life, before your spirit enjoyed the bliss of heaven in the next one[48] (this disregard of sin caused nineteenth-century historians to dub this conflict the Antinomian Controversy, although the term "antinomian" (see p. 123) was rarely thrown around during the controversy itself).[49]

Hutchinson's Familist-tinged opinions, shocking though they were, did not catch Shepard by surprise. A month before her church trial, she had been under house imprisonment awaiting banishment when he paid her a visit. He assured her that he had not come to entrap her, coaxed her opinions out of her, and then reported her to the Boston church's elders, hence her trial.[50] Shepard was now determined that Hutchinson would get what he regarded as her just deserts.

Shepard undoubtedly wanted other important Boston church members to face church trials, but they were beyond his reach. Henry Vane, the twenty-two-year-old puritan son of one of Charles's privy councilors, arrived in Massachusetts in October 1635, a few weeks after Shepard; Archbishop Laud had given him permission for the trip in the hope that the experience would get puritanism out of his system. The Cottons gave him lodging; the Boston church almost immediately admitted him; and next spring, the colony's freemen, dazzled by his high status and connections and overlooking his youth and inexperience, elected him governor.[51]

What the freemen did not know, but Shepard, who kept his ear to the ground, probably quickly realized, was that Vane had a prodigious appetite for unorthodox theological speculation. Vane recognized in Hutchinson a kindred spirit and encouraged her to set up meetings at her house, a standard puritan practice. Hutchinson was amenable to starting a meeting of her own, she explained later, because it was being put about that she was not attending religious meetings out of pride.[52]

Hutchinson's house meetings, some single and some mixed sex, proved enormously popular. Hutchinson herself led the meeting for women. Their ostensible purpose was to review Cotton's sermons, another standard puritan practice. The discussions in them, however, could range adventurously past Cotton's teachings, which was always a possibility in lay gatherings with the right mix of people and the absence of a minister. Hutchinson and a small lay group, including Vane, were guardedly exploring even more unconventional theological ideas on their own. Around this time, Hutchinson and others in her circle started spreading it about that Cotton was the only Massachusetts minister who preached the Covenant of Grace correctly.[53]

After a turbulent year as governor, Vane was voted out of office. He returned to England after promising his supporters that he would come back as royal governor over Massachusetts. Shepard called him "the prime craftsman of forging all our late novelties," and the person who raised "the opinions of Familists . . . to a great height."[54]

Another Boston church member beyond Shepard's reach was Hutchinson's brother-in-law, the ex-minister John Wheelwright. He had left involuntarily for New Hampshire two months earlier. Wheelwright had been sentenced to banishment for sedition after delivering a blistering lay sermon in Boston in January 1637, in which he all but said directly what his sister-in-law and others had started to say in private: the colony's ministers, except for John Cotton, preached a false way to salvation, the Covenant of Works (see p. 54). Some ministers, possibly at Shepard's prompting, started to worry that Wheelwright was hiding Familist doctrine in his unusual preaching.[55]

A number of times at Hutchinson's church trial, Shepard would have been sharply reminded that the great John Cotton himself was one of the Boston church's leading spreaders of Familism, as far as Shepard was concerned. That reminder certainly hit him during one of the trial's most solemn teaching moments, when Cotton admonished Hutchinson for her errors. Yet Cotton started not by condemning, but by praising Hutchinson. It might have been at this point that Shepard began to suspect that Cotton was engineering the trial to vindicate Hutchinson as much as possible.[56]

What Cotton praised was Hutchinson's ability to convince women who thought they were saved that they were erroneously relying for evidence not on Christ but "upon their own duties and performances," their works, in other words. Yet those women were doing precisely what ministers like Shepard told people to do: examining themselves for inward and outward signs that God was working genuine faith and holiness in them; signs such as pious behavior, zealous prayer, desire for Jesus, love of their fellow puritans, and the like.[57]

When Hutchinson had corrected the women, she had been following Cotton's lead. He insisted against the ministerial mainstream that none of the signs these women were relying on could be the first evidence that you were saved. They were all "works," so by themselves they could all be signs of the damnable Covenant of Works, not the Covenant of Grace. The only safe way you could initially know that God really loved you was when he told you so himself. And that he did when the Holy Spirit revealed a scripture verse promising salvation so strongly in your mind that you realized, with joy, that it was meant for you personally.[58]

For Shepard, Cotton's claim was nonsense, for no scripture verse could refer to you personally. Even worse, the claim was dangerous heretical nonsense. Cotton was preaching Familism "obscurely," according to Shepard. Once you made scripture verses say something they could not possibly say, you had thrown away all restraints on interpretation, Shepard insisted in one of his well-attended Thursday lectures, and at that point, "you may as well bring in immediate revelations and from thence come to forsake the scriptures," just like the Familists. Shepard feared revelations might even instruct these colonial crypto-Familists, like their spiritual forbears, the Anabaptists of Munster, to kill the magistrates and ministers. At the root of this potential bloody nightmare, Shepard insisted, was Cotton's claim about assurance of salvation, "the principal opinion and seed of all the rest."[59]

Calvinist theology, in its details, was vast, intricate, and responsive to a wide variety of pressures. Ministers were never going to walk in complete doctrinal lockstep, and now was not the first time that Cotton had fallen out of line with his brethren. Other ministers, however, did not draw the same horrific conclusions about Cotton's preaching that Shepard and his allies did. Cotton was not by nature confrontational; he did not insist that others agree with him; he was not entirely unique in his ideas about assurance of salvation; and he was otherwise an exemplary puritan minister.[60]

It was a frequent temptation, nonetheless, in puritan theological disputes to trace deviations from theological norms all the way to dire, deadly, and distant heresies. God's truth was narrow, while the forces besieging it were powerful, evil, and cunning, and never more so than in the late 1630s. German Protestants were being slaughtered in the Thirty Years' War, as Shepard explained from the pulpit; the English reformation was being dragged back to Catholicism; and in Massachusetts the devil was cunningly at work raising up a faction to undermine New England's reformation.[61]

Once such horrendous influences had been discovered, at least in the minds of some participants, English puritan theological debates could descend into polarized name-calling, and that happened again in Massachusetts. By making Cotton a large part of the problem, not part of the solution, in about as insulting a way as possible, Shepard only succeeded in getting Cotton's back up and guaranteeing that the problem would get a lot worse, which it started doing after Shepard first made the accusation of Familism, in early 1636.[62]

Since that time, Cotton and other ministers had been arguing about their differences in writing, at conferences, and from the pulpit. The more they argued, face to face and through manuscript exchanges, the more uncertain they grew about each other, and the more extreme Cotton's opinions became. Cotton himself started to wonder if his opponents in fact did preach a Covenant of Works for salvation as people in his congregation were now saying.[63]

The laity threw themselves into the quarrel between their ministers, while the largely subterranean theological speculation within Hutchinson's lay circle grew more extravagant. Vane was remembered for the aggressiveness of his attacks on Cotton's opponents, and Hutchinson was particularly feared because most of her activities took place among women, where men could not easily track them. Pushed to choose, most of the rest of the Boston church took Cotton's side against the other ministers. "The churches are on fire," boatmen told ships pulling into Boston harbor in the summer of 1637, as Cotton, Henry Vane, and others planned to set up a colony of their own.[64]

The planned Boston exodus would have been a grave blow to Massachusetts. But it fell through, for reasons unknown, and the crisis began to abate. Vane returned to England in August 1637, and Cotton made his peace with the other ministers in September in a synod of the New England churches in newly renamed Cambridge. At the gathering, the churches' ministers and lay representatives condemned various "errors" circulating in Massachusetts while the ministers hammered out a compromise statement affirming that both Cotton and his opponents' ways of finding assurance of salvation were acceptable. Some ministers went along with the compromise only under duress; a failed synod would possibly have broken Massachusetts, and it would have been a transatlantic scandal for puritanism.[65]

At Hutchinson's church trial six months later, Cotton resumed admonishing Hutchinson by luridly painting the ghastly consequences of her heresies. Shepard might have correctly sensed that the Boston church was growing hopeful that it could back off from excommunicating her since Hutchinson had acknowledged the error of some of her opinions.[66] Shepard not unreasonably had no trust in Hutchinson's words, and that was an outcome he desperately wanted to avoid.

His opportunity came when Cotton failed fully to call out Hutchinson on a less-than-entirely-true claim she made about when she had adopted her opinions. Shepard was furious. The crypto-Familists were still plotting together. Cotton, Shepard decided, was trying to give Hutchinson "a light to escape through the crowd with honor." Shepard interjected that Hutchinson's claim had been a "horrible" lie. After much toing and froing, Cotton and the men of the church finally agreed that she was guilty of lying and excommunicated her. One down for Shepard, but this puritan heresy hunter continued to brood publically and privately about Cotton and others who had escaped his net.[67]

Cotton himself later acknowledged that he had been insufficiently vigilant in policing his congregation. He added, however, that one reason the controversy grew so explosive was that Shepard and others tried to resolve it "with more jealousies and heats and paroxysms of spirit, than would well stand with brotherly love or the rule of the gospel." It was neither the first nor the last time that puritans tried such a take-no-prisoners approach when they found themselves in disagreement.[68]

The controversy's reverberations were long felt on both sides of the Atlantic. The "errors" of Hutchinson's circle lived on in horrified English puritan memory down to the end of the century thanks to the self-justifying accounts of them sent over by Massachusetts's leaders. Vane himself would rise to English political prominence in the next two turbulent decades while abandoning neither his controversial theological opinions nor the suspicion of puritan clergy that he picked up in Massachusetts. The urgent sermons Shepard delivered during the controversy about true and damnably false ways of finding assurance of salvation were published in London in 1660 as *The Parable of the Ten Virgins Opened and Applied*, and have been republished intermittently ever since. "One of the most useful books ever published in English," claimed the translator of the 1743 Dutch edition. The great New England theologian Jonathan Edwards drew on it heavily for his own 1746 landmark effort to set out true and false signs of conversion, *A Treatise Concerning Religious Affections*, written as he struggled to keep the Great Awakening, America's first religious revival, from spinning entirely out of ministerial control.[69]

Even before Hutchinson's church trial, voluntary—and a handful of involuntary—exiles began departing Massachusetts. Over eighty families, including the Hutchinsons, settled near Roger Williams. Most of them were disillusioned followers of Cotton and Wheelwright, while some were allies of Hutchinson. Heterodox, semi-anarchic, and religiously tolerant Rhode Island, where everyone could preach whatever they chose to anyone who wanted to listen, managed to survive among its land-hungry puritan neighbors due in no small measure to the accumulation of population and talents it acquired from this immigration.[70]

The controversy helped expand puritan New England itself. John Wheelwright's New Hampshire church stayed, shakily, within the New England communion of churches, despite some people in Massachusetts considering him a heretic. Wheelwright helped extend the reach of puritanism into Maine, territory previously associated with ungodly English fishermen. The prominent minister Thomas Hooker, Shepard's father-in-law, had already left to found Connecticut in 1636. As a parting gesture in 1636, he preached against Cotton's ideas about assurance of salvation. In 1638, another prominent, newly arrived minister, John Davenport, left Massachusetts with his followers to found New Haven. Among their reasons for departing was a fear that a royal governor, such as Vane had threatened to become, was going to descend upon Massachusetts. The ability of the godly to move away from each other and start again from scratch in New England, an option unavailable in England, went some way to defusing religious tensions.[71]

By 1638, Massachusetts Congregationalists had weathered the extremist challenges to their version of puritanism represented by Roger Williams and Hutchinson's circle. That year, however, new local challenges arose from puritans not more extreme but more conservative than the Congregationalists. One Sunday afternoon in 1638, as the Salem church's deacons distributed the Lord's Supper's bread and wine to its members, a nonmember watching in the meeting house fumed. Mary Oliver, a nonconformist and recent immigrant from the embattled, puritan-leaning city of Norwich, had refused to join the Salem church on principle. The Congregationalists' obligatory church covenant that each member had to take could be found nowhere in the Bible without enormous leaps of logic, as English puritans, including the Dod letter writers (see p. 99), kept pointing out to the Massachusetts Congregationalists, and Oliver refused to take it. On top of that, she refused to give a conversion narrative for admission, another New England novelty condemned by John Dod's circle.[72]

Oliver's frustration at being barred from the Lord's Supper for rejecting what she and many puritans regarded as unbiblical innovations moved her to stand up in the Salem meeting house and demand to be given the sacrament. John Winthrop described her as more impressive in speech and piety than Anne Hutchinson and claimed that she could have been more dangerous except that she was poor and unknown. He might have been right; there were a lot more moderate puritans like Oliver, for whom New England Congregationalism had gone too far from Church of England norms, than extremists like Hutchinson, who wanted to push it further.[73]

Around the same time, Massachusetts ministers and the General Court were busily squashing an effort in Weymouth to form a church without the Congregational church covenant (in 1636, after a church was founded along Presbyterian lines in Hingham, the General Court had passed a law requiring government approval of all new churches). Boston's pastor John Wilson told Weymouth's recently arrived non-covenant minister Robert Lenthall that it would be best if clergy like him had been "buried at the bottom of the sea" on the passage over. One of Lenthall's lay supporters found himself fined £10 for calling the covenant "stinking carrion and a human invention" and had his cow taken in payment. Another, for calling the Massachusetts ministers separatists, was whipped for lack of a cow. Mary Oliver was put in prison for her outburst until she repented, temporarily.[74]

That same year, Massachusetts ministers finally replied to the concerned letter from John Dod and his circle. They assured their English colleagues, friends, and mentors of their love for them and denied that they were separatists, despite their exclusionary churches. They admitted that they had rejected practices "received by the most Reformed churches" in Europe and "by the most godly and judicious servants of God among them." But the New England churches should be copied, not condemned, they told their brethren, for they were at the vanguard of the march of sacred history to the glorious millennium. Or, in the words of the ministers, "Churches had still need to grow from apparent defects to purity," just as the New England churches were doing, ". . . till the Lord hath utterly abolished Antichrist with . . . the brightness of his coming."[75]

The Massachusetts ministers' advice to adopt Congregationalism as the cutting edge of the approaching millennium failed to move the Dod letter signers. One, John Ball, composed a lengthy reply on behalf of the group rejecting the Massachusetts ministers' reply. At the beginning of the decade, Dod had advised John Cotton to go to Massachusetts. By the end of the decade, he was advising ministers against it.[76] Better no reformation than the New England one.

Some English puritans, however, were drawn by the blasts of this millennial bugle from across the ocean summoning them to abandon their increasingly besieged parish churches and start afresh. In 1633, an English church in Rotterdam was taken over by Congregationalists, and a steady trickle of ministers from England offset that church's ongoing brain drain to Massachusetts, while new Congregational churches were created in the Netherlands and Wales in 1639.[77]

If Archbishop Laud noticed this inter-puritan fracas, he was surely pleased. In Laud's vision, New England was a small part of a great interlocking intercontinental network that sustained puritanism. The network stretched across Charles I's three kingdoms of England, Ireland, and Scotland to America and the Netherlands. All of it was being dismantled bit by bit. The English churches in the Netherlands were being pressured to conform to the ceremonies, as were the foreign Reformed congregations in England that had previously been permitted to worship as they did in their homelands; the puritan-leaning Church of Ireland was remodeled along English lines in the 1630s. Massachusetts's charter had been vacated by an English court in 1637, and it was just a matter of time before Laud brought the colony's independence to an end.[78]

But before that could happen, one careless move wiped out Laud's progress in this multi-dimensional chess game. In 1637, Charles precipitously sprang a variation of the Book of Common Prayer on the Scots, who looked upon it as an effort to drive their own church into Catholicism. The riots that followed in the streets of Edinburgh and other Scottish cities led to the mass signing of a Scottish "National Covenant" vowing to resist the "re-establishing of Popish religion and tyranny" and to the remodeling of the Church of Scotland into full-blown Presbyterianism. That Scottish defiance led in turn to the First Bishops' War of 1639, in which a Scottish army successfully faced down Charles's attempt to invade Scotland. With the Pacification of Berwick on June 18, 1639, the armies of both sides disbanded, leaving an enraged and humiliated Charles to plot vengeance. Meanwhile Scottish propaganda flooded into England along sympathetic puritan distribution networks. The propaganda called for a Parliament, the last thing in the world Charles wanted, and blamed the crisis on evil English bishops.[79]

Now in need of more money than he could raise himself, Charles grudgingly called a Parliament in April 1640. Two signers of the Dod letter, John Ball and Simeon Ashe, hurried down to London to lobby for reforms to the

Church of England. At the same time, Ball published a condemnation of his Congregationalist brethren as unjustified separatists. Their "sin of schism," Ball wrote, was "great and heinous."[80] If Ball and his colleagues had their way, Congregationalism would play no part in any church reform.

Charles expected Parliament to loyally throw no-strings-attached money at him to defeat the Scottish army. But most MPs had long lists of grievances about church and state that they wanted settled before talking about Scottish treachery, if indeed Scotland was the nest of traitors that Charles made it out to be. The king dissolved the "Short Parliament" after three weeks, a decision for which Laud was widely blamed.[81]

Charles then cobbled together an underfunded, hastily drafted army to march north to face the Scots. Along the way, these unwilling, impoverished soldiers raided churches to demolish Laud's altar rails, rip up ceremonial garments, and smash stained glass. They brutally murdered two officers upon discovering that they were Catholics.[82]

That year a puritan trying to hasten his long-awaited national reformation by distributing Scottish propaganda might have started tracking the output of a mysterious new underground London press. He would have welcomed the press's reprints of Scottish and puritan works against the bishops; one of them even sketched out the circumstances in which the English people could legitimately rise up in arms against Charles. But this puritan would have been disturbed by the press's tract in the spirit of Roger Williams that demanded total separation from the Church of England, denied that the state could police religion, and denounced the Massachusetts puritans as persecutors just because they did the right thing by banishing dissenters. The puritan would have read with outrage and contempt a London cobbler's blistering tavern sermon arguing that an unlearned preacher was preferable to an educated clergyman.[83]

The puritan might have reflected that this fearless publisher and his authors were not striving for a puritan reformation. With their sectarian, un-puritan disdain for a learned clergy and for state policing of religion, they were aiming for something much more like the cacophonous nightmare of Rhode Island. Would it be prudent to tear down the bishops so hastily, the puritan might have wondered, if something even worse lurked on the other side?

But it is unlikely that this puritan would have lingered over such a flyspeck of a possibility. The earl of Warwick and other puritan lords invited the Scottish army to invade England. On August 28, 1640 the Scots easily defeated the English forces at Newburn, some 60 miles into England. With

his army useless for fighting, Charles had no choice but to accept the humiliating demand of these aristocratic puritan traitors that he call another
Parliament and allow it to negotiate the terms on which the Scots left
England.[84] For the first time since the English Reformation started, puritans
had more guns at their disposal than their opponents, and Laud and Charles
finally had genuine reason to be alarmed at puritanism. So too, if they only
knew it, did puritans.

# CHAPTER 10

# A MIRACULOUS YEAR GOES BAD

In 1651, eleven tumultuous years after a Scottish army had forced Charles I to call a puritan-friendly Parliament, a gaunt thirty-three-year-old London man looked out over a deeply attentive crowd and told them how God had singled him out to be an object of his everlasting love. The man's impious parents had kept him away from sermons until he was fifteen, but when he finally heard one, preached by a puritan, the result was life-changing. For the next five terrifying years, he had lain under a dreadful "spirit of bondage" (Romans 8:15) and greatly feared death. The man's recollections might have brought back memories in many of his listeners of their own protracted and painful conversions. Yet God had finally granted him joy and peace, the man told them, and he rejoiced that for two decades God had kept him from committing a scandalous sin.[1]

Such tales of grace had long been standard fare in informal gatherings of puritans. In 1651, they were part of the admission process of the state-supported Congregational churches spreading across England. "I know no higher work that saints on earth have than this," the Congregationalist standing next to the speaker had written two years earlier. He also corrected the speaker when the latter slightly misquoted a scripture verse.[2]

Standard puritan fare though the tale was, the audience listened with exceptional alertness. The speaker, Presbyterian minister Christopher Love, was about to have his head chopped off. For treason, according to the Congregationalist Robert Tichborne, the sheriff of London, who was over-seeing Love's execution. For staying faithful, according to Love, to the Solemn League and Covenant that he, Tichborne, and many others in the crowd had sworn at the command of the puritan-led Parliament in 1643.[3] They had pledged before God to reform the Church of England, protect Parliament, and defend Charles I, and certainly not, as Tichborne and his faction of Congregationalists and even more extreme Protestant religious groups had done, tear that church down, clear out Parliament with guns, and behead the king.

Many or most of that crowd would have agreed with Love about why he was being executed. This popular minister assured friend and foe alike that he was putting his head on the block with as much quietness of mind as he possessed when lying down on his bed and that he would soon change his guard of soldiers for a guard of angels. The exceptionally violent thunderstorm that broke out after the execution was widely taken as God's angry commentary on the killing of one of his saints.[4]

A decade earlier, it would have been unthinkable for puritans to kill puritans. Back then, they were united in their pursuit of the enemies of England's reformation during what they called an "annus mirabilis"—a miraculous year. Within a few years that unity of purpose began to unravel as puritans started putting reformation into practice and the tensions that had dogged Massachusetts puritanism emerged with a vengeance in England. By 1645, this unraveling was complete and rival groups of puritans, with Love and Tichborne in opposite camps, were hurling verbal hatchets at each other with an angry vehemence that had previously been reserved for opponents like bishops.

The puritans' miraculous year began in November 1640, when Charles had been forced to summon Parliament by a Scottish army occupying English soil. Under this armed blackmail, Charles agreed to the various bills Parliament sent him to protect its powers and whittle away his own. He stood by while Parliament ordered Archbishop Laud's religious innovations dismantled and had Laud himself imprisoned and eventually beheaded for high treason. Laud was followed to prison by other bishops; his clerical followers were hauled before the House of Commons and removed from their positions; and his hated Court of High Commission was abolished. Plans were afoot at high levels for moderate puritan-leaning reform of the Church of England's government and ceremonies, although these came to nothing.[5]

Puritan muscle made such changes possible. At some point in 1641 Christopher Love rode north to Scotland. Since 1639 he had been serving as the chaplain to John Warner, then sheriff of London. Love's preaching and piety were attracting attention in puritan circles, and the London parish church of St. Anne and St. Agnes, Aldergate offered Love a pulpit. But for that position, Love would have to be ordained, and Love was not going to let a bishop place his hands on his head. Nothing but a Presbyterian ordination would do, which he could only get in Scotland.[6]

In the country through which Love rode, he could have seen godly zealots taking reformation into their own hands. They were tearing down altar railings, shredding surplices and the Book of Common Prayer, smashing stained-glass windows, and pulling down crosses. Riots broke out in churches when ministers tried to compel their godly parishioners to kneel for the Lord's Supper. As a Londoner, Love would already have encountered the intimidating mobs that Charles's opponents in Parliament increasingly called on to make sure that votes went their way.[7]

Violence and threats of violence did not come only from puritans in 1641. In the fall, the long-oppressed Catholics of Ireland staged a bloody uprising, made much worse in English imaginations by horrific, exaggerated rumors of their torture and slaughter of English Protestants. The uprising gave renewed impetus to Protestant fears of popery and of Charles's duped softness toward it. Charles sent plenty of signals that he would use force against his parliamentary opponents if and when he thought he could get away with it. Yet a significant number of non-puritan parliamentarians were drifting to Charles's side. They had been initially supportive of reining in the excesses of the king and Archbishop Laud, but now they were starting to fear and loath even more the lawlessness and religious chaos triggered by puritanism.[8]

The Scots refused to ordain Love since he did not seek a Scottish pulpit. On the way back to London, Love stopped to preach in the northeastern port of Newcastle. After all the unrest he had seen on his journey, Love did not have to stick his finger too far into the wind to come up with the menacing Bible text on which to build his Newcastle sermon, Ezekiel 11:8: "Ye have feared the sword, and the sword shall come upon you." Sir John Marley, mayor of the town, scoffed at Love's grim choice of text, praised England's stability, and clapped Love briefly in jail for preaching against the Book of Common Prayer. Love's prophetic warning of war, however, was long remembered in Newcastle.[9]

For it soon came true: king and Parliament were on the verge of stumbling into a bloody civil war. Charles fled London on January 10, 1642 after his attempt to seize and arrest five parliamentary leaders failed. On July 12, Parliament voted to raise an army, appointing the earl of Essex its commander. Parliament insisted that it was fighting the king out of loyalty to him, to separate him from his evil advisors. The logic of this loyalty eluded Charles, who organized his own army and declared Essex and his followers traitors on August 22.[10]

Like many puritan ministers, Love went all in for the Civil War. A bachelor, he gave away his belongings except his clothes and his books and started making pro-Parliament preaching tours in the country around London. In the Kent town of Tenterden he was hauled up on charges of treason for preaching that it was just and proper to wage defensive war against the king—Parliament was not attacking the king, the argument went, it only was defending itself and the English people from the wicked counselors who were behind Charles's attack on religion and English liberties. A soldier wrote enthusiastically of hearing—in between stints of burning altar rails, smashing stained glass, and terrorizing Catholics—a "famous" sermon by Love. "The Lord is . . . healing a land," Love preached encouragingly to another group of soldiers, "when the people abandon and abolish all the monuments of idolatry and superstition with a spirit of indignation." To rally a larger audience to Parliament's cause, Love and a friend produced a blistering pamphlet predicting that God's arrows would soon be drunk with the blood of the king's wicked, cruel, and atheistic supporters (the imagery was from Deuteronomy 32:42).[11]

Colonel John Venn, the parliamentary governor of Windsor Castle, knew Love from their London days of fasting and prayer together before the Civil War, and he invited him to serve as an army chaplain there. Love remained at Windsor Castle for two and a half years.[12] It was probably not a difficult choice since Love still could not have served in a parish church even had he wanted to.

The obstacle for Love was that Parliament not only had to fight a war, but also had to rebuild the Church of England, which it had succeeded in smashing to bits by 1642. A few bishops were in jail and the others were largely powerless, while the church courts that handled religious and moral offenses were on their last legs. All that was more or less functioning were the church's individual parishes, where ministers continued to hold services, collect their tithes, and haul anyone into court who refused to pay them, as they would continue to do throughout the chaos and upheaval of the next two decades. But the laws had not been passed that would allow Love to receive a legal Presbyterian-style ordination.

To reform the Church of England, Parliament called an advisory assembly of ninety ministers, almost all of them puritans, along with ten lords and twenty commoners from Parliament. They started meeting at the adjacent Westminster Abbey on July 1, 1643. Most puritans did not know exactly what kind of church government and worship they wanted to replace the old ones with. For perhaps the majority at the Westminster Assembly, it would have been acceptable to retain bishops, so long as they shared a lot more of their power than they did at present.[13] The pressures of war, however, soon pushed the Westminster Assembly decisively towards Presbyterianism.

Scottish troops had left England in 1641, but Royalist military successes by early 1643 made their return urgent. The price the Scots demanded of Parliament was a formal alliance that required all English adult males, along with the Scots, to swear to a Solemn League and Covenant. This covenant bound its takers, before God, to work for a single form of church government for the British Isles, one that followed the Bible and the best Reformed churches, to repress prelacy, heresy and schism, and to defend the person of the king, the privileges of Parliament, and the liberties of the people. The Scots, and most of the English, took for granted that the covenant amounted to an English commitment to some variety of Presbyterianism.[14]

English Presbyterianism had been fairly listless for almost a half century. It quickly started to revive in the early 1640s, but most English puritans probably had only a hazy understanding of it; Love was the exception, not the rule. Nonetheless, Presbyterianism had enough clerical authority, centralized supervision, and scriptural plausibility that most puritans would be able to accept some version of it as agreeable to the Bible, if not literally commanded by scripture in all its details.[15]

Despite its broad acceptability, Presbyterianism would be hammered out neither easily nor without deep, fresh wounds to puritanism at the Westminster Assembly, in no small measure because of godly people like Robert Tichborne, the sheriff at Love's execution. Like Love, Tichborne was quick to stand up and fight. In 1642, he and other militants secured London for Parliament's cause with their elections to the city's common council. Since London was by far the wealthiest and biggest city in England (its population was around 400,000; that of Norwich, the second biggest city, was only 20,000), those elections were a major step toward victory for Parliament. Tichborne "thereby became very popular," it was remembered a decade later, "and was greatly cried up by the good people of the city." He served in London's militia as a captain, and was already fighting with Parliament's army in 1643.[16]

In the parish churches, puritan ministers were hamstrung over the reformation they could legally bring about on their own. They could finally cut out the offensive parts of the Book of Common Prayer without fear, but they had no control over discipline, and that meant that they had no control over what was for many puritans the heart of church reform, the Lord's Supper. The "pure waters" of the Lord's Supper, as one minister put it, had to be protected "from the pollution of the common feet of the wild beasts." That protection parish ministers could not provide, and increasingly, out of desperation, in the 1640s they were shutting down the Lord's Supper completely.[17]

By late 1643, Tichborne was probably already among those puritans unwilling to put the pure worship of God on hold while Parliament figured out what sort of national church it wanted. These hasty puritans took church reformation into their own hands and became Congregationalists. There were nine Congregational churches at the beginning of 1643. By the year's end, there were four more, including the one to which Tichborne belonged, and all of them illegal.[18]

Already in 1643 there was friction and even bad blood between English Congregationalists and more moderate puritans. It had been divisive enough when Congregationalists set up exclusive churches 3,000 miles away in previously churchless Massachusetts, which they insisted were spiritually superior to the parish churches. It was far more provocative to plant these exclusive churches illegally in a country already well supplied with parish churches that were themselves in the process of reformation. Love spoke for many when he denounced the Congregationalists for "gathering churches out of churches." The practice was "schism and separation," Love charged, and it was turning "London's ancient love, union, and goodness, into hatred, division, and bitterness."[19]

Opponents called Congregationalism by its other, older name of "Independency," to emphasize its corrosive effect on organic national religious unity: Congregationalists were being Independents by abandoning the parish churches when they should be working to reform them. Worse, they were helping to ensure that the parish reformation would be a failure by pinching the most zealous puritans for their own churches, the ones most likely to support a minister in a drive for discipline and protection of the Lord's Supper. God himself hated Independency, as one London puritan grimly recorded: a Congregational couple on a public fast day sinfully shunned their local parish church to worship in their own congregation, only to have the child they left at home drown in a bathtub at the hands of a careless servant.[20]

Despite the hostility coming from other puritans, the leading Congregationalist ministers in the early 1640s were, and would remain,

respectable puritan insiders. They were ordained, university-trained ministers bound by ties of friendship and mutual admiration to more conservative ministers, enjoying powerful patrons, and possessing important allies
in Parliament, where Congregationalist ministers were soon preaching.
Like the American Congregationalists, they believed—as did Tichborne—
that it was the biblically mandated obligation of the state to support religion. Five of them, newly returned from exile in the Netherlands, were
appointed initially to the Westminster Assembly to join in the work of
reforming the Church of England.[21]

The assembly's work was done in lofty Westminster Abbey, adjacent to
Westminster Palace, where Parliament met. For much of that work, the
ministers at the assembly were able to reach common ground. In November
1644, the assembly finished a replacement for the Book of Common Prayer,
called the Directory for Public Worship. In place of the earlier book's
prescribed ceremonies and liturgy, the directory offered guidelines for
worship, leaving the details and precise wording of almost all services to the
officiating minister. On January 4, 1645, Parliament banned the use of the
Book of Common Prayer, replacing it with the directory. In 1646, the
Westminster Assembly completed its firmly Calvinist confession of faith,
which was quickly adopted by the Church of Scotland. Congregationalists
openly dissented from the sections about church government and about the
power of magistrates, but everyone agreed, or at least agreed not to vocally
disagree, on the doctrines of salvation. The "Longer" and "Shorter" catechisms the assembly drew up from the confession formed the foundation of
informal and formal religious instruction for generations of Calvinists in
the British Isles and America.[22]

Church government was a much more divisive issue than theology at
the Westminster Assembly. On this topic already in 1643, friction between
Congregationalists and others at the assembly was building. Complaints
came into the assembly about the gathering of Congregational churches.
Those complaints were driven not just by the churches themselves, but by a
sense of moral and religious breakdown following the disappearance of
church courts and effective press censorship. Learned ministers found
themselves increasingly having to debate in public and in the rapidly
swelling world of print with new or newly emboldened separatist and theologically unorthodox lay preachers. Even worse, these brazen opponents
were often armed with no more intellectual weapons than urgency, sharp
wits, well-thumbed English Bibles, and, they claimed, the inspiration of the
Holy Spirit. Their assets more than made up, in their own minds, for their

ignorance of the university-trained clergy's hard-learned Latin and original Bible languages and tools of formal reasoning and disputation.[23]

The Congregationalists' affirmation of separation from the parish churches and their conviction that any group of Christians had the spiritual ability to form a valid church served as an opening wedge for what could become, it was feared, a flood of these heretics and schismatics. "Independent" became the catch-all term not just for the Congregationalists, but for all the illegal do-it-yourself churches and religious groups who claimed independence from any higher religious authority. They were widely loathed and feared as harbingers of social and religious chaos in vast disproportion to their small numbers, and their illegal meetings were sometimes violently broken up by angry mobs.[24]

By the end of 1643, opponents of the Congregationalists at the Westminster Assembly were trying to get a resolution passed to shut the door on Congregationalism, this fomenter of religious and social anarchy, as part of a national church.[25] The five Congregationalists in turn published their own tract at the start of 1644, *An Apologeticall Narration*, to explain themselves. They stressed how much they had in common with the Presbyterians and assured them that all they sought out of the church settlement was "the allowance of a latitude to some lesser differences with peaceableness." And as for the respectability of Congregationalism itself, the Apologists invoked New England: "The greatest undertaking but that of our father Abraham out of his own country," they called it, with "as holy and judicious divines as this kingdom hath bred."[26]

That Congregational request for flexibility in the reformed national church sounded benign enough, if you were willing to accept their allegedly "lesser differences" under the umbrella of a national church structure, and many puritans were not willing. But who spoke for the leaderless movement that was Congregationalism? Was it these reassuring divines in the Westminster Assembly? Or maybe it was Tichborne's minister Nicholas Lockyer, who was attacking the assembly and encouraging the godly to abandon their parish churches and gather Congregational ones. Or perhaps it was the prominent Congregationalist John Goodwin, who was creating a huge controversy in his London parish church by trying to carve an exclusive Congregational church out of its membership. Goodwin in 1644 called for the government to get out of the business of supervising religion altogether (he backed down somewhat, for the time being, in a second edition of his tract).[27]

The Congregationalist ministers at the Westminster Assembly, unlike Goodwin, insisted that there were limits to their tolerance. But they refused to say where these limits were, and their actions gave the other assembly members plenty of opportunity for dire speculation. On May 27, 1644, a London Congregational church asked four assembly Congregationalists if it should discipline members who were shunning the church after adopting the conviction that only believing adults should be baptized, not infants. As the Congregationalists certainly knew, for most members of the Westminster Assembly, the advice would have been easy—of course, discipline them. They would have agreed with Stephen Marshall, the Westminster Assembly Presbyterian most sympathetic to the Congregationalists, who that same year had denounced the refusal of baptism to infants as a "bloody" sin. What sort of a church was it that would, as Marshall put it, under "a pretense of zeal ... condemn all the infants of the whole Church of Christ" by refusing them the blessing of baptism?[28]

Yet the assembly Congregationalists advised the Congregational church not to discipline the new Baptists, as people who insisted on baptism only for adult believers were called. Instead, they should pray for their straying members and love them. The departers, they concluded, acted not out of "obstinacy," but out of "tender conscience and holiness."[29]

Refusing baptism to infants might have been a mistake, but it was, to these Congregationalists, a holy mistake. It was certainly not a "heresy," as one Westminster Assembly member called it. Many English Congregational churches would even share the Lord's Supper with the few new illegal Baptist churches that were willing to share it with them. That was not an act of fellowship they extended to the parish churches. Massachusetts, by contrast, made it illegal to try to persuade people that baptizing infants was against God's law, let alone to attempt to set up churches based on the principle, and Massachusetts ministers wrote tracts against it. By 1645, some English Congregational churches felt protective enough about their Baptist brethren that they would not give the sacraments to Congregationalist visitors from Massachusetts.[30]

Baptists were not the only unwelcome guests at the puritans' reformation who were being encouraged in English Congregational churches. In 1642 word spread in London about sensational sermons being preached by the newly arrived minister Tobias Crisp. Crisp was offering no-cost salvation to just about anyone, even, he explained, the "notablest drunkard," "greatest whore-master," and "lewdest person." All such people had to do was to say that they would have Christ, and they could immediately consider themselves among the saved—no need for anyone, no matter how great a sinner, to undergo the protracted puritan preparatory period of agonized soul-searching. After believers realized they were saved, Crisp assured his listeners, there was also no need for them ever again to repent or doubt their salvation, even if they went on to commit sins as horrible as adultery or murder.[31]

There was theological method behind this madness. Puritan ministers insisted that God pronounced the predestined elect "justified" (saved) at some point during their lifetimes. Those ministers further warned that the elect could not expect to be justified until they had probed the depths of their souls' wickedness and realized how thoroughly lost they were. Crisp, on the other hand, told his listeners that there was no need for them to discover that they were lost, for God had long ago found them, even before they were babies: he justified them not during their lifetimes but before they were born. Furthermore, God wrapped his predestined elect so thoroughly in the cloak of Christ's saving righteousness that their sins, no matter how heinous, were completely invisible to him. Repentance for any sins that happened after your discovery that you were already saved was, thus, also unnecessary.[32]

Crisp did not just explain himself; he went on the attack against his conventional puritan opponents, much as Anne Hutchinson's circle had done in Massachusetts (see p.105), although from different theological foundations. What puritan ministers really preached with their harsh, endless treadmill of self-scrutiny, guilt, and repentance, Crisp charged, was, ultimately, salvation based not on the Protestant foundation of God's free grace, but on obedience to the Ten Commandments and God's moral law. Those ministers might think themselves "the greatest Protestants," but they were in fact "ministers of Moses" and the Covenant of Works (see p. 54).[33]

Puritan ministers had faced down outbreaks of hostile, more-Protestant-than-thou preaching like Crisp's, called antinomianism, before in London, most recently in 1633. Besides their bad theology, antinomians, puritan ministers charged, dangerously failed to understand the power of sin and how much God hated it, even in those he had saved. Most of the puritan laity accepted the ministers' argument, but antinomians dismissed their concerns. True believers, Crisp explained, would "eagerly pursue" holiness, for they loved God—murder was the exception, not the rule. But they based their souls' peace only on Christ, not on any signs in themselves that they had faith or were following God's law.[34]

Smallpox swept Crisp away in February 1643, leaving behind a reinvigorated antinomian subculture among the godly. Soon there would be much ineffectual toing and froing between Parliament and the Westminster

Assembly about how best to restrain the increasingly emboldened antinomian preachers.[35]

Congregationalist ministers generally opposed antinomianism, but they did not oppose it with the single-mindedness of other puritans. They were more sympathetic than Presbyterians to theological outreach efforts to antinomians and resisted attempts in the Westminster Assembly to have antinomian preachers suppressed. In their own preaching, they tended to stress the grace and comforts of the gospel more than the harshness of the law. The old London Presbyterian wood turner and perennial busybody Nehemiah Wallington wrote letters of rebuke to Congregationalist ministers over their excessively "sweet preaching." Such preaching was good in itself, Wallington warned, but "some may lie sleeping and snorting in their sins for many years" under it. Only the "despised Presbyterians," he grumbled, were giving sin the denunciation it deserved and sinners needed.[36]

But why not tilt toward sweet preaching? The Congregational churches were, in effect, the Christian major leagues. The Presbyterians could deal with the rookies, those listeners who most needed the harsh, awakening jolt of the law, in their parish churches until they were seasoned enough to join the established "saints" in a Congregational church.

New England had no fallback churches, and American Congregationalist ministers do not seem to have had the same tendency to tilt the scales in favor of God's gospel above his law. In Massachusetts, there was no dithering about Tobias Crisp. An immigrant who had spent too much time singing his praises en route to the colony was hustled off to Rhode Island upon arrival. Massachusetts Congregationalists published against antinomianism.[37]

An English Presbyterian once grumbled that Robert Tichborne's Congregational church "bred" antinomians. He might have been thinking about Tichborne himself when he wrote that. Although Tichborne heard orthodox sermons from his minister, Nicholas Lockyer, he struck up friendships with antinomians. One of those friends, the Baptist preacher Samuel Richardson, dedicated a defense of Tobias Crisp to Tichborne and three other men for the love they had shown him "so naturally, fully, and sweetly." They could show such love, Richardson wrote, only because they themselves knew the sweetness of Christ's love.[38]

Richardson understood what he was about with his dedication. Tichborne must have been a very busy man between his business, civic, and military responsibilities, but he found time to serve his church as a lay preacher (the encouragement of lay preaching was one big difference between Congregationalists and Presbyterians, while American Congregationalists leaned more in the Presbyterian direction). Tichborne even found time to write a religious book, *A Cluster of Canaan's Grapes*. His book extols a "sweet," antinomian-esque Christian spiritual life, passive and joyful, with little place for repentance and anxious self-scrutiny for sin, while remaining relatively conventional theologically; Tichborne had neither the theological training nor drive that would push him to try to smooth out rough patches and contradictions.[39]

For Presbyterians, Tichborne's book and Richardson's warm dedication to him would have summed up everything that was wrong with Congregationalism—a dangerously erroneous Baptist schismatic like Richardson in godly embrace with a lay Congregationalist of some prominence. Had England been properly reformed, Tichborne's church would not have been able to select the minister George Cokayn, a fervent supporter of Tobias Crisp, as a successor to Nicholas Lockyer in the late 1640s. Richardson would have been either in prison or keeping very quiet about his Baptist and antinomian opinions. Tichborne would not have been allowed anywhere near a pulpit or a publisher, while his church's elders would have labored to straighten out his theological confusion.[40]

Yet the mutual embrace of Tichborne the antinomian-leaning Congregationalist and Richardson the antinomian Baptist was a feature, not a bug, in Tichborne and other Congregationalists' understanding of the godly community. Tichborne explained in his writings that the saints' loving communion with each other should transcend what Tichborne dismissed as "forms," the details of doctrine, worship, and church government that so concerned the Presbyterians. The saints, Tichborne claimed, could see through their differences about religious forms to recognize that they were all "branches of the true Vine."[41]

This mutual love did not mean that the saints of England did not try to correct each other's errors, just as Tichborne and Richardson might argue about justification and baptism. But a saint would not try to compel other saints to agree with him or her. You knew that if what you were teaching was God's will, God would lead them to it, and if it was not, they would never follow it. Tichborne warned that those who were "rigidly zealous for forms" (like the Presbyterians) would "oppose the power of godliness in others" especially if they "differ in form."[42]

Scholars have called this stance of Tichborne and others "anti-formalism." Anti-formalism envisioned a unity of the godly that respected the need and freedom of people mutually recognizing each other as saints to discover for themselves God's will. It was associated with the conviction that the

Reformation had been only the beginning of the recovery of the Bible's true message and the first dawn of the light of the coming millennium. "Since the light grows every age more and more, to the perfect day and the coming of Christ," Congregationalists explained to Presbyterians in their last formal, failed efforts to resolve their differences in 1645, "some see more and some see less." While millennialism was not the exclusive property of the Independents, it appealed to them more than it did to Presbyterians.[42]

Anti-formalism was embraced even more expansively than it was by the Congregationalists by the non-puritan groups and individuals who claimed that the state should neither support religion nor supervise it, like most Baptists and separatists (who differed in this way from earlier separatists). When these people and groups were not being lumped in with the Congregationalists as Independents, they were called "sectaries." A contemporary dictionary defined "sectary" as "one that follows private opinions in religion," and that definition had an ominous resonance to it: following private religious opinions rather than the public, authorized ones was generally frowned upon and even feared in this organic society where church and state were closely intertwined.[44]

Even most sectaries, however, had limits to their religious anti-formalism. They recognized that idolatry (i.e., Catholicism and the old Church of England), blasphemy (reviling God), and false religions like Islam and Judaism could be restrained since there was nothing genuinely religious about any of them. A small group of extremists rejected even that limitation, however, and held that the state should not interfere with any sort of religion, true or false, as long as it was peaceable. The radical Rhode Island preacher Roger Williams (see p. 97) gave this opinion wide notoriety when he published a long book, *The Bloudy Tenent of Persecution*, arguing for complete liberty of conscience while in London in 1644. Williams was visiting London to seek a parliamentary charter for Rhode Island in order to keep Massachusetts from gobbling it up. It was just as well that he left, charter in hand, while his book was being printed in July 1644; in August, the House of Commons ordered it burned by London's public hangman.[45]

On occasion, the sectaries' opinions could get very private indeed; the apocalyptic light of the 1640s had grown so bright for some of them that it allowed them to see past forms entirely and even past the Bible itself. In 1648, Elizabeth Avery sent a letter across the Atlantic to her beloved brother, the Massachusetts minister Thomas Parker. She no longer went to church, she explained to him, because she was above all forms of worship. Instead, she was being "taught immediately by the spirit." Avery still prayed in private with her husband, she acknowledged, but only in accommodation to his spiritual weakness.[46]

Like her well-known puritan father and brother, in 1647 Avery published on scripture prophecies. But unlike them, she boldly claimed in her tract that the saints now could understand Christ better than the Bible's writers did. A more glorious manifestation of Christ by his spirit was taking place, "which manifestation doth now begin to some" (Christ's new manifestation came with a Familist tinge). Avery acknowledged that only one in a thousand saints had the kind of spiritual insight she had. But that was because so few saints understood what a mercy it was to be delivered from the antichristian burden of forms of worship and church government.[47]

Parker wrote back to his sister, telling her that her "printing of a book, beyond the custom of your sex, doth rankly smell." But even worse, he warned this one-in-a-thousand saint charging headlong into damnation, was "the exaltation of yourself in the way of your opinions." Avery's equally alarmed English cousin put Parker's letter into print in 1650. It joined the attack Christopher Love and other London ministers had already made on her book in a widely endorsed Presbyterian condemnation of the "infamous and pernicious errors" coming forth from England's presses "in these wicked and licentious times."[48]

Perhaps all this negative godly feedback had an impact on Avery, for she reversed her anti-formalist course. She is last heard of giving her conversion narrative in a Dublin Congregational church in 1651, one of the rare ones that allowed women to speak at meetings and vote. "The Lord leads me on, higher and higher in himself," Avery told the church, "and for that I see so much of him here in the midst of this church, I desire to be one also with you."[49]

In 1644, at the Westminster Assembly, anti-formalism was becoming a major issue, for in that year, the assembly started grappling in earnest with the fraught, complex issue of church government for the puritanized Church of England. As the assembly majority worked their way toward a consensus about a form of Presbyterianism, would they expect the Congregationalists to go along with them? Or would the emergent Presbyterians be flexible about form and find a compromise that could accommodate restrained Congregational churches alongside parish churches underneath the national church's umbrella?

Debates with the Congregationalists about church government throughout 1644 were very long, mostly fruitless, and accompanied by a steadily growing drumbeat of Presbyterian attacks outside the assembly on the Congregationalists. Efforts at the assembly to accommodate Congregational churches within the Presbyterianized Church of England collapsed entirely at the beginning of February 1645. It was then that Congregationalists unexpectedly, but perhaps predictably, insisted on their freedom to interpret a carefully worked-out compromise about the relationship of individual churches and higher ecclesiastical bodies entirely as they saw fit. The assembly majority responded to the compromise's collapse by making little further effort to seek the Congregationalists' input as it completed its recommendations for the reformed Church of England and sent them on to Parliament.[50]

By that time, piecemeal legislation for the Presbyterianized Church of England was far enough advanced that Christopher Love could finally legally be scrutinized by his fellow ministers about his learning, preaching skills, and holiness, and then receive ordination from them. The extremely patient parishioners of St. Anne and St. Agnes, Aldergate were finally able to elect him as their minister after a four-year wait, which they did in May 1645. Love gave up his Windsor Castle army position to take the pulpit, but Colonel Venn admired his preaching so much that he bought a house in Love's parish and paid a man to take Love's sermons down in shorthand for him. Love married Mary Stone, who had been an eleven year old in John Warner's household when Love took up his chaplaincy there in 1639. With this "woman of a sorrowful spirit," as Love described her, he had five children in six years, two of them dying in infancy.[51]

Under the fast-emerging legal Presbyterian regime that made it possible for Love to be ordained, Congregational churches would have to continue, if they were allowed to continue, outside the umbrella of the national church. Such a shattering of England's organic religious unity was unimaginable and unforgivable to many Presbyterians, especially with all the erroneous and heretical sectaries that the Congregationalists refused to disavow sheltering under the Congregationalist umbrella of Independency. Out of a sense of betrayal, some Presbyterians drastically increased the verbal abuse they directed at Congregationalists, linking them with the sectaries and warning that anything was possible with people who could be so religiously destructive; Independents might even overthrow Parliament and slaughter their opponents.[52]

Congregationalist ministers, in turn, started warning their listeners that their fellow puritans the Presbyterians would be more tyrannical than the bishops. "Will you have us banished from you?" the prominent

Congregationalist minister and Westminster Assembly member Jeremiah Burroughs asked his weeping congregation. Tichborne would have heard his minister cry out against "persecution" in his sermons so frequently that a complaint was brought to the Westminster Assembly.[53]

One reason Presbyterian and Congregationalist activists attacked each other so bitterly was that theirs was a family fight. As in most family fights, other puritans often tried to avoid taking sides. In the mid-1640s, the young minister Adam Martindale was finding his vocational footing in the village of Gorton just outside Manchester in the northwest of England. Martindale admired different elements of Congregationalism and Presbyterianism and ministers in both camps, but he quickly learned that he was walking a tightrope. To be friendly with one group was to earn the hostility of the other, while avoiding both would cost him the friendship of both, all with admirable individual exceptions. The hot Protestants among his parish laity were no less divided. "The Presbyterial and Congregational governments," Martindale wrote in his diary, searching for the right biblical analogy to convey this fraught situation, "were like Jacob and Esau struggling in the womb."[54]

Martindale's choice of scripture was both appropriate and ominous. Jacob and Esau were twins, which suggested how closely Presbyterians and Congregationalists were bound together as puritans. Despite that outward resemblance, however, God chose Jacob to be the father of the Old Testament Jews, his true church until the Jews rejected Christ, while he hated Esau and wiped out his descendants. Presbyterians and Congregationalists were already hurling bitter accusations of "Esau" at each other. Tensions between the groups would only worsen as Presbyterians pressed on with building their Independency-free Church of England.

# CHAPTER 11

# THE WOBBLY RISE AND PRECIPITOUS COLLAPSE OF PRESBYTERIAN ENGLAND

One of Christopher Love's last duties as an army chaplain in 1645 was to preach at Windsor Castle to General Thomas Fairfax and his officers before they marched off to their spring campaign against King Charles's forces. Fairfax was the commander of Parliament's newly created New Model Army, a unified command that promised to do what Parliament's previous regional armies had not—deliver a decisive military blow to the king. Love wanted that knockout blow and was frustrated and angry that Parliament's soldiers had yet to deliver it. God would march forth with Israel's army, Love preached encouragingly to this new force.[1]

Possibly also present at Love's sermon was the New Model Army's soon-to-be third in command, Oliver Cromwell, a down-on-his-luck minor country gentleman and MP who had turned out to be Parliament's most effective soldier. For Cromwell, like Love, Parliament's war with the king was part of the age-old struggle between the people of God and their enemies. As a cavalry officer, he engaged those enemies with an Old Testament fury and inspired his troops to do likewise. "God made them stubble to our swords," Cromwell wrote after the important parliamentary victory of Marston Moor in 1644, won chiefly by his cavalry.[2]

Love would have approved of Cromwell's pious militancy. But there was much about Cromwell that would have made Love deeply uneasy. Cromwell leaned strongly toward Congregationalism, but he was not particularly concerned with religious formalities (he is not known to have joined a church). A Calvinist who was confident that he was among God's chosen, Cromwell believed in a non-coercive unity of the godly, built not around forms of church government or fine points of theology, but around a shared sense of the presence of the active God who was handing Cromwell his victories. Cromwell had already promoted Baptist officers and protected them from Presbyterian commanders, while gossip had it that he claimed the Westminster Assembly divines were persecutors and that he wanted only the religious Independents, the Congregationalists and sectaries, for his own troops.[3] Nonetheless, regardless of what Cromwell wanted, the army took its orders from Parliament and Parliament was in the process of legislating what would be—it was hoped—a strong national Presbyterian church. Love had no reason to think that England's public cacophony of dangerous religious opinions would last much longer.

Love's tune had changed when he next preached before General Fairfax, during the latter's triumphal entry into London in November 1645. This was to be a sermon of thanksgiving, for, to all appearances, Israel's God had marched with the New Model Army. The army won a decisive victory at the Battle of Naseby on June 14, again largely due to Cromwell's cavalry, and the mopping-up campaign over the summer that followed secured the southwest for Parliament. Parliament's final victory over Charles was in sight. The army "had been serviceable to the church of God," Love preached to Fairfax and his officers, and it "ought . . . to have a requital."[4]

Love, however, did not keep his sermon on that emollient tone of praise and support. The army's recent service to the church of God, as Love understood that church, had, in fact, been decidedly mixed. Under Cromwell's protection, the New Model Army rapidly became a hothouse of antinomian, Baptist, and even Arminian lay preaching by the soldiers, all magnified in the horrified retelling of stories about those soldiers by more conservative English people. Cromwell, from his new position of prestige and power, made it clear to Parliament repeatedly that he envisioned something like his army's godly religious tolerance for England as a whole. "All that believe have the real unity, which is most glorious, because inward and spiritual," Cromwell wrote to Parliament while describing Bristol's surrender in September 1645. "From brethren . . . we look for no compulsion, but that of light and reason."[5]

For Presbyterians like Love, light and reason were scarcely compulsions strong enough on their own to subdue men's wicked hearts. He went on to warn in his sermon before Fairfax and his officers that rewarding the soldiers for their good service "must not extend so far as to tolerate them in their evils." Love gave the "supposition" of a "commander . . . who hath been valiant and faithful" in the army, yet whose opinions were "damnable heresies," such as denying Christ's divinity, the soul's immortality, and the Bible's authority. Any requital this commander might receive, Love insisted, could not include "a toleration in these opinions."[6]

Love's predictably intolerant Presbyterian sermon did not go over well with its military audience, Love later reported. They felt Love was smearing Fairfax by associating him with opinions that no commander in the army held. Even among the soldiers, only a vanishingly small number would have held such extreme opinions (for the time being, Love might have replied). Love was not the only Presbyterian having second thoughts about the true cost of the New Model Army's links with the Independent alliance of Congregationalists and sectaries. His combative sermon was the first of his sometimes direct, increasingly desperate, and finally fatal confrontations over the next six years with the steadily more assertive army and with the Independents who sheltered themselves under its umbrella, as his hopes for a Presbyterian reformation slipped away.[7]

The New Model Army's religious diversity might have loomed larger as a threat to Love in the late fall of 1645 than it had in the spring, for, in between, the Presbyterian national church that would keep error and heresy in check had been unexpectedly stopped dead in its legislative tracks. Over the past eighty years, puritans in Parliament had done their best to run interference for puritan ministers and to help reformation where they could, while the ministers served as these influential men's spiritual advisors, chaplains, and parish clergy. Previously there had never been any reason to nail down who ultimately called the religious shots in this alliance, but now it was an urgent question, and the future of the Presbyterianized Church of England depended on how it was answered.[8]

The flashpoint in the summer of 1645 was church discipline. Presbyterian ministers believed passionately that Christ expected the government to leave his churches alone to handle it. Many MPs, however, feared that if Parliament gave its godly allies in the churches what it called "boundless power" over discipline, it might never get any of that power back. The specific issue that summer was who had the last word on suspending sinners from the Lord's Supper. Parliament, by a narrow majority, insisted that it did and legislated an intrusive and cumbersome parliamentary supervisory system that included appeals all the way up to Parliament itself. Congregationalists and their sympathizers in Parliament, happy to throw a spanner in Presbyterianism's works, provided the critical votes of support for a principle that they rejected—state control over church discipline—in order to keep Presbyterianism from coming into practice.[9]

In response, furious Presbyterians launched a massive, polarizing political mobilization against the legislation. Ministers and laypeople joined in alike, along with London's city government. Presbyterian pulpit harangues to Parliament warned of God's anger and divine judgments, and petition campaigns spread across the country. Lurid books described the swarms of heretics and political radicals who were infecting the army and the country in the absence of church discipline, while exaggerating Congregationalists' responsibility for them.[10]

Presbyterian ministers themselves collectively refused to work in this crippled system, which was otherwise all ready to go. But the more the ministers and their lay allies pushed Parliament, the more Parliament dug in its heels. To the delight of the Congregationalists, at the end of April 1646 the year-long standoff between the Presbyterians and their parliamentary allies was showing no sign of easing.[11]

And then, the king, of all people, stepped in to break this puritan deadlock. The Civil War was more or less over by the spring of 1646, at the cost of 62,000 dead, and 55,000 made homeless out of a population of around 5,000,000. On April 27, Charles slipped out of his doomed headquarters at Oxford disguised as the servant of his two attendants. His wanderings ended with him turning himself over to the Scots at Newark on May 5. Charles was always happy to fish in his opponents' troubled waters, and soon he was deep in peace negotiations with the Scottish Presbyterian army, which was angry about Parliament's delay in setting up English Presbyterianism.[12]

Parliament now had a strong incentive to make the Scots happy by patching things up with the Westminster Assembly. Accordingly, on June 3, 1646, it passed a bill about church discipline that, among other small adjustments, mandated a review of the entire disciplinary system with in three years. On June 19, London's Presbyterian ministers announced that with these slender concessions and the possibility of fundamental change in the not too distant future, they could work with Parliament's system, even though it was still not "in all points satisfactory to our consciences."[13]

Even with the law behind them, Presbyterians were in for an uphill struggle to remodel the Church of England. Almost certainly fewer than two thousand of the ministers in England's over nine thousand parishes sympathized with puritanism enough to be active supporters of Presbyterianism (and far fewer ever became Congregationalists). At least half of England's counties had so few Presbyterian-inclined parish churches that they were unable to form a single Presbyterian association of neighboring churches, called a "classis". Only London and the county of Lancashire had enough of these classes to create a regional synod. London was the center of English Presbyterianism, but even it had only enough Presbyterianized parishes to create eight of its twelve mandated classes. Love's classis had the highest number of its parishes participating, nine of eleven, while Love served on the executive committee of London's provincial synod, or assembly.[14]

Congregationalists did not stand idly by as Presbyterianism began to take institutional shape. In some parishes, hostile Congregationalists and sectaries targeted the new position of lay elder who was to govern each parish alongside its minister. They might try to hinder the parish election of the lay elders, who were often socially prominent and politically engaged Presbyterian zealots. In the English Channel town of Dover, it was claimed that they deliberately tried to elect unworthy men to the office in order to discredit Presbyterianism. On the other hand, some Congregationalists, out of their sense of civic and religious duty, themselves served as lay elders, while one prominent London Congregationalist minister, Joseph Caryl, even served in a classis.[15]

If a parish church did Presbyterianize itself, Presbyterianism could still have a hard time putting down roots. For most English people, the newly mandated lay elders were a strange, monstrous, un-English institution. No less strange and monstrous was the lay elders' practice, with the parish minister, of interrogating everyone who sought to take the Lord's Supper to see if they were godly enough.

The Presbyterian legislation only permitted the lay elders and ministers to ask their parishioners about externals—did applicants have elementary doctrinal knowledge and was their behavior "nonscandalous?" The actual questions would have varied from church to church, depending on the lay elders' and minister's zeal for the purity of the Lord's Supper and the degree of support they had in the parish. A Devon minister went into rare specifics when he said that the would-be communicant must be "such a one as performs all religious duties, as well in private, as in public" and "delights in the society of godly people."[16]

These probing new questions were criticized from all directions. To most English people, they were a rude, intrusive affront. The gentlewoman Mary Verney huffed about "questions that would make one blush to relate" (questions made all the more offensive for being asked by her social inferiors). But for Congregationalists, these questions were barely a surface probe into the holiness needed to partake in the Lord's Supper. One of Love's parishioners who later became a Congregationalist remembered that Love and his lay elders questioned her "somewhat."[17]

Nevertheless, those ministers who were able to start policing the Lord's Supper felt comfortable offering it again, and Love and his fellow London Presbyterians could begin their effort to finally transform their city into another Geneva. The London Presbyterian provincial assembly and classes encouraged preaching, strict Sabbath observance, and catechizing parishioners in the basics of Calvinist Christianity, while lay elders began scouring taverns for Sabbath-breakers. Ministers collectively organized "morning exercises," where a group of them would rotate daily preaching at a parish church for a month before the workday started, ending the month with a fast and perhaps the celebration of the Lord's Supper. As always, Presbyterians preached tough divine love; Love warned his parishioners at the end of one of these exercises that if they did not put into practice what they had been hearing, it meant that they did not love God, or God they, and that their burden would be heavier in hell than the heathens'.[18]

The beginning of official Presbyterianism was rocky, haphazard, and slow.[19] But the Church of England had never had absolute uniformity, and government-supported Protestants at the beginning of Queen Elizabeth's reign had successfully overcome much greater problems and more violent resistance than the Presbyterians faced. If there had been an extended period of time for parliamentary muscle to shore up the institutions of Presbyterianism, those institutions would eventually have become the norm in the Church of England, perhaps with some sort of accommodation for a severely restrained Congregationalism, while other dissident forms of religion and worship would have had at best a twilight existence, as had been the case before 1640.

With Presbyterianism tottering to its feet, Presbyterians could finally begin instituting another vital part of their agenda: repressing the dangerous religious errors that had come out into the open with the collapse of the old Church of England. Not for Presbyterians, thundered Love, was "a licentious, lawless toleration." In the fall of 1646, a sweeping blasphemy and heresy bill started making a very slow progress through the House of Commons.[20]

The bill would suppress, via the death penalty, the spreading of opinions that undermined what Parliament understood to be the very foundations of Christianity. Under its terms the London lace-maker and self-appointed preacher Mrs. Attaway would either have to keep to herself her conviction that God in his goodness would not damn people to hell for eternity or face execution. The zigzagging spiritual pilgrimage of the lay preacher Lawrence Clarkson, which had already taken him through episcopacy, Presbyterianism, Congregationalism, antinomianism, and believer's baptism, would end with the hangman's noose if Clarkson did not abandon his most recent position that scripture was human and could not reveal God. The raging debate about what to do with Parliament's prisoner Paul Best, who remained utterly unrepentant about his anti-Trinitarian writings denying that Christ was the equal of God the Father, would also end with his execution. The threat of a hanging might accomplish what stone-throwing and musket-firing London Presbyterian mobs had not: deter Richard Overton from sharing at the soap boiler Thomas Lambe's always lively Baptist church his opinion that bodies would not be resurrected.[21]

Prospects would not be quite so grim for Thomas Lambe himself if he still felt impelled to challenge predestination and share his belief in free will: for that, he would face only prison. Prison was the bill's alternative to silence for opinions that only threatened the superstructure of Christian belief. That provision would also sweep up Catholics and antinomians, and Baptist and separatist churches could expect constables knocking on the doors of the houses and assembly halls where they met. Congregationalists themselves were safe, even if their sectarian allies were not, but their churches would have to police the opinions circulating in them and keep tabs on lay preachers like Tichborne more vigilantly than was their inclination. The bill would have raised no qualms among New England ministers and magistrates, except perhaps for the part about separatists, but any horrified anti-formalist in England reading it and exclaiming too loudly that Presbyterianism was antichristian would face prison.[22]

Such a strong bill against blasphemy and heresy was good and necessary, as far as Presbyterians were concerned, but by 1646, political opinions were bubbling up from London's sectarian underground that were no less dangerous, from the Presbyterian perspective, than its religious ones. These new opinions were being spread by a group that in a year or so would become known as the Levellers. Presbyterians like Love wanted political reform; the Levellers wanted political revolution. To them, kings were oppressors and aristocrats were parasites. The House of Commons, as the representative of the people, was the supreme power in the English government, above the monarch and the House of Lords, and it needed to be recognized as such. What the House of Commons should have been doing over the past few years was changing the laws to treat the people more justly and allow them to worship how they pleased. Instead, a tyrannical faction in the Commons had subverted the liberating struggle against the tyranny of Charles and his bishops for its own selfish ends. Tyrannical, intolerant Presbyterianism was one of this faction's tools of oppression. Levellerism, fumed one Presbyterian in response, was a "utopian anarchy of the promiscuous multitude."[23]

In 1646, Presbyterians started seeing Leveller influence everywhere. It was bad enough for Love that Robert Tichborne and others brought a pro-toleration petition to Parliament in June 1646. But even worse was that they presented the petition to the House of Commons but not the House of Lords. This was a deliberate snub, Love claimed. Tichborne and his associates were laying the foundations for the Levellers' long-term goal of abolishing the House of Lords as an illegitimate bastion of unrepresentative hierarchical privilege.[24] The Levellers' "malignant humor," Love, like other Presbyterians, incorrectly convinced himself, "runs as blood throughout the veins of all the sectaries."[25]

The first step to gaining control over these religious and political errors spreading among the sectaries was to get rid of the sectaries' main prop, the New Model Army. Support for the New Model Army in Parliament, and with it, acceptance of the Congregationalists and, to various degrees, the sectaries, waxed and waned depending on how much the army was needed. With fighting over, except in Ireland, the need was no longer so urgent. In March 1647, a majority in Parliament moved with haste to reorganize and reduce the size of its armed forces by disbanding the New Model Army. But when doing so, it paid little attention to the legitimate concerns of the New Model Army's soldiers about back pay and legal indemnity for their military actions, and offered the soldiers no thanks for their services. When the soldiers protested about their treatment, they were called "enemies of the state." This was not the most prudent way to deal with heavily armed, angry people who had legitimate grievances, especially since Parliament would have to deal with them alone; the Scottish army had left England on January 30, 1647 after handing Charles over to Parliament's custody.[26]

Because of its mistreatment, the New Model Army, a mixture of conscripts and religiously motivated volunteers, abandoned its subordination to Parliament. The soldiers started to organize as a self-conscious religious and political force, while the Levellers and their radical political agenda made steadily increasing inroads among them. With a huge dose of wishful thinking, the soldiers managed to convince themselves that they, not the corrupt Parliament, were the true voice of the English people, defending what soon was called "the good old cause," liberty of conscience, at least for all true saints, and the liberties of the people. Parliament, in turn, reached out to London's Presbyterian-leaning Common Council to build its own counter-army out of the city's militia. By the start of the summer, Presbyterians were gearing up for war with the Congregationalists and the sects.

By August that threat had dissipated. The army had seized the king and steadily closed in on London, while frantic negotiations had taken place between Presbyterian and Congregationalist ministers to avoid bloodshed in London. Eleven leading Presbyterian MPs had fled the capital in the face of army demands that they be expelled from Parliament. A majority in the shrunken Parliament demonstrated a new sensitivity to religious toleration and other army and Independent concerns, as well it might.

Charles spent the fall of 1647 negotiating political and religious peace terms with Parliament and the New Model Army. But he did so only to buy time as he plotted renewed war while under very lightly supervised confinement on the Isle of Wight. Unrest was widespread in England. Parliamentary taxes were enormous, while the county committees that enforced its war efforts were widely resented, as was the puritan cultural revolution that they also attempted to enforce. Riots broke out widely during the recently-banned holiday of Christmas in 1647. It took three thousand militiamen and a week's time to quell the worst one, in Canterbury.[27]

Charles managed to make common cause between this English unhappiness about too much puritan control in their country and the Scottish unhappiness about too little, especially over the English heretical army. The result was a combined English–Scottish uprising and invasion in the spring of 1648. It was poorly coordinated, and the Scots were badly divided over the recruitment of the obviously insincere Charles to the sacred Presbyterian cause.[28]

The New Model Army put down the king's forces in relatively short order, but only after the army's leaders had been plunged into a spiritual crisis. The uprising caught them by surprise. Cromwell and a group of his officers wanted to learn what their sin was that caused God to inflict this wrathful judgment of a new war upon them. As was their practice in times of stress, they held an intensely emotional, three-day prayer meeting at Windsor Castle at the end of April 1648. "With bitter weeping," they saw that their sin had been to try to negotiate with their duplicitous king. After a long debate, they also resolved that they would negotiate no more with

Charles. If the Lord delivered him into their hands, he had to be called to account for the blood he had shed and the "mischief" he had done against "the Lord's cause and people." Charles was a "man of blood," they concluded, and Numbers 35:33 was ominously clear about what had to happen to such a man: "The land cannot be cleansed of the blood that is shed therein, but by the blood of him that shed it."[29]

A majority in Parliament, on the other hand, appeared uncertain who their worst enemies were, Charles and the Scots or their own fanatical, out-of-control army, with the horrid possibility of king-killing now added to its blasphemies and heresies and its political radicalism. The handful of aristocrats who still had not deserted the House of Lords refused to declare the invading Scots enemies. Instead, they republished a Scottish declaration against episcopacy, toleration, and the English sectarian army with its "leveling democracy." On May 2, 1648, Parliament finally passed its severe blasphemy and heresy bill. So far had religious radicalism advanced under the shelter of the New Model Army that even some Congregationalists voted for the bill. On August 29, as power was slipping away from it toward the army, Parliament passed an omnibus bill containing all of its various Presbyterian legislation, with no provision for toleration.[30]

Rather than put their now-captive king on trial, Parliament resumed negotiations with him in the summer. By the fall, the negotiations seemed to be making progress, largely because Charles was once again trying to buy time while organizing foreign military assistance. Although his intentions were not that secret, the House of Commons took him at face value, for it was increasingly desperate to escape the army's tightening grip. On November 20, 1648, the army demanded that Charles stand trial as the "principal author" of the Civil War. On December 5, the House of Commons confrontationally responded by voting that Charles's concessions formed a suitable basis for further talks with him.[31]

At this point, the army finally dropped all pretenses that it was under civilian control. When the MPs came to their chamber at Westminster Palace the next day, they walked into a coup. Colonel Thomas Pride, a Baptist, was standing at the door, surrounded by armed soldiers, with a very long list of members to exclude. In "Pride's Purge," around 230 MPs, out of the House of Common's functional membership, at its very rare maximum, of 471, were barred from attendance for being hostile to the army.[32]

This "Rump" Parliament, as it would be derisively nicknamed, quickly started unraveling the Presbyterians' reformation. The blasphemy and heresy bill was left a dead letter. A motion to confirm the Presbyterian

settlement of the Church of England failed by one vote, and the infant
Presbyterian national church withered away. The higher collective bodies
of churches shrank as ministers dropped out and new parish ministers did
not bother joining. Where those bodies continued, they functioned as little
more than advisory and ordination boards. Some of the small minority of
parishes that had created lay elders kept them, but many did not. In their
absence, more ministers abandoned the Lord's Supper, while others confined
it to ad hoc godly groups, a move of questionable legality that risked retali-
ation from the excluded. When Christopher Love moved to another London
parish church, St. Lawrence Jewry, in 1649, the church wanted Love to
accept everyone who was not "grossly" or "notoriously" scandalous to the
Lord's Supper without further questioning. Love seems to have refused to
lower his standards.[33]

A flood of Presbyterian sermons and pamphlets denounced Pride's
Purge. Even fiercer Presbyterian denunciations followed after the House of
Commons set up a High Court of Justice, without the cooperation of the
almost empty House of Lords, and tried King Charles for treason in January
1649. It was next to impossible to find prominent judges or lawyers willing
to participate in the trial, which was why Tichborne, keen to see Charles
executed, ended up serving with other Congregationalists and signing
Charles's death warrant. Love and his fellow London Presbyterian ministers
spent their days lobbying against Charles's execution and a large part of
their nights in fasting and prayer, beseeching God for divine intervention.
On January 30, to the general horror of educated Europe, Charles's subjects
publicly beheaded their lawful sovereign outside Whitehall Palace before a
large, sullen crowd. Presbyterians protested the execution, lest the guilt of
that horrendous sin fall on them. With the House of Lords and monarchy
formally abolished, on May 19, 1649, the Rump House of Commons
declared England a republic. Around the same time, Tichborne—who
would be elected sheriff of London in 1650—and other Independents
purged moderates from London's city government to keep it under the
republic's control.[34]

As their political influence faded, Love and other Presbyterians
continued to fight as best they could for the reformation to which they
had sworn in the Solemn League and Covenant. They worked with
Congregationalists when their reforming interests overlapped on issues
ranging from defending the Sabbath to debating ministers who spread
dangerous doctrines. The Presbyterians, however, kept reminding their
wayward Congregationalist brethren that they were schismatics whose

separation from true churches was the fount of all the "woeful mischiefs" that had befallen Christ's churches in England.[35]

Another way for Presbyterians to fulfill their covenant obligations was to defy England's illegitimate and deeply unpopular new government. Love's anti-government preaching brought him before a parliamentary committee in September 1649. No witnesses dared to appear against him, to the pleasure of the large crowd that had come out in support of Love. Parliament tried to extract a minimal loyalty pledge to the new regime, the Engagement, but it met with widespread resistance and refusal from Presbyterians, who claimed it clashed with the Solemn League and Covenant. Love warned his congregation not to take the "cursed engagement."[36]

Some Presbyterians, including Love, focused their hopes for reformation on their beheaded king's nineteen-year-old son Charles, in exile in the Netherlands. It was true that young Charles was a carousing, womanizing anti-puritan, but to Presbyterians viewing him through rose-tinted glasses, all that this ungodliness meant was that their uncrowned but lawful sovereign was in the hands of evil counselors, like his father Charles I, his grandfather James I, and Elizabeth I had been. It was these counselors who kept him from recognizing puritanism's truth. Presbyterians regarded themselves as bound by the Solemn League and Covenant to try to separate their prince from these wicked influences and get him into the safe hands of the covenanted Scots. More realistic Presbyterians recognized that this sow's ear of a teenaged reprobate could not be transformed into a godly silk purse and that to think otherwise was in itself ungodly. The Scots, meanwhile, were horrified at the execution of their monarch Charles I by an army of English lawless heretics. The Scottish government immediately recognized his son as Charles II, king of Great Britain, Ireland, and France. But the Scots told him they would let him return to his kingdom of Scotland only on one heavy condition: Charles would have to swear to the Solemn League and Covenant.[37]

In the spring of 1649, Love's house became a meeting place for London Presbyterians who were sending messages to Charles encouraging him to reject his ungodly Royalist supporters and accept the Scots' terms. Charles had no intention of placing himself in the hands of the Presbyterians, at least not while his own forces were putting up a good fight against Cromwell's army in Ireland. But who knew what the future might require? He sent the London Presbyterians a polite thank-you note, urging them to stay steadfast and promising them great favor when he was in a position to bestow it.[38]

In early 1650, Charles's army was heading to defeat in Ireland, and Charles finally started to warm to the idea of defending the Solemn League and Covenant. Negotiations between him and the Scots began at Breda in the Netherlands. London Presbyterian men and women, including Love, met in their hundreds to hold private fasts for the success of the negotiations. Love prayed at one of these fasts for God to rescue Charles from wicked and malignant counsels, redeem him from the iniquity of his family lineage, and lead him to a firm agreement with his Scottish subjects about the covenant.[39]

Presbyterian prayers seemed answered when Charles traveled to Scotland, swore to the Solemn League and Covenant, and went through the motions of humbling himself for the sins of his father's war against the godly and his Catholic mother's idolatry. The Scottish church was badly split over the godliness of forcing these pledges and acts of contrition on such an obviously insincere recipient, but the mere fact that Charles was resident in Scotland prompted the English government to launch a preemptive invasion in June 1650.

English Presbyterians were shocked by what they viewed as the unprovoked shedding of the blood of the Scottish godly by an English army riddled with heretics. They refused to pray for the army's success and wrote letters to soldiers to discourage them from fighting. Presbyterians refused to join in the days of thanksgiving that stretched from England to Congregationalist New England after Cromwell's army miraculously crushed a superior Scottish army at Dunbar on September 3, 1650 (three thousand Scottish dead to around twenty English). In Massachusetts, John Cotton emphasized the magnitude of God's goodness in granting this victory by telling his listeners that a Scottish victory would have led to bloody uprisings in England. "Scarce one of ten" in England, he said, in a rough but defensible estimate, were "true to the Parliament."[40]

After Dunbar, Love's group continued to meet sporadically at his house, where they read letters from Scotland and drafted letters in return. The group agreed to deny Scottish requests for money for weapons. Love, however, organized a collection for their English go-between in Scotland for his personal use only and wrote to tell him as much.[41]

Love was put on trial for his pro-Scottish activities in June 1651. The most damaging charges fell apart as witnesses changed their testimony, had their memories suddenly fail, or, as in the case of one minister, refused to testify under oath because the "terrors of the Lord" were upon them. Love's decision to help out an enemy agent, however, was enough to see him convicted. Throughout the trial, Love told his wife Mary, he was feeling "such ravishing manifestations of [God's] love," that he feared it was showing on his face and being misinterpreted as smiling on his judges with contempt. On July 5 the court ordered Love beheaded for "treasons and traitorous and wicked practices." Love told Mary that he hoped the judges had as much comfort at their deaths as he did when he received that sentence. Death at the hands of the persecutors of the true church was the greatest glory a Christian could enjoy.[42]

Petitions for clemency followed, from Love's wife and others. In a gesture of would-be puritan solidarity, a few leading Congregationalist ministers joined with Presbyterians for a petition. The Presbyterians wanted to petition for Love's pardon. The Congregationalists would only agree to that on one stiff condition: the Presbyterians would have to accept the present government and renounce the Scots. That betrayal of principle was more than Love's life was worth to the Presbyterians or, probably, to Love, and the petition ended up only calling for a postponement of the execution. Love's own petitions failed, for in them he too could not bring himself to unambiguously acknowledge the legitimacy of the new English government, which probably had been the whole point of his trial.[43]

Now that all other options were closed, it was time to move on to the last stage of Love's earthly pilgrimage, the "good death". For puritans that meant a death that served as an inspiring testimony to the value of the strict puritan path to all those that witnessed or heard of it. A visibly good death would also drive home the point that the new Commonwealth was condemning itself by killing a saint. Lest anyone miss that implication, Love spelled out at length in his speech before he was beheaded how his willingness to die for the Solemn League and Covenant made him a martyr. Should anyone still miss the point, the published Presbyterian funeral sermons for Love were generously peppered with examples of biblical martyrs.[44]

After Love's execution, Presbyterian ministers kept his memory alive through sermon collections of the traditional puritan divinity that Love had continued to preach throughout the last decade's turbulence. "Here are presented to thee old doctrines," said one of their prefaces to his sermons, "which will not gratify that itch of novelty which is now become epidemical." Readers found Love's presentation of the old puritan doctrines compelling enough that his sermons, like those of a number of puritans, were frequently reprinted over the next two hundred years. Love's sermons were especially popular in the Netherlands, besides being translated into French, German, and Gaelic. They are still being reprinted today.[45]

In a defiant "vindication" of his conduct written two days before his execution, Love made a grim prediction. Love had a persuasion strongly settled on his heart, he wrote, that God would avenge his blood. Cromwell and his associates would be dead soon, Love claimed, and would "not die the common deaths of men." Citing biblical precedents, Love optimistically suggested that their deaths might come at the hands of the small Scottish army that had just invaded England with Charles II at its head.[46]

Two weeks after Love's execution, however, Cromwell crushed the Scottish army at the Battle of Worcester, and it was not until seven years later that he died in his bed peacefully. Charles fled to the continent in the aftermath of the battle, and England quickly annexed Scotland. Tichborne was one of eight commissioners sent there to bring the terms of the annexation at the end of 1651. The commissioners told the Scots that they now had to tolerate anyone who worshiped peacefully in a "gospel way." Characteristically for anti-formalists, they offered no guidelines for how to recognize a gospel way. Meanwhile, a Commonwealth fleet was working its way along the North American coast and into the Caribbean, overawing the last of the six mainland and island colonies that had declared their support for Charles II after they heard of the execution of Charles I (none in New England). The wars were over, and Presbyterians had run out of options. Most of them came to a sullen resignation regarding the new English government.[47] It was up to the Congregationalists now to provide what puritan direction they could to England's reformation.

# CHAPTER 12

# SHAKING OUT ANTICHRIST IN THE 1650s

Presbyterians had experienced a string of disasters from 1648 to 1651. For Congregationalists, those same events had been "eminent discoveries of God's presence, power, and providence." So exclaimed John Owen, the rising star among Congregationalist ministers, to Parliament after Cromwell smashed an invading Scottish army in 1651 at the battle of Worcester. Owen rejoiced that God had cast down the "iron yoke" of Presbyterianism against all expectations, along with all the other civic and ecclesiastical tyrannies that threatened the godly. The biblical end-times prophecies were being fulfilled, Owen told Parliament. Jesus would soon return and God was clearly at work in England shaking out "the depths of the subtle mystery" of Antichrist. The English had no greater way of showing their thankfulness than by cooperating with him.[1]

To Owen, cooperating with God meant cooperating with the Congregationalists. Congregationalist ministers took up important positions in the universities and served as favored preachers to Parliament. Owen himself was the chief influence on the government's church policy. At the local level, after state-backed Presbyterianism died in the late 1640s, puritans seeking a thoroughly reformed church to worship in usually had little choice but to turn to the Congregationalists. A majority of the roughly two hundred English Congregational churches by 1660 were gathered between 1648 and 1653.[2]

The consequences of Congregationalism becoming English puritanism's vanguard unfold in this chapter like a play, or a tragedy in three scenes. The first is a local vignette of Congregationalism as a success story and the second a local vignette of Congregationalism as a bitter, divisive disappointment. The action of both scenes is embedded in the cacophonous religious and secular politics of the period. The final, broad scene portrays the failure and collapse of the puritan reformation.

### Scene I: Bedford, Bedfordshire

Among those puritans finally abandoning the parish churches were a group living in and around the market town of Bedford, about 50 miles north of London. Nonconformists since the 1630s, they had been meeting regularly for prayer and spiritual growth, as was a common puritan practice. In 1650, John Gifford, an ex-Royalist major, gentleman, and successful lay preacher, tried to persuade them to take the next step and transform their group into a Congregational church. Some of the group had the usual puritan reservations about Congregationalism's excessive exclusiveness. But after prayer, discussion, and conferences with other Congregational churches, the group, including two ex-mayors of Bedford, started their own church. As with 80 percent of Congregational churches in the 1650s, taking on a minister put no special financial burden on them. In 1653, Gifford received an appointment from the government to the rectory of St. John's parish church, whose parishioners were required to pay him tithes.[3]

Not that Gifford had any intention of giving the sacraments to those parishioners. For the Congregationalists and for England's new government, the parish churches still played a vital role in reformation, only not as real churches. Rather, they were endowed lecture halls or, in the words of the Congregationalists, "public meeting-places commonly called churches." In these meeting places the mass of the English population would learn their religious duties from the preaching of ministers like Gifford. There they might internalize enough Calvinist theology to be saved and discover the need to join a real church like Gifford's with its sacraments and discipline.[4]

Real churches were not the business of the government. If a preacher wanted to treat the local people attending his lectures and paying him tithes as his church and offer all of them the sacraments, as in the days of the old parish churches, that was fine with the government (and perhaps no more than 5 percent of the population sought any other kind of church). If a minister like Gifford did not want to treat them as his church, that was fine with it too.[5]

England did not have a functioning national church anymore, which suited the Congregationalists, but Owen and other Congregationalist leaders still wanted it to have a national theology. In increasingly emphatic but less-than-successful legislative initiatives in the 1650s, they tried to get the government to support the preaching of Calvinist theology and discourage as much as possible the preaching of anything else.[6]

The Congregationalists' efforts, however, brought them the intense suspicion of their awkward allies the sectaries, who had significant sympathizers and supporters in the army. The sectaries wanted the government to keep out of religion altogether, and certainly not to be ramping up its supervision of it. The Congregationalists would "bind our souls in secular chains," warned the poet and religious radical John Milton, as well he might: Milton was quietly starting to explore the horrifying (to almost all Christians) anti-Trinitarian idea that Jesus was not the equal of God the Father. Indeed, in 1655, Cromwell, now ruling over England as lord protector, saved a noisy anti-Trinitarian from Parliament's desire for his execution by banishing him to an obscure island. John Owen himself, in response to the seemingly unstoppable growth of heresy in the 1650s, was no longer as squeamish at the thought of executing anti-Trinitarians as he had been in the 1640s.[7]

One day around the time of Gifford's official appointment to his Bedford parish church, three or four women in his congregation were sitting outside on a door stoop. Women made up a majority of the Bedford Congregational church's hundred members, well over 60 percent, as was typical for Congregational churches in England and America; in some Congregational churches, the ratio was over 70 percent. Women were neither expected to be involved in church government nor to take on public roles in most Congregational churches. They were, however, expected to be active, informal evangelists. One Congregationalist chronicler wrote approvingly of how the talk of his church's female members while buying and selling at market was so "heavenly" that scoffers derided them as "women preachers."[8]

The women on the stoop were talking about religion when they were approached by an impoverished young tinker, John Bunyan. As a wandering mender of pots and pans, Bunyan ranked with peddlers and vagrants as the scum of county society. Bunyan came from a hamlet a mile away, and the women might already have heard about him: about his earlier reputation as an occasionally conscience-struck lover of sports and dancing, and an habitual blasphemer; about how he had started paying sustained attention to religion a few years previously when he married a poor devout woman with a dowry of two old puritan books that they read together; and about how he was starting to take religion seriously and reforming himself. By the time he encountered the Congregationalist women, Bunyan fancied himself a "brisk talker" on religious matters. When he overheard their discussion, he decided to join in.[9]

To Bunyan, the Bedford women spoke with such joy, fluency in the Bible, and signs of grace that he felt he had arrived in a new, unsettling world. Their discussion of the intricacies of Christ's work in the soul and the turmoil of conversion went completely and alarmingly over his cocksure head. Bunyan was plunged into doubts about his own salvation.[10]

As Bunyan subsequently traveled across the countryside mending pots and pans, he encountered members of the most unabashedly blasphemous and sinful of all the small sectarian movements popping up across England, the Ranters. The leaders, more or less, of the unorganized, nonhierarchical Ranters had published books at the turn of the decade arguing (to generalize broadly) that since God is pure and all our acts come from him, anything we do is pure, especially if it involves sex, drinking, or swearing. They put their conclusions into practice, and the horrified Rump Parliament passed a narrowly targeted blasphemy act against their doctrines in 1650 (the severe 1648 heresy and blasphemy bill was a dead letter in the new republic). The Ranters whom Bunyan encountered tried to persuade him that they had reached perfection and could do anything they wanted without sinning.[11]

Bunyan was able to pray his way out of the Ranters' temptations but not out of a spiritual crisis triggered by his meeting with the Bedford women. He became convinced that he had no true faith and, even worse, that Christ had rejected him. Bunyan finally unburdened himself to some Bedford Congregationalists, who brought him to their minister. The church associated Bunyan's struggles with a work of grace in him, even if he did not.[12]

Around 1654, the church accepted Bunyan as a member after he gave a satisfactory account of the divine work of conversion in his soul, as was customary for Congregationalists on both sides of the Atlantic. Surrounded, supported, and challenged by this experienced Christian community, Bunyan oscillated for the rest of the 1650s between collapsing into complete despair at his ongoing discovery of the depths of his corruption and gaining ever-growing hope and confidence in Christ's capacity and intention to save him.[13]

Congregationalist ministers and laypeople kept their eyes out for laymen who seemed to have a talent for preaching. Even while Bunyan was sunk in despair, his church recognized that his up and down spiritual rollercoaster ride, his heartfelt internalization of the Bible, and his gifts as a brisk talker had left him with an unusual talent for persuasive exhorting. It designated him a lay preacher and in 1656 began to send him on evangelizing missions just in time to confront what was becoming by far the most successful and alarming of the new radical Protestant movements sprouting up like mushrooms throughout England, Quakerism.[14]

The Quakers had so thoroughly shaken off what they called "the spirit of Antichrist" that horrified puritans doubted that they were even Christians. Did their lack of interest in the historical Christ mean they had also entirely shaken him off? Did their conviction that their revelations were as true as those of the Bible since they were both sent by the spirit (not to be confused with the Holy Spirit, as usually understood), mean that they had abandoned the Bible and probably the Trinity? The Quakers had certainly shaken off predestination. All humans, they insisted, possessed the divine light of Christ within them, which was much more a principle than a person, and all humans could potentially become perfect in this lifetime. Quakers had shaken off the sacraments and formal worship. At their meetings, they spontaneously trembled and quaked from what they said was the power of Christ in them; their opponents, when they were not calling them possessed by demons, called them "Quakers," and the name stuck.[15]

Quakers called themselves "Friends," but they were not so friendly to anyone who got in the way of the urgent message that male and female Quakers would preach to all and sundry, indoors and outdoors. "Thou serpent, thou liar, thou deceiver, thou child of the devil," was a typical Quaker greeting to puritan clergy, whom they often challenged in church. The Quakers' message was that the Second Coming of Jesus was taking place right now, not externally, but only in the souls of those who were following the true path of salvation, that of the Quakers. Sometimes they delivered that message symbolically, like the young Quaker woman who went naked through Oxford "in obedience to the Lord," to show Congregationalists and Presbyterians their spiritual nakedness. In this acutely status-conscious society, Quakers heightened their offensiveness by refusing to bow or take off their hats to magistrates and by addressing everyone as "thee" or "thou," instead of the formal "you."[16]

In the current unsettled state of England's laws and government, it was much easier and much more common for magistrates to convict the aggressively proselytizing Quakers for offenses against public order than for religious offenses. Cromwell stepped in occasionally when he thought local magistrates had become overzealous, but on top of mob violence and whippings, 1,200 Quakers ended up in England's loathsome prisons in the 1650s, with 32 dying there. By contrast, even though Catholicism remained illegal and its practitioners were subject to heavy fines, only one

Catholic priest was executed in the 1650s. Those who engaged in no less illegal Book of Common Prayer worship faced, at worst, occasional harassment. But the uniquely heavy-handed, sustained repression of Quakerism hardly threw the Quakers off their stride. Opponents could only explain Quakerism's rapid expansion in terms of witchcraft and Jesuit schemes to destroy Protestantism.[17]

In 1654 Quaker missionaries reached Bedfordshire. It was inevitable that they would clash with Bunyan and his church. For many spiritual pilgrims, Quakerism was the final destination of a journey that had taken them through the Congregational and Baptist churches, and Quakers were to deplete and even terminate a number of those churches in Bunyan's region. Bunyan and his fellow church members were soon debating Quakers in local churches and in Bedford's town market.[18]

Bunyan threw himself with a fury into this task, for his only hope to escape hell lay with the very historical Christ whose complex saving nature the Quakers were damnably etherealizing into a mere light within every human. In 1656 the Quakers kick-started Bunyan's career as an author, and over the next three years he wrote two theological tracts defending Jesus and attacking Quakers, as well as a pamphlet about a local Quaker who temporarily changed a woman into a horse and rode her to a Quaker meeting—the evidence against the Quaker was good enough for an indictment, but a jury refused to convict.[19]

By the end of the 1650s, Bunyan's grueling, in-depth Calvinist psychological and conceptual retraining in the Bedford church was over. He had learned enough about Jesus and himself to become confident that Christ's grace was sufficient for his salvation and that he was indeed one of the predestined elect. Bunyan had picked up a following in the region as a preacher and had started on the publishing career that would eventually make him the most-read preacher of the seventeenth century.[20]

Bunyan's extraordinary ascent could not have happened under a Presbyterian regime, for public preaching would have been the preserve only of university-trained ministers. A minister of a neighboring parish once confronted Bunyan while he was preaching in a barn, challenging his clumsy scriptural exegesis and his right as a layperson to publicly preach: if a tinker could preach, the minister fumed later, then the orderly ways of God were being overthrown, and all social order would necessarily soon disintegrate. England would become a society of bears and tigers tearing each other apart, the minister fretted, and the poorest servant would soon have as much land as a gentleman.[21]

Anxieties about social hierarchy did play a part in Presbyterian objections to lay preaching. But those objections cannot be attributed to that anxiety alone. Bunyan might have admirably battled Quakers, but if the Presbyterians had been able to create their national church, it would have kept a lid on lay preaching and made it more difficult for the Quakers to emerge in the first place. One John Bunyan was not necessarily a satisfactory trade-off for a flood of heretics. Some Presbyterian ministers locked their parish churches to keep out wandering lay preachers.[22]

Bunyan's religious world was intense, but narrow, and the connections of Congregationalism to a broader, learned religious culture meant very little to him. Bunyan's church communed only with a network of Congregational and open-minded Baptist churches, while Bunyan looked upon all learned ministers more conservative than Congregationalists as greedy vultures, keeping their listeners in darkness for their own profit. Bunyan told the minister who challenged him about his preaching to be off with his hell-bred logic to Oxford, and demanded evidence that he was converted. "Though I am not skilled in the Hebrew tongue, yet through grace, I am enlightened into the scriptures," Bunyan once said.[23]

"This man is chosen not of an earthly, but out of the heavenly university, the Church of Christ," wrote Bunyan's university-educated pastor in his preface to Bunyan's first book.[24] As a heavenly university, Bunyan's church realized the 1650s Congregationalist ideal: a voluntary, spiritually elitist, state-encouraged church actively cultivating its members' spiritual gifts, no matter how humble their background, while maintaining its evangelical and doctrinal obligations to the larger society around it.

### Scene 2: Exeter, Devon

Susanna Parr was a smart, censorious, idealistic puritan from the southwestern city of Exeter. Her uncle was probably Exeter's legendarily strict and outspoken puritan mayor, Ignatius Jurdain. Their encounters would have been regularly punctuated by Jurdain's admonitions that Parr strenuously examine herself and wrestle with God in prayer if she had not yet found assurance of salvation, which, Jurdain would have told her as he told others, he enjoyed to a high degree. It might have been from Jurdain's example that Parr imbibed the duty to fearlessly and closely adhere to what she saw as the path of righteousness.[25]

Parr's own generation, she believed, had the duty to leave to posterity "the name of God glorious in the brightness of the gospel." In 1649, a decade after her uncle's death, she worried that they were failing at this task. There were Presbyterian ministers in Exeter who managed the difficult task of restraining access to the Lord's Supper in their parish churches, even after the collapse of government support, but they were not strict enough to satisfy Parr. A partial reformation such as the Presbyterians offered, she decided, was worse than none at all.[26]

Parr was the sort of dissatisfied puritan who was ripe for the picking for Congregationalism. She admired Massachusetts and had heard that the Congregationalists had the purest, most spirit-filled churches. Around 1650, she joined some Exeter laypeople meeting to gather the city's first Congregational church. Parr's group was full of excited talk about how they had escaped Babylon, the mystical spirit of the Catholic Church that still infected the parish churches.[27]

These would-be Exeter Congregationalists kept their gatherings secret at first, on the advice of their future minister, Lewis Stuckeley, lest they come under irresistible pressure to change their minds. Exeter was not a Congregationalist-friendly place. Presbyterians dominated the city council, and Exeter's Presbyterian ministers were busy stirring up the kind of defiance against England's new republic that would end with Christopher Love's execution in 1651. An army garrison was stationed in the city, in part to keep a lid on Presbyterian unrest. An Exeter Congregationalist charged that what drove the Presbyterian defiance was the new regime's support for Congregationalism. When word got out that Exeter itself now had its own divisive Congregational church, it generated a storm of controversy among Exeter puritans.[28]

In the new church's first flush of enthusiasm, Stuckeley encouraged women as well as men to speak up in meetings.[29] Stuckeley missed a lot of those meetings; it would be a few years before he could untangle himself from other commitments. During his frequent absences, the glow of Congregationalism began to wear off for Parr. At these meetings, Parr disliked the laity's inept scriptural interpretation and clumsy prayers. Outspoken in her zeal for purity, she took an aggressive part in clashes over the suitability of prospective members and berated the other members for their "indifferency of spirit."[30]

As social friction built up, Parr began uncomfortably to feel that she was stepping outside her place as a woman by speaking in public, but Stuckeley pressed her to continue. When he finally took over the meetings, though, he informed her that now she could speak only through a man. Some of the men, he claimed, had complained to him about her speaking.[31]

After these disillusioning experiences, Parr grew uneasy that her new exclusive church had actually separated from people more godly than they were. Parr decided that she did not know enough about what made a true church. Going to Stuckeley with her concerns, he told her frankly that the New England Congregational churches considered the parish churches to be true churches. Why then separate from them, Parr wondered, and create new churches instead of working on their reformation? When one of her two children died, Parr concluded that God was sending her a sharp message. The breach that the death created in her family was like the wound the Congregationalists were making in the body of Christ by separating from the parish churches.[32]

Under the punishing hand of God, Parr started feeling the "very terrors of hell in my soul" for her separation in worship from the larger godly community. Fortunately for her, a solution was close at hand. Exeter's government had given her congregation the nave of Exeter's cathedral to use. All she had to do to cease her separation was to walk a hundred feet or so to the cathedral's choir, where the prominent local Presbyterian and ex-Westminster Assembly member Thomas Ford had his congregation.[33]

Parr was just the kind of listener Ford had been seeking. Like Presbyterians elsewhere, he was doing his best to keep something like a national church going in the face of puritan fragmentation and government indifference. Ford arranged with the other ministers in Exeter, including Congregationalists, for Tuesday sermon lectures, to ensure that the city had regular public education in the gospel. He saw to it that the Lord's Supper was offered in a parish church every other week on a rotating basis, to allow the godly in the entire city regular to access it. Ford also served as justice of the peace and as a member of Exeter's city council. In the 1650s, the government of Exeter vigorously prosecuted Quakers, enforced the Sabbath, cracked down on illicit sex, and improved the conditions of the poor. "The whole city was mightily reformed" under Ford's influence, claimed a biographer.[34]

Ford, like other Presbyterians, was willing to work with the new regime when its goals overlapped with his. One regime task Ford heartily endorsed was Cromwell's effort to improve the quality of English preaching, a long-standing puritan ambition. In 1654, Cromwell implemented one element of earlier proposed Congregationalist legislation. Under the plan, a board of "Triers," was set up in London, consisting of Congregationalists, some Presbyterians, and a few of the rare Baptists who retained the puritan belief in state involvement in religion. The Triers examined ministers heading off to preach in the parish churches for evidence of their conversion, sound life, doctrinal correctness, and pulpit skills. They were very busy: by 1659 they had examined over 3,500 men. Cromwell looked upon them as his greatest accomplishment. Anti-Calvinists grumbled that all applicants had to do to pass was to claim that they had been converted by a famous puritan. The Triers were complemented by the county-based "Ejectors," who had the task of removing inadequate clergymen from their livings. Ford joined Stuckeley to serve on the Devon committee of Ejectors.[35]

Around the time that Parr was worrying about the wound Congregationalists were creating in the body of Christ, Ford was preaching sermons designed to speed up recovery from Congregationalist spiritual exclusivity. Those sermons could even have been preached with Parr in mind. True worship, Ford told his listeners, took place among the "mixed multitudes" of a parish church. These churches were not just lecture halls, as the Congregationalists would have it, they were real churches, and hearing sermons in them, he said, was in itself a form of spiritual communion. Listening to Ford convinced Parr that she could cease her sinful separation from the larger puritan community without separating from her Congregational church. She would attend Ford's preaching on a regular basis while continuing to take the Lord's Supper with her church.[36]

Parr's one-person repair of the lamentable Congregationalist— Presbyterian fissure among puritans, however, was to the Congregationalists a heinous betrayal of her covenant with her church. Stuckeley, whose sermons she was abandoning for Ford's, told her she was like a wife delighting in another man more than her husband. The church, led by Stuckeley, pressured Parr to stop listening to Ford. To ratchet up the pressure, they raised incidents from the days when Parr spoke in public in which some members considered her to have been unduly argumentative or to have committed other sins. Back off or face disciplinary proceedings was the message. As a result of the church's heavy-handed tactics, Parr informed them in March 1654 that she was giving up her membership and joining Ford's church.[37]

She then discovered to her surprise that she could not just leave a covenanted Congregational church when she felt like it, any more than a person could just walk out of a marriage. As in New England, the church had to dismiss her. That it was not prepared to do; instead it sent a layman to her house to inform her that it had suspended her from the Lord's Supper. Her church's officers met with Ford and other Presbyterian ministers to impress upon them that Parr was in a disciplinary process and was not spiritually fit to be accepted into another church. The Presbyterian ministers dismissed those charges as groundless. To the accusation that Parr was fickle, Ford responded, according to Parr, "That is as much to say, she is a woman."[38] Ford admitted Parr into his church.

Parr had taken it for granted that pure Congregational churches would serve the national godly community; she had not anticipated how fiercely hers would attempt to fence her off from it. After Parr left, her church formally suspended her from the sacraments for her sins, as if she were still a member. Parr concluded that Congregationalists were as tyrannical and antichristian as the bishops.[39] Local Presbyterians undoubtedly reminded her that they had long predicted that the self-claimed autonomy of each Congregational church could easily lead to this kind of injustice.

The Congregationalists took no further official action against Parr for the time being—the dreadful spiritual sentence of excommunication would have been the logical next step. They confined themselves to trying to damage Parr in the court of godly public opinion, making it known around Exeter that they had rejected spiritual communion with Parr because she was a "liar, a contentious and a troublesome person." They tried to undermine Ford within the community by spreading the false story that he advocated giving the Lord's Supper to anyone. Exeter's government sold off a few redundant church buildings in 1657 to fund an interior brick wall across the cathedral, separating Stuckeley's church in the nave from Ford's in the choir.[40]

The year after Parr joined his church, Ford ventured on an even more ambitious effort to glue back together the fractured puritan reformation. In 1655, he and another Presbyterian, George Hughes, formed the Devonshire Association. Ministers who joined the association had to commit to keep unworthy sinners from the Lord's Supper in their own parish churches.[41] The Devonshire Association was part of a wave initiated by the prominent puritan minister Richard Baxter. In 1652, Baxter founded and vigorously promoted the Worcestershire Association, a self-help group for ministers who wanted to control access to the Lord's Supper in their often recalcitrant parishes and otherwise carry on with the work of evangelism in these difficult times. Baxter's grassroots rebuilding of a church network met a badly felt need, and associations were formed in at least sixteen counties, although next to nothing is known about most of them.[42]

Congregationalist ministers sometimes joined these Baxterian associations. In 1656, Stuckeley and his co-pastor Thomas Mall joined Ford's organization. Congregationalists like Stuckeley and Mall shared with the other ministers university training, friendships, and evangelical and moral reformist goals. At least in some cases, they shared the hope that the differences between Congregationalists and Presbyterians could be healed and that the puritan churches could be reunited in worship. Most Congregationalists, like the New Englanders, still claimed to aspire someday to sacramental communion with suitably reformed Presbyterian parish churches. A few Congregationalist ministers took the next step of working out elaborate terms of agreement with neighboring Presbyterian ministers that held out the possibility, at least implicitly, of this communion. But little came of such efforts. Stuckeley's own church, like Bunyan's, was typically Congregationalist in refusing to practice communion in the Lord's Supper with the insufficiently pure Presbyterian parish churches around it.[43]

It was not only religious differences that made relationships between Congregationalists and Presbyterians fraught. The Congregationalists had not forgotten that Presbyterians in the 1640s had tried to drive them all back to the parish churches. They suspected, not without reason, that Presbyterians would gladly make the effort again if the opportunity arose. But the army-backed government that gave the Congregationalists security was to the Presbyterians, and to most English people, an illegitimate government of king-killers.

That political distrust between Congregationalists and Presbyterians added to the formidable difficulties Cromwell faced in creating a stable government. On April 20, 1653, Cromwell's soldiers dissolved the Rump Parliament for reasons still not entirely clear. Cromwell thereby made permanent enemies of republicans who believed that the people's representatives should have no power above them. Soldiers were back eight months later to close the replacement governing body, the "Nominated Assembly," appointed by the army council. That assembly had become bogged down in squabbling between those members with an ambitious reforming agenda and more conservative ones. The squabbling was exacerbated by the presence of a new group, the "Fifth Monarchists," rooted in London's Baptist and Congregational churches and in the army. The Fifth Monarchists fervently believed, based on Daniel 2:31–45, that Jesus was about to return as king not just of the churches, but of the world. The world needed to prepare by replacing all merely human state institutions with a socially reformist, biblical dictatorship of the saints, if necessary by grassroots force. The Nominated Assembly should have been the first step to this interim dictatorship. After the assembly's suppression, plotters against Cromwell were as likely to be Fifth Monarchists, for whom Cromwell was now Antichrist, as they were to be republicans angry about the dissolution of the Rump Parliament, or Royalists still angry about the execution of the king.[44]

After the failure of the Nominated Assembly, Cromwell and his council opted for a more traditional form of government.[45] From 1654, he ruled as lord protector alongside a Council of State and an elected single-house Parliament, screened to keep out MPs who had supported Charles I in the Civil War. Parliament inevitably had a large number of Presbyterians, who were still no friends to religious toleration. In 1657, to push England in an even more traditional direction, Parliament offered Cromwell the Crown and proposed what they called an "other house" to substitute for the prohibited House of Lords.

Like other Congregational churches, Exeter's mounted a vigorous petitioning and prayer campaign against Parliament's offer of a crown. Its petition warned—correctly—that behind that offer was Parliament's desire to free Cromwell's government from its dependence on the army, and that the army was the barrier between the "liberty of the Saints" and Presbyterian persecutors, just as it had been in the 1640s. The petition called for Cromwell to dissolve Parliament.[46] Cromwell eventually turned down the Crown; "I will not build Jericho again," he explained, even as he took on more and more of the pomp and ceremony of a king.[47]

Cromwell's rejection of the offer, though, came well after the Exeter Congregational church's petition had triggered anxious conversation in one of its households. Tobie Allein was a prosperous clothier and a city official. Because of his social status, the elders of Allein's church wanted his signature on its petition. Allein declined on the grounds that affairs of state were none of his business. Allein, his wife Mary, and a friend were discussing the petition when the friend reminded them that Parliament had beheaded two of Charles I's counselors for advising him to dissolve Parliament, among other offenses. Mary grew alarmed at hearing this. She grew even more alarmed when she went to a prayer meeting at the church and heard a man there pray to God to humble Cromwell. This political prayer against England's ruler reminded her of the Fifth Monarchist preacher Christopher Feake, who was regularly in and out of prison for his attacks on Cromwell.[48]

Mary Allein's disillusionment with her church's meddling in politics led her to question more of its practices. The last straw came when the church wanted every member to sign a covenant that they would not listen to other preachers without Stuckeley's permission. Mary could find "no rule of Christ" for what felt to her like a separatist demand. Now she became convinced that the recent death of her children stemmed from God's wrath at her separation from her earlier Presbyterianized parish church. She rejoined it, full of sorrow for having left it in the first place.[49]

Allein, like Parr, discovered that untangling herself from Stuckeley's church was not easy. The church had not dismissed her to her new church, so as far as they were concerned, she was still a member, like it or not. Since she had neglected church fellowship and broken her covenant, along with other sins, she needed to undergo a church trial. For good measure, it decided to conclude its disciplinary process against Parr. The women refused to recognize that the church had any special spiritual bond with them; this was just a level-playing-field conflict among puritans. They offered for Presbyterian ministers to arbitrate.[50]

Stuckeley rejected their offer. Instead the church summoned Parr and Allein to attend their trials at a member's house on March 8, 1658. The women sent a letter to the meeting offering again to put their cases before impartial, outside ministers. Stuckeley scanned the letter and proceeded to pronounce a sentence of excommunication on them both. He told the church that the two women had rejected Jesus as their law-giver and were going into exile from God's people. He then formally delivered them over to Satan. The congregation made a hideous howling cry in response, which "astonished diverse then present," according to Tobie Allein. (They were mourning for the women's misery, Stuckeley replied.) Stuckeley reported the women's excommunications to the Presbyterian ministers of Exeter, but he neither explained nor justified them.[51]

After the excommunications, both sides rushed into print to protect their reputations. Stuckeley distributed 1,500 copies of his tract *Manifest Truth* across the southwest. Parr called her tract *Susanna's Apologie against the Elders*, tying Stuckeley to the biblical story in which lecherous Jewish elders slandered the virtuous Susannah and sought her death after she refused their sexual advances. Mary Allein's husband Tobie wrote a tract in which, among other topics, he defended his wife and Parr and warned that the devil had recently been seen at Stuckeley's house.[52]

Tobie also defended himself—the Congregationalists had accused him of failing to rule Mary properly. At first, Tobie explained, he had fiercely argued with Mary about her decision to leave their church. But he resented the church's harsh attitude to her, while his father advised him that preserving peace with his wife was next in importance to preserving peace with God and his conscience; Tobie would eventually join his wife's Presbyterian church. Tobie pointed out that it was only after the excommunications and in the glare of wider puritan publicity that the Congregationalists stopped their holier-than-thou habit of referring to themselves alone as the church of Christ in Exeter.[53]

Yet, as Tobie Allein acknowledged, the Congregationalists did stop. Under the floodlight of publicity, they ceased to claim that they were, in effect, the only real church in Exeter. That belated affirmation of their larger puritan community and its reformed parish churches marked an important, although profoundly conflicted, difference between most Congregationalists and the separatists and other sects, who would never make such a concession to the Presbyterians.

Nonetheless, Stuckeley's church did not retract the excommunications. Presbyterians understandably believed that Parr and Allein were correct about the real cause of their excommunications: leaving the Congregational church for Presbyterian ones. So it is probably no coincidence that at the Devonshire Association's May 1658 meeting, the Presbyterians wanted to know from the handful of Congregationalists if and or how exactly they regarded the Presbyterians' parish churches as true churches. Ever since the founding of Massachusetts, Congregationalists had been much better at affirming solidarity with England's parish churches in principle than in practice. The Congregationalists promised to give a response in two months. That promise was their last recorded participation in the association. A year later the association was still waiting for their reply. In the meantime, Stuckeley perhaps gave his own answer when he stopped participating in Ford's city-wide Tuesday lectures. The hostility between Ford and Stuckeley was by now an open secret in Exeter.[54]

The ease with which Congregationalists and Presbyterians fell out in Exeter over what could have been, and sometimes was, the mundane issue of transferring church membership, reflected the ongoing divisive brittleness of puritanism after eighteen years of power. The structure of the country's deeply unpopular government was still in flux; Presbyterians were scrambling to do what little they could to reconstruct their national church piecemeal from the bottom up. Congregationalists were still extremely conflicted about how many, if any, of those Presbyterians belonged to genuine churches, and they still only felt secure around Presbyterianism while under the protection of the army's guns. Quakerism was rapidly spreading. Parr, like other puritans, did not view Quakers as Christians, and it must have seemed to her by 1558 that her generation's duty to leave God's name glorious in the brightness of the gospel was further away than ever from being fulfilled.[55]

## Scene III: The Decline and Fall of the Puritan Reformation

On September 3, 1658, Oliver Cromwell died. At the time of his death, a group of Essex ministers summed up the period of puritan rule as "hopes of reformation given and heightened, but soon disappointed, sadly turned into tears, confusions, and vast . . . evils." It was not just the spread of religious confusion that the ministers lamented. Sin itself, they complained, "spreads farther, roots deeper, rises higher."[56]

On the face of it, that spread of sin should not have been happening. All religious groups, save the Ranters, from the most hidebound Presbyterians to the most apocalyptic Quakers, were united in opposition to sin, however much they hated each other. Parliament had passed fierce laws against sin of all sorts—theaters closed in 1641; maypoles banned in 1644; Christmas forbidden in 1647; the death penalty for adultery introduced in 1650, along with fines for swearing that increased in amount the higher the accused's social rank. Successive Sabbath bills had created a formidably long list of prohibited Sunday activities—no commerce, no games, no travel, no dancing, no secular songs, and no tippling. In 1657, Parliament was reduced to having a long and earnest debate over whether simply sitting at a gate or door should be added to the list of prohibited Sunday behavior—it was not, by two votes.[57]

Yet passing laws and enforcing them were two different matters. Before the Civil War, morality offenses were usually handled by the bishops' church courts. But those courts went out with the bishops. Cromwell had neither the means nor the will to fill local legal positions with religious zealots keen to vastly increase the workload of the secular courts by enforcing unpopular laws. In Warwickshire in the 1650s, if the court records are to be believed, only eight people swore and only six fornicated. Records from other counties show a similarly improbably low rate of offenses. Very few people were executed for adultery; grand juries refused to indict and juries refused to convict. London authorities faced pitched battles when they broke up mass Sunday recreations like cudgel fights and bear baitings, and they eventually stopped trying. Ale houses came under pressure, but individual drunkards were mostly left alone. The puritan war against Christmas had only limited success. Most shops still recognized the day by closing. Although finding a church illegally celebrating Christmas was difficult, Christmas feasting was widespread. Sinners living near the small number of activist puritan justices of the peace or in towns controlled by puritans might have to restrain themselves. But for everyone else, the years of puritan rule were more a nuisance than they were a time for serious impulse control.

Some officials were openly hostile to the new puritan order, like the assize judge who traveled across England instructing grand juries to indict puritan ministers who refused the Lord's Supper to their parishioners.[58]

Cromwell made one serious effort to beat back the tide of sin. In 1655, in between Parliaments, he and his Council of State divided England into twelve military districts, with a major-general in command of each one. Besides boosting defenses, the major-generals were charged with stamping out vice, offering relief for the poor, and improving the quality of the ministry. Some of them were starting to achieve results in the brief ten months they had in the field. But godliness was not popular to start with, and the major-generals inevitably stepped on the toes of many local leaders. Since their powers had no basis in English law, they were easily portrayed as religiously fanatical military tyrants, representatives of everything that was wrong with Cromwell's illegal, sword-backed rule. After ten months, Cromwell ended the experiment as creating more political trouble than he could afford.[59]

The major-generals were the last serious attempt at a government-supported puritan cultural revolution. Cromwell's abandonment of them left the mass of the English people mired in their dangerous exposure to old sins and new heresies. "The glory of God . . . seems almost to be departing," the leading Congregationalist John Owen warned Parliament six months after Cromwell's death and almost eight years after his rapturous sermon to that body that began this chapter.[60]

Cromwell had been at least feared, if not loved, by all the groups trying to pull the puritan reformation in their wildly different directions. After his death, it took about a year and a half for that reformation to politically implode.

Cromwell's inexperienced son and designated successor as lord protector, Richard, sympathized with the Presbyterians, who looked upon his ascension with enthusiasm. Rumors circulated that Richard would become king. His Parliament quickly started reviving the Presbyterian national church while warning that God's anger at England, manifested in poor harvests and a slowdown in trade, was due to the failure of magistrates to crack down on heresies.[61]

Congregationalists prudentially responded to resurgent intolerant Presbyterianism by vigorously reaffirming their close puritan relationship to Presbyterianism. Lay and ministerial representatives of over a hundred Congregational churches met at the Savoy Palace in London at the end of September 1658 to finally draw up a declaration of their theology and church order. The result, the Savoy Declaration, a more firmly anti-Arminian and

Congregationalism-friendly version of the Presbyterians' Westminister Confession (see p. 120), was inevitably brief and sketchy since it was thrown together in two weeks.[62]

But this rush job did what the times required. The published preface to the Savoy Declaration was written by two of the authors of *An Apologetical Narration*, Thomas Goodwin and Philip Nye. The pair updated that 1644 tract's argument—also written while Presbyterians were breathing down their necks—for peaceful coexistence between Presbyterians and Congregationalists. The new theological statement demonstrated, according to Goodwin and Nye, that Congregationalists and Presbyterians saw eye to eye on the "necessary foundations of faith and holiness." With so much in common, there was no reason why there should not be "mutual indulgence" about their differences of church government. In a gesture of godly unity with the Presbyterians, the Savoy Declaration agreed that it was at least theoretically possible for Congregationalists to welcome to their sacraments members of "less pure" but true churches, provided those members were "credibly testified to be godly."[63]

In the spring of 1659, prominent army officers belonging to John Owen's London church, perhaps with Owen's encouragement, chose another way of dealing with resurgent Presbyterianism—intimidating Richard Cromwell to make him change his advisors. But they lost control of their effort to more militant and radical junior army officers. The result was that the army pushed Richard out of office altogether and reinstated the Rump Parliament that Oliver Cromwell had shut down in 1653. For furious Presbyterians, the coup stopped their delicate and slow process of grudging reconciliation with the usurpers who had killed their king in 1649. They suspected that Catholics were behind it, on the principle that Catholics were behind everything that thwarted true reformation.[64]

For Congregationalists, the coup left them stuck between a rock and a hard place. They had escaped the possible dangers of a resurgent Presbyterianism, but their allies of necessity in the coup were religious sectaries who wanted freedom to worship as they pleased and the end of any state support for religion. Quakers enthusiastically supported Richard's overthrow.[65]

Perhaps an uncomfortable awareness of having gone too far out on a sectarian limb prompted Congregationalist ministers in northwestern England to approach Presbyterian ministers about church cooperation soon after the coup. The two groups worked out an impressive agreement to accommodate each other under what amounted to a single loose church umbrella. Fourteen Presbyterian and seven Congregationalist ministers signed the agreement in Manchester on July 13, 1659. The Congregationalists

1 The 1555 burning of the early English Protestant nonconformist and bishop John Hooper under Catholic Queen Mary (see p. 19). Soldiers and officials surround Hooper, save for a solitary woman weeping, while Hooper's arm that had fallen off as he beat his breast lies in the midst of the flames. This woodcut comes from Hooper's friend John Foxe's massively influential *Actes and Monuments* (see p. 21), commonly known as Foxe's *Book of Martyrs* (first edition, 1563).

2 From the 1563 title page of Foxe's *Actes and Monuments* comes this idealized depiction of Protestant preaching and its impact. As the preacher expounds on God's word set forth in the Bible, some listeners follow him with their own open Bibles while to the right others experience the power of God's word directly. God himself is represented only by his Hebrew name, not by an image as was the Catholic practice, idolatrous to Protestants like Foxe.

3 An anonymous mid-1570s painting of England's early Reformation. Henry VIII on his deathbed points to his young son and successor Edward VI, while Edward's Privy Council sits by. In the foreground, monks flee as the pope is struck down by a Bible open to the verse "the worde of the Lord endureth forever" (1 Peter 1:25). Protestant iconoclasts in the background destroy Catholic images. The painting was perhaps intended as a wake-up call to Queen Elizabeth to do her duty as a godly monarch and emulate her deceased half-brother Edward's Protestant zeal.

4 A posthumous portrait of John Dod, a Presbyterian activist in the 1580s and a leading nonconformist minister (see p. 51). Dod was famed as a preacher, author, and spiritual counselor and lived long enough to be harassed by Royalist soldiers in the Civil War. The second line of the accompanying verse, "and never guilty of the Churches rent," is a dig at Congregationalism, which Dod opposed, and its divisiveness.

5 The prominent funerary monument of Sir Anthony Cope (d. 1614) and his first wife Frances (d. 1600) in the parish church of Hanwell, Oxfordshire. Anthony, a local magnate, longstanding MP, and militant Presbyterian, brought John Dod to Hanwell for a twenty-year ministry in 1585 (p. 50). At the time the Cope monument was erected, the church's simple communion table when not in use might have been placed where the altar sits now, but it would not have been beautified and railed off to emphasize its sanctity, as done here. Large-scale change from communion tables to altars and railing started in the 1630s. Puritans bitterly resented the change as "popish" and, they suspected, part of a plot to drive England back to Catholicism (see p. 94).

6 A rare effort from 1640 to represent conversion visually. This man has become aware of the depths of his sinfulness and of the fiery darts of God's wrath descending on him for his sins. As a consequence, he is finally becoming truly aware of his need for Jesus as his savior (see p. 55).

7 John Cotton's early seventeenth-century pulpit in St. Botolph's parish church, Boston, Lincolnshire. Like many pulpits, this one came with a sounding board to amplify Cotton's voice in the cavernous fifteenth-century church for the crowds who would be packed in to hear him (see p. 65).

8 The relative inaccessibility of this statue of St. Botolph on the Boston church's medieval tower might have been what saved it from the sixteenth-century Protestant iconoclasts who smashed up the rest of the statues on the exterior. Its turn came in the illegal 1620 wave of lay iconoclasm that nearly cost John Cotton his pulpit (see p. 66), when Atherton Hough, future Boston mayor and subsequent Massachusetts immigrant, managed to break off its left arm, although not the preferable head. Catholics may have furtively continued to pray to it, as they did to other statues that survived Protestant iconoclasm.

9 John Winthrop, lawyer, minor member of the gentry, one of the leaders of the puritan immigration to Massachusetts Bay, and Massachusetts's frequently re-elected governor (see p. 77).

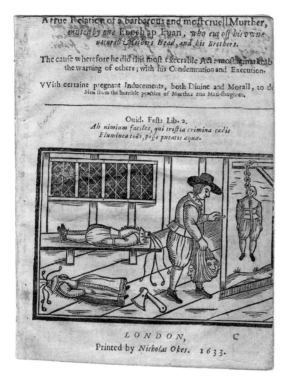

10 Enoch ap Evan's decapitation of his mother and brother in 1633 created a sensation, especially since the grisly murders came after they quarreled about Enoch's puritan-like refusal to kneel at the Lord's Supper. Besides sensationalistic short pamphlets like this one, intended to make a quick profit, the murders were used as the springboard for a sweeping, controversial attack on puritanism by a nearby minister (see p. 94).

11 Royal soldiers conscripted unwillingly to fight the Scots in 1640 are destroying "popish" Laudian innovations in a parish church as they march north—altar rails, pictures, and images are smashed, and altars turned back into communion tables (see p. 112).

12 In the early seventeenth century, the Presbyterian Thomas Brightman reintroduced the idea that the Bible predicted a glorious future millennium for Christ's church after a string of conflicts between the forces of evil and the true church (see p. 67). Millennialism was quick to be embraced, mostly by puritans, while the extraordinary religious upheavals of the 1640s drastically increased its plausibility and popularity. This title page from a 1644 edition of Brightman's commentary on the Book of Revelation depicts various prophetic scenes from that book.

The Orthodox true Minister,    the Seducer and false Prophet.

13 Religious and social disorder go hand in hand in this frontispiece from a 1648 Presbyterian refutation of unorthodox religious opinions. On the left, a trained, properly garbed minister preaches God's truth in a church, while respectably dressed men listen attentively. On the right, a self-appointed lay preacher spreads error from a tavern window, while women, children, and men of low social rank flock in a disorderly manner to hang on his false words, with scarcely a master, husband, or father in sight (see p. 120).

14 A memorial image of Christopher Love providing the date this defiant Presbyterian minister was beheaded by the English republic. Puritans disagreed about whether he died as a traitor or a Christian martyr (see p. 114).

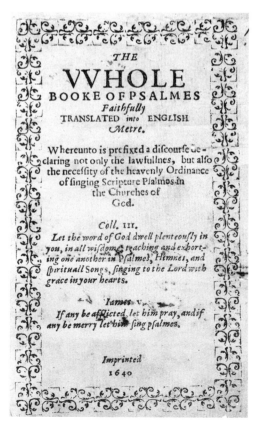

15 The Bay Psalm Book, the first English-language book printed in the Americas, somewhat clumsily, on Harvard College's printing press in 1640. It arose out of dissatisfaction among Massachusetts's ministers that earlier metrical translations of the psalms had strayed too far from the sacred Hebrew originals. "God's altar needs not our polishings," the editors explained. It became standard for New England worship up through the mid-eighteenth century.

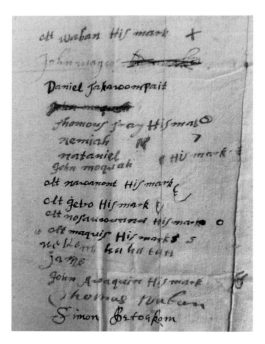

16 The signatures or marks of leading Natick Praying Indians (see p. 197) from a 1684 letter to John Eliot seeking an increase in the stipend of an English minister who preached in Natick occasionally. "Olt" (Old) Waban leads the list with his mark. The signature of Waban's son Thomas, his successor as sachem at Natick, is second from the bottom. Third from the top is the signature of Natick's minister, Daniel Takawompait, ordained by Eliot. The letter is in the hand of Simon Betoqkom, the list's bottom signature, who served as a scribe for Native Americans in their communications with the English.

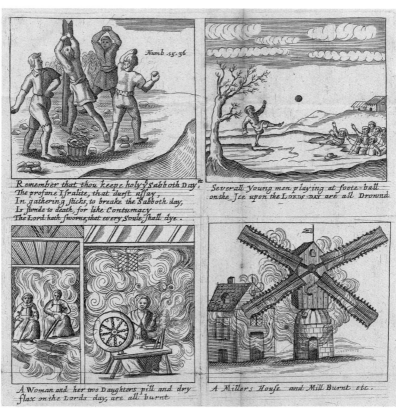

Remember that thou keepe holy y Sabboth Day.
The profane Ifralite, that durst aſſay,
In gathering fticks, to breake the Sabboth day,
Is ſtonde to death, for like Contumacy
The Lord hath ſworne, that every Soule, ſhall dye.

Severall young men playing at foote-ball on the Ice upon the LORDS-DAY are all Drownd.

A Woman and her two Daughters pill and dry flax on the Lords day, are all burnt.

A Millers Houſe and Mill Burnt etc.

17 Illustrations from a 1671 reminder of the horrific divine vengeance that could befall people who violated the Sabbath's sanctity with their secular pursuits (see p. 53).

18 John Bunyan is here portrayed dreaming his famous dream of Christian and his journey from the City of Destruction to the Celestial City (see p. 214). Christian's eyes are fixed on his Bible and on his back a pack is weighed down with the burden of his sins. The lion in its barred cave is usually taken to represent Bunyan in prison, where he wrote *Pilgrim's Progress*. This engraving appeared as the frontispiece to the 1679 third edition after the first two had quickly sold out in 1678.

The Armies in the Air: | The Three Suns seen:

Hatfield maid & Ghost | The Earthquake.

19 From a 1681 treatise by the Congregationalist minister Christopher Ness, published in the midst of the Exclusion Crisis (see p. 225). The treatise draws attention to reports of various signs and wonders foretelling great peril to England's Protestantism and its liberties from resurgent Catholicism and monarchical tyranny. "Hatfield maid & Ghost" refers to an apparition who appeared to a maiden, instructing her to tell King Charles that he must reconvene Parliament. Like Oliver Heywood during this crisis (see p. 228), Ness combined his interpretation of these prophetic signs with interpretation of Bible prophecies.

20  A detail from a depiction of puritanism as a nightmare for England, engraved in 1682 during the Tory Reaction (see p. 227). The figure of Britannia is seated next to the upside down Royal Arms. She mourns the ascendency of puritanism in the 1640s and the political, social, and religious destruction that accompany it. While a cathedral decays, a church burns, and armies clash in the background, Britannia gazes at the bloody executioner's ax that killed Charles I and the fallen royal crown, coronet, and scepter. At her feet lie a bishop's miter and crosier and the Magna Carta. A puritan minister chides Britannia, perhaps for mourning changes she should have welcomed. The minister is, in fact, a representative of the real power behind the puritans, being a two-faced Jesuit devil with his cloven hoof on a Bible. The puritan's Jesuit face talks to the demon behind him.

21 Increase Mather, a man of learning as his portrait emphasizes, was a leading Massachusetts minister, prolific author, and graduate and acting president of Harvard College. This portrait was painted in London while Mather negotiated a new royal charter for Massachusetts with the English government (see p. 265).

Farewell vain World! As thou hast been to me
Dust & a Shadow; those I leave with thee :
The unseen Vitall Substance I committ
To him that's Substance, Light & Life to it .
The Leaves & Fruit here dropt are holy seed,
Heaven's heirs to generate; to heale & feed :
Them also thou wilt flatter & molest
But shalt not keep from Everlasting Rest .

22 Richard Baxter was perhaps the most prominent minister among puritans in the later seventeenth century. A prolific author on a wide range of religious topics, some of his books became classics. Baxter's tireless work for unity among the godly was complicated by his controversial theological innovations and penchant for quarreling (see p. 269). In the poem accompanying this frontispiece portrait, Baxter explains his highest ambition for his publications.

## The Wonders of the Invisible World.

# OBSERVATIONS

As well *Hiftorical* as *Theological*, upon the NATURE, the NUMBER, and the OPERATIONS of the

# DEVILS.

Accompany'd with,

I. Some Accounts of the Grievous Moleftations, by DÆMONS and WITCHCRAFTS, which have lately annoy'd the Countrey ; and the Trials of fome eminent *Malefactors* Executed upon occafion thereof : with feveral Remarkable *Curiofities* therein occurring.

II. Some Counfils, Directing a due Improvement of the terrible things, lately done, by the Unufual & Amazing Range of EVIL SPIRITS, in Our Neighbourhood : & the methods to prevent the *Wrongs* which thofe *Evil Angels* may intend againft all forts of people among us ; efpecially in Accufations of the Innocent.

III. Some Conjectures upon the great EVENTS, likely to befall, the WORLD in General, and NEW-ENGLAND in Particular ; as alfo upon the Advances of the TIME, when we fhall fee BETTER DAYES.

IV A fhort Narrative of a late Outrage committed by a knot of WITCHES in *Swedeland*, very much Refembling, and fo far Explaining, *That* under which our parts of *America* have laboured !

V. THE DEVIL DISCOVERED : In a Brief Difcourfe upon thofe TEMPTATIONS, which are the more Ordinary *Devices*, of the Wicked One.

By **Cotton Mather.**

*Bofton* Printed by *Benj. Harris* for *Sam. Phillips*, 1693.

23 *The Wonders of the Invisble World*, Cotton Mather's government-approved, strongly supportive account of the 1692 Salem witch trials, which puts the trials in the context of European witch trials, Satan's age-long struggle against Christ's churches, and the fast-approaching millennium (see p. 285). *Wonders* came out just as public support for the Salem trials was collapsing; Mather never again went into print to praise those trials, although he occasionally made excuses for them. In 1697 he fretted in his diary that his failure to try hard enough to restrain the Salem judges could bring down the wrath of God on his family.

24 The Old Ship Meeting House, Hingham, Massachusetts, built in 1681 and later enlarged, is the oldest surviving meeting house in New England; some of the gravestones in the foreground of this picture are as old or older. The graves' tripartite rounded tops mirror the shape of bed headboards, alluding to the graves holding their bodies only until those bodies rise again at the Last Judgment.

approved the Presbyterians' standards for admission to the Lord's Supper and agreed to accept their members to that sacrament if they knew those members. Ministers would meet together regularly and swap pulpits, the Congregationalists would restrain lay preaching, and disputes between them would be resolved by jointly approved delegates. The agreement would go into effect at the ministers' next meeting on the fourth Thursday of September, after they had consulted with their colleagues.[66]

"How happy had it been . . . had both parties been of such a sweet condescending frame thirteen years before," lamented one Presbyterian, harking back to when the split between puritans began to be set in stone. Given enough time, something like a loosely united puritan church establishment might have spread across England.[67] But time was what puritanism did not have.

Unbeknownst to the Congregationalists, some Presbyterian signers of the accord were up to their necks in a Presbyterian and Royalist plot to overthrow the Rump Parliament. At the beginning of August, men in the region were summoned to arms by a terrifying false announcement in the parish churches that the Quakers were about to rebel. The real purpose of the call to arms was to overthrow Parliament. Booth's Rising, named after its leader, the Presbyterian Sir George Booth, was quickly suppressed. But the Congregationalists who had signed off on the union felt betrayed and used by their Presbyterian brethren. Those brethren had lulled them to sleep while actively plotting for a regime change that might endanger Congregationalism's very existence. The agreement died stillborn.[68]

Profoundly disunited though puritans remained in August 1659 after Booth's Rising had been quashed, Charles II, exiled in France, and what was left of the hierarchy of the Church of England appeared no closer to political power than they had been a decade previously. Charles's supporters could later explain what happened over the next nine months only as a miraculous divine intervention.

The restored Rump Parliament and the army quickly fell to quarreling with each other, and the army staged a coup against the Rump Parliament at the end of October 1659. The Presbyterian general of the most powerful army regiments, George Monck, however, marched on London and completed an almost bloodless counter-coup in February 1660. Monck reinstalled the full pre-Pride's Purge House of Commons. The result was that the large contingent of Presbyterians who had wanted to work out terms with Charles I in 1648 were now in the majority.[69]

Monck's mandate to the reassembled "Long Parliament" (so called because it had first met way back in 1640) was that it organize elections for a new Parliament and then dissolve. It accomplished that task in a month. In the meantime, it tried to legislate the clock back to 1646. It required that the Solemn League and Covenant, with its dual commitments to a uniform reformed church and monarchy, be posted and read in every church; that the national Presbyterian church structure be reactivated; and that all future parish church ministers be approved by a board made up almost entirely of Presbyterians. For good measure, it finally affirmed the Presbyterian Westminster Confession as England's official theological statement.[70]

The rejuvenated 1640s Presbyterian reformation was supposed to carry over into the "Convention Parliament" that was to succeed the Long Parliament. The filter to ensure that outcome was membership qualifications that would exclude men unsupportive of Parliament's initial revolt against Charles I. That revolt had aimed not at overthrowing Charles, which Presbyterians opposed, but at getting him to accept puritan church reform and restraints on his power. It was generally understood that the Convention Parliament would invite Charles II back.[71]

When the Convention Parliament met, the more realistic Presbyterian MPs wanted to strictly enforce the membership qualifications and set terms for Charles II's return. But their effort to purge the House of Commons of unqualified MPs failed; the king's episcopal envoys muttered soothing, empty assurances about their new-found enthusiasm for working things out with the Presbyterians; and Charles, impatiently waiting in the Netherlands, issued his Declaration of Breda on April 4, 1660, promising that no one would be punished for peaceful differences of religious opinion. On the word of the royal and episcopal leopards that they had changed their spots, Parliament threw away nineteen years of constitutional and religious struggle and invited the king and his bishops back without any conditions.

# CHAPTER 13

# CONSOLIDATING REFORMATION IN NEW ENGLAND

May 19, 1643 was a special day for New England puritanism. Representatives from the colonies of Plymouth, with eight towns, Connecticut, with six, and New Haven, with five, gathered in Boston, by far the largest of Massachusetts's thirty towns. They were there to negotiate and sign a treaty, the sort of thing, ordinarily, that only independent nations did. Massachusetts, not coincidentally, had just dropped the section in their magistrates' oath about swearing allegiance to Charles I.[1]

The novel treaty would create a "firm and perpetual league of friendship" called the United Colonies of New England. As one would expect from puritans, the treaty's authors claimed that the colonists had come to New England to "advance the kingdom of our Lord Jesus Christ." They piously wrote that the treaty's purpose was "propagating and preserving the truth and liberties of the gospel," along with defense and mutual welfare.[2] Already by the time this treaty was signed, the New Englanders were well underway in creating the governments, laws, and churches that themselves would propagate and preserve the gospel's truth and liberties in each colony. By the end of the decade, that fashioning of the only fully worked out reformations puritans ever accomplished would be largely completed.

Like their Congregational churches, the governments of all the colonies were built on popular consent. Those governments met as general courts, with the magistrates and the governor elected by colony-wide vote, while the deputies of the freemen were elected by largely self-governing towns. The magistrates, the colonies' highest judges as well as their highest rulers, tended to be their colonies' wealthiest, best-connected men. In Massachusetts, Connecticut, and New Haven, the magistrates' superior status gave them the power to veto legislation that the more numerous deputies approved.[3]

All four colonies agreed that their societies rested on the foundation of their families. Did not Adam and Eve precede the first society, and were not "nations and kingdoms" raised out of Noah's family after the Flood wiped out everyone else, as the puritan minister William Gouge asked? It was generally understood that well-governed patriarchal families produced good members of churches and commonwealths, and puritan New England tried to ensure such families with unprecedented legislative intrusiveness and zeal. Fathers were required to catechize children living in their house and teach them to read; New England children often began both tasks at the same time by memorizing catechisms and scripture passages at a very early age. Fathers were also to see to it that children were trained in a gainful and useful employment. Disorderly and abusive households risked government intervention, including the removal of children. Disorderly sex—all sex outside marriage—was vigorously, if not completely, repressed: a couple simply seen with the man's arms around the woman's neck late at night or just acting in an "unseemly and suspicious manner" could draw a court's attention. Even meeting with the possibility of eventual legal sex required patriarchal permission; a man could not try to court a woman, let alone marry her, without the approval of the woman's father. Avoiding family government in New England was not an option, at least on paper: in all the colonies, young adults and servants of all ages were required to live in a household.[4]

A web of other laws left the individual colonists wrapped up in discipline. There were laws to compel people to go to church and laws to try to hold them there once they had arrived. There were laws to keep people from traveling on the Sabbath, and laws to keep them from evading those laws. Gambling was illegal, as were games and dancing. Those prohibitions cut down the appeal of taverns, not coincidently, and taverns were carefully regulated as well, as part of a shifting kaleidoscope of laws that tried to keep a lid on drinking. The colonies oscillated between regulating smoking and banning it altogether, and did not even bother to pass laws banning plays. The colonies had an extremely low rate of reported crime, the outcome of close-knit, relatively egalitarian, watchful communities, and an extremely high conviction rate.[5]

All four colonies reformed the law itself. In England in the 1650s, puritan law reform was blocked by the flocks of lawyers and officials who enriched themselves off the legal system's countless complexities. In New England, the colonists created systems that were simple, equitable, inexpensive, speedy, transparent, and grounded in law codes crafted to protect the colonists' rights against overbearing local rulers. The colonies had their judges decide cases by scripture when their law codes failed to meet the crimes. Like many Protestant countries, all the colonies recognized marriage as a civil union, not a sacrament. Like all Protestant countries except England, courts accepted petitions for divorce, in New England for adultery, desertion, and cruelty. As in other Protestant countries, very few people availed themselves of them; the courts in each colony received on average less than one petition a year. Divorce had been one of the unrealized goals of the earlier English reformers.[6]

The greatest legal reform of all, and a long-standing puritan ambition, was to substitute God's law for man's in the legal codes, where feasible. John Lee in 1641 was fortunate that he pilfered a Bible from Widow Haffield in Massachusetts and not in England, where he might have swung for such a small theft. The laws God gave the Old Testament Jews said nothing about hanging for theft. But God did require that a thief make double restitution (Exodus 22:7). The magistrates presiding over Lee's case sentenced him to pay the widow the customary double restitution of 15 shillings. The colonies only very slowly introduced hanging for theft and then only after repeated convictions for burglary and robbery.[7]

On the other hand, had James Britten and the unhappily married Mary Letham's 1644 drunken sexual tumble outside his house taken place in England, the result at the time would probably have been nothing more than a public shaming; in Massachusetts, however, it led to their deaths, as the Old Testament commanded for adultery (Leviticus 20:10), and as all the puritan colonies except Plymouth duly legislated. In these colonies, as in the Old Testament (but not in England), the meaning of adultery was restricted to sex with another man's wife—a married woman faced death for sleeping with a man; a married man faced death for sleeping with a married woman.[8]

If you killed someone in a fit of passion you were again better off in England than in New England since the Old Testament commanded death for manslaughter as well as premeditated murder (Numbers 35:20–21). Unlike in England, however, circumstantial evidence could not send you to the gallows since the puritan colonies used the biblical two witnesses rule (Deuteronomy 19:15).[9]

The Old Testament forbade "man-stealing" (Exodus 21:16), and all the puritan colonies made kidnapping a capital offense (it was only a misdemeanor in England). In 1645 a Massachusetts sea captain and Boston church member, James Smith, kidnapped two West African men he had invited onto his ship and then launched an unsuccessful attack on a nearby town to get more to sell as slaves. Compounding his offense, he did this on the Sabbath. The General Court decided not to try him because his crimes were committed outside Massachusetts's jurisdiction. Nonetheless, it voted to return the enslaved Africans at the colony's expense, "to bear witness," as the court explained, "against the heinous and crying sin of man-stealing." But the Old Testament's God was fine with slavery itself. Massachusetts's 1641 Body of Liberties allowed for the acquisition of slaves through purchase or war, with their treatment to be guided by "the law of God established in Israel concerning such persons."[10]

Even for puritans, though, the stern legal demands of the Old Testament's God could prove too harsh. Only one other person besides Britten and Letham was hanged for adultery. Whipping became the usual punishment, although offenders sometimes had to wear shaming badges. Only one young person, John Proctor, Jr., came close to being executed for defying his parents, as called for in the Old Testament-inspired laws (Deuteronomy 21:18–21) passed by all the puritan colonies, and this was only after trying to burn his parents' house down, stabbing his brother, and calling his mother "Gammer Shithouse" and his father "Ape." His father agreed to his execution, but his mother balked.[11]

As for African man-stealing, the General Court's 1645 testimony against it was a one-off. Trade with the fast-growing, brutal West Indian sugar colonies slowly lifted New England out of the economic doldrums into which it had collapsed in 1640 when reformation finally seemed possible in England and the immigration that propped up the local economy ended. The colonists had a strong incentive not to inquire about how exactly all those Africans ended up enslaved in the Caribbean, or even how a few of them reached the end of the African slave trade's long distribution chain and arrived in New England. Enslaved Africans soon found that in New England, puritan ears were deaf to their claims that they had been kidnapped. In 1653, the Dorchester church did vote to purchase the freedom of Dorcas, one of Massachusetts's handful of enslaved Africans, whom they had admitted in 1641, but that was a gesture of love to a fellow visible saint.[12]

Beyond their shared reforming goals, the colonies pursued reformation differently. In Massachusetts, Connecticut, and New Haven, magistrates worked hand in hand with learned ministers to enforce, protect, and direct reformation, much as they had been trying to do in England for almost a century. Ensuring an ongoing supply of properly trained ministers was one of their priorities. All three colonies quickly set up schools, soon reinforced by legal mandates, that taught Latin, in preparation for the Harvard College education necessary to sustain a learned ministry. Harvard College itself, founded in 1636, was the latest of the low-budget, small-library colleges sprouting up across the Calvinist world, and there were already textbooks and curricula available for under-resourced schools like it. Girls were admitted neither to Harvard nor to the preparatory Latin schools, and only rarely to the more widespread schools—also legally mandated—that taught writing. All the colonies had "dame schools," informal kindergartens run by women where children of both sexes would learn to read but not write, building on the informal training they had probably already received at home, also as mandated by law. There was no equivalent to this religion-driven legal focus on literacy in the colonies outside New England or in England itself, and the result was a widely literate population.[13]

Plymouth's reformation was the odd one out in terms of distinguished magistrates and learned ministers. It had no distinguished magistrates to begin with. Its continually re-elected governor William Bradford came from a farming family. The magistrates' powers were steadily absorbed by the General Court until they consisted of little more than the governor's right to break a tied vote.[14]

The separatists who settled Plymouth had broken away entirely from England's church establishment and were in no hurry to create a Congregationalist equivalent. Plymouth's government, unlike that of the others, never got into the habit of regularly consulting ministers on matters of state, while the ministers themselves, unlike in the other colonies, might only have met collectively once in the colonial period. Plymouth even had a relatively high number of ministers without the college degrees expected in the other colonies. There is no hint of a formal school of any sort in the colony until the 1670s, although Plymouth had informal dame schools.[15]

All four colonies originally intended ministers to be supported voluntarily, as an expression of the laity's love and appreciation, unlike in England, where tithes were mandatory. Towns, though, were poor and ministers expensive, and even in New England, sinful humanity proved slow to prioritize the honorable maintenance of God's messengers. In 1638 a Massachusetts law made support of a town's minister compulsory, even for non-church members, who had no say in choosing him. Variations of the law were passed in the other puritan colonies in the 1640s and 1650s.

Plymouth's law was, typically, feeble, and it only passed in 1655 after Governor Bradford threatened to resign. Two decades of tinkering followed, and it was not until 1677 that Plymouth got one with teeth.[16]

While Plymouth was the reforming sluggard, New Haven, a confederation of towns scattered on both sides of Long Island Bay and centered on the town of New Haven, was the vanguard. Its region had been opened up for English settlement after the expansionist Pequot tribe made too many enemies too quickly, and were brutally crushed in 1637 by an English–Native American alliance; the lion's share of the brutality came from the English. Large-scale enslavement of the Pequots by Native Americans and English alike followed.[17]

New Haven was notable for the zeal and ambition of its reformation. Its magistrates had no juries to restrain their righteous dispensing of justice, perhaps because the Old Testament said nothing about juries. Conviction rates were high in New Haven and crime rates low, even by New England standards. In a stark reversal of ordinary practice, high-status offenders received more severe penalties than common people since more was expected of them. The town of New Haven was laid out not in the usual helter-skelter colonial fashion, but on a grid pattern possibly intended to invoke the mystical temple of the upcoming millennium's New Jerusalem. New Haven's famous minister John Davenport expected "large accounts of God's work" from would-be church members, who would tell "how [faith] was wrought, and how it works in them." Such daunting conversion narratives were the New England norm, but Davenport's church acquired the reputation of having the stiffest admissions standards in the region. New Haven was the only other colony to follow Massachusetts and require voters to be church members. A local Native American, Pawquash, found out just how seriously the New Havenites took Christianity in 1646 when he made the mistake of opining that Jesus was a fool and that he himself knew of a Native American who ascended to heaven. A severe whipping followed, with a warning that next time the consequence might be death; other colonies did not trouble themselves about the opinions of the local pagans.[18]

Connecticut did not screw its reformation quite up to the pitch of those of Massachusetts and New Haven. It required only that its governor be a church member, not its voters. The General Court threw its weight around in church affairs more freely than in the other colonies. It even crossed the church–state line to take appeals of excommunications. The colony's leading minister, Thomas Hooker of Hartford, was idiosyncratic in rejecting conversion narratives for church admission, unlike Davenport, but he still expected a thorough scrutinizing of the state of candidates' souls.[19]

When the commissioners of the United Colonies held their yearly meetings, their focus was almost entirely secular and mostly on foreign policy, dealing with Native American tribes and with the Dutch in neighboring New Amsterdam. Those foreign policy efforts did not include their treaty's charge to advance the kingdom of Christ. That sort of evangelical outreach into the dauntingly diverse and mostly ungodly English Atlantic was largely ad hoc and carried out by churches and magistrates.

Puritan laity were scattered across the other English colonies, but except for puritan-governed Bermuda, no colony had a significant number of them. Outside New England and Bermuda, ministers, puritan or otherwise, were in desperately short supply—the Church of England made no effort to send them across the Atlantic, colonial officials were reluctant to dig deeply into their own pockets to procure them, and the ones that did come over tended not to be of the highest quality. In such colonies, puritan laity usually had to make do with their social gatherings and prayer sessions as well as their books and old manuscript sermon notes to keep tottering along unsteadily on the narrow path of godliness.[20]

Now that Archbishop Laud's baleful gaze was lifted off the Atlantic, those scattered American puritans could reach out to the New England churches for help, and they did, with decidedly mixed results. Outside the puritan colonies, southeastern Virginia had the highest cluster of puritan-leaning laity, totaling possibly up to one thousand of Virginia's eight thousand English residents. In 1642, a messenger arrived in Boston with a letter from Virginia puritans asking that three ministers be sent to them.[21] Virginia's laws banned nonconformity, but the colony had been relaxed about enforcing them in earlier, more peaceful days. Now that religious conformists and nonconformists were starting to kill each other in England's Civil War, tensions were higher. The request for ministers was granted, but the mission ultimately failed.

Charles I had appointed Sir William Berkeley as Virginia's new governor in 1641. As far as Berkeley was concerned, the Church of England that Parliament was busy tearing down was still the only legal one; the three New England ministers were expelled in 1643 for their nonconformity. The Virginia Assembly passed further laws against nonconformity; local puritans continued to be occasionally harassed; and before the decade had ended, some puritans had been banished by the Virginia Assembly for belonging to what the assembly called England's "schismatical party." Most of the departing puritans went to neighboring Maryland, founded as a de facto refuge for English Catholics, where they repeatedly made trouble for the tiny colony's government. The puritans departing from Virginia left behind them a colony that had only one minister for every three thousand of its widely scattered people; in much more compact New England the ratio was one for every four hundred.[22]

New England's influence on puritan-leaning Bermuda and its two thousand people initially had more positive consequences. The ministers and governors of Bermuda, almost 800 miles south of Boston off present-day North Carolina, had long been the correspondents and trading partners of their New England counterparts; New Englanders could not have been entirely surprised in the winter of 1644 to hear that Bermuda's three ministers, filled with millennial fervor, had renounced their Church of England ordinations and gathered a Congregational church. Bermuda's governor William Sayle supported the Congregational church, and his wife belonged to it. The New England churches wrote to the new church to tell it that they recognized it as a "sister church." New England pulpits rang, they said, "with the high praises of God for what he hath done" for the Bermudans. The Bermuda Congregational church, in turn, recognized the New England churches as "the best reformed churches in the world." New Englanders were certainly pleased that Bermuda's magistrates rebuked and even punished those puritans who were in the forefront of protesting the new Congregational church.[23] North America now had another Congregationalist colony.

But not for long. Bermuda, unlike New England, was not self-governing, and this Congregationalist ecclesiastical coup brought on a string of English interventions into North American affairs, each one from the New England perspective worse than the last. Most of Bermuda's puritans supported the Congregationalists, but puritans were a minority on the island. The majority remained loudly unhappy about the sacraments being snatched away from them by a divisive church unrecognized by English law. The resulting quarrel reached the distant ears of the Bermuda Company and then Parliament. In 1645, Parliament passed a blunderbuss of an ordinance commanding the Bermuda colonists to do what the English could not: tolerate their religious differences. Following up on this measure, Parliament's Committee on Foreign Plantations sent letters to all the colonies stating, as Massachusetts governor John Winthrop summarized this entirely unwelcome communication, that "all men should enjoy their liberty of conscience."[24]

The New England colonies' sympathy lay with Parliament in its struggles with the king, although they, like the other colonies, stayed officially neutral. Nonetheless, Winthrop had no more intention of obeying this unprecedentedly intrusive interference in the colonies' affairs than did Bermuda's new governor Thomas Turner. Turner arrived in Bermuda in early 1646 with two ministers, determined to restrict worship to the Presbyterian standards recently approved by Parliament. He and the Bermuda Assembly purged the governor's council of Congregationalists, forbade Congregationalist worship, and put defiant Congregationalists on trial.[25]

The Bermuda Congregationalists eventually decided they should find a colony for themselves in the Caribbean. New Englanders would have probably looked forward to finally having a godly colony planted in a region hitherto known for brutality, religious apathy, and large numbers of sectaries and Irish Catholics; a Massachusetts minister who settled on Barbados, the largest English Caribbean island, in 1646 wondered at "God's great patience" with the amount of swearing and drinking there. In early November 1646 Bermuda's former governor William Sayle and the Congregationalist minister William Golding showed up in Boston to catch a ship bound for England where they could finalize arrangements for the prospective Caribbean colony they had located. The Massachusetts General Court called a day of fasting for them, imploring divine aid against those "seek[ing] to undermine the liberties of God's people."[26]

The liberties of God's people on Bermuda were not the only focus of this fast. God's people in New England needed divine assistance for a liberty under threat even in their own region: the liberty of ensuring that only the true worship of God took place in their society. In 1645, the wealthy and well-connected William Vassall almost succeeded in slipping an unexpected law allowing unlimited liberty of conscience through a meeting of the Plymouth General Court. He was foiled when Governor Bradford precipitously adjourned the meeting. Vassall then offered support to Robert Child, a mining engineer and alchemist recently arrived in Massachusetts. Child resented Massachusetts's lack of liberty of conscience (understandably; he was quietly an antinomian), and the exclusion of non-churchmembers from the sacraments, voting, and political office.[27]

In 1646, Child rallied six other men to sign a harshly worded petition to the Massachusetts General Court emphasizing those last points, demanding comprehensive change, and threatening to go to Parliament if their demands were not met. Vassall brought the Child petition to Parliament, despite John Cotton's fierce pulpit warning before his ship departed that God would probably sink such a cargo (another passenger prudently switched vessels). The Child petition, however, did not attract much support in Massachusetts; the appeal to Parliament failed, and the General Court loaded the petition signers with crippling fines. The liberty of God's New England people to hold their society to the narrow path of biblical truth survived this attack.[28]

But that liberty was weakening across the English world, as New Englanders were soon forcibly reminded. In 1647, their Bermuda protégés brought the *Articles and Orders*, the governing document for their new tiny colony Eleutheria, back from London. The document had been drawn up during that city's life-or-death struggle between the would-be persecuting Presbyterian Parliament and the Congregationalist- and sectarian-friendly New Model Army (see p. 138). Eleutheria's London backers were militant supporters of the army, and they had one eye on their own situation when they wrote the document.[29]

The *Articles and Orders* was a guide to the kind of radically tolerant religious settlement those London backers were imagining for England, and for English benefit, when they published it in London. On Eleutheria, the government, organized as an oligarchic republic, was to impose nothing in terms of religion. "In this state of darkness," the *Articles* explained, ". . . we know but in part," and the godly were always going to disagree with each other, for they lacked "the same measure of light." Government attempts to force uniformity as the godly moved toward the divine light at their different speeds only created factions and persecution, the *Articles* warned. Therefore, the single religious task of Eleutheria's government was to keep religious quarrels relatively peaceful. Sayle and around seventy of the Bermuda Congregationalists departed in late 1647 for Eleutheria.[30]

New England Congregationalists were aghast that their godly brethren had abandoned the government's responsibility for nurturing the gospel. After consulting with Massachusetts ministers, a Virginia puritan church turned down an offer to move to Eleutheria (the Virginians "were very orthodox, and zealous for the truth," Winthrop wrote approvingly). While many members of the Bermuda Congregational church went to Eleutheria, the church itself stayed on Bermuda, a decision perhaps connected with Pastor White's belief in religious duties for the state. In 1649, however, the Bermuda government ordered the Congregationalists to depart. White sold his African slave Toney, and he and his church finally sailed to Eleutheria.[31] This avant-garde version of the Congregationalist kingdom of Christ collapsed within a decade because of Eleutheria's poor fertility; a group of

Massachusetts churches once sent a large emergency food shipment to their misguided Caribbean brethren.[32]

Most urgent for New England Congregationalists was to advance the true kingdom of Christ in England, fount of all the errors spreading among the godly across the English world. The New England churches frequently intervened in England's struggles with fasting and prayer in the 1640s and 1650s. Prayers, one minister confidently claimed, were "murderers that will kill point blank from one end of the world to the other." Whether they were as effective to that end as the numerous New England men who served in the New Model Army is beyond the historian's remit; the punctured, bloodstained leather coat of New Englander John Leverett, a Cromwellian captain and future Massachusetts governor, survives to this day. Twenty-five of the ministers who immigrated in the 1630s returned to England in the 1640s and 1650s, while other ministers sent manuscripts to explain Congregationalism, promote cooperation between Congregationalists and Presbyterians, and try to put a damper on England's drift toward religious toleration.[33]

John Cotton contributed the lion's share of books published in England by New England ministers. His interpretations of Bible prophecies in those apocalyptic times were especially popular. "What prophecies are now fulfilling?" Oliver Cromwell eagerly wrote to him in 1651. That question might have led to New England's single most important and most disastrous contribution to the English godly cause in the 1650s. Cotton wrote back that the apocalyptic time was right to strike a mighty blow against Antichrist and send an English naval expedition to conquer the Spanish West Indies. Launching that expedition proved to be the worst military decision of Cromwell's career.[34]

In the mid-1640s, harried English Congregationalists appealed to New Englanders to take on a time-intensive task that they themselves were too overstretched to attempt, what with the Civil War and ongoing religious struggles. Presbyterians at the Westminster Assembly had long been hounding them for a platform, a detailed, scripture-backed, collective statement, of Congregationalism. Could the New Englanders provide such a platform instead? In 1646, the Massachusetts General Court issued a call for a synod of the New England churches to draft what would eventually be called the Cambridge Platform.[35]

By the mid-1640s, New England Congregationalists had their own incentive to draw up a clear, collective affirmation of Congregationalism: England's new religious diversity was emboldening dissenters in New

England. The ministers of the Newbury, Massachusetts church steered it in a Presbyterian direction in 1643, with lower admission standards and decisions usually handled by the ministers alone. A large meeting of ministers and lay elders summoned from all over the region failed to persuade the Newbury ministers to change their minds (that would take three decades and long struggles in the church). A few people with strong feelings that God wanted only believing adults to be baptized progressed from long, searching discussions with their ministers, which were permissible, to protests when an infant was being baptized, which were not, and resulted in fines and whippings. Congregationalists themselves were increasingly disagreeing about how exclusive access to baptism should be. The General Court when it called for the synod warned of "differences as will be displeasing to the Lord, offensive to others, and dangerous to ourselves" if they were not resolved.[36]

It took the synod, meeting at Harvard College, three sessions spread over three years to complete in 1648 what became known as the Cambridge Platform. God signaled his approval of the platform even while the synod was writing it. One day during the last session, the minister John Allen was preaching on the biblical basis of synods when a large snake slithered into the crowded building and headed toward the bench behind him where the other ministers were sitting. As the ministers started to edge away, one stepped forward, put his foot on the snake's head, and impaled it with a pitchfork. "It is out of doubt," John Winthrop wrote, that God revealed his mind in what happened. The minister and the snake, Winthrop explained, acted out the prophecy in Genesis 3:15 that the serpent who had just lured Adam and Eve into sin (i.e., the devil) would eventually have his head crushed. The minister represented Christ's New England churches who were crushing the devil through their outline of the kind of churches that would triumph over him. At the synod's closing, the lay and clerical delegates, awed by the magnitude of their grace-assisted accomplishment—the most accurate recovery, they believed, of New Testament church government since the Reformation's recovery effort began—sang Revelation 19:1–2, merging themselves with the multitude of heavenly saints in those prophetic verses who were to cry "Hallelujah" shortly before the glorious millennium began, after God had cast down the Catholic Church and avenged the blood of his martyrs.[37]

The Cambridge Platform was a coming-of-age statement for New England Congregationalism, summarizing the region's standard church practices as they had evolved over two decades, and vigorously reasserting in these unstable times the government's responsibility to restrain idolatry, heresy, blasphemy, dangerous errors, and wayward churches, all backed up by scriptural citations. The platform eventually acquired a patina of informal authority in New England, while English Congregational churches occasionally consulted it. But it was never perceived as having binding force; such force would have been the onset of antichristian tyranny over the individual churches.[38]

Nonetheless, a collective Congregationalist affirmation of anything, even if non-compulsory and even if God himself sent a message of approval, easily set off hair-trigger Congregationalist fears about incipient assaults on the freedom of Christ's churches. The call for a synod met with initial lay opposition from deputies in the General Court and from members of the Salem and Boston churches. These laity, some of them "come lately from England," John Winthrop noted ominously, smelled a Presbyterianish trap set by the magistrates and ministers to force uniformity on the churches. In 1651, a third of the General Court's deputies refused to approve the finished Cambridge Platform for that reason, even though the court stressed that it did not intend to impose the platform on any church. The reason John Allen preached his snake-interrupted sermon was because of lay grumbling about synods being unscriptural.[39] Such laity, loath to be religiously tied down by larger-than-local commitments, leery of taking guidance from ministers and magistrates, and suspicious of innovation and potential coercion, were empowered by Congregationalism's democratic, consensus-driven form of church government. Their protests during the process of creating and ratifying the Cambridge Platform served as a warning of the challenges that lay ahead for New England's reformation in the 1650s.

# CHAPTER 14

# OLD ENGLAND'S CORRUPTIONS COME TO NEW ENGLAND

In the fall of 1652, New England's leading minister John Cotton caught a fatal chill while being rowed back to Boston across the Charles River after preaching in Cambridge. Shortly before he died on December 23, Cotton had a prophetic dream in which he saw nearby Ipswich's minister John Norton riding to Boston on a white horse to succeed him. Cotton, his church, and the magistrates all agreed that the multi-talented Norton was the right person for this important pulpit. He was much admired for his long extempore prayers, and he struck an awed fear into people's hearts by the solemn majesty with which he conducted church disciplinary cases. Norton had acquired international respect for a Latin treatise he wrote defending Congregationalism, while the General Court turned to him for tasks as various as diplomatic discussions with the English government and the writing of a learned treatise refuting heresy.[1]

It suited Norton's larger reforming agenda to be based at Boston. Boston was where the General Court met, and magistrates frequently consulted Norton on matters of state. It was where ministers routinely gathered, and a seventeenth-century historian claimed that Norton "maintained a care of all the churches." Norton had been planning to return to England, but he agreed to take Cotton's position.[2]

Like Cotton, Norton believed that the success of New England's reformation in church and state hinged on making sure that the unruly, fickle, and sometimes ignorant impulses of the laity did not overwhelm the guidance of the wise and learned in both church and state. Boston laity had been especially active in resisting the Cambridge Platform. To keep them in line,

Norton insisted as a condition of accepting the Boston pulpit that the church's male members had to "particularly consent" to the platform. They wanted him badly enough that they agreed.[3]

From his new Boston perch, New England Congregationalism's informal superintendent would do his part to steer it through the turbulence of the 1650s and early 1660s. Some of that turbulence was churned up by the assertive, populist impulses of the laity, both within and without Congregationalism; some by England's changing religious and political dynamics; and some by emergent design problems within Congregationalism itself. Controversy inevitably followed in the wake of Norton's interventions, and his activism would result in, among other things, accusations of treason and dead bodies, including, finally, his own.


One member of Norton's new congregation, the young goldsmith John Hull, was busy in the 1650s becoming an overseas merchant, grafting himself into rapidly growing and dizzyingly complicated, high-risk networks of trade, credit, and debt stretching from England to the West Indies. Yet Hull remained a deeply pious puritan. He had a steady appetite for sermons, which he jotted down in typical puritan fashion for later study-ing and sharing. That appetite is what brought him on April 9, 1656 to Boston's Second Church, founded in 1652.[4] The preacher that day was Michael Powell, whose sermons Hull frequently attended.

The fifty-four-year-old Powell was an earnest, well-organized preacher. He was good at conveying that he spoke out of a deep love and fear of God and out of his own spiritual struggle and joy. Powell's theme that Sunday was the mystery of why people rejected Christ, even though he spoke so clearly through his ministers. Among the many explanations Powell offered was that listeners did not appreciate what they had in their ministers: "they look upon a poor man but consider not of Christ that speaketh."[5]

Hull might have sensed a personal edge to Powell's words. Powell was himself a poor man, an ex-inn keeper whose formal education is unknown. He had slowly climbed through the lay puritan spiritual ranks up to his pulpit before crashing into a glass ceiling because of his lack of college training. In 1649, Powell and his wife moved to Boston from Dedham, where Powell had served in various town offices and as a deputy to the General Court. On their first Sunday in Boston, the Powells discovered that there was no room for them in the crammed meeting house. The church elders directed them to Second Church, in the process of being created. The six men founding the church invited him to join them in the protracted fasting, prayer, and sharing of spiritual experiences that went into that process. They wrote their church covenant and took it on June 5, 1650.[6]

Then the minister Samuel Mather, freshly graduated from Harvard, whom they had lined up to lead their newly founded church, sailed off to England, as did almost half of Harvard's 108 graduates in the 1640s and 1650s, propelled by a shortage of vacant pulpits in New England and a shortage of godly ministers in the British Isles. Powell's spiritually edifying contributions to Second Church's preparatory meetings had made a deep impression on the other organizers, and they invited him to fill in as a lay preacher while they looked in vain for another learned minister. In the meantime, Powell's preaching edified them beyond their expectations, while local Bostonians attending the conveniently located new church also approved of him. Since God was clearly blessing Powell's preaching, the church decided to call him to the ministry in 1652.[7]

With that calling, Second Church stumbled into the middle of a tense standoff between the General Court and England's Rump Parliament. In 1650, a book fresh off a boat from England alarmed the General Court. Bad enough was the fact that its title page alone revealed it to teach heretical opinions about Christ's sufferings on the cross. Even worse, this book flaunted its author's name William Pynchon on its title page and identified him as a "gentleman of New England." Worst of all, Pynchon was a Massachusetts magistrate. One of the court's members, to its shocked surprise, was undermining the efforts of the last godly magistrates in the English Atlantic committed to repressing error and heresy and had made sure that all the world knew. The court demanded that Pynchon retract his opinions and publish a signed rebuttal in England. It gave John Norton the task of writing a refutation, had the public executioner burn the book to testify to its righteous indignation, and sent notice of its action to England, undoubtedly partly as a broad hint to the English government as to how it should handle some of the books that were issuing from English presses.[8]

At Pynchon's request, Norton, Cotton, and another minister love-bombed him with their erudition in an effort to bring him back to ortho-doxy. After some months, they appeared to be making progress, or so the court thought and granted Pynchon more time to recant before sentencing him. But letters of encouragement from England persuaded Pynchon to give the court the slip and return to England himself in 1651. In Massachusetts, Pynchon created a scandal and received sustained critical, concerned attention from the colony's most important ministers; in England, where he went on vanity-publishing his theological novelties, he would be a mostly ignored, idiosyncratic minnow swimming in a sea of heterodoxy. That same year, 1651, the court offered three proselytizing Rhode Island Baptists the choice of fines or whippings, as was its wont with aggressive Baptists. One of them, John Clarke, also left for England.[9]

Once in England, Pynchon and Clarke complained to English friends in high places about their treatment. Sharp, critical letters to Massachusetts ministers and magistrates followed. The Massachusetts General Court in turn sent a sharp, critical petition to the Rump Parliament in October 1652. The court lamented Parliament's failure to repress the heresies rampant in England and its failure to sufficiently encourage the learned clergy who could refute those heresies. God's judgments would surely fall on England for Parliament's failures, the court warned. The General Court's bluntness might have been driven in part by worry about objections that were being voiced in Massachusetts at its repressive actions, even from within the court itself. How could Massachusetts magistrates and ministers hold up the old puritan standards when their English counterparts were abandoning them?[10]

Massachusetts's magistrates then explained to the men of Second Church that having just chastized Parliament for failing to support learned clergy, they were not about to accept Powell as a clergyman, especially in a town as important as Boston. Powell simply lacked the "learning and quali-fications . . . rightly to divide the word of truth and be able to convince gainsayers," the court told them, as well it might. The Bible in its original Greek and Hebrew was a closed book to Powell, as was Latin, the language of European learned culture. A Latin-literate heretic like Pynchon might have made intellectual mincemeat of him in a debate.[11]

The laymen of Second Church were unconvinced by the court's argu-ments, however, and a two-year tug of war followed. Powell defiantly told the court that he feared he might "break a rule of Christ" if he did not accept the church's calling, even without the court's approval. Magistrates and ministers, John Norton claimed, privately came to the church, eyes brim-ming with tears and on their knees, explaining about the dangers of unlearned clergy. But the only answer these unleashed democrats gave their superiors in learning and social status was "That is your judgment, and this is ours."[12]

No other churches came to Second Church's support; occasional lay preaching was one thing, but a Massachusetts minister regularly expounding scripture without the college training needed to properly unlock it was something entirely different. In 1654, Second Church finally accepted the court's longstanding compromise offer. The church would have to have a college-trained man as its minister. Powell could still supplement the learned sermons of the minister with his own preaching and the church could pay him a salary, but he would have to be ordained as a ruling lay elder, which meant that he could not administer the sacraments.[13]

That outcome was, from Norton's viewpoint, a happy example of ministers and magistrates saving the people from themselves. Less happy was a battle he and the magistrates lost in 1656. Anne Hibbens, an abrasive, quarrelsome magistrate's widow and an accused witch, had demonstrated her dark powers when she accosted two of her enemies talking on the street and asked them, correctly, why they were talking about her. As was often the way in witchcraft cases, the people were keener to see her hanged than the magistrates. The magistrates overturned a jury's guilty verdict, but Hibbens lost the case again in the General Court, where the people's representatives, the deputies, outvoted the magistrates. Hibbens was hanged "only for having more wit than her neighbors," was how Norton put it. He was perhaps among those who noted strokes of God's wrath on Hibbens's accusers. Hibbens was the fourth person executed for witchcraft in Massachusetts, and the last until 1689.[14]

In 1656, the nightmarish apogee of unrestrained religious populism reached the shores of Massachusetts. A Boston ship returning from Barbados on July 11, 1656 carried two Quaker missionaries, Ann Austin, a London matron, and Mary Fisher, a thirty-year-old former servant. "Conquer the whole earth," Fisher had exhorted Barbados's fledgling Quakers before leaving, "and rule over the inhabitants thereof." Suffering was one of the most powerful weapons by which these Quakers would complete their world conquest, and Fisher already bore the scars of three English whippings on her back.[15]

The Massachusetts authorities acted decisively to quarantine this plague. They jailed the missionaries and had them searched for marks that they were witches. Their books were burned, their prison windows boarded up to keep them from sharing their message with passersby, and they were soon shipped back to Barbados.[16]

But before they were removed, an old Bostonian innkeeper, Nicholas Upshall, bribed their jailer in order to make contact with them. Upshall was an excommunicated Boston church member and "Seeker." As a Seeker, Upshall believed that there would be no true church on earth until new apostles emerged to found it. Two other excommunicated Boston Seekers had returned to England and become Quakers. Perhaps they had already written to Upshall that the church he sought would not be found in outward forms like sacraments and ordained ministers, but within the saints, guided by revelations and by Christ himself, who was the light within all humans. It was George Fox's conversion of Seekers in 1652 that gave Quakerism its explosive initial English lift-off. Upshall seems to have slipped the missionaries the good news that even in puritan New England, they would find Seekers meeting in Salem and more Seekers in Sandwich in Plymouth colony.[17]

Upshall was soon banished for protesting a new anti-Quaker law. But he turned banishment into a missionary trip and brought news of the Quakers to the Sandwich Seekers. The Plymouth magistrates moved Upshall along, too late, to the semi-anarchic four-town confederation of Rhode Island, where religious liberty was written into the colony's charter, where there was no meeting house and no paid ministers, and where the largest religious affiliation was Baptist.[18]

There Upshall would have met another ex-Boston church member, Mary Dyer. Dyer had been Anne Hutchinson's right-hand woman in Boston in the 1630s, and she had recently returned from England a Quaker. Dyer had perhaps already converted Hutchinson's sister Katherine Scott and her husband Richard to Quakerism (Anne Hutchinson had died at the hands of Native Americans in 1643). When two Quaker missionaries, Christopher Holder and John Copeland, landed in Rhode Island on August 3, 1657, they learned from Dyer, Scott, and other ex-Bostonians that Quakerism, in their own minds at least, was the culmination of why they had immigrated over two decades previously: what John Cotton, John Wheelwright, and Anne Hutchinson had been preaching twenty years earlier in Boston was the Quakers' inner light (the only one of this trio still alive to speak for himself, John Wheelwright, supported whipping Quakers) (see p. 103). As one of the ex-Bostonian Quakers put it, they were "then called puritans, now Quakers."[19]

Later that summer, the two missionaries made trips to the proto-Quakers of Salem and Sandwich and solidified them into their new religious identities before being expelled. New England's Seekers had become its nascent Quaker movement (Quakers neither made a sustained effort nor succeeded in establishing beachheads in Connecticut and New Haven, which lacked local Seeker groups).[20]

The next year, 1658, an angry John Norton found himself amidst a wave of Rhode Island-based Quaker missionaries descending on Massachusetts. In June, the Boston jailer, a member of Norton's church, whipped a Quaker missionary, William Brend, so severely that he passed out. A Quaker posted a call for the jailer's arrest on the door of First Church's meeting house, and Norton tore it down. "William Brend endeavored to beat our gospel ordinances black and blue." Norton shrugged, according to the Quakers, "If he was beaten black and blue, it was just." To suffer for false belief, Norton wrote, as the Quakers were doing, was an even greater sin than to hold it in the first place.[21]

On the Thursday after the whipping, Norton was giving his usual weekday sermon. Two indignant Quaker missionaries listened as Norton launched into a denunciation of Quakerism, while his devoted audience, the missionaries complained, "gaped on him, as if they expected honey should have dropped from his lips." After Norton finished, one of the missionaries stood up and cried, "Verily this is the sacrifice which the Lord God accepts not." He was going on about Norton being an abomination to the Lord as angry laymen pulled him down. The two missionaries were hustled off to the magistrates, whipped repeatedly, and expelled. Interruptions like this were a regular part of Norton's ministry in 1658.[22]

The shock of the Quakers' abrasive, confrontational proselytizing provoked even sleepy Plymouth into aggressive religious repression. Missionaries were banished, with a whipping thrown in if they were too defiant and rude to the magistrates (their refusal to take off their hats to magistrates was already enough of a provocation). But the missionaries kept returning. Local Quakers were harassed and fined, which in this cash-starved society, as elsewhere in the English world, usually meant seizing cows, sheep, tools, and other necessities of survival. These repressive measures were popular—a magistrate who opposed them was voted out of office—but the Plymouth government never escalated the harshness of its laws, despite those laws doing little to slow the Quakers down.[23]

Massachusetts, on the other hand, moved from whippings to ear-slicings in 1658 to solve the novel problem of aggressive heretics who would not stay banished. By the end of August 1658 there had been enough back and forth of Quaker missionaries to Massachusetts that three lay in a Boston jail cell awaiting their mutilation. It was not a good sign for puritanism that their coming ordeal bothered them no more than it did John Norton. Rather, it made them more confident of their ultimate victory. The "seed is ripe in Boston and Plymouth . . ." one of the imprisoned missionaries wrote exultantly back to England on September 3, and once Boston was "brought into subjugation to the truth, the others will not stand out long."[24]

The Quakers' delusory confidence that they were on the verge of toppling the Massachusetts churches was matched by the equally delusory fear of enemies like Norton that they might be right. The General Court, at its wits' end in dealing with Quakers, passed a law the next month mandating hanging for any that returned after being banished. Only two deputies disapproved enough of the final bill to record their dissent. Quakers claimed that Norton was particularly influential in passing the hanging law.[25]

To make sure the people understood how dangerous the Quakers were, Norton wrote a treatise, at the request of the General Court, to be given to every minister, town, and legislator in the colony. Massachusetts would violate its covenant with God and bring down his wrath on itself if it did not suppress the heretical Quakers, Norton warned. Even worse, the form that God's wrath would take would probably be a revelation-driven Quaker bloodbath of the Massachusetts puritans, provoked by the evil powers behind them, Satan and the Jesuits. Others shared Norton's fear of Quaker violence (in 1661, Quakers committed themselves to pacifism).[26]

Norton was right that Quaker confidence in their revelations would lead to deaths, but the only deaths would be their own. Early in 1659, two missionaries, Marmaduke Stephenson and William Robinson, received revelations telling them to go to Boston to challenge the hanging law, and they soon found themselves in the Boston jail. God moved Mary Dyer to come to Boston to visit them, knowing that she too would be jailed. "I choose rather to suffer with the people of God than to enjoy the pleasures of Egypt," Dyer wrote to the General Court. Upon the three Quakers' refusals to abide by banishment, they were sentenced to death. Their crimes, according to the court, were "rebellion, sedition, and presumptuous obtruding themselves upon us."[27]

Quakers claimed that most magistrates would have accepted the offer of the governor of Nova Scotia to send the condemned Quakers to him for perpetual banishment. But the people's representatives, the deputies, wanted them dead, and Norton set to work successfully persuading the magistrates to go along with this. Dyer warned the court that killing them would solve nothing; God would continue sending his servants among them and would "overturn you and your law by his righteous judgments and plagues."[28]

She and the two young Englishmen soon found themselves with nooses around their necks and their arms and legs tied on ladders propped against a gallows. As Stevenson and Robinson's ladders were yanked away and they suffocated to death, Dyer lost herself in religious contemplation, freely offering up her life to God in anticipation of her own death. But then, as she would write in complaint the next day, a buzz of unwelcome words broke off God's "presence, peace, and love in me." All that Dyer could make out of the words was that she was to return to prison and remain there for forty-eight hours. The Massachusetts authorities' plan had been to shock Dyer enough that she would not return after her son, by prior agreement, had taken her back to Rhode Island. Dyer had to be forcibly pulled off her ladder.[29]

Dyer was still keen to offer the ultimate testimony of martyrdom against those who vainly tried to repress the message of the inner light. Eight months later, she was back in Boston, having given the slip to her non-Quaker family, who were in desperation over what her husband called her "inconsiderate madness." Dyer rejected another offer to spare her if she would leave the colony. "I have been in Paradise several days," she was reported to have said on the gallows before she swung off into eternity. Attending militia fired a volley in celebration. Massachusetts was to hang another Quaker the next year, after he too had refused an offer to spare his life if he promised to leave the colony for good.[30]

Quakers were the most aggressive outside religious threat to New England's puritan reformation in the 1650s. But the most insidious and dangerous threat was internal: young people. New England's English population was rapidly expanding and growing steadily younger, plunging to a point where the median age reached sixteen. In the 1650s, the Massachusetts General Court repeatedly passed laws to rein in young people's fondness for drinking, gaming, strolling around on the Sabbath, and acting disrespectfully during the church services of very long prayers, sermons, and communal psalm singing that could last for three hours or more each Sunday morning and afternoon. The court called for the churches to pray for the young and ordered colony-wide days of fasting for them.[31]

This rising tide of young people made it impossible to ignore any longer what Norton and many other ministers and laypeople had already concluded was a grievous error the original settlers had built into their churches. Children's membership, which came with their parents' admission, was not worth very much. It brought them only one privilege, their own right to be baptized. Children could not take the Lord's Supper, and their moral and spiritual supervision was usually handled by the parents, not the church. When they grew old enough to claim the membership privileges of the Lord's Supper and baptism for their own children, they had to demonstrate their visible sainthood by giving a convincing conversion narrative, just like newcomers applying for membership.[32]

But admissions standards set in the 1630s for and by self-selected middle-aged religious zealots proved terrifyingly daunting to their offspring raised in more routine times. The children were not rising to the challenge. They were drifting out of the churches' orbits, while the first generation of settlers was starting to die off. That steady shrinkage of the churches could not have been why God sent the settlers to New England. "The Lord hath not set up churches," as one alarmed minister put it, "only that a few old Christians may keep one another warm while they live, and then carry away the church into the cold grave with them when they die."[33]

And since the Lord could not have intended to shovel his New England churches into the cold grave, where had the New Englanders originally gone wrong in trying to understand his intentions? Since the 1640s, John Cotton, John Norton, and other prescient ministers and laity had been rethinking Christ's intentions in order to allow the churches to hold on to their children as they became adults and started having children of their own who needed baptism. John Norton wanted that rethinking written into the Cambridge Platform of 1648, but he was vehemently opposed at the Cambridge synod by an "eminent person" who was dead set against any change. Since Congregationalists tried to work consensually as much as possible, the synod ducked the issue. Out of the same impulse for consensus, individual churches were reluctant to test the waters and expand baptism to their children's children on their own, even though it was their Congregationalist right.[34]

Finally, in 1656, 30 miles northwest of Boston in the new frontier town of Chelmsford, the town's church used ministerial blueprints to put a more inclusive, long-term approach to their descendants into practice. It did so after a characteristically long and careful debate, spread out over a quarter of a year. In the Congregationalist consensual system, in order for change to take place the lay debaters all had the heavy responsibility of either satisfying themselves that the learned ministers' blueprints were what Christ intended, or of being at least willing to live with them.[35] The Chelmsford church decided that the churches had been wrong in the 1630s to think that Christ intended the one-off event of baptism to be the only membership benefit for children. In fact, children were supposed to have access to a lot more privileges before they faced the high hurdle of telling a tale of their conversion to their church.

One privilege that came automatically, they agreed, was the church's life-long disciplinary scrutiny—grow old enough to escape from your parents, the Chelmsford church decided, and you still had the church keeping watch over you for your own benefit. A few months after their decision, eighteen-year-old Nathaniel Shipley started spreading a story about its consequences. He had been sleeping on a plank by Thomas Adams's recently dammed millpond when he suddenly found himself awake and dangling by his heels over the water. Adams was holding him upside down and telling him to attend Reverend Fiske's catechism meeting, as was Adams's new disciplinary responsibility to grownup children like Shipley, or he would drop him. Another pillar of the church, Abraham Parker, was encouraging Adams to drown the rogue. As it turned out, most of the story was just Shipley's imaginative way of expressing how irritated he had felt at being woken up for a catechism meeting. Perhaps he did not mind terribly when the church freed him of its watch shortly thereafter by excommunicating him for his lying.[36]

Those grown children who avoided the sins that would get them into church trouble were only one step away from another hitherto unrecognized membership privilege. If they publically accepted the church covenant, the Chelmsford church decided, and showed that they had a solid grasp of doctrine, who could say for certain that they were not saints? That ambiguous sliver of visible sainthood was enough for them to have their own children baptized without needing to give a conversion narrative. Those children, in turn, could have their children baptized, and so on to the Second Coming of Jesus. The Chelmsford church's continuity was assured.[37]

Where Christ still wanted high walls of purity maintained forever, the Chelmsford church concluded, was around the last and most important privilege of church membership, the Lord's Supper. No one could share in that sacrament until they could give a conversion narrative. And only men who got over this last hurdle would have a vote in the church. Chelmsford church would now have a large number of adult members who were not super-saints, but the super-saints remained the church's sacramental core and the ones who would guide the church. Six months after the Chelmsford church came to its conclusions, a meeting of ministers from Massachusetts and Connecticut affirmed them in general terms.[38] From Norton's perspective, Congregationalism was getting back on track to ensuring its long-term New England future.

Or was it? On September 27, 1657, John and Lydia Minot proposed in the Dorchester meeting house that the church's minister Richard Mather baptize their baby daughter. Undoubtedly, Mather had told John Minot that he had that right since he had received his membership through his parents as a child. Mather had been softening up his church for this moment for seven years, and he had probably cleared the Minot baptism with the congregation. But if he had, laity like deacon John Wiswall were getting cold feet. As the Minots stood up to offer their child, Wiswall might have been remembering his church covenant's solemn charge that members like himself resist "to the utmost of [their] powers" "polluting" themselves "with any sinful inventions of men." And what was it if not pollution to baptize the children of people who could not demonstrate saving grace? Once you cracked the doors of the church open like this, where would you stop? Would you push those doors wider and wider until you ended up not with a pure church of visible saints but a hopelessly corrupt parish church? Wiswall saw standing before him not faintly visible saints, but ungodly parents with an uncovenanted baby presumptuously claiming a right to have her baptized. And that novel claim of a baptismal right itself was nothing but "a corruption creeping in," as he wrote in the church record book, and "an harbinger to old England practice viz. to make all members, which," Wiswall added, "God prevent in mercy."[39]

What did it matter to Wiswall that almost all the learned ministers in Massachusetts disagreed with him? His memory of the puritan struggle with England's corruption was still fresh, and the saints would have to answer one day to God, not the ministers. Because of Dorchester laymen like Wiswall, Martha Minot was not baptized. In a church trying to run on consensus, it would have taken only a few laymen as determined as Wiswall to thwart the effort. Only a few churches followed Chelmsford and expanded baptism. When Norton and his fellow minister John Wilson tried in 1657 to get the Boston church to help its children, they could only bring the church to agree to keep adult children under disciplinary watch, not to expand baptism.[40] Ignorant laity were determined to drive the New England churches into extinction, or so it seemed to Norton, and given Congregationalism's emphasis on consensus and lay empowerment, there was little he could do to stop them. In 1661, he preached the warning to the Massachusetts General Court that observers were raising the "sad query . . . whether the Congregational way be practicable, yea or not?"[41]

At least the quarrel about baptism took place among the saints. An even bigger threat to New England's Congregationalism rose up when the startling, completely unexpected report reached the region in July 1660 that Charles II had been restored to the throne of England. Most New Englanders probably hoped that the news was just one of the many wild rumors that crossed the Atlantic during these turbulent times, and the first reaction was to ignore it. Even when it became clear that the king was firmly

in power, in Massachusetts the dominant attitude remained that the colony's reformation was no one's business but its own as long as it abided by the
minimal terms of its royal charter (see p. 96).[42]

So Norton knew he was treading on very thin ice in 1660 when he
pushed in vain for the General Court to immediately address their king.
Norton had always placed a heavy emphasis on deference to all but the
most ungodly government. At this time, he might have been among the
puritans who hoped that Charles II would bring order to the chaotic English
world and finally rein in the Quakers. In any case, Norton's insistence that
Massachusetts was subservient to the king left him fending off accusations
that he was a traitor to the colony's liberties.[43]

Two years later, Norton was on a ship sailing back to Massachusetts
from his official visit to Charles's court. Getting him to England had been a
slow process. By early 1661 word might already have reached New England
that ignoring the king was a risky strategy. Charles was showing favor to
Quakers, releasing them from prison, and assuring them that he intended
to let them worship as long as they were peaceable, and Quakers quickly
publicized the good news. Plymouth was a squatter colony, without any
legal foundation; it needed to keep on Charles's good side. In the face of that
cool royal wind blowing across the Atlantic, Plymouth stopped cold its own
persecution of Quakers in 1661.[44]

Massachusetts also started to dial down the harshness of its punishment
of Quakers in early 1661. But the General Court did not pull its head
entirely out of the sand about the new Atlantic political order until
November, when a banished Salem Quaker disembarked in Boston harbor
brandishing a letter from Charles ordering that the whipping and killing of
Quakers end. The horrified General Court complied, but only as a gesture
of respect to Charles, it insisted, not because it had to obey his orders. The
shock of Quakers being untouchable by whips or nooses finally gave political traction to the idea of sending agents to Charles. In December, the
deeply divided General Court agreed to send Norton and, as second fiddle,
the magistrate Simon Bradstreet, to England. It took a great deal of coaxing
to get Governor Endicott, no friend to monarchy, to sign this order, a
humiliating de facto acknowledgment of Massachusetts's subordination to
the English king.[45]

Norton's trip meant that he was able to experience firsthand the raw
atmosphere of hatred of puritanism in England. While he was there,
Parliament passed unprecedentedly harsh laws intended to purge the
Church of England of puritanism and puritans. In June 1662, Norton might

have been in the large London crowd watching Charles II's vindictive judicial murder of former Massachusetts governor Henry Vane (Vane had been protected, or so he thought, under the terms of an amnesty passed by Parliament after Charles's return). Norton and Bradstreet faced Quaker threats to prosecute them for Massachusetts's illegal executions of Quakers.[46]

So, all in all, given the climate of hostility, Norton did not do badly out of his visit. He was carrying back to Massachusetts a letter from the king confirming Massachusetts's charter. Moreover, the letter gave a royal green light to the renewed whipping of Quakers—Norton and the archbishop of Canterbury had talked that issue over, one of the rare topics on which the two agreed. The letter did order the colony to end the restriction of voting to church members, and it commanded toleration of the small number of colonists who wanted Book of Common Prayer worship. Both would be blows of sorts to Massachusetts's reformation, but nothing compared to the scheme that Norton had fought off. That would have put New England under the rule of an English governor-general and installed a bishop for the region.[47]

Norton had other reasons to look forward to returning to Massachusetts. The same General Court that had sent him to England had agreed to call a synod of the churches. The synod's chief task was to come up with a definitive statement about the requirements for baptism and other membership privileges. Norton could rightly anticipate that it would come out with a ringing endorsement of what Chelmsford had done about discipline and baptism for its children. So the churches were getting on track to remain the long-term spiritual centers of their towns; the Quakers could be whipped out of the colony; and relations with Charles II had been stabilized without fatal concessions.

The reaction to Norton's return was quite different than what he might have expected. The dominant response was that Norton had failed badly in his mission to England. He had wantonly allowed Charles to believe, mistakenly, that he could make demands on Massachusetts outside the terms of its charter. Beyond a few token gestures, the unmoved General Court chose to stonewall the royal letter, although it gladly resumed the whipping of Quakers. Norton, fresh from the London executions, was said to have warned the stubborn court that "if they complied not with the king's letter, the blood that should be spilt would lie at their doors."[48]

The synod, though, worked out as Norton had hoped, and he returned in time to participate in it. It overwhelmingly agreed that the baptismal inclusiveness of the Chelmsford church reflected the mind of Christ.

Norton, however, might not have anticipated just how bitterly the handful of dissenters and their supporters would fear and loathe this retreat from earlier New England standards. "Halfway Covenant" was the inaccurate, derogatory name the new model was given by opponents almost a century later; "large Congregationalism" was the term used at the time. Hostile gossip wove the synod and Norton's mission to England together into a plot to take away the civil and spiritual liberties of Massachusetts's freemen. The synod's dissenters defiantly published their objections in England, in order, they claimed, to "let the world know that the Lord hath still a few names in New England who ... detest the abominations of Antichrist."[49] The old Massachusetts of bristling pure churches and chartered independence from England's ungodly rulers would not go down without a fight.

It was not a fight that Norton lived to see. He had been deeply wounded by the hostility to his efforts to adapt New England's reformation to a changing world. To add insult to injury, in his own church a faction tried to get a recently arrived Englishman, a kind of anti-Norton who disapproved of expanding baptism and of sending agents to England, appointed as another minister. Convinced that even friends were judging him unjustly and turning away from him, Norton sank into a deep, sustained gloom. On Sunday, April 6, 1663, while sitting by his fireside, the fifty-six-year-old reformer, worn out and bitter, fell into a swoon and expired after "a very few groans and gasps." The way Quakers told the story, before Norton slipped into unconsciousness, guilt about the blood on his hands overwhelmed him and he "confessed that the hand of the Lord was upon him."[50]

# CHAPTER 15

# WABAN'S REFORMATION

About 20 miles southwest of Boston, Massachusetts lived an ambitious reformer. Even as a child shortly after 1600, Waban had possessed big aspirations; he would become a sachem, the ruler of a village or villages among the Massachusett tribe, or maybe even a powwow who could heal, or possibly hurt, through his spiritual powers. But Waban reached middle age with those childhood ambitions unfulfilled. He had risen to be an influential man in Nonantum, a village about 5 miles west of the English settlement of Roxbury, but he was still no sachem, although he married a sachem's daughter. Nor had he become a powwow, for the spirit Cheptain had never visited his dreams as a horned snake to confer upon him a powwow's powers.[1]

But Waban had not entirely lacked for good fortune. Although a devastating three-year epidemic in the late 1610s had cleared a large area of the coast for European settlement and ripped Waban's world apart—villages extinguished, bands collapsing and regrouping, the powwows overwhelmed by these new diseases—Waban was among the 750 members of his 4,500-strong tribe who survived it. He took note when further grim epidemics in the 1630s and 1640s left the English largely unscathed while pounding the Native American population throughout the entire region. The spirits of the English clearly had powers that the spirits of the Native Americans lacked. Waban decided that the locals must do as the English did.[2]

Waban's early efforts to unlock the spiritual secrets of the English did not go well. It was commonly known among the English settlers that the fastest way to get Native Americans out of a house was to discuss religion with them in the usual ethnocentric English way—Native Americans took badly to being told that their complicated relationship to the world of spirits was nothing more than devil worship. "You know the devil; I do not know the devil," Waban exclaimed as he stormed out of one English house; the family might have had a young Native American servant or slave who could translate what their departed visitor had just said. Yet Waban liked the unfamiliar food pious English people plied him with on these visits, and that was incentive enough to keep coming back.[3]

In the course of his visits, Waban's hostility to English religion started to recede. He slowly became convinced that long before the English arrived, what he had been doing was "sinning," and that the English had a good God. He learned, too, that his ideas about the afterlife had been wrong and that if he wanted the eternal life of heaven and not the eternal death of hell for his soul, he would have to pray to this God. He had observed the English closely enough, too, to worry that if the Native Americans did not learn to pray, the newcomers might kill them. Armed with his new insights, Waban spread the word around Nonantum about the urgency of praying. As a result, on October 28, 1646, a large group of men, women, and children gathered in Waban's wigwam to listen to two Massachusetts ministers, Thomas Shepard and John Eliot, pray and preach to them.[4]

The ministers had probably not come to Nonantum with high expectations. Waban's language and his topsy-turvy world alike were almost impenetrable to the English. The tattooed, scarred, and painted Native Americans had sex freely before marriage and divorced easily. The men practiced polygamy. Women sometimes served as powwows and sachems, and they were in charge of the male job of agriculture. The men, as far as the English could tell, did next to nothing when they were not wandering off to hunt and fish, sometimes taking their villages with them, and these activities, from the English perspective, hardly counted as work. Spirit was everywhere in the Native Americans' world, as were other-than-human personalities. Some of these personalities were more good-natured than others, but Native Americans took the pragmatic view that placating malevolent spirits was more sensible than fussing about the benign ones. Native Americans told stories of an afterlife in the southwest for their souls much like this life, only more pleasant, and devoid of the great Christian afterlife dramas of judgment, heaven, and hell. Englishmen disagreed on whether the Native Americans believed that good people had it better in that afterlife than bad ones; Native Americans often might have been responding politely to their leading questions.[5]

The English had always made pious, empty noises about the mission-izing goals of their colonies. "Come over and help us," says the Native American on the 1629 seal of the Massachusetts Bay Company. Yet for already overworked New England ministers faced with what one called the "veriest ruins of mankind," it was easier to agree with the illustrious John Cotton about the Native Americans' place in God's plan for humanity. The Native Americans' mass conversion was to take place only after the mass conversion of the Jews. Since the Jews remained stubbornly Jewish, the Native Americans must remain, for the time being, Native American, and there was no point in putting energy into trying to convert them.[6]

But in March 1644 a number of sachems placed themselves and their followers under Massachusetts sovereignty. They agreed that the General Court's requirement that they learn about the English God made sense: "We do see he doth better to the English," they explained, "than other gods do to others." In November 1644, the General Court ordered the county courts to "civilize" the now-subordinate Native Americans and teach them about God. The order seems to have drawn a mostly listless response from the colonists. The same order given to the colony's ministers a year later might have been the spur that goaded Roxbury's minister John Eliot to study the local Native American language, Massachusett, a necessary tool for any serious effort to convert the Native Americans.[7]

To Shepard and Eliot's surprise, the meeting in Waban's wigwam in 1646 went very well. The Native Americans listened to a prayer in English, and then to Eliot's halting Massachusett-language sermon, delivered with an interpreter's help, and peppered the ministers with questions. In answer to a major concern of Waban and others, the ministers assured them that God could understand prayers in their language. In answer to another question, they promised the Native Americans that they would ask the General Court to give them an English legal title to the land the village was on. The minis-ters left after passing out apples to the children and tobacco to the men. Eliot accelerated his study of Massachusett, and started making bi-monthly visits to Nonantum.[8]

Waban now threw himself into praying, making up simple ones like "Lord lead me to heaven when I die." But praying was much harder than Waban had expected. Under Eliot's instruction, Waban discovered that he was trying to pray with an entirely evil heart. Moreover, he could not conceal that wickedness from the English God. God was everywhere at once, a diffi-cult enough, novel concept, and he knew everything, including all of Waban's thoughts and sins. Waban soon found himself growing weary of this exhausting praying, and he could not help reflecting that he used to love praying to what he now understood to have been the devil back in less psychologically conflicted times.[9]

In spite of his struggles, Waban kept up his evangelical zeal. He and his circle set about reforming Nonantum. Even before the General Court granted his village title to its land, Waban and others drew up an English-style code of laws for the village. The code fined, among other offenses, fornication, female toplessness, and both sexes' extravagantly coifed long hair. Women's hair now had to be tied up, men's had to be short. Waban instituted the puritan practice of organized group prayer sessions and meetings to review Eliot's sermons. The Native American villagers started their own Sabbath meetings in which some of them exhorted and led prayers, while they collected questions to ask Eliot on his next visit. Many of them attended these meetings in English clothes. Some built partitions in their wigwams so they could have sex in decent Christian privacy. No less important for the inculcation of English Christian values, the Native Americans, with Eliot's prodding, began accustoming themselves to "labor," engaging in steady manual work. They built stone walls around their fields and started regularly taking brooms, baskets, berries, and fish to sell at English markets. Women started to spin. Idleness became a finable offense in Nonantum. Waban later remembered thinking that he would "quickly die" when he first tried to "labor." He found himself sometimes longing for his old "wild courses" and "wandering about."[10]

Waban took his evangelizing zeal to other Native American villages, as did other Native Americans. By the end of 1648 Elliot concluded that the "Praying Indians," as they were called, needed a town entirely of their own, away from the temptations and trials of their old culture, much like the puritans who left sinful England for Massachusetts. There they could learn to leave behind their wandering ways, labor like the English, read and write their own language, and eventually gather their own church—Eliot had no appreciation of Native American cultures, but he had a high regard for Native American abilities and already thought that some Praying Indians were more likely to be among God's elect than some Massachusetts church members. This ambitious project became feasible when Parliament chartered a charity, the New England Company, in 1649 to support Eliot, who had become well known in England for his heavily publicized missionizing. In 1650 the Praying Indians persuaded—or manipulated—him to choose a site where some of them had Native American rights to the land, thereby securing precious English legal title.[11]

On the morning of October 13, 1652, a year after the Praying Indian town of Natick had been set up with about a hundred inhabitants, a stream of magistrates, ministers, and other church delegates crossed the Charles River over a long, sturdy, Native American-built, English-style footbridge. They walked down one of Natick's three streets—lined with the wigwams the Native Americans preferred to the English houses Eliot had wanted— until they reached the Native American-built meeting house. Eliot had set up a biblical republican government for the town, with Waban at its head. The visitors might not have been as convinced as Eliot was that this sort of government would rapidly spread across the world in preparation for the imminent millennial reign of the world's only legitimate monarch, Jesus. Nor were they probably anywhere nearly as convinced as he and a few others in England and America at this time that Waban and the other locals might be descended from one of the ten lost tribes of the Old Testament Jews and that their conversion was part of the millennium's prophesied preparation.[12]

They would have been most uncertain of all about the conviction of Eliot and the Praying Indians that brought them here: enough of the Praying Indians were now truly converted that the Native Americans could gather their own church. Some visitors had already attended Natick services and had been impressed with the zeal and piety of the Native Americans. But they still might have wondered how unbaptized, illiterate, recent devil worshipers could be genuinely converted when conversion took much longer for many English people. Other visitors might have been among those English settlers who thought that the mission itself was a fraud. As was the Massachusetts practice, the would-be church founders had to give their conversion accounts in front of the visitors, who could stop the proceedings if they were not convinced the candidates were ready, as happened on rare occasions in Massachusetts.[13]

The visitors had no plans to spend the night. Yet once the ceremony started, it quickly became clear to them that Eliot had badly underestimated how long the proceedings would take. The Native Americans spoke slowly, and their speeches had to be transcribed and then read out in translation. Even before the Native Americans offered their accounts, the visitors were restless and edgy, while the Native Americans were visibly nervous.[14]

Waban was the second speaker, and with him the already problematic event began a rapid downhill slide. The English had long regarded Waban as not being very articulate about his Christianity. In tears, he told the audi-ence that he did not know if he either truly believed or prayed and did not know what grace was in his heart. But he did desire Christ. Eliot tried to perform damage control while giving his translation by explaining that Waban's gifts lay in ruling and evangelism, not in "expressing himself this way." The next candidate, Nataôus, went disastrously off-script at the end, perhaps from nerves, saying that he was angry with himself because "I do not believe the word of God, and gospel of Jesus Christ." The fourth candidate gave a solid, biblically and theologically informed account, but the uncomprehending English audience was already lost. While he was talking in the local language, some English started whispering while others left, and "great confusion" spread through the meeting house. Eliot cut him off. The visitors ended the proceedings after the fifth candidate failed to perform as well as he had in the preliminaries. The Native Americans were told that the closure was because of the lateness and lack of translators, but they could hardly have failed to notice that the English were in no hurry to reschedule.[15]

No record survives of the Praying Indians' reaction to being judged by the impatient and disrespectful English as falling short of real Christianity. One glimpse, possibly, comes seven years later when they finally got the chance to try again, this time before Eliot's Roxbury church. Perhaps it was Waban's memory of that crushing earlier rejection that prompted him to remind his Roxbury audience that God was not European. At least, that is one way to interpret how he began, saying through a translator, "I do understand but little of the English language. The word of God came not first unto my heart by the English language."[16]

Waban went on to conform much better to English expectations in Roxbury than he had last time around, telling of how, after discovering his heart's hardness and wickedness, he came to truly understand that only Christ could save him. Waban and the seven other Praying Indian men speaking with him now had the benefit of Native American school teachers and books printed locally in their own language, including a catechism and two books of what would eventually become Eliot's complete translation of the Bible into Massachusett. They were approved as Christians, accepted into the Roxbury church, and they and their families were baptized. Shortly thereafter, in 1660, they gathered a church at Natick, with all the spiritual powers and privileges of any other of Christ's true churches, including not having to subject future applicants to English grilling. By the time the Natick church was gathered, four other, smaller Praying Indian towns had been created in Massachusetts. Conversion of Native Americans was beginning in Cape Cod and was far along on the adjacent island of Martha's Vineyard.[17]

Waban's acceptance of Christianity had one idiosyncrasy to it. He never adopted the practice, common among Praying Indians, of taking a Christian first name. Perhaps that was because he felt he did not need to, for his name was already charged with Christian significance. "Waban" meant "wind," and Eliot's first sermon to the Notamun Indians was on Ezekiel 37:1–14, which speaks of wind stirring up dry bones. Native Americans and English alike made the connection between the verse and Waban and his evangelizing activities. For Waban, his prophetic name meant that the coming of Christianity started before the arrival of Europeans. Other Native Americans recalled pre-contact dreams of the arrival of black-clothed missionaries, while still others were convinced that the missionaries were restoring wisdom the Native Americans had forgotten.[18]

These newest of Native American stories, about how their God used the English to complete his bringing of his truth to them, meant nothing to most of the colonists. To the dismay of Eliot and the Praying Indians the other churches did not extend to the Natick church the standard Congregationalist courtesy of allowing its members to take the sacraments with them.[19] As would soon be violently re-emphasized to the Native Americans, the very best Waban and the other new Christians could hope for was second-class citizenship of the puritan city on a hill that they had climbed so hard and from so far away to enter.

# Part III

## TWILIGHT, c. 1660–c. 1689

# CHAPTER 16

# ENGLISH PURITANISM UNDER PERSECUTION

O n the eve of Charles II's return to England in 1660, Joseph Alleine could look back on five successful years in the ministry at Taunton, Somerset—in the unlikely event that he would have considered his ministry successful as long as he thought there was one soul left to save. Alleine had received Presbyterian ordination in 1655 and come to work as an assistant to George Newton, minister at St. Mary Magdalene parish church. Alleine was no narrow Presbyterian. He got along with people possessing a wide range of opinions about ceremonies and church government as long as their piety was strict and serious like his. Alleine had a boundless energy for evangelical work, always ready to substitute for other ministers and otherwise make himself available wherever preaching was needed.[1]

Joseph married Theodosia Alleine (perhaps a cousin), whose father and uncle were both Presbyterian ministers, in 1655. Theodosia's only real complaint about Joseph was that she saw so little of him. His absences left her too often uncomfortably in the role of spiritual and practical governor of their sizable household, including her thriving boarding school. "I know thy soul is safe," was Joseph's explanation whenever she pressed him to spend more time at home.[2]

Joseph regularly discussed his work and other matters with his wife and disapproved of married men who did not. The restoration of Charles II in 1660 gave the Alleines plenty to discuss. However Theodosia might have felt about it, Joseph would have seen supporting the return of Charles as a moral imperative. Like other Presbyterians, he had taken the Solemn League and Covenant, initially sworn before God en masse in England

and Scotland in 1643 and 1644, and vowed "to preserve and defend the king's Majesty's person and authority." It was the Presbyterians' faithfulness to that covenant that had led them to oppose Charles I's execution, to refuse to take an oath to the Rump Parliament, and to work to bring Charles II back to England.[3] Unlike Congregationalists, Presbyterians believed in a national church and had been busy restoring England's when they had finally been returned to brief political power just before Charles II's restoration.

Nonetheless, Joseph and Theodosia might have wondered how wise it had been of the Presbyterians not to press for specific reforms to the Church of England, instead accepting vague, general promises before agreeing to Charles's return. They both would have had only distant childhood memories of the old, unreformed Church of England which was rapidly reemerging all around them, along with the old festive culture of maypoles, dancing, theaters, and lavish public ceremony. If their affairs took them to Wells, 25 miles away, they might have had the same visual and aural culture shock as another young Presbyterian minister in 1661 when he encountered for the first time the utterly un-New-Testament pomp and splendor of cathedral worship: "Diverse I saw with the white surplices, and red tippets [long ceremonial scarves] upon their backs, their worshiping toward the east at saying 'gloria patri,' their singing the Lord's Prayer and the creed, and resounding of the organs, . . . I saw enough to make me hate vain inventions and to love God's perfect word and pure worship better." The modest, parish-scale formal ceremony of Book of Common Prayer worship rapidly burst out from the semi-underground existence it had maintained in the 1650s. In some areas overzealous justices of the peace ran ahead of the law and started fining ministers who failed to use it. The Alleines must have started wondering if Joseph would be allowed to keep his parish pulpit, or even if he could keep it in good conscience.[4]

The Alleines would have done well to wonder. Anti-puritans were about to set off a fierce gale of persecution intended to blow puritanism entirely out of the Church of England and batter down all Protestant worship outside it. In ministers like Alleine, who, like earlier puritans, valued their membership in a national church, the persecution triggered an unprecedentedly defiant response. Congregationalists had no desire to be part of the Church of England, and for them the persecution meant no more than increased alienation from that church and keeping their own heads down when necessary. Puritans would reach safe, if not entirely desirable and—as it turned out—only temporary harbor from this storm in 1672.

\* \* \*

Seemingly wonderful news would have reached Alleine shortly after October 24, 1660. On that day, Charles II issued a long-awaited statement on church principles, the Worcester House Declaration. Almost all English Presbyterians, unlike Congregationalists, were prepared to be flexible about church government, and the declaration went a long way to creating the kind of church that most puritans had sought since the 1560s: improved discipline, power-sharing with the bishops, and still-unspecified modifications of the ceremonies. If this statement was anything like what the final settlement would be, then Joseph would gladly keep his pulpit.[5]

To be on the safe side, in November 1660, Presbyterians rushed to have Parliament enshrine the Worcester House Declaration in law. From this point on, things went downhill fast for them. Congregationalists had no intention of returning to the Church of England under any circumstances, and the bill made no provision for tolerating them.

Presbyterians were well aware that the bill offered the Congregationalists no protection. They pleaded with the Congregationalists that their hands were tied, but that was not the whole story. They still leaned toward the old one-nation, one-church ideal. Many of them still hoped for no worship outside that church, and if you did grant toleration to the Congregationalists, where did you stop, especially given the breadth of Charles's easygoing personal religious toleration? He showed sympathy for Catholics, and there were even rumors that he was one himself, while his sympathetic interviews with Quakers embarrassed and alarmed his advisors.[6]

But for the Congregationalists, safety lay in numbers. If they were going to be left unprotected, it was in their interest to keep the much more numerous Presbyterians unprotected alongside them. The bill narrowly died in the House of Commons, in part because the Congregationalists all voted against it.[7]

News for puritans got steadily worse after this defeat. The 1661 elections for the new Parliament were the first in decades in which there were no anti-Royalist restrictions on membership. The consequence was a House of Commons that for the first time believed, by a sizable majority, that the route to religious peace in England lay in repressing puritanism. In that majority's eyes, it was puritanism that was responsible for the Civil War, and the fact that Presbyterians did not want to kill Charles I when they went to war with him hardly absolved them of responsibility for his death. In the spring of 1662, Parliament passed a legislative ultimatum, the Act of Uniformity, aimed at ministers like Alleine. It presented them with a stark choice: abandon your puritan principles or abandon your pulpit.[8] The act was passed over the objections of Charles II, who went on encouraging religious toleration in the steadily increasing number of American colonies, where Parliament could not interfere.[9]

Theodosia and others expected Alleine to agree to the bill's demands rather than give up the ministry that meant so much to him. But the more he thought those demands over, the more unacceptable they seemed to him. Could he really agree to a re-ordination from a bishop? Ordination was a once-and-for-all event, like baptism, and if Alleine needed it again, that meant that Presbyterian ordination did not work and that nothing he had done as a minister all these years had any validity. Could he really renounce his sacred oath to abide by the Solemn League and Covenant? There was nothing wrong with swearing loyalty to the king, as it required. True, that covenant did bind those who took it to "endeavor the extirpation of . . . prelacy," but all that clause meant, Presbyterians argued, was that the covenant-takers could work by legal means to improve the Church of England's government.[10] Perhaps most daunting of all, could Alleine really stand in front of his congregation and tell them with a clear conscience that he gave his "unfeigned assent and consent to all and everything contained and prescribed" in the Book of Common Prayer (as if it had "dropped immediately out of heaven," grumbled one nonconformist minister). This was the stiffest commitment puritan ministers had ever had to make to a book of worship that they regarded as deeply flawed at best. All new ministers would have to make that commitment in the future.[11]

Alleine finally decided that he could not comply. On the Sunday before the Act of Uniformity was to come into force, a "black and mournful Sabbath," according to Alleine's wife, he "took his farewell with much affection of his beloved people," as almost a thousand other ministers were doing across England. The next Sunday, August 24, 1662, was remembered by puritans as "Black Bartholomew's Day," when the ancient feast of Saint Bartholomew was marked by the emptying out of the Church of England's puritan ministry. Puritans recorded an alarmingly large number of churches being hit by lightning around that time, but the authorities paid no heed to that divine commentary. More to the point for them was that the riots and even rebellion that they feared might break out never took place.[12]

The Act of Uniformity's broom did not sweep all puritan ministers out of the Church of England. There were men anxious enough to keep their positions that they persuaded themselves that the oaths did not mean what they clearly did, sometimes with the encouragement of a sympathetic bishop. These puritans might continue to try to pick and choose their way around the ceremonies, just like in the old days, and hope, with lesser or greater success, that the authorities would not notice. Other ministers could take the oaths and conform with utterly clear consciences, but they were also prepared to be flexible enough about the ceremonies so as not to drive their most zealous puritan parishioners off—no kneeling at the sacrament, if you felt that strongly about it; a discrete private baptism for your baby that omitted godparents and the sign of the cross, and so forth. The puritan gentry did their best to present such flexible clergy to churches under their control and hope that the church authorities did not catch on.[13]

But while Black Bartholomew's Day did not entirely drive puritans from the pulpits of the Church of England, it did effectively drive those puritans almost underground. Charles II tried to be inclusive when he appointed his first bench of bishops. The bench included a few Calvinist and moderate bishops and even one former member of the Westminster Assembly. All the key posts, however, went to Laudians (although they did not get the blank check that Archbishop Laud had enjoyed). It is telling that the most effective clerical advocates within the Church of England for the nonconforming ministers over the next few decades were either not Calvinists, or, at the most, kept their Calvinist cards very close to their chests. The old, wary alliance between evangelical Calvinist bishops and flexible nonconformists that Laud had done his best to end would not be resumed.[14] There was an anti-puritan sea-change in the Church of England's pulpits, and a determination among most of the church's hierarchy to keep it that way. This book will from here use the term "Anglican" to refer to the supporters of that sea-change.

The Act of Uniformity, despite its severity, had a weakness that Anglicans had failed to anticipate. While it removed the most committed puritans from their pulpits on a scale vastly greater than ever before attempted, it did not and could not by itself remove them from the ministries that they had ritually sealed with God. That was not a serious problem for Anglicans if the men ejected from their pulpits opted to leave the country. Twenty-five went to the Americas, while fifty went to the continent, mostly to the Netherlands. The real problem was the ministers who stayed put, like Alleine. As far as Alleine was concerned, once he had gotten over the shock of his removal, his ministry remained as it always had been, with his people in Taunton. Compounding the problem for Anglicans was that there was now an unprecedented number of laity who felt as Alleine did. Soon Alleine was preaching in houses to large groups of people, in Taunton and in neighboring villages, between seven and fourteen times a week.[15]

Alleine was knowingly breaking the law when he resumed preaching, but he would never have thought of his activities as rebellious. He was nothing like the handful of armed Fifth Monarchists (see p. 156) led by a former New Englander who stormed out of a London alley on January 6, 1661, intent on conquering London for Jesus as a first step to conquering the world. The uprising was quickly and easily put down. But there were enough abortive and feeble small-scale plots and rumors of plots for the next couple of years to keep suspicions about all nonconformists high; who knew exactly where the next Oliver Cromwell was going to come from?[16]

Alleine, in his own mind, by continuing his ministry, was playing a vital role in preventing rebellion. He made a point of attending Church of England services, encouraged others to do likewise, and praised good preaching by conformists when he heard it. But too many of the ministers who replaced the ejected nonconformists like him were, according to Alleine, incapable of gospel preaching. They hated the "power of godliness," Alleine was convinced, and as a result, in their hostile, graceless hands, religion in England was "sinking, falling, dying away." Those laity who already had felt the power of godliness under preachers like Alleine would certainly never "sit down under" the "formal Pharisees" who had replaced the puritan ministers, Alleine predicted. If the ejected ministers were not willing to keep preaching to them, godly laypeople would drift away from the public ministry entirely and turn to sectarian "seducers, and despisers of government."[17] Everyone knew all too well from recent English history what damage religious despisers of government could cause.

Alleine's argument—that the godly laity were dangerous if they did not have guides they trusted—was a standard and long-standing puritan defense of the puritan ministry. The old rebuttal was that it was the puritan ministers' preaching that had stirred up these laity's discontent with the Church of England in the first place. The rebuttal had always been only partially true; the laity made their own judgments. But there was some justice to it. Alleine, his wife remembered, was "urgent" with people he judged to be unconverted after Black Bartholomew's Day especially since, as he explained to them, they had now "fallen into the hands" of replacement ministers who often "had neither skill nor will to save souls." He warned would-be converts that "moral persons, punctual in their formal devotion" (like the devotion, for example, in the Book of Common Prayer) would condemn and dismiss the "strictness of religion" that Alleine was insisting on as "intemperate zeal." Such critics, Alleine warned his listeners, were undoubtedly "rotten at heart," for their moral veneer covered their graceless souls.[18]

This sort of divisive critique of the Church of England and the majority of its ministers was conventional enough for puritans. But memories were very fresh of the damage that the dissatisfied, self-selected, judgmental saints that Alleine and others were illegally nurturing had done to the Church of England and to England itself. These so-called saints were in fact no saints at all, according to Anglicans. They were nothing more than "fanatics"—the new insult against puritans and anyone else who could be connected with the religious and political turmoil of the last two decades. "To be called a puritan or fanatic for the bold and constant owning of the power of Christianity," Alleine retorted, was a greater title than "earthly princes can bestow."[19]

In the summer of 1663 the law caught up with Alleine, and he was placed on trial at Taunton Castle for breaking the Act of Uniformity. His judge called Alleine "a ringleader of evil men" and his meetings with his followers "seditious." Members of the local gentry attending the trial told Alleine that he deserved to be hanged.[20]

If you believed that Alleine's preaching was seditiously undermining the Church of England, the way he occupied himself subsequently in prison would not have put you at ease. Alleine wrote and illegally published a small tract for his fellow ejected ministers, encouraging them to follow him in breaking the law. Alleine reminded them that their ministry was conferred by Christ, not by Parliament, and that Parliament could not end their sacred office by legislation. Since they were still in office, they still had to carry out the office's duties and keep preaching, legally or not. Did they really want to argue with Jesus at the Last Judgment that Parliament had removed that responsibility from them? To the "people of God" in Somerset, Alleine wrote letters warning that it was Satan who was spreading a fear of prison and suffering among them.[21]

In order to ratchet up the fear of prison among godly laypeople, Parliament passed a new law, the Conventicle Act, while Alleine languished in prison in 1664. The law made it a crime for more than four unrelated people to assemble for a religious meeting. The act had barely come into force when in 1665 London was hit by a devastating outbreak of the plague. Around 100,000 people, perhaps a third of London's population, succumbed to this fast-acting, fatal, agonizing disease in 1665, and those who could fled the city, including many of the Church of England's clergy. Nonconformist ministers, rather than leave the city's pulpits empty in this hour of need, took them over; what better time to warn of the wrath of God and the need to prepare for another world than when rapid, horrible death could strike anyone at any moment? At least some of the ministers preached that the persecution of puritans was one of the sins that brought about the plague.[22]

Parliament, which had fled to the relative safety of Oxford, showed no appreciation that nonconformists were keeping up the work of Christianity under such dangerous circumstances. Instead, it was outraged and alarmed that they brazenly dared to preach in public. Prodded by the bishops, it passed the Five Mile Act, the last in this series of laws against noncon-formity, collectively called the Clarendon Code. The act banned ejected ministers like Alleine from coming within 5 miles of any town or any place where they had ministered unless they had taken an extremely harsh oath of loyalty. Some nonconformists, having convinced themselves that the oath meant something other than it clearly did, took it, but most refused.[23]

Thirty miles southwest of Taunton, the Five Mile Act left Exeter's puritans contemplating the dreary prospect of a city depleted of its most active and vigorous puritan ministers. To prepare for this misfortune, those soon-to-be departing ministers approached a pious young man, George Trosse, in 1666. Trosse had gone to Oxford University in the late 1650s with the intention of becoming a minister. The return of Charles II had brought that plan to a halt. After much soul-searching and reading of old conformist and nonconformist authors, Trosse decided that he could not conform to the Church of England, although with no hard feelings to those who decided differently.[24]

Trosse's equanimity was shaken soon after on a Sunday morning. The college chaplain gave his typically puritan extempore prayer "with more than ordinary elevation of soul," according to Trosse, and it moved Trosse deeply. Yet as soon as the chaplain was finished, the new master of the college, Henry Wrightwick, attacked him in front of all the students. Wrightwick charged the chaplain with impudence and pride for thinking that what Wrightwick called his "crude notions" were better than the prayers of the Book of Common Prayer. To Trosse, the attack was all the more shocking, even blasphemous, because its real target, intended or not, was "the spirit of prayer, by whom the chaplain had been so eminently assisted." To heap insult upon injury, Wrightwick then went into the pulpit himself with the Book of Common Prayer. For Trosse, his reading had no more warmth than that of a schoolboy reciting his lessons, and Wrightwick rushed through it with no feeling of reverence.[25]

Wrightwick's performance was as far removed from real worship for Trosse as it could be, and it left Trosse debating whether he should abandon Church of England services altogether. A minister he trusted, Henry Hickman, talked him down off that separatist ledge by explaining that he could join in Anglican services as long as he was not active in anything of which he disapproved. To drive his point home, Hickman gave Trosse an old puritan book against separatism. Once back in Exeter, Trosse attended his parish church on a regular basis, for the minister was a "very good practical preacher," but he refused to take the Lord's Supper since for that he would have to unbiblically kneel. Meanwhile he attended nonconformist meetings. All across England, puritan laity were making that sort of calibrated adjustment to the country's new religious order.[26]

What the Exeter ministers wanted from Trosse in 1666 was that he be illegally ordained. He had a talent for preaching and preached occasionally at the nonconformists' meetings. But laity were pushing for more, as another ejected minister, Phillip Henry, found out that same year. A group of laity told Henry that their otherwise admirable parish minister had refused to give them the Lord's Supper without kneeling, explaining that his hands were tied. They wanted the sacrament from Henry. Henry had previously rejected the idea because of "a fear of separation"—to preach like he was doing was to augment the work of the parish churches; to give the sacraments was to compete with them like separatists. That controversy-filled decision was not one a Presbyterian would make lightly—a bullet was fired into the room where the leading Presbyterian Richard Baxter was partaking in one of his first private Presbyterian Lord's Suppers in the 1660s.[27]

But it was not these laity's fault that they were in this bind, Henry decided; it was Parliament and the bishops who had deliberately upset the status quo in the parish churches. Henry did not see how he could deny them without, as he put it, "betraying my ministerial trust, and incurring the guilt of a grievous omission." Henry perhaps also feared that if he denied the Lord's Supper to this group, some of them might turn Congregationalist, or worse, and be lost forever to the parish churches.[28]

Henry was not alone in his decision to administer the Lord's Supper. Alleine and other ministers in his circle did the same, as had Presbyterians elsewhere, including, probably, Exeter. If Trosse were ordained, he could administer it himself in place of the ministers who had to leave Exeter. Since he had never been a minister, the authorities would not be on the lookout for him for violating the Five Mile Act.[29]

Trosse agreed to be ordained. He and the Exeter Presbyterian minister Richard Atkins rode to Taunton, where Alleine and four other ministers grilled Trosse and two other men on their suitability as ministers. They examined the three prospective ministers on their knowledge of theology and received their confessions of faith. Then, using the spiritual authority they had received through their own ordinations, the ministers laid their hands on the men and prayed over them. Trosse long remembered Alleine's prayers. Trosse went on to offer the Lord's Supper regularly in Exeter.[30]

The authorities might have anticipated that, after Black Bartholomew's Day, the ejected ministers would have dutifully behaved like pre-Civil War nonconformist ministers. Once those earlier ministers had been removed from their pulpits, their days of attempting anything more than preaching, and that usually only in private settings, were over. Exercising their full ministry by administering sacraments, let alone usurping the bishops' power by performing ordinations, as Alleine and the others were, and would go on, doing, was out of the question.[31]

Many of the ministers ejected in 1662 would proceed no further than the old nonconformists, and only preach privately. The average age of the ejected clergy, however, in 1662 was just under forty-two.[32] Many of these clergy had little to no experience of ministering in an episcopal church. Unlike older puritans, neither they nor their lay admirers had any reason to regard the bishops who had been thrust upon them as anything more than a regrettably powerful usurping faction in their church. Usurpers were owed no deference, and they often got none, either from these ministers or from the laity who valued the ministers' services.

The result was something unprecedented in puritanism, a full-service, self-replicating Presbyterian wing of the Church of England. In 1689, one nonconformist estimated that most of the Presbyterian ministers then serving had been ordained illegally since 1660. This Presbyterian wing even had its own distinctive national ritual, possibly started by Alleine, with Congregationalists eventually participating. Every Monday morning, across the country, between six and eight a.m., puritan ministers and laity paused what they were doing and prayed for what they considered to be best for their church and country.[33]

Before or soon after Trosse's ordination, Alleine found himself thrown in jail again for violating the Five Mile Act. He was released in time to make a donation to those affected by the 1666 Great Fire of London (New Englanders raised money as well). That fire (set by the Catholics, it was widely believed) raged for three days and destroyed most of the city and its churches. The next year saw the climax of a disastrous, unnecessary war with the Dutch instigated by Charles and his advisors in 1665. A Dutch fleet humiliatingly sailed up the Medway River unopposed and burned the English fleet in the naval docks at Chatham.[34]

The string of disasters demonstrated that God was clearly angry at England, although that anger could be interpreted in various ways— Anglicans argued that London's suffering stemmed from the unrepented role it took in the downfall of Charles I, while nonconformists took it for granted that their persecution was a major cause.[35] Whatever the causes of God's wrath, however, vigorous persecution of nonconformists did not seem to abate it, and public hostility against them started to recede in the mid-1660s. That change in opinion was abetted by a change in Charles's ministry in 1667, which brought in men who were sympathetic to noncon- formists and to religious tolerance.[36]

As pressure from the top levels of government subsided, so did the rigorous enforcement of the new, divisive, and controversial religious laws at the local, mostly volunteer level (church courts were slightly more effi- cient in punishing nonconformists). Often at that local level, the system was administered by people who sympathized with nonconformists, or who were simply reluctant to prosecute their neighbors for religious reasons. Without the pressure from above, only local anti-puritan zealots would go to any trouble to try to enforce the religious laws. Nonconformists grew more relaxed about meeting openly; they started erecting their own meeting houses; and, if Richard Baxter is to be believed, by the late 1660s, more Londoners were attending nonconformist meetings than the parish churches (although there were too few parish churches to hold London's swelling population to begin with). This good news about nonconformist staying power came too late for Alleine, however. His stays in prison broke his health, and he died in 1668.[37]

At some point, Alleine's preaching came to the attention of Richard Baxter, who looked upon Alleine as a model Christian and nonconformist minister. Baxter arranged for a book of recollections of Alleine, including Theodosia's, to be published in 1672, as well as a passionate, urgent evan- gelical tract, *An Alarm to the Unconverted. Alarm*, a phenomenally popular book, was reprinted frequently into the nineteenth century and sporadi- cally since then in numerous languages, including Korean.[38]

At the time of Alleine's death, perhaps 5 percent or more of England's adult population of around two million people were committed nonconformists of all persuasions, including Quakers and Baptists. More than half of these were Presbyterians. Congregationalists ran a distant second with perhaps a third of the Presbyterians' numbers. But these estimates certainly substantially undercount the laity who attended both nonconformist meetings and their

parish churches. "I have coach hearers, but foot payers," grumbled a prominent Presbyterian about the fashionable, wealthy Londoners who attended
his Wednesday lectures but who went to Church of England services on
Sundays. In London itself, 15 to 20 percent of the population might have
been nonconformists, and some other towns had similarly high numbers.[39]

Unlike the Presbyterians, the 171 Congregationalist ministers who had
parish pulpits to lose when the king returned never thought that those pulpits
were attached to real churches. They could let go of them far more easily than
the Presbyterians. While Presbyterians wrestled with the issue of how much
they should worship outside the parish churches, Congregationalists argued
about setting so much as a foot in those unprecedentedly wicked churches. An
old leading Congregationalist, William Bridge, threatened to excommunicate
any member of his Yarmouth church who attended any part of parish church
services. The equally old and even more prominent Congregationalist Philip
Nye reminded the Congregationalists that this position was more extreme
than the position of the "soberest separatists" (like the founders of Plymouth
colony), for whom hearing sermons was acceptable. The Congregationalist
leader John Owen wrote that the Church of England had degenerated so far
from the principles of the Reformation that it was heading for an apostasy
from God's truth worse than Catholicism.[40]

John Bunyan's Congregationalist pastor could not lose his parish pulpit,
for he died in August 1660. But his congregation was unceremoniously
turfed out of the Bedford parish church whose tithes had supported him.
Bunyan himself had a target on his back as an uneducated, well-known lay
preacher. In November 1660, a local Royalist justice of the peace had him
arrested for preaching in a house. The justice was surprised that neither
weapons nor any other evidence were found to prove that Bunyan and his
listeners were plotting violence. When Bunyan refused to promise to stop
preaching, he was thrown into prison, which would be his residence most
of the time for the next twelve years.[41]

While in prison Bunyan probably finished *The Pilgrim's Progress from
This World, to That Which Is to Come*, an allegorical dream about the
pilgrim Christian and his peril-ridden journey of salvation to the Celestial
City. By the nineteenth century, *Pilgrim's Progress* was, after the Bible, the
most common book in Protestant households in the English world. By
1938, there had been over 1,300 editions, and it had been translated into
more than 200 languages.[42]

*Pilgrim's Progress*, for all its global and age-long appeal, is firmly rooted
in the gathered congregations of the Restoration and their piety. It reasserts

the protracted turbulence and struggle of the traditional puritan path to heaven—Christian is saved early on in his journey, yet thereafter, like earlier puritans, he strays frequently from the path to the Celestial City and comes close to committing suicide in the dungeon of Doubting Castle at the urging of its owner, the Giant Despair. Unlike earlier puritans, however, Bunyan does not give the slightest hint that the bleak social landscape of *Pilgrim's Progress* could be reformed into a new Israel. Christian initially flees from the city of Destruction; in the graceless village of Morality, Mr. Worldly Wiseman tries to entice him into fatally halting his journey; Lord Turn-Around, Mr. Facing-Both-Ways, and other puritans who conformed after the Restoration live in the village of Fair-Speech; and wicked judges routinely order the execution of the godly in the city of Vanity, where "lusts, pleasures; and delights of all sorts" can be found at its one-day-to-be-famous fair. The only spiritual shelter in the grim, perilous landscape of *Pilgrim's Progress* is Palace Beautiful, a vivid depiction of Restoration-era gathered congregations and the sustaining warmth of their fellowship.[43]

At a late stage of his journey, Christian acquires a traveling companion, Ignorance. Christian is dubious about Ignorance, as well he might be since Ignorance emerges from a crooked lane that begins in the country of Conceit. Christian bids Ignorance tell him how it is with his soul. Ignorance answers complacently that he follows God's commandments and that through the merits of Christ, God will accept that obedience and declare him justified, or saved. Christian tries to explain in standard puritan fashion that God will never accept Ignorance's righteousness; Adam's fall into complete depravity had put an end to that possibility. Christ's righteousness alone will get Ignorance into heaven, and only after Ignorance has probed the depths of his soul and discovered its complete wickedness. Such talk, Ignorance replies dismissively, is "the fruit of distracted brains," and he leaves Christian's company. Ignorance's confidence in his salvation remains unshaken right up to the gates of the Celestial City where, in the final lines of *Pilgrim's Progress*, angels swoop down, seize him, and drop him into hell.[44]

Bunyan's readers would probably have noticed that Ignorance's fatal misunderstanding about salvation could also be found in the most up-to-date Anglican spiritual guidebooks. Like Ignorance himself, these Arminian books heavily emphasized the saving effect of moral behavior unbalanced by any stress on God's grace, introspection, and a turbulent period of conversion, and they denied that a person's freedom to choose heaven was crippled by any alleged total sinfulness of the human heart.[45]

As Bunyan was finishing *Pilgrim's Progress*, Anglican ministers were increasingly smothering their servings of their new Arminian piety in a sauce of no-holds-barred attacks on Calvinism and puritan piety (among Anglicans, the once-dominant Calvinists had become a steadily diminishing minority). That old puritan theology and piety, Anglicans claimed, was nothing but delusive, morose incitements to seditious faction and rebellion. Rather than concentrate on reason and on the great truths of morality and obedience to superiors, the Anglicans charged, preachers like Bunyan dwelt obscurely on grace and nonsensical gospel mysteries and on an equally nonsensical long, inwardly and outwardly arduous path of salvation, both of which required that listeners adhere to the preachers' allegedly spirit-illuminated expertise for safe passage. To better further their seditious aims, these puritan preachers inculcated in their listeners a hothouse fervency, encouraging them to believe that they were the predestined "godly," and thus superior to everyone else in England.[46]

The increasing vehemence of these Anglican attacks was driven by nonconformity's increasing visibility. In the late 1660s there were even high-level talks about "comprehension" (inclusion in the Church of England) for Presbyterians and "indulgence" (toleration) for Congregationalists. Disagreements between Presbyterians and Congregationalists again helped to scuttle what would have been a steeply uphill effort, at best.[47]

Anglicans pushed back against this growing tolerance with a renewed Conventicle Act in 1670. Striking at the ministers, the supposed collective serpent's head of puritanism, the renewed act drastically increased fines for the preachers at conventicles while lowering them for attendees. It also allowed informers to take a share of any fines.[48]

After the act's passage, informers infiltrated their way into nonconformist circles, anticipating great profits from fines, and jails started to fill up again. Troops broke up nonconformist services and destroyed the meeting houses, sometimes battling their way through stone- and brick-throwing crowds to do so. In London, they seized meeting houses for use as parish churches.[49]

Within a year, however, the push from above for enforcement began to slacken, for Charles's devious mind had turned elsewhere. In 1670, he signed a treaty with Louis XIV, the militantly Catholic expansionist king of France. In exchange for a healthy financial subsidy, Charles was to join Louis in his war against the Protestant Netherlands, lighten the burdens of English Catholics, and, when conditions permitted, announce his own conversion to Catholicism. Needless to say, this treaty was negotiated entirely behind the backs of Charles's subjects and was kept hush-hush afterwards, although rumors of it soon leaked out.[50]

The treaty gave Charles a new incentive to attempt something that Parliament had warned him off in 1662. In 1672, on his own authority, he simply suspended the laws against nonconformity for Protestants and Catholics alike with a Declaration of Indulgence. Protestant nonconformists could make the trek down to Whitehall Palace in London to get properly signed licenses for ministers and for public meeting houses; Catholics would be allowed to worship privately.[51]

Nonconformists did not greet the declaration with entirely open arms. Congregationalists and Presbyterians suspected that they were being used as pawns in a larger game whose only winners would be England's Catholics, roughly 1 percent of the population; Catholics were in some ways already better off than the nonconformists: there had been virtually no pressure from above to enforce the laws against them. Some nonconformists had constitutional scruples about the Declaration of Indulgence, fearing that Charles was employing a legal power that did not belong to him. Quakers did not believe that the state could dictate to anyone as to when and where they could hold religious assemblies. For that reason, they refused to apply for licenses, as did some Baptists and a few Congregationalists.[52]

Nonetheless, the licenses proved immensely popular. As many as 1,610 were given out in England and Wales: 939 licenses identified the minister as Presbyterian, 458 as Congregationalist, and 210 as Baptist. John Bunyan chose to receive his as a Congregationalist, although he was personally a non-dogmatic Baptist by this point. A number of ministers took out more than one preaching license, usually Presbyterian and Congregationalist, a sign in part that good and willing preachers were in short supply, in part that scraping together a living was usually hard for them, and in part that differences between these two groups of puritans did not necessarily appear so weighty now that they were equally politically powerless. Among the gentry, widows were the most forward in offering their houses to be licensed for meetings; men could lose more by exposing their nonconformist religious preferences too openly. In licensed private buildings as various as houses, barns, sheds, malt houses, and purpose-built meeting houses, ministers and laity recommenced a public worship that had once taken place in parish churches and even great cathedrals.[53] But how long this freedom created by the arbitrary action of the king would last remained to be seen.

# CHAPTER 17

# ENGLISH PURITANISM GOES PUBLIC AGAIN

Unchained by the Declaration of Indulgence, Restoration puritanism lurched in new and much more visible directions. That lurching can be followed through the fortunes of two ministers, Thomas Jollie, a Congregationalist, and Oliver Heywood, a Presbyterian. Friends from Cambridge University who still prayed and preached together, they lived about 30 miles apart across the moors of west Yorkshire and Lancashire. Both took full advantage of the Declaration of Indulgence and of the period of relative freedom that followed it to reinvigorate their ministries and to attempt to heal the rupture between Congregationalists and Presbyterians. They labored in the midst of turbulent political tides, pulled in shifting directions by still-raw historical memories. By the 1680s, those tides were once again threatening to overwhelm puritanism.

Heywood and Jollie both lost their pulpits around Black Bartholomew's Day. They agreed that their ejections did not break their bond with their people, but for entirely different reasons. Jollie's bond was only with the small Congregational church he had carved out of Altham chapel, a satellite of Whalley parish church (a common arrangement in the vast parishes of northern England). One of the reasons he was ejected before Black Bartholomew's Day was that he had alienated the rest of his parishioners by denying them the sacraments. Jollie's Congregational church left Altham chapel with him.[1]

The only time Jollie now heard Church of England ministers preach was at funerals, when family and social duties left him little choice. Those experiences only gave him more "cause to question whether many of them be the ministers of Christ." In Jollie's church, attending a Church of England service could lead to disciplinary action, while the congregation resolved that it was their duty to bear witness against anyone at all who attended the Church of England regularly, lest they take on the guilt of that sin themselves.[2]

This hardline attitude to the religious life of most of the Congregational church's neighbors could help explain why those neighbors offered Jollie little help when the authorities went after him for his nonconformity. Exceptionally unlucky in the attention he attracted, Jollie was jailed briefly for his church's private meetings in 1663, jailed again for a month that same year on suspicion of participation in an abortive uprising, jailed for three months in 1665 for private meetings, and jailed for most of a year in 1669 for violating the Five Mile Act. Jollie finally converted the door in front of his house's stairwell into a folding pulpit, so he could leap backwards, shut the top of the door, and head up and out if the house was raided during a meeting or service. Otherwise, all that Jollie, like other nonconformists, could do about his church's persecution was take note when God executed a wrathful judgment on one of its persecutors: the one forced to flee the area because he had fallen into deep poverty, for example, or the one who died when the Lord smote him with an unquenchable thirst, or the one lifted off his horse by an invisible hand while crossing a river, spun around three times, and thrown into the water dead. That persecutor's wife confessed, according to Jollie's informant, that he had told her the previous evening that the devil would fetch him shortly.[3]

For Jollie, the Declaration of Indulgence was a deliverance from this harassment and persecution. He could sleep in his house again, and his church could finally function freely and openly. "A good presence of God was manifested in the church," Jollie concluded after a year of freedom, especially in the church's government and its firm use of discipline. He noted that while the church's membership did not grow much during this time of public worship and public access, others were "convinced" and "better satisfied" about Congregationalism. That rise in respect was enough for Jollie to conclude that the church's "liberty was not in vain."[4]

Visibility, though, brought its own challenges. It was no secret that most Congregationalists had not wanted Charles II to return, including Jollie. Even Presbyterians still sometimes lashed out at them as king-killers. The Church of England had made the anniversary of Charles's return, May 29, a day of thanksgiving. Jollie's church knew that they had to offer some affirmative gesture on that day about the blessings of having a king "to avoid offense" to their neighbors. The best they could think of, though, was to meet privately and thank God for prompting Charles to issue the Indulgence. On the other hand, they gobbled up the impeccably sourced story that the devil attended a dance at Whitehall Palace; Charles's court had become notorious for its dissolute behavior, with the king taking the lead.[5]

The Presbyterian Oliver Heywood's bond with his congregation had been created by his appointment in 1650 at Coley chapel, a satellite of Halifax's parish church (Halifax's huge parish sprawled across twenty-six townships). After Heywood's ejection in 1662, groups of up to a hundred would come to his house to hear his preaching. When the Five Mile Act forced Heywood to move to an isolated house, he was pleased that he could now sing and preach as loudly as he wished without worrying about hostile ears over-hearing him.[6]

To keep up the work of reformation, Heywood regularly made two- to three-week tours through Yorkshire and Lancashire, sometimes with Jollie, preaching, fasting, praying, and celebrating the sacraments. Most of this itinerant work took place in the homes of gentry, farmers, tradespeople, and relatives along the old puritan networks of the region. But these tours included two churches, Denton and Peniston, whose nonconformist minis-ters had somehow slipped through the Church of England's cracks and never agreed to the Act of Uniformity. They remained little oases of uncom-promised puritanism in a vast parish church desert. Here Heywood could lay aside his private, furtive work and once again be a public minister, and here is where he most consistently found intense spiritual satisfaction in his ministry, if his diary is any measure.[7]

Heywood never entirely severed his bonds with the Church of England in Coley. He continued to attend parish church services, and he urged others to do likewise. Heywood maintained a good relationship with his Church of England successors at the chapel and with much of the local laity. When there was no preaching at the Church of England chapel, his house became especially crowded with people coming to hear him. Heywood even preached by invitation in the chapel himself a few times when there was no minister. He also kept up a tactful pastoral concern for those former charges who did not consider themselves among the godly. Heywood's cultivation of his local community paid off in tips from local officials when-ever it looked like a meeting he was holding might get raided. By 1672, Heywood had suffered only a £10 fine and the emotional wear and tear that came from having to constantly fret about being arrested.[8]

The Declaration of Indulgence transformed Heywood's ministry. He and his lay supporters decided that it gave them royal permission to start acting again like the public church they had been before Black Bartholomew's Day. There would be no more infrequent private celebrations of the Lord's Supper to floating groups of people whose Christian watch over each other was at best haphazard.[9] That sacrament would be offered regularly and openly within a rejuvenated spiritual community that maintained disciplinary care of its members.

The process of rejuvenating Heywood's church commenced on June 12, 1672, with a sermon, prayer, and celebration of the Lord's Supper at Heywood's house. These exercises, Heywood wrote afterwards, "carried" him "out to God," who "united our spirits." The laity then signed a document affirming their shared religious beliefs and their conviction that they "still" recognized Heywood as their "rightful pastor." They pledged to "believe and practice" the "truths and duties" he taught, even in the face of persecution. Heywood pledged in turn to serve his people faithfully, also in the face of persecution.[10] The church at Coley chapel, obscured by the spiritually illegitimate Act of Uniformity, was visible once again.

Now Heywood could resume the old Presbyterian goal of guiding people into lives of godliness and self-examination that would eventually revolve around participation in a carefully policed Lord's Supper. In 1682, a young man, Joseph Wood, explained to Heywood how, after hearing sermons Heywood had preached five years earlier on the perennial puritan theme of the heart's deceitfulness, God had "laid" him "very low." Wood was thrown, he remembered, into "many sad days and nights of sorrow." Heywood himself might have been weeping during those sermons that moved Wood so much, as he often did, while Wood might have been among those listeners who wept so hard that the notes they were taking of his sermons became unreadable.[11]

There was an abundance of lay groups for prayer and mutual spiritual guidance in Heywood's congregation to help Wood along during the process of his conversion. He joined a group of young men for prayer and conference. As Wood grew more proficient and comfortable in the ways of social godliness, he might have been invited to participate in the frequent fasts that the laity held for a variety of causes, including the weather, national politics, illnesses, childbirth, and harvests. Wood finally grew secure enough about the state of his soul to present himself for the Lord's Supper. Heywood examined him, and on November 20, 1681, Wood participated for the first time. He could join now in the customary post-sacrament meal at Heywood's house.[12]

Two and a half months later Wood came to Heywood's house during family
devotions. Heywood invited him to pray. To Heywood's increasing admiration, Wood, now thoroughly at home in the ways of the godly, launched into a
heartfelt and highly skilled extempore prayer lasting over an hour, "confessing
sin, self-loathing, pleading with God for grace, pardon, communion with God,
for the church, souls' conversion, for me, my wife, sons, blessing God for us."
So impressed was Heywood with Wood's "warmth, solidity and extraordinary
workings," that he concluded Wood would either soon die or was being
prepared by God for some great service. "Oh blessed, blessed be my God,"
Heywood wrote in his diary, "for this fruit of my poor labors."[13]

For Anglicans, including the local vicar, all that Heywood and his congregation's labors with Wood had produced was another fanatic to undermine
the Church of England. It did not take long after the Declaration of
Indulgence for Anglicans to start hurling angry charges of schism and separation at the Presbyterians because of what the Anglicans claimed were their
new churches, like Heywood's. A few Presbyterians were, indeed, starting
to wonder if they would be better off abandoning the Church of England
and going their own way as a separate group, like the Congregationalists.
Most, though, rejected both that goal and the Anglican accusation that
churches like Heywood's represented such a separation. The real schismatics
and separatists, they charged, were those Anglicans who removed ministers
like Heywood from their rightful Church of England pulpits and put
usurpers in their places.[14]

Rejuvenating the Presbyterian churches might have opened up for
Anglicans a fresh wound of separation. For some Congregationalists,
however, it healed an older wound, the split in puritanism. Now that
Heywood's group was finally acting like a real church, independent of any
connection with the ungodly masses in the parish churches, a neighboring
Congregational church that had recently lost its minister was willing to
look them over.

A delegation from that church met with Heywood's church six days after
its momentous Lord's Supper. After a discussion, they agreed that in the
main their churches were run the same way, "though our principles were
different," and that they were willing to overlook any differences (Heywood
retained control of admissions and discipline in his church). More discussion followed, and the Congregationalists agreed that Heywood showed
"fidelity as to admission" of members.[15]

That agreement allowed the Congregationalists to approach and cross
the point at which discussions between them and Presbyterians had always

maddeningly broken down as far back as 1630s Massachusetts. Heywood's members, they decided, could take the sacraments at their church without further inquiry into their godliness and they would be glad to take the sacraments at Heywood's church. "This is the strange work of God!" Heywood commented with astonishment, "Men's spirits are strangely altered." The two churches agreed to celebrate the Lord's Supper together on July 14 and they both went away "abundantly satisfied." Some of the Congregationalists eventually joined Heywood's church.[16] What to Presbyterians had always been their unnatural divide from the Congregationalists was healed, at least in this tiny corner of England.

The new puritan freedom of worship hit a snag when Parliament reconvened in 1673. Rumors abounded about the depth of Charles's sympathy for Catholicism and the control Louis XIV had over him through his corrupt ministers. Even worse, Charles had been unable to produce a legitimate heir, and it was fast becoming all but public knowledge that his brother who would succeed him, James, duke of York, had himself converted to Catholicism. In this climate, it was straightforward to interpret the Delaration of Indulgence, along with other problematic kingly actions, as stemming from a sinister plot by Catholics to manipulate the king to abuse his power to their own ends. Tyranny and Catholicism were raising their familiar, monstrous twinned heads again.[17]

The sight of that old specter produced an increased appreciation in the House of Commons for the rock-solidly anti-Catholic puritan nonconformists. The House successfully petitioned the king for the revocation of the Declaration of Indulgence, or else no money for him. But the purpose of this petition was strictly to stop Catholic worship, not to harm the nonconformists. In a striking turn-around, the Commons also passed a bill that would have removed some of the scruples of those ministers who wanted their parish pulpits back and provided terms of toleration for the rest. The bill would have been acceptable to many Presbyterians and Congregationalists (although not to Quakers or Baptists). Unfortunately, the House of Lords, where the bishops made up a large voting bloc, loaded the bill with unacceptable amendments, and it died when Parliament was adjourned in March. But the bill marked a watershed. The century-old alliance between puritans and an anti-Catholic House of Commons majority was re-emerging.[18]

Charles did not call in the nonconformists' preaching licenses after he withdrew the Indulgence until 1675. That delay created a legal gray area, and in most places, rigorous enforcement of the penal laws did not resume in 1673. There was enough harassment, though, that Jollie's ambitious effort to rejuvenate a regional association of Congregational churches ground to a halt in 1674 after only four meetings in a mutually convenient tavern.[19]

That harassment and the lack of good ministerial candidates in the pipeline plunged Jollie into the depths of despair about the future of English Congregationalism. His fresh despair was loaded on top of sadness over the recent death of his fourth wife that repeated fasts with friends had done little to abate. Perhaps it was time, Jollie wondered, to immigrate to New England—Jollie's church, like other Congregational churches, had a web of personal and spiritual connections with New England Congregationalists.[20]

With the support of his church, Jollie traveled down to London in 1675, to confer with Congregationalist leaders about emigration and about the long-term viability of English Congregationalism. The London Congregationalists talked him out of leaving for New England (Congregationalist immigration to New England was steady but small). Instead, they turned their attention to ways of strengthening ties between Congregationalists and Presbyterians, a project already in process, and helping overstressed churches and aspiring would-be ministers. Most hearteningly of all, Jollie was told that "the Lord was leading our rulers into counsels for our liberty in a signal manner."[21]

The Lord, in fact, was doing no such thing, but by the time Jollie realized as much back in Yorkshire, he could see that sustained persecution was over. Jollie was soon writing in his notebook about how his church could now meet safely out in the open, and about how in its worship "we had some sights of blessed Jesus and some tastes of his love."[22]

Charles's attention was focused elsewhere, on a mass of activities that to many English people were growing increasingly sinister. One of those observing Charles closely was Andrew Marvell, former secretary to Oliver Cromwell, poet, and long-time member of Parliament for the northern port of Hull. Marvell, a puritan-leaning conformist, had recently made a name for himself with illegal publications that defended the nonconformists and their goals for church reform while updating the old, enduring puritan conspiracy theory about the wicked bishops' plot to drag England back into popery and tyranny. The tracts' deadly serious arguments were seasoned with a lot of outrageously funny, malicious, skillful satire that gave them a wide, appreciative audience, including the king.[23]

In 1677, Marvell's attention turned to another alleged conspiracy, this one even more alarming since its tentacles reached deep into the royal family. Marvell broadcast the news of this conspiracy to the world in another illegal tract, *An Account of the Growth of Popery and Arbitrary Government in England*, published in late 1677. In this widely distributed tract, Marvell wove the government's increasingly authoritarian, arbitrary and pro-French conduct into a high-level plot to drive England into "French slavery and Roman idolatry." The conspirators would accomplish this goal by starting another civil war or by intimidating their opponents with the threat of one. Marvell never named the conspirators. But the leading candidates appeared to be the king's advisors, his now openly Catholic brother and heir to the throne James, duke of York, and possibly Charles himself.[24]

When he sounded this warning, Marvell was speaking not only for himself but for a growing faction in Parliament that in a couple of years would be called "Whigs," along with "fanatics," "Presbyterians," and, on occasion, "puritans." Many leading Whigs had been Presbyterian politicians at the time of the Civil War, and their intertwined religious and political goals remained the same now as they were then, and had been, off and on, for puritans since the sixteenth century: keep the monarch's power limited, reform the church, and fight popery. Circumstances had made many of them conformists, but they retained a strict puritan piety and had close relationships with nonconformist ministers.[25]

The existence of a hugely dangerous Catholic-leaning conspiracy was apparently confirmed when word broke in the late summer of 1678 of a Catholic plot to assassinate Charles II and plunge his kingdoms of England, Scotland, and Ireland into bloody chaos for France to pick off, bit by bit. As a result of this so-called Popish Plot, seemingly confirmed by a series of bizarre coincidences, dread of Catholicism swept the country, more intense than any that had been felt since 1641. Support for the Whigs swelled, thanks in part to extensive Whig demonstrations and propaganda, and Charles had no choice but to dissolve Parliament and call for new elections.[26]

From 1679 to 1681 he called three Parliaments. They were all dominated by the Whigs, they all quickly collided with Charles and were quickly dissolved, and they all shared three objectives. The first was to crush the Popish Plot. That goal had wide support until it slowly became obvious to everyone but the Whigs that the plot was the murderous fiction of a gifted, shameless liar, Titus Oates, a fiction that led to the execution of twenty-four innocent Catholics and the imprisonment of hundreds more.[27]

The second goal was to keep Charles's Catholic brother James off the throne when Charles died. Charles himself was willing to legislate strict limitations on James's power, but the Whigs had no confidence that these would be enforced; they insisted on excluding James from the throne. Charles regarded giving Parliament control over who became king equivalent to making England a republic, which he believed was the Whigs' real goal, and exclusion was thus unacceptable to him. This unbreakable deadlock has made "Exclusion Crisis" the blanket term for the whole controversy.[28]

The Whigs' third goal was to work out a scheme of comprehension (inclusion) in the Church of England for the Presbyterians and indulgence (toleration) for the rest of the nonconformists. In the fall of 1680, the second of these three Whig Parliaments met. This Parliament, meeting amid fears that Catholics would soon start murdering Protestants in their beds, kill the king, and burn London a second time, was the most hopeful for a wide range of puritans since the early 1640s. Bills for comprehension and indulgence were drawn up in the House of Commons and passed on to the House of Lords. Presbyterians by now generally accepted the inevitability of some form of Protestant religious pluralism. Nonetheless, most of them, along with the Congregationalists, still had grave doubts about whether Quakers were Christians, and there was heated debate before Quakers were included in the broad indulgence bill.[29]

The comprehension bill to put Presbyterian ministers back in their parish pulpits offered much to please them. Ministers gained control over the Lord's Supper and for them the surplice was gone. The ceremonies were optional and the hated parts of the Act of Uniformity were removed. Where the bill clearly fell short was that it did not allow them to pick and choose their way around the liturgy. That limitation itself seems to have been enough for most Presbyterians to conclude that indulgence outside the Church of England was preferable to this comprehension bill. Panicky Anglicans interpreted their lack of enthusiasm as meaning that with the Whigs in the ascendant, Presbyterians smelled Anglican blood. They were "so near the carrying all before them" that no more compromise was necessary.[30] Why go through any inconvenience to board the Church of England's sinking ship?

An Anglican observer who happened to be at New Hall, a large building near the center of Sheffield, on April 25, 1681 might well have surmised that Presbyterians were finally striking out on their own. The observer would have been incensed or alarmed to see that Oliver Heywood was brazenly leading an illegal ordination in public. Even more threatening was just how learned the young nonconformist candidate for ordination was. He passed a grilling by the assembled ministers in logic, philosophy, languages, and theology and held his own in a Latin disputation about infant baptism, yet he would never have set foot in one of England's two universities, Cambridge or Oxford—those institutions required the swearing of oaths unacceptable to nonconformists. Rather, the candidate was a product of one of the illegal so-called dissenting academies founded by ejected ministers in the 1660s. With a pipeline for producing new learned clergymen in place, Presbyterians and Congregationalists now had everything they needed to keep their churches running forever.[31]

The ordination might also have unsettled this Anglican observer as a show of puritan unity. It was being conducted by Heywood in a typical Presbyterian manner; the assembled ministers, not the congregation, determined the candidate's fitness for the ministry and ordained him. But it was, in fact, for a Congregational church. The candidate was Thomas Jollie's son Timothy, and participating alongside Heywood were Jollie and two other Congregationalist ministers. Jollie pushed his fellow Congregationalists hard to make this unusual ordination happen; Heywood called it "an olive-branch of peace amongst God's people," although a couple of church members had boycotted it.[32] Puritans were coming together, even as Presbyterians were pulling away from the Church of England.

But that new solidarity masked fundamental differences in Congregationalist and Presbyterian aspirations. A little over a year after this separatist expression of puritan unity, on the twentieth anniversary of Black Bartholomew's Day, Heywood's church met for a solemn day of fasting. They collectively lamented their two-decades-long "woeful, mournful separation from the public assemblies" and prayed for "our restoration."[33] With their churches and academies, the Presbyterians' severance from England's national, public church might have become sustainable, and even desirable unless the terms for return to Church of England pulpits were good, but that did not make it any less of a tragedy for them.

The lingering attraction of Presbyterians like Heywood to the Church of England elicited no sympathy from the Whigs' Anglican opponents, now called Tories. Instead, that undesirable attraction provided more material for a potent story the Tories were vigorously spreading about the causes of England's recent troubles. This concerned "the church-rending and nation-confounding puritan[s]" who were launching yet another assault on the English monarchy and the legal order of the Church of England, just as they had done with such devastating consequences in 1641. If the Whigs were not vigorously repressed, Tories warned, the country would slip back into illegal parliamentary tyranny and Presbyterianism, and in that chaos, the

Jesuits, who were the masterminds behind the nonconformists, would introduce Catholicism. There was no need to fear James, the Tories argued. He was of excellent character and had promised to protect the legal privileges of the Church of England. For the Tories, to truly save England from popery, nonconformity needed to be crushed once and for all. Also needing to be crushed was the destructive idea, propagated by Presbyterians and others in Queen Elizabeth's time, aggressively promoted during the Civil War by puritans, and now being spread again by the Whigs, that in England the monarch fundamentally shared power with Parliament. On the contrary, England was an absolute monarchy.[34]

The third and last Whig Parliament met briefly and unsuccessfully in March 1681. But even before it did, Whig hopes that they could prevent Charles's Catholic brother James from succeeding him were fading fast. Two months earlier, Charles had dissolved the second Whig Parliament before it had time to complete its puritan-friendly legislation. Oliver Heywood, responding to the news, wrote a gloomy memorandum listing all the evidence that England would soon lapse back into Catholicism. There was that second Parliament's failure; there was Charles's "arbitrary government," which was a "companion of popery"; there was the unreconstructed popery of the Church of England's government and ceremonies; and there were any number of prophetic signs of doom. "A late astonishing comet," Heywood noted, signaled impending disaster, as did the reports, "if true," of armies seen fighting in the sky.[35]

The Bible's end-times prophecies, too, seemed to predict an approaching English religious catastrophe. Heywood reasoned, like other nonconformists, that the Presbyterians' eighteen years of "exclusion" from the national church made it likely that they had been prophesied by the Book of Revelation's faithful two witnesses who preached God's truth in sackcloth. Revelation 11:7 prophesied that a dreadful beast rising from the bottomless pit would slay the witnesses, and that beast clearly represented the Catholic Church.[36]

Heywood soon received ample confirmation that his ominous reading of biblical prophecies was correct. The third Whig Parliament proved no more cooperative with Charles than the previous ones, and Charles dissolved it after a week. Louis XIV had started to provide him with a handsome secret subsidy, and by now he was satisfied that Tory sentiments among the population had swelled enough that he need neither fear the Whigs nor call a Parliament to ask it for money. Instead, his government threw its weight behind the "Tory Reaction," with the fervent support of most of the Church of England's clergy. During the Tory Reaction local governments were purged of Whigs and nonconformists and an unprecedentedly sustained repression of nonconformists was launched.[37]

The shock of this repression resonated across the country. Heywood was among the many nonconformists whose luck in avoiding legal trouble finally ran out, and in 1685 he began almost a year of imprisonment in York. There Heywood might have consoled himself by remembering that Revelation prophesied the eventual resurrection of the slain two witnesses and recalling what he had written in 1681 about the glorious time for Protestantism that would follow that resurrection. "Even in England," Heywood had predicted, God would finally "raise up faithful magistrates . . . [and] pastors" who together would "take away our heavy grievances in church and state."[38]

In heavily nonconformist Taunton, the Anglican mayor Stephen Timewell resolved to do his part for the Tory Reaction in early 1682 by cracking down on local nonconformist meetings. These meetings centered around the large meeting house built in 1672 by friends and followers of the late Joseph Alleine. Timewell was soon complaining of his inability to catch the Presbyterians in the act of worshiping at their meeting house, perhaps because of the vigilant nonconformists who patrolled the streets, allegedly armed with pistols.[39]

In the summer of 1683, Timewell took another tack. A mob, at his direction, stripped the Presbyterian meeting house of its roof and anything combustible and made a gigantic bonfire in the town marketplace. Parish church bells rang all night in celebration. "The church is now full . . . The fanatics dare not open their mouths," Timewell wrote exultantly to the secretary of state. Timewell moved on to breaking up conventicles in private houses. His campaign of repression was effective enough that local nonconformists started talking about armed resistance. The government suspected, but could not prove, that nonconformists from Taunton were involved in the 1683 Rye House Plot, a desperate Whig conspiracy to assassinate Charles and his brother James. In 1684 agents for the duke of Monmouth, the ostentatiously Protestant illegitimate son of Charles II, reported to Monmouth in the Netherlands that Taunton could provide men for the invasion he was planning against his father and Catholic uncle.[40]

Charles II died on February 6, 1685, after making a deathbed conversion to Catholicism. James was crowned at Westminster Abbey on April 23, to great enthusiasm across the nation, at least among the now-dominant Tories. On June 11, the duke of Monmouth landed about 25 miles south of

Taunton in a tiny, badly planned invasion, coordinated with an equally badly planned invasion of Scotland by the duke of Argyll to overthrow their new Catholic monarch.[41] Most Whigs would have nothing to do with the invasions, partly out of principle and partly because they rightly smelled disaster.

But across the West Country, a ragtag would-be army of Baptists, Congregationalists, and Presbyterians, including old Cromwellian officers, flocked to join the duke of Monmouth. They were eager to fight against popery for the "good old cause of God and religion," as a local Congregational church put it. The inhabitants of Taunton received the duke's 3,000-man army joyously. In the town's marketplace, Monmouth was proclaimed king before leading his men to their own slaughter against King James's smaller but much better trained and equipped army at nearby Sedgemoor. The ferocious royal judicial mopping-up that followed resulted in over 300 hangings, with nonconformist limbs, torsos, and heads subsequently dangling from trees all across Somerset, and hundreds more of Monmouth's soldiers sent for long terms of slavery in the Caribbean.[42]

Anglican enthusiasm for James, however, quickly dimmed. For years Anglicans had been defending his right to the throne, crying up the unaccountable authority of kings, and reassuring themselves that a Catholic king like James in a sea of Protestants could do no harm, especially since he told all and sundry that he would be a faithful protector of the Church of England. But James had neglected to share with Anglicans that his real, secret goal was to re-Catholicize England. Once on the throne, he wasted little time putting his agenda into action. He intruded Catholic officers into the army, opened up Catholic chapels across the country, forced Catholic masters on the two universities, tried to restrain Anglicans from preaching against Catholicism, and selected new Church of England bishops by their willingness to go along with his plan.[43]

Nonconformists got dragged into James's growing confrontation with the Church of England when James, switching gears from persecution, tried to build an alliance with them against the increasingly unhappy Anglicans. In April 1687, he issued his own Declaration of Indulgence suspending the penal laws against nonconformists and Catholics. Nonconformists were glad to be able to worship without harassment or fear. But, with some exceptions, they were suspicious of his motives, reluctant to send him the formal letters of gratitude that he wanted, and still more reluctant to acknowledge in those letters that it was within his power to dispense with the enforcement of laws. They were likewise leery, with some exceptions, of his scheme to remodel local governments for an upcoming parliamentary election in order to get MPs who would repeal the penal laws against nonconformists altogether.[44]

Out of these dark and confusing times came one unequivocally good development for nonconformists. James woke a significant mass of Anglicans up to the possibility that nonconformists might be more useful as friends than enemies. That awareness did more to persuade them of the merits of reaching out to nonconformists, at least the more religiously conservative nonconformists, than had all the treatises arguing for toleration written by nonconformists in the last couple of decades.[45]

The biggest conversion came as seven bishops, including the archbishop of Canterbury William Sancroft, defied James's order for their clergy to read the Declaration of Indulgence from the pulpit in May 1688. James sent the bishops to the Tower of London after they petitioned him against the order. Moderate Presbyterians had a series of meetings with leading churchmen. The Presbyterians concluded that supporting James in his assault against the bishops would amount to "separating from the English church," which had always been against Presbyterian principles. They decided to support the bishops, whom a jury refused to convict, to the rejoicing of the English nation. Seeing the bishops putting their personal liberty on the line in defiance of popery rejuvenated the Presbyterians' interest in comprehension, and Archbishop Sancroft started drawing up wide-ranging proposals to bring that about.[46]

For Anglicans, the only tolerable things left about James were that he had not produced a son, and that his daughters in the line of succession, Mary and Anne, were Protestant. He was in his mid-fifties, the age when his brother had died. Anglicans hoped they could sit him out and clean up the damage after he was gone. Those hopes were shattered by the birth of a son and heir on June 10, 1688. On June 30, seven leading Englishmen wrote to Mary's husband, the Presbyterian William of Orange, the Netherlands's *stadhouder* (the closest political office the Dutch republic had to a king). They promised the support of the vast majority of the people if he invaded England. When William's army landed on November 7, James's English support melted away and he fled the country. William was crowned monarch of England, alongside his wife Mary, on April 11, 1689. The deposition of King James forcibly settled once and for all the old puritan (but not only puritan) issues of whether English monarchs shared power with their subjects and, even more, whether those subjects could remove their monarchs.[47]

However, by this time puritanism was on its last legs. The national church had swung so far away from Calvinism, while hot Protestantism had fractured so entirely, that it would take enormous doses of self-delusion for a puritan to look in a mirror now and see reflected the old puritan self-image— the evangelical vanguard of what was, or could be made to be, a doctrinally united Calvinist Church of England, one in which all of England's people would worship each Sunday, like it or not. The collapse of doctrinal unity also dissolved the Congregationalists' hope for a national network of autonomous churches held together by a state-supported Calvinist national doctrine. Presbyterians themselves were trying out their own independent churches, something that would have been inconceivable before Parliament passed its reckless persecutory laws against nonconformists.

But that Presbyterian experiment in separation was not by choice, and most Presbyterians at least retained the old puritan aspiration of a state church with its government and ceremonies reformed to what they took to be New Testament standards. Once the Church of England was finally properly reformed, Richard Baxter wrote in 1684, those nonconformist churches like the Congregationalists' that still insisted on staying outside it would be nothing more than "hospitals for the sick," watched over by the government.[48] Presbyterians now had a bushelful of Anglican promises about reformation, while the English throne had sitting upon it what had hitherto been a figment of their wildest dreams: a Presbyterian. They thus had good reason to think themselves closer to the core puritan aspiration of a properly reformed Church of England than ever before.

# CHAPTER 18

# RELIGIOUS PLURALISM COMES TO PURITAN NEW ENGLAND

The Massachusetts General Court met in a somber and anxious mood on Wednesday, September 12, 1666. As was customary, ministers gave extensive guidance to this assembly of magistrates, elected from the colony's leading men, and deputies, elected from each town. The court spent the morning listening to six ministers extemporizing long prayers and the afternoon asking their advice on state matters. The Thursday lecture sermon took up the next morning.[1] Finally, after a day and a half of religious guidance, the court was ready to debate a momentous question that struck close to the heart of puritanism: when godliness and obedience to the monarch clashed, what were puritans to do?

That recurring puritan dilemma was staring these puritans in the face because they had repeatedly disobeyed Charles II's representatives when four of them had appeared on Massachusetts soil two years earlier. The representatives were there to establish once and for all to these rebels and schismatics that obeying their monarch was not a choice.[2]

The representatives' visits to the other New England colonies went smoothly, for those colonies had everything to gain and nothing to lose by playing up their obedience. Plymouth was a squatter colony desperately trying to acquire a royal charter that would make it legal, and it treated the visiting commissioners obsequiously. Connecticut gave the commissioners the same welcome. It had finally received a royal charter in 1662, but its land claims clashed with newly conquered New York's, now the possession of Charles's brother James, and it needed all the support it could get.

Massachusetts, by far the largest and wealthiest colony and the one most defiantly protective of its distinctive form of puritanism, was the real prize. The General Court relentlessly stonewalled the commissioners. There would be no oath of allegiance to the king unadulterated by reference to the Massachusetts charter and no freedom of worship for the Anglicans who were starting to arrive in its bustling port towns ("it will disturb our peace," the court explained). The godly franchise ensuring that only Congregationalists could elect the colony's leaders would remain intact— with the very slight concession that exceptionally wealthy men who were approved by a local minister could also vote.[3] When the royal commissioners tried to strike at the heart of Massachusetts's autonomy and set up an appeals court in Boston, the General Court forbade colonists to attend.

Now in 1666 the court was convened because it had received a very angry letter from Charles. He demanded that five men come immediately to England to answer for the court's treatment of his servants. Charles warned that he expected "full obedience." He specified two magistrates by name, Governor Richard Bellingham and William Hathorne, whom the commissioners had singled out for their disloyalty. This was the supreme test for Massachusetts's theocracy. Would they continue to insist, even in the face of royal wrath, that they had no obligations to Charles II except the ones outlined in their charter: giving the Crown 5 percent of their non-existent gold and silver ore and making no law repugnant to the laws of England? (They defined "repugnant" very loosely.) And that, therefore, they had no obligation to send the men to Charles?[4]

As far as a majority of the magistrates were concerned, both God and law were on their side. Hathorne made a legal argument that puritans had been making for a century in their struggle with the bishops and the monarch—the king's "prerogative [i.e., rights and privileges] is not above law, but limited by it." Therefore, the king had to abide by the charter. Francis Willoughby, the deputy governor, reminded the magistrates of their religious obligations: "We must as well consider God's displeasure as the king's."[5] Theirs was the traditional defiant Massachusetts view, the one that had prompted the General Court in the 1630s to build up the colony's fortifications when threatened by Archbishop Laud.

But now some magistrates were prepared to argue the opposite. The king's prerogative overrode the charter's terms, they insisted, and the magistrates must go to England. Simon Bradstreet threw in another pragmatic concern of these magistrates. The merchants who traded with England "are afraid that they will suffer there, if nothing be done," he warned. Backing up Bradstreet was a petition signed by 135 men from four Massachusetts port towns where mercantile interests predominated. The prevalent anti-monarchical interpretation of the charter was "doubtful," as the petition bluntly and correctly pointed out. And since it was false, Massachusetts had neither the legal nor religious right to defy Charles. By clinging to this doubtful interpretation, the petitioners warned, also correctly, the General Court risked losing all the liberties that the colony enjoyed.[6]

Some of the people who signed the petition were church members, and one was a former speaker of the Court of Deputies. Others, though, blended with a godly commonwealth as poorly as oil with water. There was the merchant and land speculator Thomas Breedon, for example, resident in Massachusetts only to make money. When he returned from London in 1662 fashionably and unpuritanically clothed in a strange four-cornered hat and trousers bedecked with ribbons, children in the streets hooted and called him a devil. In London, Breedon had given a blistering account to the king's ministers of Massachusetts's disloyalty, and he had urged Charles to take it over. On his return, Breedon found himself fined and imprisoned for his disloyalty, insolence, and contempt. But puritan friends and business partners, who included Connecticut's governor, John Winthrop, Jr., bailed Breedon and paid his fine. The unrepentant Breedon had housed Charles's commissioners in Boston.[7] He would try to destroy puritan New England; his puritan friends would attempt in their different ways to preserve it; and in the meantime they would build their fortunes together in the fast-growing, slavery-driven Atlantic economy.

The magistrates narrowly agreed with the deputies from the towns that the General Court should stand its ground against Charles. It would send no one, but as a goodwill gesture, it would make Charles a present of two fine New England masts for the Royal Navy. Yet even that gesture was controversial. Some people regarded the gift as too deferential, others as not deferential enough, and the court had problems raising money to pay for it.[8]

Neither the colony's defiance nor its internal divisions had cost it anything yet; the disastrous war with the Netherlands and a major shake-up of Charles's ministers distracted the king's attention from Massachusetts for the time being (see p. 212). But this bitter quarrel, extending to the heart of the colony's government, immediately played into a sometimes convulsive process that within a decade would drag New England's puritans to a grudging, hitherto unthinkable acceptance of limited religious toleration.

*  *  *

For many in New England, the quarrel over the relationship with the king was one more sign of the region's spiritual declension. New England's spiritual glory was fading, as could be easily seen by this and other bitter disagreements among the saints, declining church membership, and a general slackening of zeal. God was abandoning the region, or soon might, and he was sending New England sharp tokens of his wrath, including steeply declining crop yields (the region's bug population had exploded, thanks to the feasts provided by the colonists' monoculture agriculture, but that cause-and-effect relationship eluded the colonists).[9]

In New Haven, this spiritual declension stared one of New England's most prominent ministers, John Davenport, hard in the face in the early 1660s. Davenport and the wealthy London merchants who immigrated with him in 1637 had intended to make their colony a great commercial trading center, prosperous enough to have its own college to add to the luster of its exemplarily strict godly government. But its location did not meet its purposes, and the colony withered into provincial obscurity, too poor even to afford the college. Its last jewel, its godly government, disappeared when Connecticut gobbled up the colony by arranging for expanded boundaries in its 1662 royal charter.[10]

It was not only his own colony's decline that ate away at Davenport. For him, the most lethal symptom of New England's declension was the novel push to lower the protective walls around the Congregational churches by expanding baptism, as affirmed by the 1662 Massachusetts synod. Allowing the children of church members to have their own children baptized without first leaping the high hurdles of church membership would, the synod hoped, reverse the alarming decline in membership (see p. 186). But that reversal, opponents like Davenport insisted, came at the cost of polluting the churches with ungodly members and throwing away the churches' hard-won separation from the wickedness of the world. For "strict" Congregationalists like Davenport, the "large" Congregationalists, as they were called, were leaving New England's "ancient paths, to comply with old England, in their corruptions." New England, Davenport wrote to his regional network of strict Congregationalists, would soon feel God's wrath if it did not repent for this transgression.[11]

From his backwater, Davenport's thoughts inevitably turned to Massachusetts, where the struggle against English corruption was still political as well as religious. God himself had an interest in Massachusetts's charter, Davenport wrote to the Massachusetts magistrate John Leverett in 1665 in a letter supporting the General Court's firm stand against the royal commissioners, "and he will be with you while you are with him." The strict Congregationalists' expansive dread of England's religious corruptions made them more likely than large Congregationalists to support Massachusetts's resistance to the king's political demands.[12]

In 1667, members of Boston's First Church wrote to Davenport with immensely encouraging prospects. Their church's founding minister John Wilson had just died, leaving the church without ministers. The church had committed to expanding baptism, but largely as a courtesy to its ministers Wilson and John Norton, who had died in 1663; it had not actually put it into practice. Now a majority of the laymen wanted to make Davenport their minister, do a complete turn-around on baptism, and reverse this decline into England's corruptions.[13]

The hitch was that a substantial minority among the church's laity neither wanted to reverse course nor have Davenport as their minister. The majority went ahead anyway, as did Davenport. Congregational churches ran on consensus, and more than a few dissident men should have been enough to stop the proceedings. The fact that it did not left the dissidents feeling that their church had been hijacked, and they wished to leave it. But you could only leave a Congregational church properly, in New England as well as old, if the church dismissed you. First Church refused to do that, even after a council of churches it called in November 1667 for advice recommended this course of action. The council also recommended that the dissidents start their own church, for Boston's population had far outstripped the size of its two meeting houses.[14]

One would not need to practice astrology (which, according to puritans, worked when it did only because of demonic intervention) to predict that this deadlocked situation was not going to end well. The dissidents finally walked out in April 1668 without a dismissal, after taking the precaution of calling a second council of churches on their own. The council affirmed that Congregationalism, properly understood, granted them the right to leave. That same year a majority of magistrates gave them the legal green light needed to set up their own Boston church. Davenport and First Church, though, insisted that they were still members: as such, the second council had lacked the spiritual right to even listen to them; they had no spiritual right to set up their own church; the magistrates had no legal right to give them permission; and the members of all three groups had grievously sinned because of their actions. A protracted controversy within this swelling controversy followed when First Church refused to dismiss the dissident men's wives to join the new church, and they left anyway.[15]

In itself, this dispute was nothing but an intense church squabble caused by an unlikely line up of circumstances, personalities, and principles. "The like may not be seen in an age," noted the minister who replaced Davenport in his pulpit, John Oxenbridge, after things had calmed down (Davenport died in March 1670). But in the heat of the moment, the quarrel grew at explosive speed. For Davenport and his partisans, the quarrel shined a flood of light on the large Congregationalists' unprecedented betrayal of New England principles. If First Church wanted to keep hugging its dissident members with their dangerously corrupt ideas about baptism tight to itself where they could do no damage, it was its God-given Congregationalist right to do so. And the fact that other churches actually encouraged these members to illicitly leave and that magistrates allowed these unrepentant sinners to create their own corrupt church demonstrated how determined the large Congregationalists were to subvert Congregationalism.[16]

What was truly horrifying about the large Congregationalists in this organic, consensual society, where unity was expected to prevail and dissidents had always been a small minority, was that there were so many of them. Large Congregationalism was a disease that could kill Massachusetts, a "corrupting gangrene," and an "infecting, spreading plague," as a jaw-dropping 1670 report by the General Court's deputies called it. It was "threatening the ruin of our foundations," the report went on. Its proponents, most of Massachusetts's ministers and over half of its magistrates, were no better than the tyrannical bishops who had been left behind in England. They were exercising "a lordly, prelatical power over God's heritage."[17] "Let us walk by the same rule and be of one mind," the deputies concluded this angry, fevered threnody for a lost, unified New England. The General Court's deliberations were supposed to be confidential, but the deputies circulated their inflammatory papers against the large Congregationalists outside the court in order to do maximum damage to the large Congregationalists' wicked plans.[18]

In the 1671 election, the people gave their verdict on their deputies' angry quest to return to New England's old single-minded times before the rise of large Congregationalism. They saw a disastrous confrontation ahead between large and strict Congregationalist partisans and wanted no part of it. More than half of the strict Congregationalist hotheads were voted out of office. With this change of direction, large Congregationalist ministers, furious about the attack on them, saw their own chance to make Massachusetts of one mind again. They sent a petition to the court denouncing strict Congregationalism and asking the court to call a new synod or public disputation to settle the issue of baptism once and for all.[19]

But these new deputies wanted to pull the government out of the flames of church quarrels, not thrust it in deeper. The majority did vote to take back all the nasty things the last court had said about the large Congregationalist ministers. But it also ignored the ministers' harsh words about strict Congregationalism and their request for a new debate about baptismal standards. As far as the government was concerned, if the churches of Christ could no longer agree on what the biblical qualifications for baptism were, they were going to have to finally learn the virtues of tolerating each other. Strict Congregationalists at least had the satisfaction of seeing all this contention, unprecedented in its scale, effectively put a damper on the desire of any more churches to stoke the fires of controversy by adopting large Congregationalism.[20]

Yet even the strict Congregationalists knew that the idealized days of organic unity were over in Massachusetts. In 1665, seven men and two women, some recent immigrants and some longstanding local church members, satisfied themselves that the Bible restricted baptism to believing adults. In order to obey this scriptural command, they gathered a Baptist church, the first in Massachusetts, in a house in Charlestown. Would God allow the colony to survive "so dangerous a malady?" the General Court asked. It answered itself by fining and imprisoning them.[21]

But the court only fined and imprisoned the stubborn Baptists intermittently. It had to pull its punches because by the 1660s, the weight of public opinion was shifting against its old-school puritan intolerance. Many strict Congregationalists flocked to defend the Baptists, including John Davenport. If Massachusetts could survive the large Congregationalists' dangerously corrupt ideas about baptism, their argument went, then it could survive these non-confrontational Baptists. Baptists organized their churches pretty much like Congregationalists, though they were much more relaxed about unlearned ministers and lay preaching, and if they erred by confining baptism to believers, at least they erred on the side of purity, unlike the large Congregationalists. Prominent English Congregationalists, too, weighed in by letter to protest against this persecution. A short way down Massachusetts Bay, Plymouth colony was demonstrating that Baptists and Congregationalists could co-exist, at least given some distance. In 1668, it allowed Baptists who had disruptively and illegally gathered a church at Rehoboth the previous year to form their own town, Swansea, with the crucial understanding that Swansea's Baptist church would tolerate members who believed in infant baptism. But in Massachusetts, it was not until the former New Model Army officer John Leverett became governor in 1673 that the half-hearted persecution of

Baptists tapered off. In 1674, the Baptists were grudgingly allowed by the magistrates to worship privately in Boston, and another old Massachusetts puritan line in the sand was washed away.[22]

In Connecticut, there were no Baptists to complicate disputes over baptism. What Connecticut did have, besides strict and large Congregationalists, was a few Presbyterian-leaning ministers and dissatisfied laity who pushed for lower standards of admission and baptism in their towns. In 1669, Connecticut's General Court, after an abortive effort to weigh in on the controversy on the side of the Presbyterian-leaners, washed its hands of it entirely. It declared that any doctrinally orthodox group could organize their church in whatever way seemed best to them. With this unmistakable official green light for expanding baptism, large Congregationalism rapidly took off. Connecticut churches drifted into a wide variety of practices later given the portmanteau name of "presbygationalism."[23]

Even the Quakers were finding their own niche in puritan New England. On both sides of the Atlantic by the late 1660s, Quakers' unbounded enthusiasm for exhibitionist, disruptive, and aggressive missionizing had faded as it became clear that the religious darkness of the puritans and other Protestants around them was remarkably, if inexplicably, impenetrable by the Quakers' apocalyptic inner light. Massachusetts puritans, in turn, were learning grudgingly to tolerate Quakers; the more time that passed without any Quaker neighbors, relatives, or business associates hearing the murderous inner voices suspected by fearful puritans that would command them to rise up and massacre everyone else, the less urgent the repression of this tiny, but very tenacious group seemed. In the 1670s, except for one brief period, the worst that Quakers faced from magistrates were occasional and mostly token fines for absence from Congregational church services.[24]

This acceptance of de facto toleration for pushy fellow Protestants was more a surrender to social realities than a change of principles. In 1679, a synod of Massachusetts churches denounced the small number of local Quakers and Baptists as being among the "evils of the times" that were bringing God's wrath down on New England and called for the laws against them to be once again enforced. Ministers continued to preach against religious toleration for fellow Protestants up until the final crisis of Massachusetts's charter in the mid-1680s, when decisions about toleration were taken out of local hands.[25]

# CHAPTER 19

# NEW ENGLAND'S REFORMATIONS
# COME OF AGE

Lancaster, Massachusetts came into existence when twenty families covenanted together in 1652 to create a town, with the General Court's permission, on the western edge of English settlement. They had purchased the land from a group of Englishmen who had purchased it from Shaumauw, the sachem of the Nashaways, in 1643. As the General Court expected, the second, successful group of settlers agreed not to admit anyone to the town who was impious or "notoriously erring" in religion, or disloyal to Massachusetts's government. And as the General Court also insisted, they agreed to build a meeting house and support a "godly minister."[1]

Lancaster found its minister in 1654: Joseph Rowlandson, Harvard's only 1652 graduate. The previous generation of Massachusetts ministers had studied at great English universities and had built up experience and reputations before immigrating, often with followers and admirers. The ministers who succeeded them, like Rowlandson, were young men from an undistinguished provincial college, with no background of heroic puritan struggle to justify salaries that swallowed up a town's budget and put them in the wealthiest 15 percent of colonists. As happened to many other ministers of Rowlandson's generation, Lancaster dragged its feet about making his position permanent. He called their bluff in 1658 when he informed them of an offer from another town.[2]

That same year, Lancaster built its meeting house, undoubtedly an unadorned, barn-like building. Its dark interior would probably only have had a single, unglazed window, shuttered in wintertime to prevent drafts. Glass and more windows would come later, as would pews to replace the long benches. Women and children would sit on one side, men on the other.[3]

It was not until 1660 that there were enough visible saints in Lancaster to gather a church. The communal, fresh-off-the-boat puritan zeal of the earliest decades of settlement was starting to fade, and if Lancaster's new church was like others at this time, candidates for admission might have been able to give their conversion narratives privately to the church elders and then have them read to the congregation. Church members would have been more willing than before to clog up church discipline with petty and personal disputes. Rowlandson would not have enjoyed as much deference from his congregation as had first-generation ministers. But he probably would not have had to share his executive powers with a lay elder since lay men were increasingly reluctant to take on this demanding job.[4]

Perhaps Lancaster was among the towns that were starting the soon-to-be-ubiquitous practice of assigning meeting-house seating, as in the English parish churches. The formula always involved some combination of age, wealth, and honors or office holding. Rowlandson, up front in his simple pulpit, was in the top rank of the town's social hierarchy as a minister. He was the only man in the town to bear the honorific "Mister" before his name, a title that only the highest ranks of Massachusetts men enjoyed. Sitting up near him would have been the family of Lancaster's wealthiest land owner, John White. It was fitting that Mr. Rowlandson had already married White's daughter Mary in 1656, for in New England a minister was always a suitable addition to a wealthy family.[5] Mary White thereby automatically received the rare honorific "Mistress" along with her new last name.

Mrs. Rowlandson had arrived as an infant in the farming and port town of Salem in 1639. There land was already getting so scarce that her father's grant of land was 6 miles away from the town center. No record exists of John ever joining a church. His wife Joan joined the Salem church on February 26, 1643. From the beginning of the colony women went through the ordeal of becoming members in greater proportion than men, and the imbalance grew steadily during the century. Joan doubtless saw to it that her children were well acquainted with the Bible, which was certainly among the few books in the White household. In 1645, Joan transferred her church membership to the new church in Wenham, a town that had been carved out of their part of Salem. In Wenham, Mary went to Pastor John Fiske's house on Tuesdays, where Fiske would have drilled her and the other children in the catechism to make sure their basic doctrinal understanding was sound, and probed them on what they had learned from his sermon on Sunday.[6]

Soon, Mary Rowlandson had four children. She later shared her warm memories of how her large extended family and their neighbors would gather at her house on Saturday evenings for dinner, prayer and psalm singing, as English puritans had been doing for a century. On Sunday evenings, after the long morning and afternoon church services, family, friends, neighbors, and a Native American servant would gather for more prayers and psalms, and a sermon review.[7]

The only thing that Mary Rowlandson found seriously wrong with her puritan-legacy life in Lancaster was there was so little wrong with it. Other people whose piety seemed greater than hers, Rowlandson worriedly observed, struggled with poverty, sickness, and other afflictions. Rowlandson brooded over the ominous words of Hebrews 12:6: "For whom the Lord loveth, he chasteneth." She wondered if this lack of divine chastening attention meant that God did not love her and that the satisfactions of this life would be more than made up for by the eternal torments of the next.[8]

In 1675, Rowlandson would find herself drenched in God's chastening attention, as would New England as a whole. A war would break out with Native Americans that would ravage Massachusetts's Christian communities, Native American and English alike, and drastically accelerate the English movement toward large Congregationalism, even as the Christian Native Americans' own reformation was reaching maturity.

The previous year, Waban and other Praying Indians had repeatedly warned their fellow Christians that the Wampanoag sachem Metacomet, or King Philip, was about to turn violently on Plymouth colony, which had been treating him with sustained, heavy-handed disrespect while eating away at his tribe's land. Their warnings went unheeded, and what could have been a small, contained war then flared up into a regional conflagration as the English colonists treated neutral and even allied Native Americans with suspicion and yet more heavy-handed disrespect, driving many Native Americans, including some Christians, to side with King Philip. At some point, the Rowlandsons' Native American servant seems to have joined them.[9]

The colonists had seen no war with the Native Americans for almost forty years and had no idea what they were in for. Demography encouraged complacency. Disease and dislocation had reduced the Native American population to around eighteen thousand, while the English population had grown to around sixty thousand.[10] But the highly mobile Native Americans' deadly hit-and-run raids caught the ill-trained English militias completely unprepared. Towns soon started going up in flames all the way to Maine.

Lancaster's turn came in the early morning of February 11, 1676, while Joseph Rowlandson was in Boston seeking troops for his town. Shortly before, a neighboring Praying Indian, James Quanapohit, had shared information gathered at the risk of his life about a planned raid on Lancaster, but he had been ignored. Native Americans laid siege to Mary Rowlandson's well-fortified, crowded house for two hours. If the siege was anything like others in this war, the Native Americans would have mocked the defenders' desperate prayers and shouted "Now see how your God delivers you!" Finally, the Native Americans got close enough to set the house on fire and force the defenders out. Twelve people from the house died, including Mary Rowlandson's sister and baby, while twenty-four others were carried off by different groups of Native Americans to captivity.[11]

Mary Rowlandson spent eleven weeks as a captive before being ransomed, frequently on the move and, like her captors, frequently close to starvation. What would have been in any case a harrowing emotional crisis, was for Rowlandson also a deeply spiritual one. Why was God putting her through this ordeal?

Introspection was the first step to finding an answer. God had to have a reason, and, inevitably, that reason had to do with Rowlandson's sinfulness. Her conscience, she found, did not accuse her of unrighteousness to anyone (more critical puritans might have raised their eyebrows at such a complacent claim). The wickedness that Rowlandson discovered and was willing to share with the readers of the manuscript she later wrote, was more routine than revealing. She had used her time carelessly, a frequent snare for the godly, so out went her tobacco habit; the devil laid it as bait to make people lose their precious time, she now realized. Also routine was Rowlandson's realization that she had been careless in her observance of the Sabbath, a day so relentlessly stringent that, in principle, even dreams were supposed to be pious. For that sin alone, it would have been entirely righteous of God to cut off her life and send her to hell.[12]

Rowlandson, to her relief, soon discovered that, despite her sins, God had not abandoned her in her captivity. When her badly wounded six-year-old daughter finally died, she entreated God to send her a sign of comfort. In swift succession, her son visited from a neighboring Native American encampment with news that her other daughter was also alive, and then a Native American returning from a raid on an English town gave her a Bible he had plundered. When Rowlandson opened up the Bible, apparently at random, God repeatedly had her eyes land on appropriate Old Testament verses; the experience of such divine guidance was common for godly people who knew their Bibles well. She read those verses in the standard puritan manner she had learned from family, friends, and ministers. Since Rowlandson was one of God's people and God was unchanging, what God had said to his people thousands of years ago was no less applicable to her. Happily, the verses mostly delivered the same message: God was sending her these afflictions, but he would also deliver her from them. Rowlandson marveled at God's goodness in bringing her so many comforting scriptures in her distress.[13]

Finally ransomed and reunited with her family, and with no Lancaster to return to, Rowlandson and her family were housed by well-heeled Boston friends until Joseph received a new pulpit in Connecticut. Life returned to a semblance of normality. But late at night while her family lay sleeping, Rowlandson would lie awake, thinking of her experiences and weeping. What ran through her mind, or at least what she shared in her manuscript for the benefit of friends and family (its admirers finally decided to publish it in 1682), were the exemplary religious insights she gleaned from her travails: the power, might, and love of God carrying her through all her troubles, the transitory nature of the things of this world, and how God alone could be depended upon. Most of all, she had discovered that whatever trouble God led his saints into, he would carry them through, and make them the better for it.[14] These were all standard discoveries that ministers taught the godly to make from their afflictions, but Rowlandson did not seek original insights. The point for her was that having lived those truisms, she could affirm them to others out of her own experience, as was her godly responsibility.

Many of the Christians who endured the horrors of King Philip's War lacked a soft landing like Rowlandson's. "We do, with all thankfulness, acknowledge God's great goodness to us, in preserving us alive to this day," was how Waban, the very old leader of the Praying Indian town of Natick (see p. 197), accurately summarized the extent of what God did for the Praying Indians during the conflict. At the war's beginning, Waban's Praying Indians fought alongside the English, but prejudice quickly pushed them out. They spent most of the war forcibly interned under miserable conditions on a barren island in Boston harbor—the terrified, hostile, and contemptuous English were mostly incapable of distinguishing between friendly and enemy Native Americans. While the Praying Indians were interned, their English neighbors plundered their town. Praying Indians fought again at the end of the war, after it finally dawned on the English that they needed Native American fighting techniques to fight Native Americans.[15]

The war would leave the Massachusetts Praying Indians confined to four much shrunken towns, while Native American numbers dwindled from 25 percent of New England's population to around 10 percent as a result of the fighting. Waban came to the end of his very long life around 1685. Perhaps family, friends and members of his community placed pipes, beads, and other traditional Native American grave goods in his coffin, as was the custom with many Natick Praying Indian burials.[16]

As Native American Christianity declined in Massachusetts, it was putting down roots in relatively peaceful areas south of the colony. On the Native American-majority island of Martha's Vineyard, the Native American church's officers, ordained in 1670, were all Native Americans, including the minister, a first in the Americas. English settlers who understood the local language took the Lord's Supper there when there was no English pastor on the island. The Martha's Vineyard Native Americans evangelized neighboring Nantucket Island, which had an all-Native American church by 1674. Around Plymouth and Cape Cod a few English ministers and laymen and Native American lay preachers and school teachers expanded missionary work after the war, as did the Vineyard Native Americans. The English charity the New England Company continued to provide financial support for Native American Christianity. All this activity, increasingly Native American initiated and directed, was creating new post-tribal Native American Christian networks and providing new survival skills for dealing with the fast encroaching English.[17]

In the decades after King Philip's War, it would become possible for well-situated Native Americans to pursue lives of piety in their own language much like those of their English neighbors. On exceptionally well-documented Martha's Vineyard, Christian Native American families and friends engaged in prayer, scripture reading, and psalm singing, along with spiritual discussion, counseling and exhortation. Some Native Americans, both male and female, were especially admired for their praying abilities, and Native Americans noted, like the English, when God appeared to answer their prayers. Particularly edifying deaths might be written down for posterity; one woman's apparition appeared to her father after he failed to transcribe her dying exhortations, as she had requested. Literate Native Americans read godly books—published in their own language by John Eliot's printing press—"with delight," and wrote comments and reflections in them. Some Native Americans attended sermons with Eliot Bibles at hand, to check the preacher's scripture references. Native Americans applying for church membership gave their conversion relations with much emotion and at length. Like the English, many apparently genuine Native American Christians hesitated to offer themselves for membership out of fear that they were not worthy. Native American godly magistrates campaigned against sin in their communities, and, as with the English, those campaigns could be resented by their neighbors. And like the English, by the 1690s, the Wampanoag Christians had splintered into Congregational and Baptist churches, with disagreements about how much toleration they should show each other.[18]

The Native Americans' piety had its own cultural inflections. In the absence of a learned ministry, rising in church ranks depended on communal approbation, much as it could among the Baptists. A church might ask a man particularly vigorous in reproving sin to be a ruling lay elder. A church member given to exhorting his neighbors might become a lay preacher whose task was to preach to outlying Native American settlements, a position without counterpart in the English churches. Native American churches chose their indigenous clergy with input from the New England Company, but they did not hesitate to ignore that input. On Martha's Vineyard, and probably elsewhere, churches celebrated days of thanksgiving with communal feasts sponsored by the most prosperous Native Americans, while on days of fasting, leading laymen prayed, as well as the pastor. At least on Nantucket, when a service was over, the Native Americans would pass a pipe of tobacco around and say "I thank you."[19]

"It was God that sent [the English]," the Martha's Vineyard pastor Japeth Hannit explained to his fellow Wampanoags in 1684, "that they might bring the gospel to us." But even on Martha's Vineyard, the Englishman's gospel was accompanied by grinding collateral damage: racism, poverty, debt, alcoholism, internal political turmoil, and demographic collapse. There were perhaps 3,500 Native Americans on Martha's Vineyard in 1640; there were around 800 in 1720.[20]

King Philip's War ended, as puritans noticed at the time, only after Plymouth colony pulled out new spiritual heavy artillery. Throughout the war the colonies' governments called for days of humiliation, on which the churches would fast, lament their members' sins and those of New England, and implore God to cease their well-deserved punishment. God's response to these days of humiliation was, it appeared, demoralizingly erratic. As a consequence, in June 1676, Plymouth's General Court instructed all the colony's churches to set another day of humiliation, this time deploying the rarely used but much more thorough ceremony of covenant renewal.[21]

In Plymouth town, July 18 was the day for its church to renew the covenant made by its founders and taken by all subsequent members when they joined. After a morning of pastor John Cotton, Jr.'s praying and preaching, ruling lay elder Thomas Cushman delivered a long prayer. He then read out a covenant renewal statement for the church's full members to affirm. It listed the many sinful ways they had strayed from the covenant—slackness at church services, slackness in keeping the Sabbath, slackness in family government, and slackness in keeping up "brotherly love and holy watch-fulness" with each other, among other sins. The paper acknowledged the justice of God's punishment of them and vowed reformation and renewal of their covenant. Then Cushman, Cotton, and all the full church members, including the women, stood up to show their affirmation of the statement and thus their recommitment to the ideals of the original pact between the church and God.[22]

Pastor Cotton then spoke for the children of the church who had yet to take the church's covenant themselves. Through Cotton, they affirmed that they had violated the covenant that God made with them through their parents by not embracing Jesus as their savior. They agreed, Cotton read out, that they were "descended of a noble vine, yet become the degenerate plant"—that imagery of declension, from the Old Testament prophet Jeremiah, was wildly popular in New England. They agreed, too, that they had a "deep hand" in bringing the wrath of God down on the colony. Their many sins ranged from irreverence during the very long church services to misspending their "precious time in idleness and sensuality." Those children who had families of their own acknowledged their failures of family government. Through Cotton, all the children affirmed their "interest in the covenant of the Lord God of our fathers" and vowed to "endeavor a thorough reformation." The children then all stood up to show their consent to what Cotton had read out. The covenant renewal allowed them to demonstrate in public for the first time before their parents and to the watching townspeople their commitment to the church and to the ideals of "their fathers'" covenant.[23]

The result of the colony's reaffirmations of its church covenants was dramatic and quick. "Immediately," as John Cotton put it in the church's record book, "God turned his hand against our heathen enemies." Less than a month later, Philip was killed and, Cotton added, his head "was brought into Plymouth in great triumph." There it stayed on a tall pole for decades until it disappeared; Native Americans may have removed it for a proper, secret burial.[24]

The cause and effect lesson of covenant renewal was obvious to the Congregationalists. The saints of New England had been erroneously wrapped up in the purity of their churches, focusing all their efforts on keeping others from sullying that purity, including their own children. But as far as God was concerned, the saints and sinners of New England were all connected, and the wrath God expressed in King Philip's War showed the consequences of the saints turning their backs on the sinners in the extreme way of the strict Congregationalists. It had left seventeen of the region's roughly eighty towns charred ruins, over fifty severely damaged, and the colonies over their heads in debt and dislocation (war with Native Americans on the Maine frontier continued until 1678).[25]

The saints took that spiritual lesson to heart. The churches must reach out to the sinners all around them if they wanted God to bless them. The use of covenant renewals, like the ones in Plymouth colony, gradually spread, allowing the children of the churches to affirm their connection to them.[26]

An even more expansive way to reach out was for the churches to make it easier for their children to baptize their own children by adopting large Congregationalism. Large Congregationalism had been hitherto expanding at a glacial pace in Massachusetts, but it picked up rapidly after the disaster of King Philip's War. After 1675, new churches commonly started as large Congregationalist and many older churches adopted it. By the early 1690s, large Congregationalism had been adopted by three quarters of the Massachusetts churches. Some churches extended their reach even further than the synod of 1662 recommended. They used large Congregationalism's less intimidating interrogation standards for the church's children to admit people with no previous connection to their churches who wanted their children baptized.[27]

In a final step at casting the churches' spiritual nets widely, a 1679 Massachusetts synod approved ministers baptizing the children of people who could pass minimum muster as Christians, even if they belonged to no church. This practice, too, spread widely, despite it clashing with two fundamental Congregationalist principles: ministers had no special spiritual powers outside their own congregation, and laity had no sacramental privileges except through their membership in a congregation. Those tight, exclusionary principles had been firmly laid down in Massachusetts in 1630 when the Winthrop fleet's members were denied the sacraments at the Salem church (see p. 86), yet if there was any resistance five decades later to gutting them, it has left no trace.[28]

In some churches the influx of people taking the covenant under large Congregationalism was substantial. Many of these new covenant-takers, however, did not attempt to jump the higher hurdles required for the Lord's Supper, either out of spiritual timorousness, fearing that they would eat and drink their own damnation if they were not really among the saved (see p. 69), or because their current level gave them what they wanted from church membership for themselves and their children. It became common to take the church covenant around the time of marriage, making it as much a routine post-puritan lifecycle ritual as it was the fruit of soul-searching and an expression of commitment to the church.[29]

Most of the full communicants in the churches were women. The ratio of females to males in a church could be two to one or even greater, another change from early Congregationalism. Women, ministers suggested, were less entangled with the cares of secular business than men and, through the perils of childbirth, were compelled to contemplate their own deaths on a regular basis. Historians have suggested that men, once the initial communal zeal of settlement had passed, would have been more uncomfortable with the total self-abnegating submission to Christ insisted upon by the ministers, and less interested in the cleric-dominated church environment.[30]

The promoters of this church membership expansion believed that as long as an inner core of saints kept their hands on the churches' tillers and alone took the Lord's Supper, the churches would preserve their intended purity and not risk capsizing from all the new ballast they had taken on board. In fact, in this new wave of evangelical energy, even the steady shrinkage in members in full communion finally reversed itself, even though it did not keep up proportionately with population growth.[31] With all their new members scattered among many families, the drift of the New England churches away from the larger communities around them had been stopped. Those churches started out in the 1630s as sharp, exclusionary, puritan protests against old England's inclusive parish churches, while trying to maintain the same spiritual monopoly in their communities that the English parish churches enjoyed. Now they were deep into the process of making themselves over, as far as they were going to, into post-puritan equivalents of those parish churches.

# CHAPTER 20

# NEW ENGLAND'S PURITAN AUTONOMY ENDS

In 1676, Edward Randolph, busy carving out a niche for himself in England's expanding colonial civil service, arrived in Massachusetts. He came to the colony not to confront its leaders as rebels and fanatics, unlike the last royal servants to visit in 1664–65, but as tax evaders and real-estate swindlers. On a private visit to Governor Leverett, Randolph wanted to know about the ships from all over Europe he had seen in Boston's harbor. They were in obvious violation of the recent navigation acts that controlled the English Atlantic's fast-growing trade for the mother country's benefit and the king's revenue. Randolph did not respond well to Leverett's explanation that His Majesty's laws were not enforceable in Massachusetts. When the governor and magistrates assembled together in Boston's townhouse, built in 1658 for civic business, Randolph told them that the king demanded an explanation of how Massachusetts had managed to stretch its boundaries to encompass New Hampshire and Maine; neither of those colonies, as far as Charles was concerned, belonged to it. Randolph noticed that when he removed his hat while Charles's letter was being read, only three magistrates followed his example. Randolph then went on a tour of the colony, making contact with people dissatisfied with its government.[1]

Before Randolph finished the first of what would be many friction-filled sojourns in Massachusetts, Governor Leverett warned him that God would bless those who blessed Massachusetts and curse those who cursed it.[2] It was the kind of warning that Massachusetts officials had been making to their opponents for almost fifty years, and previously, empirical evidence gave some support to their conviction that God had the colony's back. This time, it would not; a half-century of Massachusetts puritans successfully fending off the English government was coming to an end. Over the next fifteen years, Massachusetts would lose its royal charter; its reformation would fall apart; a revolt would kindle hopes that this reformation might be rebuilt; and Boston would witness the last confrontations between puritans and their opponents. In the midst of this political stormy weather, Massachusetts would be the stage for a dramatic case of witchcraft and demonic possession.

Edward Randolph's blistering report on his Massachusetts visit to the Lords of Trade and Plantations (a new committee of the king's Privy Council) was followed by seven years of cat and mouse between the committee and Massachusetts's General Court. The court repeatedly sent agents to Charles's increasingly exasperated ministry but it gave them no power to negotiate anything, while in response to English demands for major changes to its practices, it made the most minimal adjustments. Along the way, New Hampshire became a royal colony, and the General Court angered Charles further by buying Maine from its original proprietors just as the king was intending to purchase it. There was a brief respite as English authorities' attention turned elsewhere during the Exclusion Crisis, when Whigs tried to remove Charles's Catholic brother James from the line of succession to the throne. The pressure soon resumed in the Tory Reaction (see p. 228). At this point, whipping Massachusetts into line became part of the English government's general goal of crushing the Whigs and religious nonconformity (English nonconformists kept their New England friends well informed of events in England, and merchants traveled regularly in both directions).[3]

The cat-and-mouse game between the General Court and the Lords of Trade and Plantations came to a crashing halt in 1683. Randolph returned from one of his periodic trips to England with an ultimatum from Charles for the court: submit the charter to Charles for modification or lose it. Randolph had been assiduously wooing the moderate party in Massachusetts all the while. Now with the support of some of the ministers, there was finally a majority among the magistrates for complying with the king. Charles promised in a letter that if the General Court surrendered the charter, he would leave the colonists' property rights intact and that he would only make such changes to the charter as were necessary for good government.[4]

The king said nothing about religion in his letter, however, leaving the colonists' imaginations to run wild at a time when the persecution of English nonconformists was reaching its peak. And run wild those imaginations did, in alarmed, semi-hysterical manuscripts that circulated through the colony.

One manuscript suggested that the settlers could declare independence upon revocation of the charter and, if necessary, withdraw to the interior towns, where it would be too expensive for the king to subdue them. Another manuscript claimed that the ministers and magistrates who wished to accommodate the king were "backsliders and betrayers of their liberties and country." A third manuscript ominously warned that "popish councils" might lead to Church of England worship becoming mandatory in Massachusetts; the good news, according to this paper, was that if the colonists suffered for their refusal to submit to Charles's demand, they would "be accounted martyrs in the next generation." The deputies decided to issue a high-stakes rejection of Charles's ultimatum on December 5, 1683.[5]

Soon after the deputies' vote, martyrdom began to look like a real possibility. On December 10, Lionel Cranfield, the new autocratic royal governor of neighboring New Hampshire, instructed the tiny colony's three ministers that from now on they would have to administer the sacraments using the Book of Common Prayer to anyone who requested it or face prison. Cranfield's quick, harsh follow-through with his order ensured that the Massachusetts magistrates' desperate efforts to get the deputies to change their minds and agree to surrender the Massachusetts charter to their persecuting Anglican king were futile.[6]

Cranfield was particularly concerned with the Portsmouth, New Hampshire minister Joshua Moodey: a danger, as far as Cranfield was concerned, to the king, to the Church of England, and to Cranfield's autocratic rule. He passed word to Moodey near the end of January 1684 that he would be attending one of Moodey's services and would take the Lord's Supper by the Book of Common Prayer. Moodey would have refused to give the Lord's Supper to a man like Cranfield anyway, and probably to any Anglican, and he certainly was not going to use the Book of Common Prayer. He soon found himself in prison under the English Act of Uniformity both for his refusal and for "administering the sacraments contrary to the laws and statutes of England." Cranfield refused to allow any ministers to preach in Portsmouth for Moodey while he was imprisoned. Cranfield's mere threat that he was heading up to Hampton, New Hampshire to make the same demand of Seaborn Cotton, was enough to send Cotton fleeing to Boston. The New Englanders, Cranfield wrote to England's secretary of state, would "never make good subjects," until Harvard College was suppressed and "their ministers silenced."[7] New England puritans had succeeded in keeping the struggle with the Church of England's dominant faction at an ocean's distance for a half-century, but that period was over.

Moodey soon came to Boston and took up a post at First Church, ready to hit back at Anglicans as hard as they had hit him in New Hampshire. In 1685, he joined with Increase Mather, Massachusetts's most prominent minister, in a successful campaign to harass and intimidate a wandering Huguenot-turned-Church of England minister out of the colony. The minister had started to offer Anglican baptisms, including one, allegedly, to "a noted whore," and marriages. He left the colony when he heard there was a warrant out for his arrest.[8] Should push come to shove, the grudgingly tolerated local Baptists and Quakers did not have much to shove with; Anglican ministers had an enormous, hostile national church behind them, which was all the more reason to try to keep them from getting a toehold in Massachusetts.

Moodey and Mather perhaps threw themselves into their task with extra urgency because they already knew that their half-century-old puritan quasi-republic was living on borrowed time. The colonists learned by September 1684 that their charter was legally dead. Nonetheless, they continued to elect their own government and pray that God would intervene in their favor. Without that divine intervention, they knew that whatever change of regime was to follow would, at the very least, involve an Anglican church in Boston, smallish, but with the weight of a new government behind it (there were not enough Anglicans in the region to make a church viable anywhere else). On December 25, 1685, the magistrate Samuel Sewall looked out at Boston's bustling, business-as-usual streets and gave thanks to God that the colonists were not required to celebrate Christmas "yet."[9]

Fifty-six years of puritan self-rule came to a formal end on May 14, 1686. Randolph arrived on a well-armed naval frigate with an Anglican minister in tow, Robert Ratcliffe, along with the long-delayed instructions for a provisional government with an appointed local governor and council, but no elected assembly. Tears flowed copiously at the General Court's final meeting amid long extempore prayers and psalm singing, but for all the previous bluster, there was no resistance to this change; the colony had had months to digest the news of how mercilessly the newly crowned King James II had put down Monmouth's Rebellion (see p. 230).[10]

On June 6, Bostonians, curious, indignant, or both, crowded into the Boston townhouse to gape at what must have been for most of them their first Church of England service, complete with the white surplice and Book of Common Prayer.[11] Bostonians started calling Ratcliffe "Baal's priest" (a standard puritan insult thrown at conformist ministers, referring to Old Testament idolaters), while Boston pulpits rang with disparaging anti-

Anglican remarks about the "leeks, garlic and trash" of Egypt that the Old Testament Jews preferred while wandering in the Sinai Desert above heavenly manna (Numbers 11:5). Ratcliffe does not seem to have picked quarrels with the Congregationalists in return; he might have been chosen because he was the son-in-law of a prominent Presbyterian minister and thus well schooled in being diplomatic around puritans.[12]

Soon thereafter, Increase Mather published a short tract reminding anyone who might have forgotten that the Book of Common Prayer was superstitious, sinful, and rooted in popery. What made the tract significant was that it came without an author's name, publisher, place, or date on the title page—the latest in a long line of clandestine puritan books, but a first for Massachusetts. The old puritan extralegal struggle against the Book of Common Prayer had been revived in New England.[13]

The short-lived local provisional government avoided ruffling Congregationalist feathers. Things changed with the arrival in Boston of the new governor, Edmund Andros, on December 19, 1686, along with sixty soldiers. Andros, a seasoned colonial administrator, was tasked with uniting all of New England into one super-colony, the Dominion of New England, and if he ruffled local feathers in the process, it did not worry him.[14]

Andros quickly knocked the Congregationalists off of the privileged perch they had crossed the Atlantic to erect for themselves. He came with orders to maintain liberty of conscience, and one thing that order meant for him was no more laws forcing people to pay for Congregationalist ministers. "Many fear the ministry will be starved out," John Baily, a minister and former member of Thomas Jollie's church, wrote back to his Lancashire brethren as alarmed clergy watched their incomes starting to plummet. The three Boston churches steadfastly refused Andros's demand that they share one of their meeting houses with the Anglicans, aghast at the thought that the words of the Book of Common Prayer might resonate within their walls. Andros, in turn, dismissed these ministers as nothing more than laymen since they had not received ordination from a bishop. He took matters into his own hands on March 25, 1687, showing up at Third Church's meeting house with his entourage. The forewarned sexton had locked the door, but his brave vow to defy the governor (and perhaps experience the tang of Christian martyrdom) melted away at Andros's command to let him in. Two years of very unhappy forced sharing followed until the Anglicans finally built King's Chapel. Andros introduced the new (for New England) and idolatrous (according to many local laypeople and ministers) courtroom requirement of swearing on a Bible rather than raising a hand. If scrupulous New Englanders found themselves in front of one of Andros's new, non-Congregationalist judges, they might pay for their anti-idolatry with a fine or jail time.[15]

Having to put your hand on a Bible in a courtroom or sharing a meeting house with another religious group would barely register as religious persecution from the perspective of English nonconformists watching their own meeting houses burning, and facing crippling fines and jail. Still, for these New England Congregationalists, to be left with no more privileges than that of worshiping as they pleased was a huge, unsettling step down. Puritans had created Massachusetts in order to steer it as they wanted, as God demanded, and as Book of Common Prayer worshipers were incapable of doing. And now the Anglicans had finally thwarted them in America, just as they had done in England.

Congregationalists knew from stories passed down to them that with the Book of Common Prayer inevitably came sin and corruption. It was no accident that under Andros's censorship regime, the local press was now publishing, along with Anglican books, almanacs with Anglican saints' days and humor that was, by easily breached New England standards, off color. It was no accident that the holy stillness of a Sabbath night in Boston was shattered by the bonfires, music, and cannons of English naval officers celebrating the birthday of King James's Catholic wife, and no accident that Samuel Shrimpton, a wealthy merchant and recent appointee to Andros's council, rolled along in a coach at 9 p.m. one night drunk and singing loudly with his friends without a constable so much as laying a hand on him. "Promiscuous dancing," Increase Mather noted with horror, "was openly practiced and too much countenanced in this degenerated town." When the Charlestown night watch chopped down a new maypole, a larger one was erected, with a garland festively dangling from it.[16]

Many New England puritans would have seen it as even more of the same old English pattern that along with the Book of Common Prayer came arbitrary and even tyrannical government. Charles II had taken the colonists' land back along with their charter, and the colonists discovered that if they wanted clean titles to their acreage they had to pay stiff fees. The new phenomenon, for New Englanders, of official profit-taking meant that government fees in general went up sharply, while new officials introduced the English practice of selling now-lucrative government positions. Heavy fines and jail sentences crushed the fledgling no-taxation-without-representation resistance movement that sprung up after Andros introduced new taxes. Andros was at least honest enough that he shielded no one, friend or foe, from his measures. Everyone suffered when he enforced the English navigation acts that regulated shipping and trade with a strictness unmatched until just before the American Revolution, and thereby pushed the unprepared region into an economic slump. On April 7, 1688, Increase Mather slipped off to England to appeal to King James against Andros.[17]

Below this swirl of politics, in the summer of 1688, a pious Boston stone-mason, John Goodwin, and his wife faced a heartrending personal crisis, one that parents continuously had to brace themselves for in an age when death was always close at hand. The second oldest of their six living chil-dren, thirteen-year-old Martha had been struck down with some dreadful and apparently life-threatening illness. To add to the horror of Martha's shrieks, groans and fits, she was crying out that she did not know if she was saved.[18]

This was a dreadful divine judgment, and the Goodwins struggled to understand what sins had provoked God to inflict it. Then Martha's symp-toms got worse and stranger, and three younger siblings started behaving similarly. Their joints stiffened and then went impossibly slack. They cried out that they were being stabbed and beaten. They all got sudden pains at the same time in different parts of their bodies. These once dutiful children, whose parents kept them continually busy, would take forever to do the simplest chores and would break into "most grievous woeful heart-breaking agonies" when they were scolded. Sometimes they would shriek or seemingly go deaf when someone was praying or reading from the Bible. It was a mercy that they managed to shout out a warning when they were about to hurt themselves or someone else and that they always got a good night's sleep.[19]

People starting flocking to the Goodwins' house to watch and share their concerns and opinions about this extraordinary group illness. "The devil and his instruments had a hand in it," they told the Goodwins. A prominent and pious physician, Thomas Oakes, confirmed that nothing but witchcraft could have triggered the children's behavior.[20]

The news that their children were not just sick, but in the hands of devils unleashed by witchcraft plunged the parents into even deeper spiritual despair. John Goodwin concluded that God was slaying his children to drive the point home to Goodwin that he had been insufficiently strict in admonishing and instructing them. Goodwin found some comfort in reflecting on how severely God treated Job before making everything all right in the end.[21]

Some of the Goodwins' neighbors told them that if it were their chil-dren, they would try "tricks," or counter-magic. The Goodwins could use time-honored remedies like boiling the children's urine over a fire, perhaps with nails thrown in, to end the children's suffering and attack the witch. Even godly people were giving this advice, John Goodwin noted, though they surely knew that ministers condemned fighting the devil with the devil's own tools. The Goodwins finally rejected such means of alleviating the children's suffering since they came with the risk of "ensnar[ing] our souls." The only remedies good Christians used against devils and witches, ministers emphasized to their never-entirely-convinced congregations, were the biblical ones of fasting and prayer. Ministers and pious laypeople set up such a regime in the Goodwin household.[22]

On a different front, John recalled how just before Martha had come down with her symptoms, she had confronted their washerwoman over some missing linen. The woman's mother was a poor Irish Catholic widow named Glover, and she stepped in to give Martha a piece of her mind, possibly in Gaelic (how well she spoke or understood English is not certain). To John, Glover's witchery was obvious, not least because she was poor, old, and a woman, the clearest warning signs of a witch in both old and New England.[23]

Goodwin probably recognized that the confrontation, like most mani-festations of witchcraft, was not robust enough cause-and-effect evidence for a conviction. Evidence convincing enough for a court was always hard to come by, which was why conviction rates for witchcraft in New England ran at only around 25 percent. For example, the fact that six years ago a woman named Howen had seen Glover repeatedly come down her chimney while she, as she believed, lay dying from bewitchment had not been enough for her to drag herself to a magistrate and make a complaint againt Glover. Instead, Howen had simply complained to a neighbor. Goodwin, driven by his children's dire state, nonetheless filed a complaint with the magistrates against Glover and her daughter.[24]

The daughter was released for lack of evidence, although suspicion about her lingered. The mother, on the other hand, in her preliminary questioning, made unsatisfactory answers when asked if she believed in God, and she failed to repeat the Lord's Prayer. These were reasons enough for her to stand trial. At the trial, she had to speak through translators, and all that is known of the proceedings comes from brief descriptions by Cotton Mather, Increase Mather's son, who was convinced of her guilt. Mather noted that suspicious ragdolls stuffed with goat's hair were found in Glover's house, and that when Glover was given them to handle, one of the Goodwin children had fits. Like Mather, the jury was satisfied that she had also confessed to being in league with the devil—the surest route to a conviction. They found her guilty. A critic who read the transcript claimed that most of her answers were nonsensical, that the court tripped her up with leading questions on the answers that convicted her, and that she acted throughout as if she were distracted. The judges were uneasy enough that they took the unusual precaution of having six doctors examine her to determine her mental state. They gave her a clean bill of health and two weeks later, she was hanged. There were proportionately more witches tried and executed in New England than England, but there had not been a witchcraft execution in the region for over twenty years (England's most recent, and last, witch-craft execution had happened five years earlier in 1683).[25]

Going to her death on November 16, Glover gave an angry warning to the crowd that had gathered to watch her die. She was understood to say that the children's afflictions would not stop with her execution, for others had a hand in them, and after her death there was, indeed, a sharp increase in the sighting of witches. Soon, one of the Goodwin boys started seeing the specters of three or four women he recognized. When bystanders vigorously struck at the specters, though they were invisible to them, the boy felt pain in his body. Writing about this incident, Cotton Mather noted that an "obnoxious woman" in the town was seen afterward with a fresh wound, although he did not mention her name. No further inquiry had been made, he explained, and he did not want to "wrong the reputation of the innocent." Mather also did nothing with the names of three women whose specters, Martha Goodwin claimed, assisted the devils that tormented her. Mather's caution about unleashing witch-hunts was typical of ministers and magistrates.[26]

At the end of November 1688 a large fast was held in Goodwin's home, with five ministers present and "other good praying people," as John Goodwin called them. Goodwin, to his shame and mortification, had to hold his oldest boy down with all his might to keep him from kicking the ministers as they prayed. But God heard the prayers of this fast, according to Goodwin, for the severity of the children's afflictions was greatly dimin-ished. They stopped altogether, Cotton Mather noted, when a "horrible old woman" suspected of being involved in the children's bewitchment died as strange "fearful noises" resounded through her almshouse.[27]

Having seen his family through this demonic onslaught, Goodwin took much the same positive lesson from it that Mary Rowlandson had taken from her troubles (see p. 245): "If we want [i.e., lack] afflictions we shall have them, and sanctified afflictions are choice mercies." Goodwin had learned more about God's goodness "in these few weeks of affliction, than in many years of prosperity," and among the time-honored truths that he now learned first-hand was "how ready the devils are to catch us" and that "God would hear the prayer of the destitute."[28]

A few days before Glover's execution, Cotton Mather took Martha Goodwin into his house.[29] He hoped that with professional close attention, the devils that afflicted her might be driven off more quickly. Mather, an extremely ambitious twenty-seven-year-old, also probably already had in mind a book featuring this episode. He knew there was a transatlantic audience that might be interested in this case, and one not necessarily limited to nonconformists.

It was true that nonconformists on both sides of the Atlantic were far more wrapped up in the world of witches, possessions, and devils than were conformists. Their piety was all about an intensely experienced, pressing supernatural world where evil and sin loomed large. But the lines were not hard and fast. Robert Boyle, for example, the conformist president of the Royal Society, the center of English science, besides making groundbreaking discoveries in physics, was intensely interested in witches and the demonic. What scientist, or natural philosopher, as they were then called, would not want to read about Mather's discovery that the demons would not let Martha Goodwin read puritan books or the Bible but were quite willing to let her read Quaker books, the Book of Common Prayer, and books of jokes? And what natural philosopher would not want to know whether or not demons could read the thoughts of people they were not directly harassing? After a few tests with Martha, Mather concluded that some could and some could not.[30]

Mather had evangelical reasons, as well as scientific ones, for writing about the Goodwin children. Nothing was more likely to convince the scoffers and irreligious—who, it was feared, were flourishing in the late seventeenth century—that God was real than to demonstrate the reality of witchcraft. Prove Satan and you proved God, this line of reasoning went. Nonconformists on both sides of the Atlantic wrote much more on this topic than conformists, but again, lines were not hard and fast.[31]

With Andros in power, however, it was not the safest time for Mather to let the world know about the fondness of demons for the Book of Common Prayer. During the winter of 1688–89, he faced a charge of violating the English Act of Uniformity. He was also indicted for "scattering" his father's tract against the Book of Common Prayer and other "scandalous libels," around Massachusetts. Mather's purpose in spreading these writings, his opponents claimed, was to persuade the "common people" that "the governor and all of the Church of England were papists and idolators."[32]

Persuading them would not have been hard that winter. Andros was spending the season on the Maine frontier with unhappy and badly treated drafted colonial militia, making ineffectual efforts to end the war with Native Americans he had ignited in the spring with a bungled raid. Rumors started to spread that he was working with the hostile Native Americans, not against them, rumors, too, that he was, like his master the king, a Catholic. These rumors mingled with ones slowly coming over from England about William of Orange's invasion (see p. 231), at which point they took a final, terrifying form: for his master King James, Andros was preparing to turn New England over to the French (who were, in fact, active among the Native Americans from their base in Quebec). In a spontaneous, bloodless uprising on April 18, 1689 Andros was swept out of office and into the Boston jail, thereby sparing Mather imprisonment in the nick of time.[33]

Mather could now publish his account of the Goodwin children, which he finished in June. It came with a preface vouching for its accuracy from the four other ministers who fasted with the Goodwins, including Samuel Willard, the future president of Harvard College, and the recently arrived prominent nonconformist Charles Morton, who would have become Harvard's president had its board not worried about antagonizing Andros.[34] Two years later came republication in London, with a glowing preface by the great puritan Richard Baxter.

Meanwhile, there was the more pressing issue of what was to replace Andros's government. Three years of English control left the old godly, quasi-independent Massachusetts republic shattered. A convention of representatives of fifty-one Massachusetts towns met in Boston near the end of May 1689 and resolutely resolved in the old puritan spirit to venture their "lives and estates for the reviving and maintaining of" their "former liberties and enjoyments both civil and sacred." One faction at the convention managed to convince itself that the old charter was still legally in effect and that they could pick up where they had been rudely interrupted in 1686.[35] But most of the magistrates the convention wanted to serve in the government refused to sign up until a grudgingly worded acknowledgment was made that their government's permanent form would be ultimately decided by the "higher powers in England."[36] Since the new government was on record that its authority was ultimately provisional, allegiance to it

was also provisional. There was no going back; King William was in ultimate control of Massachusetts's destiny.

A few Anglicans were initially prominent in the uprising against Andros,
but they dropped out as the rebellion's religious edge grew sharper. The revolutionaries briefly jailed most of the Anglicans. Hostile Congregationalists
called them "papists dogs" on the street, ripped up the Book of Common
Prayer, broke the windows of their church, and smeared crosses of shit on its
doors, and stuffed feces into their keyholes. There was threatening talk of
turning the church into a school or of giving it to French Huguenot refugees.
According to Anglicans, one Congregationalist minister called for all their
throats to be cut. The Anglican minister Robert Ratcliffe finally went back to
England in July 1689 for his own safety.[37]

This Congregationalist intimidation of the Anglicans came fresh on the
aborted prosecution of Cotton Mather. No one in Massachusetts knew at
the time that Parliament had already all but settled permanently the relationship of puritanism to the Church of England. Ratcliffe was the last
Anglican minister to be run out of Boston and Mather probably the last
minister on either side of the Atlantic to face prosecution under the old
terms of the Act of Uniformity. The Boston confrontations had been the
final spasm of the 150-year-old struggle that had created and defined puritanism.

# Part IV

ENDINGS, 1689–1690s

# CHAPTER 21

## HOPES RAISED AND DASHED

In January 1689, three of England's leading Presbyterians, Richard Baxter, William Bates, and John Howe, met in London. The three men, whose ministries went back to Cromwell's time and further, must have been in very good spirits. James II had fled England, while the Dutch Presbyterian William of Orange was only waiting for Parliament to convene to declare him king with his wife Mary, James's daughter, as co-reigning queen. It was time for the Presbyterians to start collecting on all those reforming IOUs that Anglicans had given them when they needed allies against James's Catholicizing.

With the unfamiliar heady feeling of being on the winning side, the three Presbyterians allowed themselves to think big about the reformation in store for the Church of England, starting with the bishops. They were finally going to be cut down to size and would have to make all their decisions with the consent and advice of their ministers. The next month, Bates publically called on the new king and queen for terms of union between the Presbyterians and the Anglicans "wherein all the Reformed churches agree." Those terms would have required drastic changes to the Church of England's ceremonies and government.[1] After almost 150 years of puritan struggle, something like victory was in sight.

In idle moments during their January meeting, the three men might have chatted about their friend Increase Mather. He had slipped out of Massachusetts and appeared unexpectedly in England in 1688 with his thirteen-year-old son Samuel in tow. Mather had last left England in 1661 to return to his native Massachusetts after he refused to conform. A consummate networker, Mather had kept up his English profile with London publications, much-appreciated correspondence about Congregationalism, among other topics, and gifts of his Massachusetts books. Within two weeks of arrival, he wrangled an audience with James II to lodge a complaint about Governor Andros and an introductory visit to Baxter soon after. Bates's meeting house had become one of many in which Mather guest-preached and sometimes took the Lord's Supper. Mather had already befriended Howe in the 1650s when Howe was a chaplain to Oliver Cromwell and Mather was a recently arrived Harvard graduate.[2]

Mather, like the other ministers, would have been in very good spirits that January. What had started out as an effort to get James to replace Governor Andros was, with James's overthrow, changing into something much more ambitious—restoring Massachusetts's old charter and having the colony pick up again as much as possible with its old puritan quasi-republic.

Within a year, the hopes of all four ministers for something like a successful conclusion of puritanism had been dashed. Tories had backed William's invasion in order to put James on a very short leash, not to overthrow him for a foreigner in violation of their heartfelt principle of hereditary monarchy. It made matters even worse for the Tories, who were already feeling vulnerable, that Presbyterians in England were visibly excited about the changes in store, while in William's other new kingdom of Scotland, Presbyterians were turfing episcopal ministers out of their pulpits and homes on a grand scale (in payback for three decades of brutal oppression). William soon convinced the already alarmed Tories that he was at best tone deaf and possibly much worse concerning the rightly privileged place in his new kingdom occupied by bishops and the Church of England.[3]

In this menacing climate, earlier half-hearted Anglican promises to reach out to the nonconformists evaporated. Efforts to legislate political equality for them failed in Parliament. After a few rough starts, Parliament abandoned responsibility for drawing up a plan of comprehension to bring Presbyterian ministers back into Church of England pulpits. It kicked that task over to Convocation, the Church of England's two-house legislature. The only religious bill Parliament passed in 1689 was one for toleration, and even that bill was grudging. The Toleration Act did not repeal the religious penal laws but only suspended their penalties, on a few slight conditions, for all Protestant nonconformists who believed in the Holy Trinity. Nonconformists still had to pay tithes to the Church of England minister in whose parish they lived, while their sons, being nonconformists, could not go to Oxford or Cambridge University. Earlier Restoration legislation barring men from political office who would not participate in a Church of England Lord's Supper remained in force.[4]

Initially, it looked as if Convocation might work out better for Presbyterians. In preparation for its meeting in November 1689, a Church of England committee sketched out a package of extremely promising changes to the Book of Common Prayer. When Convocation met, the bishops supported the commission's proposals. With some small additions, the package could have placed two thirds of the Presbyterian ministers in, or back in, parish pulpits according to one leading nonconformist. The militantly Tory lower house of the clergy, however, refused to consider any changes, no matter how slight. Their uncompromising, unbreakable stance was widely recognized as signaling the end of the long, intermittently bloody, and entirely unsuccessful puritan campaign to reshape the Church of England along the lines of the continental Reformed churches. It was thus the end of English puritanism.[5]

While Convocation met, a bill restoring Massachusetts's old charter was moving through Parliament, thanks to Mather's tireless lobbying. But when William dissolved Parliament in January 1690, the bill still had not passed. It died with the Parliament. That dissolution ended the last opportunity for such a generous bill, and with it the last flicker of hope for a rebirth of Massachusetts's puritan quasi-republic, the most long-lasting puritan gesture of defiance against ungodly English monarchs.[6]

The failure of that bill confirmed that puritanism's long political struggle with England's monarchs was over on both sides of the Atlantic. But there was still unfinished puritan business for the godly to contend with on both sides of the Atlantic.

# CHAPTER 22

# THE FINAL PARTING OF THE WAYS FOR ENGLISH PURITANS

A major piece of unfinished business for English puritans was resolving the split between Presbyterians and Congregationalists. There was good reason to think that this split was closer to being healed than it ever had been, a silver lining to puritanism's cloud of failure. But that effort collapsed when other discordant pieces of unfinished personal and theological business became wound up with it and produced a toxic fin-de-siècle send-off for post-puritanism.

Unresolved theological business prompted Samuel Crisp, a pious, wealthy London merchant, to ask Increase Mather and other London ministers for a favor in 1690. When Crisp was a young boy in the early 1640s, his father Tobias raised an uproar among puritans by preaching variations on his doctrine that God had not the slightest concern about the sins of those whom he had predestined for salvation, no matter how heinous. Crisp compounded the shock of this antinomianism by attacking mainstream puritan ministers for arguing otherwise. They in turn fiercely disagreed with what they took to be Crisp's bad theology and his offer to his listeners of a license to sin (see p. 122).

Perhaps Increase went to Samuel Crisp's house to talk this requested favor over. Mather might have listened politely while Crisp expressed admiration for a wide range of Congregationalist and Presbyterian ministers and showed him his notebooks, in which he claimed to have recorded 5,200 sermons. If Mather grew restless, he would have reminded himself that his host was an important patron of the broad-minded Tuesday lectures at

Pinners Hall, where since 1672, a well-compensated weekly sermon had rotated between six prominent puritan ministers—four Presbyterian and two Congregationalist.[1]

Eventually Crisp would have explained the point of the visit. A publisher had approached him about reprinting his beloved father's sermons. To ward off attacks that his father had encouraged sin, Samuel was including old manuscript sermons that made it clear he had not. Samuel wanted Mather and the other ministers to attest that these sermons were genuinely his father's. Besides Mather, two Baptists, five Congregationalists, and four Presbyterians signed the attestation. Among the signers were Mather's prominent old Presbyterian friend John Howe and another old friend of Howe's, Mather's brother Nathaniel. Nathaniel Mather had long been a Congregationalist minister in Dublin, but moved to London in 1688 when persecution in Ireland became too intense.[2]

Five decades earlier, Crisp would have been hard pressed to get such a wide range of signatures, even for so narrow a purpose. Back then, strict Calvinism was in the ascendant. His father's sermons would have been measured by its rigid, narrow standards and rejected as a dangerous misunderstanding of the predestinarian processes of salvation. Now, the all-but-official doctrine of the Church of England was Arminianism, which dismissed predestination and stressed the capacity of grace-assisted human reason to freely follow God's law sufficiently for salvation. Calvinism, emphasizing helpless humanity's complete dependence on Christ for salvation, was dismissed by Arminians as over-intricate, irrational mystery-mongering.

Given the Church of England's close-to-complete abandonment of predestination as the end of the century approached, some Calvinists were more forgiving of Tobias Crisp's predestinarian excesses than they would have been in the 1640s. A Presbyterian remarked in 1690 that the reigning dangerous inclination to "neglect Christ under pretense of exalting reason and goodness" called for more tolerance of Crisp. The critical but cautiously sympathetic assessment that Mather and six other attestation signers later gave of Crisp was that he had been "greatly affected with the grace of God to sinners" and that parts of his writing were "very apt to make good impressions upon men's hearts." Passages that were objectionable were "in some measure" cancelled out by other passages.[3]

Samuel Crisp's taste in puritan preachers was broadminded but it stopped short before Mather's friend, the prominent Presbyterian Richard Baxter. Long ago, in 1647, Baxter's fear of antinomianism pushed him to a drastic surmise: the Calvinist way of salvation itself might be responsible for antinomianism and, therefore, Calvinism might have a fatal misunderstanding about how the elect were saved built into it. At the time, Baxter, believing himself to be at death's door, was busy working on what he thought would be his only book (over 160 were to come), *The Saints' Everlasting Rest*. That book, about the joys of heaven and how to ensure you ended up there, would become massively popular—twelve editions during his lifetime, and, in abridged form, a steady seller to this day, including translations in numerous European and non-European languages. Baxter set the book's manuscript aside, however, when his difficulties in making sense of one scripture verse compelled him to pursue his probe into Calvinism.[4]

Where did Calvinism go wrong about salvation? According to Calvinists, Christ was able to save the elect because he was their surety (Hebrews 7:22). That meant that Christ and each of the elect were one person in the eyes of God the Father as a matter of law. At the moment of an elect person's justification, God would legally recognize Christ's earthly deeds—his perfect obedience to God's law over the course of his life, and his suffering God's just wrath against the sins of the elect on the cross—as the elect's own deeds. The infinite debt for their sin that the elect would otherwise have had to pay off for eternity in hell was thereby cancelled, since Christ had paid it, while the doors of heaven that could only be opened by a perfectly sinless life were opened for them by Christ's life.[5]

But, Baxter reasoned, if Christ really had fully paid the elect's debt, there was no reason for them not to keep sinning away to their hearts' content after they had been justified. Calvinism, he decided, inescapably laid the foundations of antinomianism and, therefore, had to be dangerously wrong. Baxter prayed and pored over the Bible to discover what God's plan of salvation really might be. Then "an overpowering light," as he remembered it, "suddenly" gave him dazzling new insight about God's work in the human soul. Justification, it turned out, was not a once-and-for-all event, as the Calvinists insisted. God justified his elect over time, "proportionably and by degrees."[6]

The reason that justification was not once and for all was that Christ did not pay the elect's actual debt to God, as the Calvinists taught. He paid an equivalent that did not in itself get the elect into heaven. What it did was drastically lower the terms of their salvation. Instead of the perfect obedience that God demanded under the Covenant of Works he made with Adam, the new terms for justification under the Covenant of Grace were ongoing sincere (instead of perfect), grace-enabled faith and righteousness until justification had been completed after death.[7]

Baxter's theological innovations, much more subtle and intricate than a brief, bald summary can hope to convey, opened up what one of his followers called the "middle way" between Calvinism and Arminianism. For Baxter, it combined the best of both.[8] From Calvinism it took predestination, for only the elect were able to fulfill the protracted conditions for justification, and from Arminianism, the need for continuing good works though life for justification to be finalized. Predestination was now cemented firmly to good works, and, according to Baxter, the door was slammed shut on antinomianism.

Four decades after Baxter launched his immensely controversial non-Calvinist theological ideas into print, many of the godly had still not made peace with them. "Neither fish nor flesh, nor good red herring!" scoffed one old woman at Baxter's middle way. Increase Mather and his son Cotton, like most puritans, immensely admired Baxter's continually reprinted guides to conversion and the spiritual life. But if Baxter shepherded the elect to heaven, it was in spite of his dubious theological innovations, not because of them. According to Cotton, Baxter, with his insistence that ongoing good works were necessary for justification, had only created a false new Covenant of Works. Increase agreed that those innovations were "very offensive" to "judicious" ministers.[9]

Adding to Baxter's offense was that he did not simply disagree with the Calvinist scheme of salvation; having abandoned it, he rubbished it ferociously. The churches of New England observed "with grief," according to Cotton Mather, that Baxter was not content to politely disagree with "the [Calvinist] glorious truths of the gospel" about how God saved his elect. Rather, he went out of his way to insult those sacred truths as "fictions, falsehoods, forgeries, ignorant confusions, and gross errors."[10]

Congregationalists like the Mathers were all too aware that Baxter was not the only Presbyterian departing from the glorious old Calvinist truths of the gospel. The Church of England exerted a strong gravitational pull on Presbyterians, and they were sensitive to its mounting criticisms of Calvinism. John Howe did not go as far as Baxter, but, like Baxter, he abandoned double predestination, the Calvinist conviction that God not only actively appointed the elect to heaven, he appointed the damned to hell. From "the horror of so black a conception of God," Howe insisted, the "common sense of mankind" recoiled. He concluded, as did some other Presbyterians, that God predestined only the elect to heaven and that everyone else got to hell on their own sin-befouled steam.[11] The more that

Presbyterians grew comfortable with moderated Calvinism of this sort, the easier it was for them to tolerate Baxter's more extreme revisionism and perhaps even to adopt it.

Congregationalists, unlike Presbyterians, did not feel the gravitational pull of the Church of England and its dangerous, even damnable theological apostasy from the Calvinism that had been the Church of England's semi-official doctrine at the turn of the seventeenth century. If the glorious truths and all-powerful God of Calvinism, affirmed by careful, prayerful study of the Bible, appeared harsh and unreasonable, that appearance just showed the folly of insisting that the unfathomable wisdom of God be dragged down to the level of sinful humanity's "common sense." Rather than backing off from those Calvinist truths, for the previous forty years leading Congregationalist theologians had been elaborating them, emphasizing God's absolute sovereignty, human passivity in justification, and the mystery of the elect's union with Christ.[12]

Cotton Mather was moved to his own outburst against Baxter after reading an angry book Baxter published in response to the new edition of Tobias Crisp's sermons. When Samuel Crisp solicited signatures from Increase Mather and the other ministers, he left out one major detail about the book, probably deliberately: he was going to use a new preface to attack Baxter. Crisp's attack was not so much about Baxter's hostility to antinomianism, although there was some of that, it was about how far Baxter's theology had strayed from the puritan mainstream—Baxter was the dangerous deviant from orthodoxy, not Crisp's father. To make his point, Crisp selectively quoted at length from Congregationalists, Presbyterians, and earlier puritans.[13]

Old friends tried in vain to restrain Baxter from responding; Baxter, on top of his hatred of antinomianism, was notorious for his scorched-earth responses to criticism. One such friend, the Presbyterian minister Francis Tallents, told Baxter that if he really felt he had to attack Crisp, he should focus only on Crisp's greatest errors and not lump in England's "best divines" (meaning Calvinist ministers) with the antinomians; Baxter ignored him. Another, John Howe, pointed out that people thought there were errors in Baxter's books, just as there were in Crisp's sermons, but that those errors did not stop them from appreciating the good they found in them.[14]

It was especially important to Howe right now that the godly avoid a bare-knuckle theological fight. Howe and Increase Mather, along with others, were trying to build something positive from puritanism's ruins in 1691. The ministers were working out a formal union between the Congregationalists and Presbyterians, creating a unity of religious fellowship and worship among the godly that had not existed since Congregationalists began separating from more moderate puritans in the 1630s.[15]

Now that Presbyterians were no longer chasing their phantasm of parish pulpits, they quickly came to terms with Congregationalists about uniting under a mega-organizational umbrella. The founding document for this umbrella, the "Heads of Agreement," described individual churches generically enough that they could be either Presbyterian or Congregationalist, committed these churches to admit each other's members to the sacraments unless they had a "just exception" to them; and committed their ministers to meet regularly for consultation. The "Heads of Agreement" announced that henceforth these ministers "formerly known as Congregationalists and Presbyterians" would be called the "United Brethren."[16]

Increase's brother Nathaniel had been busy alongside Increase in this drive for unity. He was one of the managers of the Common Fund, founded in 1690 to provide support for prospective Presbyterian and Congregationalist ministers, and one of the six Congregationalists on the committee that wrote up the Heads of Agreement. But Nathaniel froze at the last minute and became one of only three London Congregationalist ministers who refused to sign on to the United Brethren.[17]

Nathaniel was a strict Congregationalist and vigilant against efforts on both sides of the Atlantic to dilute what he understood as Congregationalism's biblical purity. He had long been writing to Increase with exasperated objections to Increase's prominent role in expanding access to baptism in Massachusetts. Nathaniel undoubtedly shared with Increase face to face his reasons for rejecting the United Brethren, making the same points he raised in a letter to an inquirer. The way the Heads of Agreement had been created was "sinful": it had been rushed through with insufficient openness; it should have been discussed among the churches before the agreement of those churches' ministers was announced; and the terms agreed upon with the much greater number of Presbyterians, under close examination, secured "not one principle of the Congregational way."[18]

The defection of a few Congregationalists like Mather from this long-sought-for reunification of God's people scarcely dampened the apocalyptically expectant mood at the thanksgiving service launching the London United Brethren on April 6, 1691. "Are not your names among the angels who are to pour out the vials upon the earth?" the sixty-one-year-old Congregationalist minister Matthew Mead asked his listeners (Revelation

15:6–7). And was not the godly's new unity a part of the prophesied preparation for the final battle against Antichrist at Armageddon, "for Zion's
building and Babylon's ruin . . . do go together" (Revelation 19:7–20)? And
did not Revelation 21:2–3, with its vision of the descent of the millennium's
New Jerusalem, give "farther light" to what was happening now in London?
"God," exclaimed Mead to the assembled nonconformists, "is accomplishing
the latter-day promises upon you." Puritanism might have lost its long battle
to purge Antichrist from the Church of England, but the creation of the
United Brethren showed that the godly were still on track for their final
victory against him (although Mead hedged his predictions with variations
on "it may be").[19]

Richard Baxter had been trying to reunify God's people in his own contentious way since the 1650s, and on December 8, 1691, eight months after the
day of thanksgiving for the formation of the United Brethren, he died. At
Baxter's funeral procession, the coaches of the wealthy stretched almost a mile
behind the hearse, and thousands of people attended.[20] Younger ministers
might have wondered if any of them would have a funeral remotely as impressive. Baxter represented the rapidly vanishing old puritan world with its inti-
mate ties to the Church of England (Baxter had been offered a bishopric in
1660), and to the upper reaches of England's social order. Like Baxter, the
older members of the aristocratic and gentry families that had given puritanism much of its clout were dying off, and their offspring had already started
to show that they had no intention of going off into the wilderness of nonconformity. That vital alliance, more than a hundred years old, between nonconformist ministers and the gentry and aristocracy was fading. The numbers of
nonconformists employed by these families as chaplains and teachers would
drop precipitously in the 1690s, and nonconformity would rapidly accelerate
its process of becoming a mostly urban, middle-class movement.[21]

Optimistic Congregationalists thought that, with Baxter's death, the
tension over antinomianism and Baxter's theology would slacken. It might
have, were it not for Baxter's protégé, Daniel Williams, fast rising into a
leadership position among London Presbyterians. Williams shared Baxter's
alarm over antinomianism and, to a lesser extent, his discomfort about
Calvinism, while admiring elements of Baxter's theological innovations. He
took it upon himself to create his own theological middle way, not, like
Baxter's, between Calvinism and Arminianism, but between Calvinism and
Baxterism, by working Baxter's emphases on continued human initiative in
justification into a more traditionally Calvinist framework. Williams would
thereby avoid what he called the "excess" of "both extremes."[22]

Williams had set himself an extremely ambitious project, especially for someone without any formal theological training and perhaps without much of a gift for original theological work (which might explain why he could be touchy about criticism). The old, respected Baxterian, John Humfrey, claimed that the internal logic of Williams's alleged middle way was entirely Baxterian, regardless of Williams's protests to the contrary. A sympathetic Presbyterian, on the other hand, called Williams a "semi-Baxterian," while noting that, at least in theological matters, Williams had "a sounder heart than head."[23]

Williams's theological middle way died with him, but not before it had precipitated the destruction of the United Brethren. Alarmed Congregationalists agreed with Humfrey that Williams's theology was actually warmed-over Baxterianism, but they disagreed that Williams came to his confusion honestly. To them, that confusion was both deliberate and sinister. Williams designed his alleged middle way to be a Baxterian Trojan horse, involving "many ambages [i.e., ambiguities] and subterfuges," in order to infiltrate Baxter's pestilent doctrines deeply into the godly community.[24]

Tensions between Williams and Congregationalists were already flaring up publicly in 1691. After Williams gave an anti-Crispian guest sermon at Pinners Hall that year, the old Congregationalist lecturer there, Thomas Cole, disputed his theology in his own sermons, albeit relatively politely. But the laity at the lectures found it disconcerting that their godly guides were quarreling, and, given the eternal stakes, they wondered if they should take sides. Cole and Williams managed to patch things up and affirm each other's orthodoxy, for now. Williams wrote that their difference "lies (I hope) more in words than some unthinking men imagine." Baxter had wanted Williams to replace him as a regular Pinners Hall lecturer, but Williams hardly received a rousing endorsement from the lay subscribers who paid for the lectures. He had created enough unease by his sermon that their vote was tied and had to be resolved in Williams's favor by casting lots, as the apostles did (Acts 1:26).[25]

Almost four months after Baxter's death, on March 29, 1692, Increase Mather set sail for Massachusetts. He had stayed in London long enough to witness the emerging friction between Williams and Cole, and he might have started to worry that his handiwork, the United Brethren, was not taking root. Only six months after he left, the London Congregationalist minister (and ex-New Englander) Isaac Chauncy, who had already taken printed potshots at Williams, stormed into one of the United Brethren's meetings. He told them that the union had been "broken and perverted from its right end" and that he would no longer be a member.[26]

Chauncy was angry about two things. The first was that the London United Brethren had taken it upon themselves to arbitrate disputes in a wide radius around London, as if they had a Presbyterian "synodical jurisdiction," as Chauncy put it. Their arbitration, according to Chauncy, showed prejudice both against Congregationalism and against Congregationalist ways of resolving differences among churches.[27]

The other reason for Chauncy's anger was explained in a paper signed by him and five other Congregationalists, including Nathaniel Mather, and supported by still more. Chauncy handed the paper over to the ministers to let them see for themselves what it said and left the United Brethren for good.[28]

The paper had a list of objections to *Gospel Truth*, an attack on antinomianism that Daniel Williams had published that year. Williams's "truths" themselves were not terribly controversial, and Williams mostly tried to avoid saying anything that was in dispute among the United Brethren in his explications. But he could not restrain himself from making an unusual Baxteresque interpretation of the scripture verse, Philippians 3:9, despite being warned by a Congregationalist that it was problematic. That interpretation spurred the Congregationalists to go on a microscopic search for snippets of Baxterianism in the rest of *Gospel Truth*. They believed their search was successful, even while acknowledging that they did not try to reconcile Williams's "inconsistencies and contradictions."[29]

But those alleged Baxteresque errors were not what prompted the group protest to the United Brethren. The real problem was that *Gospel Truth* came with endorsements from forty-nine Presbyterian members of the United Brethren (efforts to get Congregationalist endorsements had failed). For suspicious Congregationalists, those endorsements represented a backdoor United Brethren stamp of approval for Williams's effort to "craftily undermine . . . the great truths of the Bible taught by the first reformers."[30]

After much back and forth, the Congregationalists reluctantly agreed to a watered-down United Brethren statement that the endorsements pertained only to the book's gospel truths, not to Williams's elaborations of those truths. But most of the Congregationalists stopped coming to the United Brethren meetings on a regular basis, if at all, and set up their own meeting, while a spate of tracts about *Gospel Truth* were published, most of them attacking Williams. One tract by Chauncy called Williams and Baxter Neonomians, for turning the gospel into a new law, and "Neonomian Controversy" has become the usual name for this dispute.[31]

In 1693, another, sharper spat between Cole and Williams broke out at Pinners Hall before quietening down. The precarious peace that followed lasted until 1694 when a lecturer fell ill and Nathaniel Mather was invited to substitute for two lectures. He mulled about preaching something uncontroversial, which would have been diplomatic, given that the United Brethren were on the verge of collapse. But the Church of England was already deeply sunk in apostasy from the truths of Calvinism, Mather decided, and apostasy was spreading among the nonconformists. Mather's duty, therefore, was to bear witness against this flood of error and preach the unvarnished truth about Williams's theology.[32]

Mather's whistle-blowing decision could have only been helped by his long, fraught, competitive history with Williams. They had known each other in Dublin, where there was already Congregationalist unease about Williams's theology and where Williams moved on from Congregationalism to Presbyterianism, which would not have endeared him to Congregationalists. They had left for London around the same time, and both had vied for the Congregationalist pulpit Mather now held. Mather had won out in part because Williams made no secret of being Presbyterian and in part because Mather let the congregation know that Williams's doctrine was unsound.[33] In his Pinners Hall lectures, Mather would finish his longstanding doctrinal quarrel with Williams by unmasking him as the covert Baxterian Mather knew him to be, while unmasking Baxterianism as worse than the teaching of many Catholics.

Before Mather began this unmasking, he laid out the truth, as he saw it, to his audience about Christ's righteousness and salvation. Antinomianism, Mather then acknowledged, was a "wide mistake" (Mather preached against Crisp to his own congregation).[34] That out of the way, Mather laid into Williams and Baxter, maintaining a slight fig leaf of anonymity for decorum's sake. He cited "one who is among ourselves" saying that the benefits of the gospel were given as a reward (as opposed to being the free gift of God). There was probably a buzz of whispers in the hall as listeners shared the fairly easy identification of Williams. Mather moved on to "another" who spoke "less covertly" when he said that God saved people only for their believing. The whispers might have become more quizzical since this was a bit esoteric, but some listeners who had read widely enough might have passed around that Mather was referring to another Baxterian, Joseph Truman. The third and final figure, Mather told his listeners, "saith plainly" what the others only implied: salvation was a reward for merit, which made him, Mather warned, "grosser" than some "learned papists." That figure would have been easy to identify as Baxter.[35]

The loudest buzz of whispers would have come as Mather then told his audience that what those three Baxterians taught, openly or covertly, was "soul-destroying"—"damning," he added in the published version. Follow Baxterians, be they open or covert, and you went to hell. Mather might have been among the London godly who assumed that hell was where Baxter's theological innovations had deposited him.[36]

Williams pushed back against Mather in two subsequent Pinners Hall sermons. He defended his theological soundness, of course. But probably more important, goaded by Mather's attack, he did something he had previously avoided, wisely, at least in such a public forum. That was to openly attack the Calvinist theology of salvation that Mather had vigorously reasserted. Williams did so with arguments like Baxter's, linked that theology to antinomianism, as Baxter did, and disparaged it in a Baxterian manner as "vulgar mistakes and dangerous notions" —no more pretenses that the disagreement between him and the Congregationalists lay only in words.[37] But what Williams was scornfully dismissing was for many of his listeners the foundation of their hope for eternal life. Any of those listeners who had taken on Mather's less-than-fair accusation that Williams covertly taught the same doctrine as Baxter would have heard plenty to back it up.

Even the slowest of the listeners at Pinners Hall would have grasped that Mather and Williams each thought that the other's allegedly godly theology put immortal souls in grave peril. Now the lectures, the last public face of a united puritan heritage in London, dissolved into acrimonious infighting. On November 7, 1694, Howe and the two remaining Presbyterian lecturers finally left the hall for good, along with Williams, to start their own lecture series. To drive home the point that the godly party was now irreversibly split, the Presbyterians scheduled their new lecture series at Salters Hall to meet at the same time as those at Pinners Hall. Mather was heavily involved in the decision of the Congregationalists the next year to abandon the last official London joint Presbyterian–Congregationalist venture, the Common Fund for prospective ministers, and start their own.[38] Perhaps Mather felt a certain satisfaction in knowing that while he could not undo the Presbyterian corruptions about baptism his younger brother had helped to introduce into New England Congregationalism, he had at least succeeded in freeing English Congregationalists from the Presbyterian yoke his brother had helped to slip on them.

The United Brethren continued to function in the provinces into the early eighteenth century. Its failure in London, however, ensured that the two groups of puritans, Congregationalists and Presbyterians, both of whom had once laid claim to being England's religious establishment, went into the post-puritan future as small, separate denominations. Around 1720, Presbyterians made up some 3.3 percent of England's 5.5 million people and Congregationalists 1.1 percent. Both denominations were finally firmly committed to liberty of conscience for all Protestants, unlike the Church of England's still-vengeful Anglicans, for whom the two groups remained the same dangerous schismatical rebels they had been in the 1640s. They both looked to the reconstituted Whig party to shield them from the Anglicans' ongoing fury, mostly successfully.[39]

With the final surgical separation of the two groups, the Presbyterian retreat from the stern puritan doctrines of predestination became a headlong flight. It was reported in 1731 that twenty-seven of London's thirty-one Congregationalist ministers were Calvinists, while three were antinomian extremists, and, as for one, "it is difficult to say what he is." Among the forty-four Presbyterians, on the other hand, the nineteen Calvinists were now outnumbered by twelve "middle-way" ministers hovering between Calvinism and Arminianism, like Richard Baxter, and thirteen who had entirely embraced Arminianism.[40]

As the heirs of the puritans continued to drift apart in the 1730s, puritanism itself cemented its long-term relevance. During that decade, the British Atlantic world started to be stirred by broad, novel, interdenominational religious revivals playing up the urgency and necessity of conversion. Revivalists included large numbers of Arminians newly discovering conversion's importance, most prominent among them John Wesley, one of the founders of the Church of England movement Methodism (later a separate denomination). Who better than puritans to serve as guides to conversion and to the devotional life that went along with it? They were, after all, the pioneers of this kind of evangelical Protestant piety. On both sides of the Atlantic, puritan books were eagerly rediscovered and reprinted by Calvinist and even Arminian revivalists, sometimes in abridged and adapted form to speak more readily to new religious audiences. They have continued to speak to those audiences down to the present day.[41]

# CHAPTER 23

# A GODLY MASSACRE OF THE INNOCENTS IN POST-PURITAN MASSACHUSETTS

Increase Mather arrived back in Massachusetts on May 14, 1692, bearing with him Massachusetts's new royal charter. During his four-year absence, his wife Maria had been regularly using his newly free study, their house's only truly private room, for days of fasting and prayer for the success of his mission. Increase only discovered Maria's appropriation of his study after her death in 1714 when he went through her papers. Perhaps Maria, like many other people in Massachusetts, was bitterly disappointed with the new charter Increase was bringing back with him and did not wish to discuss with him her efforts to produce a better result.[1]

The charter gave Plymouth colony to Massachusetts, which was small consolation for bringing Massachusetts's autonomy and its tight relationship between its government and its churches emphatically to an end. The governor would be appointed by the Crown and have a veto over all appointments and laws. Property, not godliness, would be the requirement to vote for deputies to the General Court. All Protestants would have religious liberty. At least there would be no strangers in this new government, at first, for Mather had been allowed to nominate the governor and council. But that was a one-off.[2]

In London since his departure in early 1688, Increase would have been kept abreast by travelers and letters of all but the last four months or so of the mostly dismal events in Massachusetts. He would have known that the colony had endured a long string of what looked like divine punishments for its sins. In 1689, the French, servants of Antichrist, allied with the Native Americans, servants of the devil, in their attacks on the English in Maine.

Thanks to the accession of William of Orange to the English throne, this local conflict became one of the front lines of a new war between England and its allies and France, the Nine Years' War (known as King William's War in America). Massachusetts launched a retaliatory invasion of Quebec in 1691 that failed disastrously, leaving the provisional Massachusetts government with nothing to show for it except large numbers of men dead from smallpox, an empty treasury, and widespread public contempt. After this "awful frown of God," more devastating Native American raids left most of Maine empty of the English.[3]

Increase would also have heard about another assault launched on Massachusetts in his absence, this one by the aggressive Quaker missionary George Keith. Keith appeared in Boston briefly in 1688 and had been firing printed broadsides at Massachusetts Congregationalists ever since. Increase would have agreed with his son Cotton's 1690 warning about Keith and Quakers that they were a "spiritual plague" sent by God as punishment for people's sins. Quakerism itself, Cotton went on, was "antichristian paganism" and a "snare of the devil" filled with "venomous and contagious" and "damnable heresies." So horrid was Quakerism, wrote Cotton and three other leading ministers, that conversion to it was "not seldom" accompanied by the "very sensible possession of Satan."[4] An old Quaker-hanging puritan like John Norton could not have described that soul-destroying group of heretics better.

Norton, however, would have been startled and alarmed to hear Cotton go on to claim that magistrates, on principle, should not punish Quakers. God would surely destroy Quakers, Cotton acknowledged, but even Quakers, he insisted, were entitled in the meantime to "liberty of conscience." As a puritan, Norton had taken for granted what Cotton appeared to have forgotten: God punished Christian societies that failed to punish heretics. Did Cotton know that his father, in old-school puritan fashion, had tried unsuccessfully to keep liberty of conscience for all Protestants out of the new Massachusetts charter?[5]

As soon as Increase Mather stepped off his boat in 1692, he would have heard for the first time about a new satanic assault that dwarfed the Quakers and even the Native Americans in menace. This assault was aimed directly at the very institutions that Massachusetts's old puritan government had been set up to protect, Christ's churches. The new assault, however, would be met not by the old puritan government, but the post-puritan new charter government. The result of that collision of Satan's old, familiar wiles with Massachusetts's new, untested, secular government was the debacle of the Salem witch trials.

\* \* \*

Increase would quickly have been informed that in a field by the meeting
house of Salem Village, an outlying parish of Salem, vastly larger numbers
of witches than New England had ever known were reported to be meeting
regularly in spectral form. There they were said to listen to diabolical
preaching and participate in a satanic version of the Lord's Supper (both
firsts for New England), led by the specter of a minister (another first),
George Burroughs, whom Salem Village had tried out for its prospective
church and rejected in 1683. These witches, it was said, were bent on making
Salem Village "the first seat of Satan's tyranny." Thirty-eight accused witches
were already crammed into the stinking, badly overcrowded jails of Boston
and Salem, awaiting the setting up of courts under the new charter.[6]

At some point, Increase Mather would have paid a courtesy call on
Simon Bradstreet, the eighty-eight-year-old outgoing governor, at his house
in Boston. Mather would not have been surprised to have one of Bradstreet's
two enslaved Africans lead him into Bradstreet's parlor, for the importation
of African slaves was rapidly increasing, and they would soon make up 2 to
3 percent of New England's population. Once in Bradstreet's parlor, Increase
might have heard him tell a drastically different story about the devil's work
at Salem.[7] In January 1692, the niece and the daughter of Salem Village's
minister Samuel Parris started to have inexplicable fits. These were soon
attributed to witchcraft and three suspects were named. In a normal New
England witchcraft case, one or two of the suspects might have been
executed, and the authorities, as in the recent Glover witchcraft case (see
p. 258), would have been in no hurry to tie up loose threads.

Bradstreet would have gone on to explain to Mather how the magistrates who initially investigated the charges had started off disastrously on
the wrong foot. They had foolishly opened their preliminary hearings to the
public, thrown the mostly female accusers and accused together, and let the
hearings dissolve into pandemonium. Very soon, ten or more self-identified
victims at these hearings would be shrieking and having fits when, they
claimed, a suspect's specter attacked them, leaving teeth marks and bruises
for all to see. Even a glance or a flick of the wrist from a suspect could result
in an uproar that could be heard far away from the Salem Village meeting
house where the examinations took place. The fits stopped when the
accused witches were restrained or confessed their guilt.[8]

In a witchcraft case a decade earlier dominated by similar spectral
evidence, Governor Bradstreet, presiding over the old Court of Assistants,
along with a majority of his fellow magistrates, had overturned a jury's
guilty verdict. Bradstreet had remembered then, as had the investigators of

the 1688 Glover witchcraft case, that the devil was a great trickster and that phenomena like witches' specters had to be treated with a great deal of caution.[9]

The over-impressionable Salem magistrates, however, had forgotten that conventional wisdom, and in the hothouse courtroom atmosphere they permitted it would have been hard to remember it. Instead, the magistrates took as a given that the accusers were reliable witnesses and that they themselves had found a reliable way of determining guilt. Perhaps they were chasing witches so aggressively to compensate for failing so abysmally to protect the colony from its satanic enemies on the Maine frontier, as was the magistrates' duty. Whatever the reason for their lack of caution, the old puritan order of things—magistrates serving as a brake on popular demands for witch-hunting—had been flipped on its head. The more that Salem magistrates exposed witches, the more that fear spread through the area and the more afflicted victims and accused witches emerged into legal daylight.[10]

The man who was ultimately in charge of the Salem witchcraft investigations, the newly appointed, recently arrived royal governor Sir William Phips, would hardly pass muster as a godly magistrate. Maine-born, he had become a sea captain and spectacularly successful Spanish sunken treasure-hunter, for which he won a knighthood and the favor of the English government. But as everyone in Massachusetts was no doubt aware, under the old charter, he would never have been elected governor. He had no formal education and perhaps could not even read, let alone write. Far from being an experienced saint and Congregationalist, Phips had only been baptized and joined Boston's Second Church, whose ministers were Increase and Cotton Mather, in 1690, at the age of thirty-nine, conveniently one day after the colony made him its major general. Hot-tempered Phips's visible sainthood was not so apparent to others, but his association with the influential Mathers had stood him in good worldly stead over the last couple of years. Nonetheless, in 1691 Phips had to leave Boston for London hastily to avoid the legal consequences of some of his more questionable business and military practices.[11] In almost every sense of the word, Phips was Massachusetts's first post-puritan governor.

On May 27, Phips set up a temporary court to try the accused witches while the legislature created a new permanent legal system. For its presiding judge, he chose William Stoughton, the Crown-appointed deputy governor. Stoughton had been a commanding, forceful presence in the Massachusetts courts over which he previously presided and had no patience for questioning of their methods, both of which character traits might help explain why Massachusetts voters had never elected him to an office as high as the one he now occupied.[12] For Stoughton, like Phips, the new post-puritan charter meant a promotion.

Stoughton embraced the procedures and assumptions for dealing with the witch suspects already set in place by the examining magistrates, and in his hands, New England's old witchcraft conviction rate of 25 percent leapt to 100 percent. The colony's last elected deputy governor, Thomas Danforth, opposed the witch trials. Under the old charter, Governor Bradstreet, who also opposed them, would have presided over appeals from the jury verdicts of the county courts where witchcraft cases like the ones in Salem were heard. The Salem disaster is often treated as the defining expression of American puritanism. But it was an expression of American puritanism in its fevered death throes, after it had been thrown into a disastrous, terrifying imperial war and the old brakes on witch-hunts had been removed, both by powers beyond puritanism's control.[13]

At the beginning of June, there was still one old puritan brake against witch-hunting left to slam. Phips and his council requested a report from twelve ministers, including Increase and Cotton Mather, about procedures in the trials. In their report, presented on June 15, the ministers made the obligatory deferential courtesies about the good job the new court had started to do, and then suggested that its approach "may be perfected." Whereupon they lowered the boom—perfection meant no more public initial inquiries; more regard for the previous reputations of suspects (by this point, the magistrates had jailed several church members and another magistrate); much less reliance on specters and similar evidence; and close attention to what the old prominent English puritan ministers William Perkins and Richard Bernard had to say about how to try witches (their advice was more of the same sort of caution that the Massachusetts ministers advised). The devil, the ministers warned, was very likely scheming to get as many innocent people jailed and executed as possible. The greatest "affront" the judges could give him would be to disbelieve testimony based on spectral evidence. With those necessary precautions laid out, the ministers urged "a speedy and vigorous prosecution."[14]

In the old Massachusetts theocracy, such strong recommendations coming from the colony's leading ministers would have drastically reduced the damage inflicted by the court. But the report did not sway Chief Justice Stoughton at all; there is some evidence that he had long resented the insufficient vigor that had gone into pursuing witches in Massachusetts. Phips was in no position to study the recommended old, dense puritan witchcraft treatises himself, being barely literate at best, and he did nothing to bring Stoughton into line.[15]

In June and July, Stoughton's court moved from preliminary examinations and arrests to indictments, trials, and executions. The dangers of the court's unconventional methods were perhaps not immediately obvious because the results they were initially getting made sense. Of the first six people hanged, in June and July, all women, five had already accumulated accusations of witchcraft, or, in two cases, had been tried and acquitted on witchcraft charges before they appeared on these new charges.[16]

In the second half of July, the witchcraft prosecution took a gigantic leap forward in urgency, and even credibility. A witch's voluntary confession was by far the most reliable evidence of witchcraft. Up until then in this witch-hunt, only six out of eighty or more accused witches had confessed. In itself, that was not unusual; people accused of witchcraft rarely had anything to confess. But in the last two weeks of July, the first five of what would eventually be thirty-nine confessing witches from Andover, a town near Salem, started to tell their stories of their lives as witches.[17]

What these witches revealed was that the devil's conspiracy was far more horrifically ambitious than previously realized. "Throughout all the whole country," according to one witch, the plan was to overthrow Christ's kingdom and set up the devil's. The confessors revealed that at the great diabolical sacramental meetings in Salem the devil was urging the participants to make as many witches as they could, while another witch estimated that there might already be over three hundred witches in Massachusetts. These new confessors added that the devil was baptizing his proselytes in a nearby river.[18]

Perhaps the magnitude of the voluntary Andover confessions gave the ministers second thoughts about their June reservations. Cotton Mather, for one, concluded that, despite all the flaws in the court's procedures, which he always acknowledged, the sheer volume of roughly consistent confessions demonstrated just how important the court's task was. As Mather explained in print and pulpit, those confessions showed that the devil was laying a plot for "rooting out the Christian religion from this country." In its place, he would substitute "perhaps a more gross diabolism, than ever the world saw before." Given the scale of the immediate crisis, it scarcely mattered that, by Mather's interpretation of Revelation's prophecies, which he was sharing at the time, the millennium would probably begin in five years.[19]

Up to this time, the devil had opposed the true church, of which New England had the purest examples, with his own diabolical worship only in disguised form, through his agent Antichrist and the false Catholic Church. Now there were no more intermediaries. The true church at its purest and the religion of Satan at its most wickedly brazen were confronting each other face to face, on a vast continent that had belonged entirely to the devil before the English started erecting their churches and converting Native Americans. When Mather put his thoughts on the devil's terrifying plot into print in October 1692, they came with an endorsement by William Stoughton, making them the quasi-official explanation for what was happening in Massachusetts.[20]

But the story of this unprecedented epic confrontation between the godly and the forces of evil was already falling apart by the time it appeared in print. On August 19, an exceptionally large crowd turned out in Salem to see the next five executions. George Burroughs, the clerical leader of the witches, along with three other men and a woman were to hang. For puritans, the gallows could offer moving dramas of redemption, provided that the condemned felons died well in the eyes of the spectators. This they did by convincingly acknowledging the wickedness of the crimes of which they were accused, making tearful confessions of how they went wrong, and professing newfound hope in redemption through Jesus' blood before their souls were launched into the afterlife.[21]

But none of these condemned witches had yet confessed, and none of these men who were to be hanged had reputations as witches until the afflicted women started seeing their specters. It was open knowledge that the court's methods for identifying witches were under dispute.[22] If these convicted but unconfessing witches appeared to die like good Christians while expressing no repentance for the heinous sin of witchcraft, it would be a powerful argument that they had no such sin to repent for and that the court was killing innocent people.

At least three of the men did die well on August 19 without making a gallows confession of witchcraft. It must have surprised many of those watching that Burroughs was one of them. The way he prayed and said the Lord's Prayer "did much move unthinking persons," grumbled one of the judges present, and the crowd started to mutter against his execution. After he was hanged, Cotton Mather exhorted the crowd that the devil could appear as an angel of light (2 Corinthians 11:14), which somewhat calmed it down, and the executions continued.[23]

But two other men, John Willard and John Proctor, are known to have died impressively well that day. They were not church members, but they had learned from friends, family and church attendance the proper godly way to face death. According to Thomas Brattle, a Boston merchant who was present, they forgave their accusers, spoke without bitterness of the judges and jurors, implored Cotton Mather "with great affection" to pray with them in their final moments (Mather almost certainly refused since they refused to admit to their sin of witchcraft), and finally prayed that God might pardon their sins and save them by Jesus' blood. Their manner of leaving the world was "very affecting and melting to the hearts of some considerable spectators," said Brattle. He did not need to add that this was almost certainly not how an unrepentant genuine witch would die.[24]

An outbreak of new confessions in Andover at the end of August could not wipe away the growing concern about innocent deaths. Instead, it provided new grounds for it—could there really be so many witches in "a place of so much knowledge" as Massachusetts, it was asked, or was the sheer number of alleged witches another sign that the court was doing something wrong? Most of the accused Andover witches had never been suspected previously and several of them were church members in full communion.[25]

By September, the shedding of innocent blood was starting to haunt the colony's collective psyche. Seventeen-year-old Mary Herrick of Wenham must have been terrified when the specter of the soon-to-be-executed witch Mary Easty from neighboring Topsfield appeared to her one day in the middle of September. If Herrick was attuned to local gossip, she would have known that Easty was insisting that she was innocent and that her minister, church, and fellow townspeople had been willing to testify on her behalf. Herrick might also have known that Easty had submitted a petition addressed to the court and to the ministers. The petition did not ask for pardon for herself, although in it she asserted her innocence. Instead, she asked the court to prevent the shedding of any more innocent blood by tightening up its procedures.[26]

Nonetheless, Herrick believed that Easty was a witch. She undoubtedly anticipated that Easty's specter was about to unleash a barrage of painful physical torment on her, as she would have heard that other specters did, and possibly demand that Herrick choose either death or signing the devil's book and becoming a witch herself. But all Easty's specter did was tell Herrick that within a year, Herrick would agree that Easty was innocent. Herrick may have heard subsequently that when Easty was hanged on September 22, along with one male and six female unconfessing witches, her "serious, religious, distinct, and affectionate" final words brought tears to most of those present. Nonetheless, Herrick persisted in believing in Easty's guilt.[27]

Was Herrick gnawed, though, by an unacknowledged possibility that Easty's specter was correct, and did that unsettling uncertainty about the guilt of the witches open a space for new visits by specters? One of those fresh specters pinching, pricking, and choking Herrick came in the shape of Sarah, wife of the minister John Hale, a strong supporter of the trials. On November 12, Easty's ghost returned with Sarah. The ghost repeated her claim that she was innocent of witchcraft, cried "Vengeance, vengeance," and told Herrick to reveal her encounter to Reverend Hale and Reverend Joseph Gerrish. Easty would then rise no more from the grave and Sarah Hale's specter would not afflict Herrick. Herrick did as she was told two days later. Learning that the devil could even take on the shape of his own wife might be what jolted John Hale to finally start questioning the witch trials.[28]

One of the changes in court procedure Easty had urged in her petition was more-thorough questioning of the confessed witches. At least some of them had "belied" themselves, she had warned. By the end of September, the signs started piling up that Easty had been right. Talk was circulating about how some Andover confessors were recanting their allegedly voluntary confessions, with stories of the psychological but occasionally physical torture—another first for New England—that had been used to extract them. Those tales were reinforced by an Andover petition signed on October 19 by the town's two ministers and twenty-four other men. It made the same charge that the confessions had been forced. Increase Mather went to the Salem jail himself on October 20 to talk to the Andover witches. Eight of the twelve women he spoke to confirmed those claims with their own stories about the pressures that led them to confess to such a heinous crime.[29]

In October, tracts started circulating criticizing the court's methods; fourteen leading ministers endorsed the fierce critique in Increase Mather's tract. Another tract argued that the accusers were either possessed by the devil or were witches themselves. Another more cautiously said that the devil was manipulating their brains. Cotton Mather's was the only tract to defend the court and its work vigorously, although selectively, while noting its flaws; he was afraid that all the one-sided emphasis on those flaws would cause it to be shut down. It was said that only three ministers now agreed with the court's procedures.[30]

The closest thing to a poll of public opinion about the witch-hunt came on October 26. That day the General Court debated a bill about the witchcraft outbreak. The bill warned of the forthcoming "utter ruin and destruction of this poor country," and it was not being hyperbolic. If the court continued to stick to its standards, the people already in jail, a hundred or more, perhaps a third of them church members, would die, and although arrests were drastically slowing down, there was no sign of when they would stop. The bill called for a fast and a convocation of ministers to "know the mind of God in this difficult case." The General Court's bill was recognized as a vote of no-confidence on the court. It was significant that it passed and also significant that even with nineteen dead convicted witches, the margin was thin, thirty-three to twenty-nine.[31]

This move to formally reject the court and throw the colony's legal and political problem into the collective laps of the ministers for guidance would have been standard practice in puritan Massachusetts. There ministers and magistrates worked hand in hand, just as they had in Calvin's Geneva. But it never happened. The witchcraft executions began under, and perhaps because of, the new London-controlled regime, and they ended because of it. At the beginning of November, on his own authority, Phips decided to suspend the court, which he could have done at any time. One factor in his decision, Phips explained in a letter to his London superiors, was that he had come to a belated recognition of something he had been warned about from the very beginning: spectral evidence was unreliable. He was certain, he wrote, that the devil was taking on the shape of innocent people. Phips may have come to this certainty after accusers identified one specter as his wife.[32]

Phips also had on his mind pressures entirely outside the orbit of puritanism and unknown to earlier Massachusetts governors. His royal masters 3,000 miles away could take his job away at any moment. Phips fretted in the same letter that "enemies" seeking to have him fired were pointing to the disastrous trials to undermine him. Phips was right to fret. Joseph Dudley, a politically nimble imperial administrator and native of Massachusetts, ended a short stay in the colony sometime before February 1693 and sailed off to London to lobby for Phips's position for himself (he would win the job in 1702, long after Phips was dead). Dudley could point out there that when he presided over the Glover witchcraft trial in 1688, as a member of Edmund Andros's council, his court, unlike the new one, had not followed up on spectral evidence that led to other suspected witches.[33]

Phips permitted the court to meet again in January, with the understanding that spectral evidence and the like "had not the same stress laid upon them as before." Under the stricter rules of evidence, only three of fifty-two people tried were condemned. Phips reprieved them and the five other prisoners awaiting execution. Stoughton had already signed their death warrants and was furious when he heard the news. He refused to sit on the court, claiming that the drive to clear the land of witches had been undermined. Luck of the draw had determined whether suspected witches came out of this year-long legal process convicted and executed, convicted but reprieved, acquitted, or unindicted. A similar witchcraft case unfolded in Connecticut over the same period, but it followed a more conventional course—the judges took to heart the advice of the colony's ministers to be cautious. Only two of eight accused women went to trial; the jury convicted only one of them, Mercy Disborough; and the colony's assembly overturned that verdict on the recommendation of a panel of magistrates, who, by this time, had the disastrous example of Salem to guide them. Disborough barely survived a lynch mob a year later.[34]

The horrific fluke of Salem brought to an end a twenty-nine-year interlude during which only one person had been hanged for witchcraft, whereas fifteen had been hanged in the previous twenty years. That precipitous collapse in executions roughly tracked the grudging acceptance of religious pluralism in the region, as was true elsewhere, and the correlation is unsurprising. Witchcraft for New England's godly magistrates had always been purely a religious offense. Witches were "the most detestable enemies to God and his people that can be," as the renowned English puritan William Perkins put it, and it was the magistrates' divine charge "to discover and to punish the enemies of God and his church." The old laws of puritan New England, unlike English witchcraft laws, had perfectly embodied this puritan priority. They referred only to evidence of a witch's alliance with the devil, not to the malicious harm witches inflicted upon their neighbors.[35]

Legally, in New England it had been strictly this dreadful religious alliance that brought witches to the gallows, not the trail they left behind them of dead farm animals, sick children, and bewitched puddings, among other damage. When detestable religious offenders like Baptists and even the demon-possessed, heretical Quakers stopped being the concern of the magistrates in the later seventeenth century, why should witches be treated much differently? The subsequent Salem legal disaster drove home just how blunt and unreliable the courts were as tools for dealing with a crime about which godly magistrates had always been cautious and recently had grown even more so. Massachusetts held no more witch trials after Salem. Connecticut held one, in 1697, which resulted in an easy dismissal.[36]

That legal disappearance of the crime of witchcraft was neither driven nor followed by a rapid, smooth rise in skepticism about witchcraft itself. In the eighteenth century, New Englanders long continued to suspect neighbors as witches, mainly older women, and fear that they were their victims, while the dark, heavy, supernatural mist raised by the Salem witch frenzy dissipated only slowly. Thomas Hutchinson, a future Massachusetts governor, lamented in the early 1760s that the colonists remained stuck in the old debate about whether it was the accused or the accusers who were "under some preternatural or diabolical possession" instead of debating whether the accusers were ill or imposters. As late as 1795, James Sullivan, another future Massachusetts governor, opted for "possessed by evil spirits" to explain the accusers.[37]

In 1692, what the relationship between magistrates and God's church and its enemies should be—quite apart from the witch trials—was an urgent issue in Massachusetts. All the laws written under the old Massachusetts charter legally died with it. The General Court needed to write new ones, including laws regulating religion. In drafting the laws concerning religion, the General Court labored under the handicap of the charter's insistence on Protestant liberty of conscience, which prevented it from giving Congregationalism any legal privileges.

Nonetheless, the General Court did its best to legislate something of Massachusetts's lost puritanism back into life. It was true that towns could not be compelled to support a Congregationalist minister. They could, however, be made to support an "able, learned, and orthodox" one. The townsmen would choose that minister at a town meeting. If Congregationalists dominated the meeting, as they would pretty much everywhere, and if the result was that Congregationalism would enjoy the same government-supported domination of Massachusetts towns as the Church of England did of English ones, that was serendipity, not a violation of liberty of conscience. Towns would also still have to pay for a school and schoolmaster to ensure a Bible-literate population, another puritan legacy, and to ensure a steady stream of would-be ministers heading to Congregationalist-controlled Harvard, yet another legacy. Who could object to strict laws regulating public activity on Sunday, whether or not they agreed with puritans that Sunday was the divinely mandated Sabbath? And if you removed from the law code the scripture verses that justified certain offenses being punished by death, what did it matter that those laws were still based on the Old Testament and not on English law?[38]

The legislation still only gave a limited taste of Massachusetts's old puritanism. The godly under the new charter had no control over who their governor was and, with the new property-based franchise, no formal way of ensuring that their own representatives were godly. Certainly, no one would extoll Massachusetts's new secular government as a "glorious specimen of the kingly government of Christ," as they had done the old, increasingly threadbare government right into the 1680s.[39] Yet thanks to the new legislation, Massachusetts at least came out of its change of charters with a de facto state-supported Congregationalist church establishment, along with a theocratic thread, albeit drastically pared back, running through its laws.

These puritan-legacy accomplishments, however, collided with the new reality of life in the English empire. The Privy Council disallowed the theocratic death penalty laws; the laws of England, not the laws of the Old Testament, were to be the norm for England's colonies. The General Court's sleight-of-hand re-establishment of Congregationalism escaped the Privy Council's attention, but decades of protests by Baptists, Quakers, and Anglicans followed, locally and to the English government. The General Court belatedly carved out tax exemptions for them, which was more than religious nonconformists in England were given, to avoid a worse reaction from the English government. It knew that the government's official position on Massachusetts was that the colony was a Protestant free-for-all with no established church.[40]

By overwhelming weight of numbers, Calvinist Congregationalism would continue to religiously dominate New England, along with its cultural baggage: anti-Catholicism, high intellectual endeavor, communitarianism, visionary zeal, coercive, moralistic evangelism, and a participatory culture in church and state. But puritanism itself, aspiring to a Christian commonwealth governed and guided by an intolerant state and a purified Calvinist church establishment, belonged on both sides of the Atlantic to an older world.

# GLOSSARY

These terms are mostly defined as the subjects of this book would have understood them.

**Anabaptism** The belief that baptism should be limited to believing adults. The term in England unfavorably connoted a mainly Swiss and German movement associated with various heresies (sv) and a bloody sixteenth-century rebellion in the city of Münster.

**Antichrist** A special enemy of Christ prophesied, it was thought, in various books of the Bible and generally believed by Protestants to be the pope. Puritans believed, to varying degrees, that Antichrist's influence pervaded the Church of England.

**antinomianism** The belief that those whom God has saved are freed from the commanding power of his laws. Puritans were convinced that antinomianism offered a license to sin.

**archbishop** A bishop presiding over a province consisting of a number of dioceses (sv) and their bishops. England had two provinces, Canterbury and York, with Canterbury by far the bigger and more important.

**Arminianism** A theological system denying predestination and affirming that God genuinely gave people the ability to choose whether or not to accept salvation.

**Baptist** Holding that only believing adults should be baptized, not infants. Calling people "Baptist" was more neutral than calling them "Anabaptist" (sv).

**Calvinism** A theological system, with many variations, built around justification (sv) by faith (sv) and double predestination (sv).

**Congregationalism** A form of church government in which the laymen of each church elected the elders (sv) and participated in making decisions. Each individual church cooperated with others strictly on a voluntary basis.

**consistory** See Presbyterianism.

**Covenant of Grace** An agreement made by God that the predestined elect (sv) would be saved through God-granted faith (sv) in Jesus.

**Covenant of Works** An agreement God made offering salvation for perfect obedience to his law. Adam and Eve broke the agreement by eating the forbidden fruit, and no one has been able to meet its terms since.

**diocese**  An ecclesiastical administrative area made up of parishes (sv) and governed by a bishop.

**elders**  Lay and clerical governors of a Congregational (sv) or Presbyterian (sv) church.

**elect**  Those people whom God predestined to go to heaven before he created the world.

**episcopacy**  Government by bishops.

**faith**  A gift of God whereby the elect received Christ as their savior.

**Family of Love**  A small, secretive religious movement whose adherents believed that Christians could eventually enjoy perfect union with God and freedom from sin and that their own revelations superseded those of the Bible. By the 1630s, the terms "Familism" and "Familists" were often used very loosely to refer to eclectic Protestants who explored ideas associated with the Family of Love.

**General Courts**  Legislative and chief judicial bodies of the New England colonies, comprised of deputies, assistants, and a governor. Their deputies were elected annually by each town, while the smaller number of assistants and the governor were elected colony-wide.

**heresy**  Any Christian belief obviously contrary to the Bible and thus very dangerous to the souls of those who stubbornly adhered to it. Reaching a consensus about which beliefs fell into that category was difficult.

**heterodoxy**  Deviation from what was considered to be orthodox Christian truth.

**Independent**  Could refer to the Congregationalists (sv) or to Congregationalists and sectaries (sv).

**justification**  God's declaring a sinner righteous and pardoned from sin.

**magistrate**  A term used expansively to designate a person with the power to enforce law and order. The monarch was the chief magistrate.

**millennium**  A glorious thousand years for Christ's church, which many puritans and other Protestants believed would begin sometime in the not-too-distant future.

**MP (abbr.)**  Member of Parliament, referring to a member of the House of Commons.

**parish**  The Church of England's basic administrative district, which had a minister.

**popery**  Pertaining to the Catholic Church.

**predestination, double**  The belief that, before the world was created, God had inalterably predestined a certain portion of humanity—the elect (sv)—for heaven, and another portion—reprobates—for hell.

**predestination, single**  The belief that God's predestination applied only to the elect.

**prelacy**  Church government by a hierarchy of bishops and lower officers.

**Presbyterianism**  A church system with many variations, in which a board of clerical and lay elders called a consistory or presbytery, with higher bodies above it, supervised one or a number of churches. The amount of lay input in the membership of the presbytery and its decisions also varied greatly. Prebyterianism had no hierarchy among ministers.

**Privy Council**  A Crown-appointed board of aristocrats and prominent commoners who advised England's monarch and administered its government.

**Reformed churches**  European family of Calvinist Protestant churches, as distinguished from the Lutheran churches, with which the Church of England identified itself in the sixteenth century. That identification grew more contested as the seventeenth century progressed.

**sanctification** The creation of a new holiness in believers that followed justification (sv).

**schism** Spiritually and/or legally unlawful separation from a church to create another church.

**sectary** A member of a fringe Protestant group that had broken away from the Church of England.

**separatists** Congregationalists (sv) who rejected all the Church of England's parish churches as false.

**synod** An assembly of churches.

**tithes** A tax on produce intended for the maintenance of the clergy.

# ENDNOTES

Place of publication is London unless otherwise noted.

## Abbreviations

| | |
|---|---|
| Baxter, *RB* | Richard Baxter, *Reliquiae Baxterianae* (1696) |
| BL | British Library |
| Bremer, *CC* | Francis J. Bremer, *Congregational Communion: Clerical Friendship in the Anglo-American Community* (Boston, MA, 1994) |
| Bush, *CJC* | Sargent Bush, Jr. (ed.), *The Correspondence of John Cotton* (Chapel Hill, NC, 2002) |
| Calamy, *ABH* | Edmund Calamy, *An Abridgment of Mr. Baxter's History of his Life and Times*, 2 vols. (2nd edn., 1713) |
| CH | *Church History* |
| Collinson, *EPM* | Patrick Collinson, *The Elizabethan Puritan Movement* (1967) |
| Collinson, *GP* | Patrick Collinson, *Godly People: Essays on English Protestantism and Puritanism* (1983) |
| Cooper, *TTL* | James F. Cooper, Jr., *Tenacious of Their Liberties: The Congregationalists in Colonial Massachusetts* (New York, 1999) |
| CSMP | *Publications of the Colonial Society of Massachusetts* |
| CSPC | *Calendar of State Papers, Colonial Series, America and West Indies*, ed. W. Noel Sainsbury et al., 44 vols. (1860–1969) |
| CSPD | *Calendar of State Papers, Domestic Series, 1603–1704*, ed. Mary Anne Everett Green et al., 85 vols. (1857–1972) |
| DWL | Dr. Williams's Library |
| Foster, *LA* | Stephen Foster, *The Long Argument: English Puritanism and the Shaping of New England Culture, 1570–1700* (Chapel Hill, NC, 1991) |
| Goldie, *RM* | Mark Goldie, *Roger Morrice and the Puritan Whigs* [vol. 1 of *The Entring Book of Roger Morrice, 1677–1691*] (Woodbridge, Suffolk, 2007) |
| Halcomb, "SH" | Joel Halcomb, "A Social History of Congregational Religious Practice during the Puritan Revolution" (Ph.D. thesis, University of Cambridge, 2009) |

| | |
|---|---|
| Hall, *FS* | David D. Hall, *The Faithful Shepherd: A History of the New England Ministry in the Seventeenth Century* (Chapel Hill, NC, 1972) |
| Hall, *WW* | David D. Hall, *Worlds of Wonder, Days of Judgment: Popular Religious Belief in Early New England* (New York, 1989) |
| Hall, *LAP* | Michael G. Hall, *The Last American Puritan: The Life of Increase Mather, 1639–1723* (Hanover, NH, 1988) |
| *Hartlib* | J. Crawford et al. (eds.), *The Hartlib Papers: A Complete Text and Image Database of the Papers of Samuel Hartlib (c. 1600–1662) Held in Sheffield University Library* (Ann Arbor, MI, 1995) |
| *HJ* | *Historical Journal* |
| *HP* | Thomas Hutchinson (ed.), *The Hutchinson Papers*, 2 vols. (Albany, MA, 1865) |
| Hutchinson, *HC* | Thomas Hutchinson, *History of the Colony and Province of Massachusetts-Bay*, ed. Lawrence Shaw Mayo, 3 vols. (Cambridge, MA, 1936). |
| *JBS* | *Journal of British Studies* |
| *JEH* | *Journal of Ecclesiastical History* |
| Johnson, *AE* | Richard R. Johnson, *Adjustment to Empire: The New England Colonies, 1675–1715* (Newark, NJ, 1981) |
| Keeble and Nuttall, *CCRB* | N.H. Keeble and Geoffrey F. Nuttall (eds.), *Calendar of the Correspondence of Richard Baxter*, 2 vols. (Oxford, 1991) |
| MA | Massachusetts Archives |
| Mather, *MCA* | Cotton Mather, *Magnalia Christi Americana: Or, The Ecclesiastical History of New-England*, 2 vols. (Hartford, CT, 1853) |
| "Mather Papers" | "The Mather Papers," *MHSC*, 4th ser., 8 (1868) |
| *MHSC* | *Collections of the Massachusetts Historical Society* |
| *MHSP* | *Publications of the Massachusetts Historical Society* |
| Moore, *P* | Susan Hardman Moore, *Pilgrims: New World Settlers and the Call of Home* (New Haven, CT, 2008) |
| *MR* | *Records of the Governor and Company of the Massachusetts Bay in New England, 1628–1686*, ed. Nathaniel B. Shurtleff, 5 vols. in 6 (Boston, MA, 1853–54) |
| *NEQ* | *New England Quarterly* |
| ODNB | Oxford Dictionary of National Biography |
| *OHA* | Anthony Milton (ed.), *The Oxford History of Anglicanism*, vol. 1 (Oxford, 2017) |
| Pope, *HWC* | Robert G. Pope, *The Half-Way Covenant: Church Membership in Puritan New England* (Princeton, NJ, 1969) |
| Sewall, "Diary" | Samuel Sewall, "Diary," *Collections of the Massachusetts Historical Society*, 5th ser., 7 (1878) |
| Shaw, *HEC* | William A. Shaw, *A History of the English Church during the Civil Wars and under the Commonwealth, 1640–1660*, 2 vols. (1900) |
| Vernon, "SCC" | Elliot Vernon, "The Sion College Conclave and London Presbyterianism during the English Revolution" (Ph.D. thesis, University of Cambridge, 1999) |
| Winship, *GR* | Michael P. Winship, *Godly Republicanism: Puritans, Pilgrims, and a City on a Hill* (Cambridge, MA, 2012) |
| Winship, *MH* | Michael P. Winship, *Making Heretics: Militant Protestantism and Free Grace in Massachusetts, 1636–1641* (Princeton, NJ, 2001) |
| *WJ* | *The Journal of John Winthrop, 1630–1649*, ed. Richard S. Dunn, James Savage and Laetitia Yeandle (Cambridge, MA, 1996) |
| *WP* | *Winthrop Papers, 1498–1649*, 5 vols. (Boston, MA, 1929–47) |

## Introduction

1. John Strype, *The Life and Times of the Most Reverend Father in God, Rev. John Whitgift, D.D.* (1718), p. 139.
2. Alexander Grossart (ed.), *The Complete Works of Richard Sibbes*, 7 vols. (Edinburgh, 1862–64), vol. 1, p. 97; John Stachniewski and Anita Pacheco (eds.), *Grace Abounding with Other Autobiographies* (Oxford, 1998), p. 14; John Rogers, *Ohel or Beth-shemesh* (1653), pp. 426–7; Thomas Fuller, *The Holy State* (1642), pp. 91–2.
3. *WP*, vol. 3, p. 344; Charles E. Hambrick-Stowe, *The Practice of Piety: Puritan Devotional Disciplines in Seventeenth-Century New England* (Chapel Hill, NC, 1982), p. 19; Michael P. Winship, "Briget Cooke and the Art of Godly Female Self-Advancement," *Sixteenth Century Journal* 33 (2002), p. 1,048.
4. A number of emergent English Protestant groups during this period, Quakers, Baptists, semi-Familists, and antinomians among them, had at least some roots in puritanism. But, for the most part, they rejected the fundamental puritan goal of a government and reformed Calvinist church establishment working closely hand in hand. Such groups come within the scope of *Hot Protestants* only to the extent that they interacted with puritanism. Some scholars, nonetheless, call these groups puritans or "radical" puritans. For scholars associating Quakerism, for example, tightly with puritanism, see Geoffrey F. Nuttall, *The Holy Spirit in Puritan Faith and Experience* (Oxford, 1941; reprinted with a new introduction by Peter Lake, Chicago, IL, 1992), and Hugh Barbour, *The Quakers in Puritan England* (New Haven, CT, 1964). For representative critiques of that tight association, see Melvin B. Endy, Jr., "Puritanism, Spiritualism, and Quakerism: An Historiographical Essay," in Richard S. Dunn and Mary Maples Dunn (eds.), *The World of William Penn* (Philadelphia, PA, 1986), pp. 281–302; Rosemary Moore, *The Light in Their Consciences: The Early Quakers in Britain 1646–1666* (University Park, PA, 2000), pp. 109, 268n37; Ariel Hessayon, "Jacob Boehme and the Early Quakers," *Journal of the Friends Historical Society* 60 (2005), pp. 191–223. On whether antinomians should be considered puritans, see the following exchange: Theodore Dwight Bozeman, "The Glory of the 'Third Time': John Eaton as Contra-Puritan," *JEH* 47 (1996), pp. 638–54; David R. Como, *Blown by the Spirit: Puritanism and the Emergence of an Antinomian Underground in Pre-Civil-War England* (Stanford, CA, 2004), pp. 29–31, 29n36; Theodore Dwight Bozeman, *The Precisionist Strain: Disciplinary Religion & Antinomian Backlash in Puritanism to 1638* (Chapel Hill, NC, 2004), pp. 209–10. For the tenuousness of John Milton's connections with puritanism, see Catherine Gimelli Martin, *Milton among the Puritans: The Case for Historical Revisionism* (Aldershot, Hants, 2010). In a different case, whether and at what point Scotland, with its close ties to England but an entirely separate church, had Protestants who can be usefully considered puritans is debated among scholars. For a discussion, see John Coffey, "The Problem of 'Scottish Puritanism,' 1590–1638," in Elizabethann Boran and Crawford Gribben (eds.), *Enforcing Reformation in Ireland and Scotland, 1550–1700* (Aldershot, Hants, 2006), pp. 66–90. See ibid., pp. 67–71, for a succinct discussion of scholarly disputes, now largely subsided, since the mid-twentieth century over how to use the term "puritan" in an English context. For the utility of continuing to use "puritan" in the latter part of the seventeenth century, see my "Defining Puritanism in Restoration England: Richard Baxter and Others Respond to *A Friendly Debate*," *HJ* 54 (2011), pp. 689–715. On using the term "puritan" in a New England context, see my "Were There Any Puritans in New England?" *NEQ* 74 (2001), pp. 118–38.

## Chapter 1  The Seeds of Puritanism

1. Robert W. Dunnin, "The Last Days of Cleeve Abbey," in Caroline M. Barron and Christopher Harper-Bill (eds.), *The Church in Pre-Reformation Society: Essays in Honour of F.R.H. Du Boulay* (Woodbridge, Suffolk, 1985), pp. 58–67; Peter Marshall, *Heretics and Believers: A History of the English Reformation* (New Haven, CT, 2017), pp. 226–9.

2. Dunnin, "Last Days," p. 59; D.C. Newcombe, *John Hooper: Tudor Bishop and Martyr* (Oxford, 2009), p. 6; *Victoria History of Somerset*, vol. 2, ed. William Page (1911), p. 118.

3. Hastings Robinson, *Original Letters Relative to the English Reformation*, 2 vols. (Cambridge, 1846–47), vol. 1, p. 34.

4. Diarmaid MacCulloch, *Tudor Church Militant: Edward VI and the Protestant Reformation* (1999), pp. 109–12; Christopher Haigh, *English Reformations: Religion, Politics, and Society under the Tudors* (New York, 1993), p. 195; Robinson, *Original Letters*, vol. 1, p. 35; Newcombe, *John Hooper*, pp. 6–19.

5. Diarmaid MacCulloch, *The Reformation* (New York, 2004), pp. 337–43.

6. W.M.S. West, "John Hooper and the Origins of Puritanism," *Baptist Quarterly* 15 (1953–54), pp. 354–5.

7. John Strype, *Ecclesiastical Memorials; Relating Chiefly to Religion*, 6 vols. (Oxford 1822), vol. 2, pt. 2, pp. 289–311, 293.

8. Haigh, *English Reformations*, p. 171; Eamon Duffy, *Saints, Sacrilege and Sedition: Religion and Conflict in the Tudor Reformations* (2012), pp. 242–3.

9. Haigh, *English Reformations*, pp. 176–7.

10. Diarmaid MacCulloch, *Thomas Cranmer: A Life* (New Haven, CT, 1996), p. 405; Eamon Duffy, *The Stripping of the Altars: Traditional Religion in England 1400–1580* (New Haven, CT, 1992), p. 100.

11. MacCulloch, *Cranmer*, pp. 410–20, 461–2, 504–8; Barrett L. Beer, *Rebellion and Riot: Popular Disorder in England during the Reign of Edward VI* (Kent, OH, 1982), pp. 78–81.

12. Newcombe, *John Hooper*, pp. 27–9; Robinson, *Original Letters*, vol. 1, p. 75; Strype, *Ecclesiastical Memorials*, vol. 2, pt. 1, p. 66.

13. MacCulloch, *Cranmer*, p. 361; John Foxe, *Actes and Monuments* (1563), p. 1,050; MacCulloch, *Tudor Church*, p. 23.

14. John Hooper, *The Early Writings of John Hooper*, ed. Samuel Carr (Cambridge, 1853), pp. 534, 536.

15. Bernard J. Verkamp, *The Indifferent Mean: Adiaphorism in the English Reformation to 1554* (Athens, OH, 1977).

16. Hooper, *Early Writings*, pp. 479, 534, 554.

17. Richard Bauckham, *Tudor Apocalypse: Sixteenth Century Apocalypticism, Millenarianism and the English Reformation—From John Bale to John Foxe and Thomas Brightman* (Appleford, Oxon., 1978), chaps. 3, 4.

18. Hooper, *Early Writings*, p. 398; Robinson, *Original Letters*, vol. 1, p. 72.

19. Robinson, *Original Letters*, vol. 2, pp. 465–6, 563; John H. Primus, *The Vestments Controversy: An Historical Study of the Earliest Tensions within the Church of England in the Reigns of Edward VI and Elizabeth* (Kampen, 1960), pp. 16–70; *Writings of John Bradford*, 2 vols. (Cambridge, 1848, 1853), vol. 2, p. 390; John Strype, *Annals of the Reformation* (1709), p. 432; Anthony Gilby, *A Pleasant Dialogue, Betweene a Souldior of Barwicke, and an English Chaplaine* (Middleburgh?, 1581), sig. g[viii]r–v.

20. MacCulloch, *Cranmer*, pp. 483–4.

21. Primus, *Vestments Controversy*, pp. 6, 61; Robinson, *Original Letters*, vol. 2, pp. 468, 568.

22. Foxe, *Actes*, p. 1,053.

23. F.D. Price, "Gloucester Diocese under Bishop Hooper 1551–1553," *Transactions of the Bristol and Gloucestershire Archaeological Society* 60 (1938), pp. 51–151, quote from p. 91.

24. Francis Proctor and Walter Howard Frere, *A New History of the Book of Common Prayer* (1908), pp. 35–6; MacCulloch, *Cranmer*, pp. 506–9; George Cornelius Gorham, *Gleanings of a Few Scattered Ears during the Period of the Reformation in England* (1857), p. 232; Thomas S. Freeman, "'The Reformation of the Church in this Parliament': Thomas Norton, John Foxe and the Parliament of 1571," *Parliamentary History* 16 (1997), p. 139; Torrance Kirby, *Persuasion and Conversion: Essays on Religion, Politics, and the Public Sphere* (Leiden, 2013), chap. 3.

## Chapter 2 Proto-Puritans in Exile

1. Jennifer Loach, *Edward VI* (New Haven, CT, 2002), pp. 161–2; Newcombe, *John Hooper*, pp. 207–8; Foxe, *Actes*, pp. 1,061–2; Eamon Duffy, *Fires of Faith: Catholic England under Mary Tudor* (New Haven, CT, 2009), chaps. 4–8.
2. Brett Usher, " 'In a Time of Persecution': New Light on the Secret Protestant Congregation in Marian London," in David Loades (ed.), *John Foxe and the English Reformation* (Aldershot, Hants, 1997), pp. 233–51.
3. Andrew Pettegree, *Marian Protestantism: Six Studies* (Aldershot, Hants, 1996), p. 87; Susan Brigden, *London and the Reformation* (Oxford, 1989), pp. 559–61; Christina Hallowell Garrett, *The Marian Exiles: A Study in the Origins of Elizabethan Puritanism* (Cambridge, 1938), pp. 32, 41; Thomas S. Freeman, " 'The Good Ministrye of Godlye and Vertuouse Women': The Elizabethan Martyrologists and the Female Supporters of the Marian Martyrs," *JBS* 39 (2000), p. 16.
4. Peter Lorimer, *John Knox and the Church of England* (1875), pp. 104, 150–2, 175; MacCulloch, *Cranmer*, pp. 527–8.
5. Peter Lake, " 'Puritans' and 'Anglicans' in the History of the Post-Reformation English Church," in *OHA*, pp. 354, 356–8. For the following incident, see Jane Dawson, *John Knox* (New Haven, CT, 2015), chap. 7; Karl Gunther, *Reformation Unbound: Protestant Visions of Reform in England, 1525–1590* (Cambridge, 2014), chap. 5.
6. *The Forme of Prayers* (Geneva, 1556), pp. 89–90.
7. Michael S. Springer, *Restoring Christ's Church: John a Lasco and the Forma ac ratio* (Aldershot, Hants, 2007), pp. 126–32.
8. *Forme of Prayers*, pp. 49, 89–90, 92, 93.
9. Beth Quitslund, *The Reformation in Rhyme: Sternhold, Hopkins and the English Metrical Psalter, 1547–1603* (Aldershot, Hants, 2008), pp. 115–20, 142–53, chaps. 4, 5; Andrew Pettegree, *Reformation and the Culture of Persuasion* (Cambridge, 2005), pp. 54–65.
10. Anon., *A Brief Discourse of the Troubles at Frankfort, 1554–1558 A.D.*, ed. Edward Arber (1908), p. 66; *Forme of Prayers*, p. 14.
11. Anon., *Brief Discourse*, pp. 38, 64.
12. "John Bale to Catharytes," in Jane E. A. Dawson, "Letters from Exile: New Documents on the Marian Exile, 1553–9"; online at http://www.marianexile.div.ed.ac.uk/resources/Bale-Catharytes-Winter.shtml#letters (accessed July 21, 2016).
13. Robin A. Leaver (ed.), *The Liturgy of the Frankfurt Exiles* (Cambridge, 1984); Gunter, *Reformation*, pp. 176–9.
14. Bryan D. Spinks, *From the Lord and "the Best Reformed Churches": A Study of the Eucharistic Liturgy in the English Puritan and Separatist Traditions, 1550–1633* (Eugene, OR, 2004), p. 28.
15. Duffy, *Fires of Faith*, pp. 87–8; Lake, " 'Puritans' and 'Anglicans,' " pp. 356–8.
16. John Calvin, *Institutes of the Christian Religion*, ed. John T. McNeill, trans. Ford Lewis Battles, 2 vols. (Philadelphia, PA, 1960), vol. 2, pp. 1,215–16.
17. Diarmaid MacCulloch, *Reformation: Europe's House Divided 1490–1700* (New York, 2003), p. 239; F. Bruce Gordon, *Calvin* (New Haven, CT, 2009), pp. 215–16.
18. Philip Benedict, *Christ's Churches Purely Reformed: A Social History of Calvinism* (New Haven, CT, 2002), pp. 102–4.
19. Ibid., pp. 109–14.
20. John Knox, *The Works of John Knox*, ed. David Laing, 6 vols. (Edinburgh, 1846–64), vol. 4, p. 240.
21. Jane E. A. Dawson, "Knox, Goodman, and the Example of Geneva," in Patrick Collinson and Polly Ha (eds.), *The Reception of Continental Reformation in Britain* (Oxford, 2010), p. 128; Roger Williams, *The Bloudy Tenent of Persecution* (1644), p. 120; Collinson, *GP*, chap. 10.
22. David Daniell, *The Bible in English: Its History and Influence* (New Haven, CT, 2003), chaps. 16, 17.

23. *The Bible and Holy Scriptures Conteyned in the Olde and Newe Testament* (Geneva, 1560), sig. ***iiiv, GGgiir (Rev. 11:7), GGgiiiir (Rev. 17:4); Andrew Penny, *Freewill or Predestination: The Battle over Saving Grace in Mid-Tudor England* (Woodbridge, Suffolk, 1990); Duffy, *Fires of Faith*, pp. 175–6.

24. *Bible*, 1st fol., fol. 341r (Ezekiel 18:23), 2nd fol., fol. 97r (2 Thess. 2:13); Richard G. Kyle, *God's Watchman: John Knox's Faith and Vocation* (Eugene, OR, 2014), pp. 97–103.

25. Gordon, *Calvin*, pp. 206–7, 281; Frank A. James, *Peter Martyr Vermigli and Predestination: The Augustinian Inheritance of an Italian Reformer* (Oxford, 1998), p. 34; Anthony Milton, "Attitudes towards the Protestant and Catholic Churches," in *OHA*, pp. 354–5; Pettegree, *Reformation*, p. 199.

26. Daniell, *Bible in English*, pp. 294–5, 434, chap. 26.

27. Ryan M. Reeves, *English Evangelicals and Tudor Obedience, c. 1527–1570* (Leiden, 2014), chap. 4, for this and next paragraph.

28. Christopher Goodman, *How Superior Powers Oght to be Obeyd of Their Subjects* (Geneva, 1558), pp. 35–7, 52–4; Knox, *Works*, vol. 4, pp. 373, 416.

29. Pettegree, *Marian Protestantism*, pp. 143–9.

30. Anon, *Brief Discourse*, pp. 223–4, 225–7.

## Chapter 3  The Birth Pangs of Puritan England

1. Edmund Grindal, *Remains* (Cambridge, 1843), pp. 288–9, for an account of this incident; Brett Usher, "Bartlett, John (fl. 1562–1567)," ODNB.

2. Collinson, *EPM*, pp. 75–9; Usher, "Bartlett."

3. Collinson, *EPM*, pp. 75–9; James Gairdner (ed.), *Three Fifteenth-Century Chronicles with Historical Memoranda*, Camden Society, N.S. 28 (1880), p. 139.

4. Isabel M. Calder, "The St. Antholin Lectures," *Church Quarterly Review* 160 (1959), pp. 49–50; Gairdner (ed.), *Three Fifteenth-Century Chronicles*, p. 140.

5. Patrick Collinson, *Archbishop Grindal, 1519–1583: The Struggle for a Reformed Church* (Berkeley, CA, 1979), pp. 61, 64–5, chap. 9.

6. *Calendar of Letters and State Papers Relating to English Affairs Preserved Primarily in the Archives of Simancas* (1892), vol. 1, p. 37; John Strype, *The Life and Acts of Matthew Parker* (1711), pp. 46, 107, 310; Anne Llewellyn Barstow, "The First Generation of Anglican Clergy Wives: Heroines or Whores?," *Historical Magazine of the Protestant Episcopal Church* 52 (1983), pp. 3–16; Norman L. Jones, *Faith by Statute: Parliament and the Settlement of Religion, 1559* (1982), pp. 9, 134–7; Roger Bowers, "The Chapel Royal, the First Edwardian Prayer Book, and Elizabeth's Settlement of Religion, 1559," *HJ* 43 (2000), pp. 317–44. Some of Bowers's examples are more convincing than others.

7. Peter Marshall and John Morgan, "Clerical Conformity and the Elizabethan Settlement Revisited," *HJ* 59 (2016), pp. 1–22; Collinson, *EPM*, pp. 63–8.

8. Brett Usher, "Edward Brocklesby, 'the first put out of his living for the surplice,'" in Stephen Taylor (ed.), *From Cranmer to Davidson: a Church of England Miscellany* (Woodbridge, Suffolk, 1999), pp. 47–68.

9. Jones, *Faith*, pp. 130–2; Collinson, *EPM*, pp. 68–71; Gunther, *Reformation Unbound*, pp. 99, 211–13.

10. Strype, *Life of Parker*, p. 184.

11. Patrick Collinson, *Richard Bancroft and Elizabethan Anti-Puritanism* (Cambridge, 2013), p. 3.

12. Perceval Wiburn, *A Checke or Reproofe of M. Howlets Untimely Shreeching in her Maiesties Eares* (1581), fol. 15v; Brett Usher, "Participants in the vestiarian controversy (act. c. 1563–c. 1570)," ODNB.

13. Collinson, *EPM*, pp. 48, 79–81; Richard W. Dixon, *The History of the Church of England from the Abolition of the Roman Jurisdiction*, 6 vols. (1878–1902), vol. 6, pp. 126–36, 153–60; Hastings Robinson (ed.), *The Zurich Letters* (Cambridge, 1845), pp. ii, 153–4.

14. Anon., *A Parte of a Register* (Middleburg, 1593), p. 27; Brett Usher, "The Deanery of Bocking and the Demise of the Vestiarian Controversy," *JEH* 52 (2001), p. 453; Collinson, *EPM*, pp. 73, 82.

15. Collinson, *EPM*, pp. 142–3; Felicity Heal and Clive Holmes, *The Gentry in England and Wales, 1500–1700* (Stanford, CA, 1994), p. 12.

16. "Carleton, George (1529–90), of Overstone, Northants., Wisbech and Coldham, Isle of Ely", *The History of Parliament: The House of Commons 1558–1603*, ed. P.W. Hasler (1981); online at http://www.historyofparliamentonline.org/volume/1558-1603/member/carleton-george-1529-90 (accessed May 7, 2017); Alan G. R. Smith, *The Government of Elizabethan England* (New York, 1967), pp. 90–5.

17. Richard Cust and Peter Lake, "Sir Richard Grosvenor and the Rhetoric of Magistracy," *Bulletin of the Institute of Historical Research* 54 (1981), pp. 40–53; Jacqueline Rose, "The Godly Magistrate", in *OHA*, pp. 103–21.

18. Collinson, *EPM*, p. 141.

19. William J. Sheils, "The Puritans in the Diocese of Peterborough," *Northamptonshire Record Society Publications* 30 (1979), p. 28; Collinson, *EPM*, pp. 168–76.

20. Sheils, "Puritans," pp. 21, 24; Stanford E. Lehmberg, "Archbishop Grindal and the Prophesyings," *Historical Magazine of the Protestant Episcopal Church* 34 (1965), pp. 91, 106, 111.

21. Lehmberg, "Archbishop Grindal", p. 124.

22. William Weston, *An Autobiography from the Jesuit Underground*, trans. Philip Caraman (New York, 1955), pp. 164–5.

23. R.M. Serjeantson, *A History of the Church of All Saints, Northampton* (Northampton, 1901), pp. 104–6.

24. Ibid., pp. 105–6.

25. Sheils, "Puritans," pp. 28, 45; Thomas Knell, *An Answer at Large, to a Most Hereticall, Trayterous, and Papisticall Byll* (1570), sigs. Bir, Biir.

26. Sheils, "Puritans," pp. 26–7; Collinson, *EPM*, p. 63.

27. Sheils, "Puritans," pp. 31–2, 37–8, 40–1, 114, 122–3; Anon., *Parte*, pp. 383, 386; Joseph Lemuel Chester, "The Hutchinson Family," *New England Historical & Genealogical Register* (1866), p. 366; Collinson, *EPM*, pp. 357–8.

28. Thomas Cornell Doumaux, "Fast Days and Faction: The Struggle for Reformation, Order, and Unity in England, 1558–c. 1640" (Ph.D. diss., Vanderbilt University, 2008), p. 170; Arnold Hunt, *The Art of Hearing: English Preachers and Their Audiences, 1590–1640* (Cambridge, 2010), p. 66.

29. Hunt, *Art*, pp. 81–94, 131–2; John Craig, "Psalms, Groans and Dog-Whippers: The Soundscape of Sacred Space in the English Parish Church, 1547–1642," in Will Coster and Andrew Spicer (eds.), *Sacred Space in Early Modern Europe* (Cambridge 2005), pp. 110–11.

30. Francis J. Bremer, *Lay Empowerment and the Development of Puritanism* (Basingstoke, Hants, 2015), pp. 39–40; Hunt, *Art*, pp. 72–81; Collinson, *EPM*, pp. 375–80; idem, *From Cranmer to Sancroft* (2006), pp. 145–72.

31. John Knewstubs, *A Confutation of Monstrous and Horrible Heresies, Taught by H.N.* (1579), sig. **5[i]r.

32. Thomas Cartwright, *Cartwrightiana*, ed. Albert Peel and Leland H. Carlson (1951), pp. 120, 130–6.

33. Doumaux, "Fast Days," pp. 81–118, 161.

34. Patrick Collinson, "John Foxe and National Consciousness", in Christopher Highley and John N. King (eds.), *John Foxe and His World* (Aldershot, Hants, 2002), pp. 10, 36; Patrick Collinson, "Biblical Rhetoric: The English Nation and National Sentiment in the Prophetic Mode," in Claire McEachern and Debora Shuger (eds.), *Religion and Culture in Renaissance England* (Cambridge, 1997), pp. 15–45; Michael McGiffert, "God's Controversy with Jacobean England," *American Historical Review* 88 (1983), pp. 1, 151–76. Theodore Dwight Bozeman, "Federal Theology and the 'National Covenant': An Elizabethan Presbyterian Case Study," *CH* 61 (1992), pp. 400–1.

35. Natalie Mears, "Public Worship and Political Participation in Elizabethan England," *JBS* 51 (2012), pp. 4–25; Alexandra Walsham, *Providence in Early Modern England* (Oxford, 1999), p. 146; Collinson, *EPM*, p. 215; Wiburn, *Checke*, fol. 59r; Richard Cosin, *Conspiracie, for Pretended Reformation* (1592), sig. Bv; Cartwright, *Cartwrightiana*, pp. 129, 143–52.
36. Doumaux, "Fast Days," pp. 122–4, 136; Cartwright, *Cartwrightiana*, p. 129; Laurence Chaderton, *An Excellent and Godly Sermon* (1578), sig. Fiir–v.
37. Patrick Collinson, "The Shearman's Tree and the Preacher: The Strange Death of Merry England in Shrewsbury and Beyond," in Patrick Collinson and John Craig (eds.), *The Reformation in English Towns, 1500–1640* (Basingstoke, Hants, 1998), p. 213; Collinson, *GP*, pp. 445–66.

### Chapter 4 The Elizabeth Puritan Political Movement

1. Job Throkmorton, *The Defence of Job Throkmorton* (1694), pp. 26–7. The prayer is adapted from Walter Howard Frere (ed.), *Puritan Manifestoes: A Study of the Origin of the Puritan Revolt* (1907), p. 41.
2. Michael A.R. Graves, *Elizabethan Parliaments 1559–1601* (2nd edn., 1996), pp. 29, 36.
3. Simonds D'Ewes, *Journals of all the Parliaments during the Reign of Queen Elizabeth* (1682), 176, 240; J.E. Neale, *Elizabeth I and Her Parliaments*, 2 vols. (New York, 1958), vol. 1, pp. 194–6, 200–7.
4. Neale, *Elizabeth I*, vol. 1, pp. 247–302; D'Ewes, *Journals*, p. 213.
5. A. Peel and C.H. Firth (eds.), *The Second Parte of a Register*, 2 vols. (Cambridge, 1915), vol. 1, p. 89.
6. Frere (ed.), *Puritan Manifestoes*, p. 19; Winship, *GR*, pp. 14–25, 257n27; Thomas Cartwright, *The Rest of the Second Replie* (Basel, 1577), p. 65.
7. Collinson, *EPM*, p. 149; Stephen Alford, *The Early Elizabethan Polity: William Cecil and the British Succession Crisis, 1558–1569* (Cambridge, 1998), pp. 94–5, 184; H.H. Leonard, "The Huguenots and the St Bartholomew's Massacre," in D.J. Trim (ed.), *The Huguenots: History and Memory in Transnational Context: Essays in Honour and Memory of Walter C. Utt* (Leiden, 2011), pp. 43–68.
8. Collinson, *EPM*, pp. 131–41, 146–9; Frere (ed.), *Puritan Manifestoes*, p. xix.
9. Andrew Forret Scott Pearson, *Thomas Cartwright and Elizabethan Puritanism, 1535–1603* (1925), pp. 28–54; Collinson, *GP*, p. 332. Collinson, *EPM*, p. 123.
10. Pearson, *Cartwright*, pp. 85–6, 120.
11. Winship, *GR*, pp. 14, 25–6.
12. John Whitgift, *The Defense of the Aunswere* (1574), pp. 171–2. The Shakespeare quotation is from *Henry V*, act IV, scene 1, ll. 37–8.
13. Winship, *GR*, p. 13; Peter Lake, "Puritanism (Monarchical) Republicanism, and Monarchy; or John Whitgift, Antipuritanism, and the 'Invention' of Popularity," *Journal of Medieval and Early Modern Studies* 40 (2010), pp. 463–95.
14. John Strype, *The Life and Acts of Matthew Parker* (1711), pp. 461, 491; Pearson, *Cartwright*, pp. 125–6, 129.
15. Strype, *Life of Parker*, appendix, p. 178; Collinson, *EPM*, pp. 159–61.
16. Collinson, *Archbishop Grindal*, chaps. 12, 13: Winship, *GR*, pp. 467–98.
17. Winship, *GR*, p. 351; Peter Lake, *Bad Queen Bess?: Libels, Secret Histories, and the Politics of Publicity in the Reign of Queen Elizabeth I* (New York, 2016), pp. 109–11; Diarmaid MacCulloch, *Reformation: A History* (New York, 2003), p. 40.
18. Collinson, *EPM*, pp. 350–5.
19. Collinson, *GP*, pp. 339, 343, 345–6, 348–9.
20. Patrick Collinson, John Craig and Brett Usher (eds.), *Conferences and Combination Lectures in the Elizabethan Church: Dedham and Bury St Edmunds, 1582–1590* (Woodbridge, Suffolk, 2003), pp. lxxviii–lxxxi, 3–10.
21. Peter Lake, *Moderate Puritans and the Elizabethan Church* (Cambridge, 1982), p. 47; Pearson, *Cartwright*, p. 152, Collinson, *GP*, p. 348.

22. Collinson, *EPM*, pp. 205–6, 243–8.
23. Collinson, Craig and Usher (eds.), *Conferences*, pp. 15, 17, 13; Collinson, *EPM*, p. 260.
24. Collinson, *EPM*, pp. 242, 263, 268, 270; Winship, *GR*, pp. 31, 33.
25. Winship, *GR*, pp. 31–4, for this and next paragraph.
26. Winship, *GR*, pp. 279–82, 303–7.
27. Winship, *GR*, pp. 286–8, 303–15; John Strype, *The Life and Acts of the Most Reverend Father in God John Whitgift* (1718), appendix, pp. 70–3.
28. Neale, *Elizabeth I*, vol. 2, pp. 69–71.
29. Collinson, *EPM*, pp. 386–7; Michael P. Winship, "Puritans, Politics, and Lunacy: The Copinger-Hacket Conspiracy as the Apotheosis of Elizabethan Presbyterianism," *Sixteenth Century Journal* 38 (2007), p. 59.
30. Collinson, Craig and Usher (eds.), *Conferences*, pp. 85–7, xcvii–xcviii.
31. Ibid., pp. 38, 39.
32. Ibid., pp. 317–29, 352–4.
33. George Gifford, *A Short Treatise against the Donatists of England* (1590), sig. a2r, pp. 1–2.
34. Winship, *GR*, pp. 39–51.
35. Ibid., pp. 60–4.
36. Ibid., pp. 53–4.
37. Ibid., pp. 51–60.
38. Gifford, *Short Treatise*, sig. a2r–v.
39. Winship, *GR*, p. 35.
40. "Martin Marprelate," *The Protestatyon of Martin Marprelat* (n.p., 1589), p. 23; Winship, *GR*, pp. 35–6, 261n56.
41. Winship, "Puritans," p. 348; Collinson, *EPM*, p. 391.
42. Winship, "Puritans," p. 349; Strype, *Whitgift*, p. 289; Collinson, *EPM*, pp. 391–2.
43. Collinson, *EPM*, pp. 403–31, 428, 437–43.

## Chapter 5   The Puritan Path to Heaven

1. Christopher Hill, *Economic Problems of the Church: From Archbishop Whitgift to the Long Parliament* (1971), pp. 56–7, 63–9; Collinson, *EPM*, pp. 357–8.
2. Lake, *Moderate Puritans*, pp. 38–40, 46; Samuel Clarke, *The Lives of Two and Twenty English Divines* (1660), p. 200.
3. Hunt, *Art*, pp. 83–94.
4. John Dod, *The Bright Star which Leadeth Wise Men to Our Lord Jesus Christ* (1603), 1st fol., fol. 2v.
5. Ibid., 1st fol., fols. 39v–40v; 2nd fol., fols. 52r, 55r, 56r–v, 57r; Anthony Fletcher, "The Protestant Idea of Marriage in Early Modern England," in Anthony Fletcher and Peter Roberts (eds.), *Religion, Culture, and Society in Early Modern Britain: Essays in Honour of Patrick Collinson* (Cambridge, 1994), pp. 161–81; Thomas W. Laqueur, *Making Sex: Body and Gender from the Greeks to Freud* (Cambridge, MA, 1990), pp. 98–103.
6. Dod, *Bright Star*, 2nd fol., fol. 57r.
7. Ibid., 2nd fol., fol. 56v.
8. John Dod, "Dods Droppings," DWL, MS 28.2, pp. 102–3, 104–5; Piers Beirne, *Confronting Animal Abuse: Law, Criminology, and Human-Animal Relationships* (Lanham, MD, 2009), pp. 74–86; Francis J. Bremer, *John Winthrop: America's Forgotten Founding Father* (New York, 2003), pp. 94.
9. Dod, *Bright Star*, 1st fol., fol. 51v. Cf., John Edwards, *Theologia Reformata*, 2 vols. (1713), vol. 2, p. 422.
10. Dod, *Bright Star*, 1st fol., fols. 45r (incorrectly foliated as 54r), 46r, 55v.
11. Ibid., 1st fol., fol. 43v.
12. Ibid., 1st fol., fol. 60r; idem, "Dods Droppings," p. 192; Winship, *GR*, pp. 162–3; Clarke, *Lives of Two and Twenty*, p. 203.

13. Dod, "Dods Droppings," p. 196; idem, *Bright Star*, 2nd fol., fol. 46v; Patrick Collinson, *Elizabethans* (2003), p. 237.
14. Nicholas Bownde, *Sabbathum Veteris et Novi Testamenti* (1606), p. 264.
15. John H. Primus, *Holy Time: Moderate Puritanism and the Sabbath* (Macon, GA, 1989); Dod, *Bright Star*, 1st fol., fols. 71v–72r, 73r, 92v; 2nd fol., fol. 79v.
16. Barton John Blankenfeld, "Puritans in the Provinces: Banbury, Oxfordshire, 1554–1660" (Ph.D. diss., Yale University, 1985), pp. 154–69; Strype, *Whitgift*, p. 315; Richard Brathwaite, *Barnabæ Itinerarium; Or, Barnabee's Journal* (1818), p. 15.
17. James Ussher, *The Annals of the World* (1658), p. 2.
18. Dod, *Bright Star*, 1st fol., fol. 3r.
19. Ibid., 2nd fol., fol. 83r; Michael P. Winship, "Weak Christians, Backsliders, and Carnal Gospelers: Assurance of Salvation and the Pastoral Origins of Puritan Practical Divinity in the 1580s," *CH* 70 (2001), pp. 462–81 for next six paragraphs.
20. Dod, *Bright Star*, 1st fol., fol. 41v.
21. Ibid., 1st fol., fol. 10r; Hambrick-Stowe, *Practice of Piety*, pp. 168–75.
22. Clarke, *Lives of Two and Twenty*, pp. 210–11; Dod, *Bright Star*, 2nd fol., fol. 86v; 1st fol., fol. 89r.
23. Dod, *Bright Star*, 1st fol., fol. 86v; 2nd fol., fol. 10v.
24. Winship, *MH*, pp. 18–19; idem, "Weak Christians," p. 478; John Flavel, *The Whole Works*, 6 vols. (1820), vol. 3, pp. 564, 566; Giles Firmin, *The Real Christian* (1670), "To the Reader"; Dod, "Dods Droppings," pp. 117–18; John Stachniewski, *The Persecutory Imagination: English Puritanism and the Literature of Religious Despair* (Oxford, 1991), pp. 219–41; Alec Ryrie, *Being Protestant in Reformation Britain* (Oxford, 2013), p. 83; J.T. Cliffe, *The Puritan Gentry: The Great Puritan Families of Early Stuart England* (1984), p. 14. The collective claim about the difficulty of assurance of salvation came at the Westminster Assembly. See Robert Letham, *The Westminster Assembly: Reading Its Theology in Historical Context* (Phillipsburg, NJ, 2009), pp. 283–8.
25. Paul S. Seaver, *Wallington's World: A Puritan Artisan in Seventeenth-Century London* (Stanford, CA, 1985), pp. 22–3, 25, 43–4, 109–10.
26. Ibid., p. 5; Foster, *LA*, pp. 86–92; Andrew Cambers, *Godly Reading: Print, Manuscript and Puritanism in England, 1580–1720* (Cambridge, 2011), chaps. 2,3.
27. Samuel Clarke, *Lives of Sundry Eminent Persons* (1683), 2nd pag., pp. 154, 155, 161, 164–5; Kate Narveson, *Bible Readers and Lay Writers in Early Modern England: Gender and Self-Definition in an Emergent Writing Culture* (Farnham, Surrey, 2012), chap. 2.
28. Clarke, *Lives of Sundry Eminent Persons*, 2nd pag., p. 159.
29. Ibid., p. 161; Michael P. Winship, *Seers of God: Puritan Providentialism in the Restoration and Early Enlightenment* (Baltimore, MD, 1996), chap. 1.
30. Clarke, *Lives of Sundry Eminent Persons*, 2nd pag., pp. 159, 161.
31. Ibid., p. 157.
32. Ibid.
33. Clarke, *Lives of Two and Twenty*, p. 212; Ralph Houlebrooke, "The Puritan Death Bed, *c.* 1560–*c.* 1660," in Christopher Durston and Jacqueline Eales (eds.), *The Culture of English Puritanism, 1560–1700* (Basingstoke, Hants, 1966), pp. 122–44; Matthew Mead, *A Funeral Sermon Preached upon the Sad Occasion of the Death of That Eminent and Faithful Servant of Christ, Mr Thomas Rosewell* (1692), p. 28.

### Chapter 6  Taming Puritanism

1. Willem J. op 't Hof, "The Eventful Sojourn of Willem Teellinck (1579–1629) at Banbury in 1605," *Journal for the History of Reformed Pietism* 1 (2015), pp. 5–34; Philip Benedict, *Christ's Churches Purely Reformed: A Social History of Calvinism* (New Haven, CT, 2002), pp. 522–5.
2. Winship, *GR*, p. 68; *Royal Commission on Historical Manuscripts Report on the Manuscripts of Lord Montagu of Beaulieu* (1900), pp. 32–40.

3. Winship, *GR*, p. 68; William Barlow, *The Summe and Substance of the Conference* (1604), pp. 36, 83.
4. Gerald Bray, "Canon Law and the Church of England," in *OHA*, pp. 181–3; Winship, *GR*, pp. 70–80. Kenneth Fincham puts the number of beneficed ministers who lost their positions at between seventy-three and eighty-three, along with an unknown number of curates and lecturers. Nonconformists put the total figure at around three hundred. See Kenneth Fincham, *Prelate as Pastor: The Episcopate of James I* (Oxford, 1990), pp. 323–6; idem, "Clerical Conformity from Whitgift to Laud," in Peter Lake and Michael Questier (eds.), *Conformity and Orthodoxy in the English Church, c. 1560–1660* (Woodbridge, Suffolk, 2000), pp. 139–41; Samuel Hieron, *A Short Dialogue* (1605), p. 1; Robert Parker, *A Scholasticall Discourse* (1607), p. 120; Henry Jacob, *A Christian and Modest Offer* (1606), sig. *3r. See also Foster, *LA*, pp. 99–101.
5. Tom Webster, *Godly Clergy in Early Stuart England: The Caroline Puritan Movement, c. 1620–1643* (Cambridge, 1997), pp. 159–62, 167.
6. William Durham, *The Life and Death of that Judicious Divine, and Accomplish'd Preacher, Robert Harris* (1660), pp. 11–17.
7. Winship, *GR*, p 163.
8. Blankenfeld, "Puritans in the Provinces," p. 275; Webster, *Godly Clergy*, pp. 159–60; William Whately, *Prototypes* (1649), sig. a5r–v; C. Richardson, *Puritanism in North-West England: A Regional Study of the Diocese of Chester to 1642* (Manchester, 1972), pp. 81–3; Jacqueline Eales, "Whately, William (1583–1639)," ODNB.
9. Durham, *Life and Death*, p. 25; Collinson, *GP*, chap. 18; Alfred Beesley, *The History of Banbury* (1841), p. 269; William Whately, *The New Birth* (1618), pp. 139, 142, 146–7.
10. C.M. Newman, "'An Honourable and Elect Lady': The Faith of Isabel, Lady Bowes," in D. Wood (ed.), *Life and Thought in the Northern Church, c. 1100–c.1700: Essays in Honour of Claire Cross* (1999), pp. 407–19; Thomas S. Freeman, "Darcy, Isabel, Lady Darcy (d. 1622)," ODNB.
11. Winship, *GR*, p. 67.
12. Amy Gant Tan, "Richard Bernard and His Publics: A Puritan Minister as Author" (Ph.D. diss., Vanderbilt University, 2015), pp. 39–41; Winship, *GR*, p. 85.
13. Winship, *GR*, pp. 86–8.
14. Ibid., pp. 93–5.
15. Ibid., p. 70.
16. John Fielding, "Conformists, Puritans and the Church Courts: The Diocese of Peterborough, 1603–1642" (Ph.D. thesis, University of Birmingham, 1989), p. 67.
17. Peter Lake and Isaac Stephens, *Scandal and Religious Identity in Early Stuart England: A Northamptonshire Maid's Tragedy* (Woodbridge, Suffolk, 2015), pp. 298, 320.
18. Ibid., pp. 298, 341; Isaac Stephens, "The Courtship and Singlehood of Elizabeth Isham, 1630–1634," *HJ* 51 (2008), pp. 1–25.
19. Lake and Stephens, *Scandal*, p. 343; William Perkins, *The Workes*, 3 vols. (1617), vol. 2, pp. 141–2; Lake and Stephens, *Scandal*, pp. 344–5.
20. Thomas Freeman, "Demons, Deviance and Defiance: John Darrell and the Politics of Exorcism in Late Elizabethan England," in Lake and Questier (eds.), *Conformity and Orthodoxy*, pp. 34–68.
21. Clarke, *Lives of Two and Twenty*, pp. 88, 91–5; Freeman, "Demons," p. 62n143.
22. Clarke, *Lives of Two and Twenty*, p. 87; Samuel Whiting, "Concerning the Life of the Famous Mr. Cotton," in *Chronicles of the First Planters of the Colony of Massachusetts Bay*, ed. Alexander Young (Boston, MA, 1846), pp. 422–3; Mather, *MCA*, vol. 1, p. 257; Bremer, *CC*, p. 21; Larzer Ziff, *The Career of John Cotton: Puritanism and the American Experience* (Princeton, NJ, 1962), pp. 36–7.
23. Whiting, *Life*, pp. 425–6; Bush, *CJC*, pp. 18–23; Percentor Venables, "The Primary Visitation of the Diocese of Lincoln by Bishop Neile, A.D. 1614," *Associated Architectural Societies' Reports and Papers* 16 (1881), p. 50.

24. Whiting, *Life*, pp. 423–4; John Cotton, *Some Treasure Fetched Out of Rubbish* (1660), pp. 1–52; Ziff, *Career*, pp. 50–1.

25. Margaret Aston, *Broken Idols of the English Reformation* (Cambridge, 2016), pp. 666–73, 686–7, 670, 804–8; Jesper Rosenmeier, "'Eaters and Non-Eaters': John Cotton's *A Brief Exposition of . . . Canticles* (1642) in Light of Boston's (Lincs.) Religious and Civil Conflicts, 1619–22," *Early American Literature* 36 (2001), pp. 157–60.

26. Ibid., pp. 160, 151; Whiting, *Life*, pp. 426–7; Bush, *CJC*, pp. 91–103; Alan Ford, "The Church of Ireland 1558–1634, a Puritan Church?" in Alan Ford, J.I. McGuire and Kenneth Milne (eds.), *As by Law Established: The Church of Ireland Since the Reformation* (Dublin, 1996), pp. 52–68.

27. Mather, *MCA*, vol. 1, pp. 259–60; Hartlib, 29/2/51A, 29/2/54A, 29/2/59B; Walter Scott (ed.), *The Somers Tracts* 13 vols. (1809–15), vol. 4, pp. 583–4.

28. Venables, "Primary Visitation," p. 41; Mather, *MCA*, vol. 1, pp. 258, 259

29. Bauckham, *Tudor Apocalypse*, chaps 3,4.

30. Andrew Crome, *The Restoration of the Jews: Early Modern Hermeneutics, Eschatology, and National Identity in the Works of Thomas Brightman* (Dordrecht, 2014), pp. 16–26, chaps 3, 4.

31. John Cotton, *A Brief Exposition of the Whole Book of Canticles* (1642), pp. 209–10, 213, 214, 219–20, 225, 226, 229; Winship, *MH*, p. 61. Cotton's historicizing of the Old Testament Song of Songs in these passages came from Brightman: see Crome, *Restoration*, pp. 81–93.

32. Paul Christianson, *Reformers and Babylon: English Apocalyptic Visions from the Reformation to the Eve of the Civil War* (Buffalo, NY, 1978), p. 105.

33. Cliffe, *Puritan Gentry*, pp. 182–3; Fielding, "Conformists," p. 14.

34. Samuel Clarke, *A Generall Martyrologie* (1651), pp. 413–14.

35. David Underdown, *Fire from Heaven: Life in an English Town in the Seventeenth Century* (New Haven, CT, 1994), pp. 18, 31, 92.

36. Ibid., pp. 2–3; William Whately, *Sinne No More* (1626), pp. 5–6.

37. Underdown, *Fire*, pp. 90–109, 155–6.

38. Winship, *GR*, p. 165.

39. Frances Rose-Troup, *John White, the Patriarch of Dorchester Dorset and the Founder of Massachusetts, 1575–1648* (New York, 1930), pp. 220, 418–19; Eamon Duffy, *Reformation Divided: Catholics, Protestants and the Conversion of England* (2017), pp. 334–7.

40. Duffy, *Reformation Divided*, pp. 110–29; Paul Slack, *From Reformation to Improvement: Public Welfare in Early Modern England* (Oxford, 1999), chap. 2.

41. Rose-Troup, *John White*, pp. 50–63, chap. 15.

42. Patrick Collinson, *The Religion of Protestants: The Church in English Society 1559–1625* (Oxford, 1982), 159.

43. Winship, *GR*, p. 73; Underdown, *Fire*, p. 153.

## Chapter 7  The Lure of the Atlantic

1. Jeremiah Dyke, *A Sermon Preached at the Publicke Fast to the Commons House of Parliament. April. 5th. 1628* (1629), p. 25.

2. Winship, *GR*, pp. 112–17; Babette M. Levy, "Early Puritanism in the Southern and Island Colonies," *American Antiquarian Society Proceedings* 70 (1960), pp. 93–112.

3. Winship, *GR*, pp. 117–18; Hambrick-Stowe, *Practice of Piety*, chap. 3.

4. William Bradford, *Bradford's History "Of Plimouth Plantation"* (Boston, MA, 1898), p. 123; Neal Salisbury, *Manitou and Providence: Indians, Europeans, and the Making of New England, 1500–1643* (New York, 1982), p. 104; Winship, *GR*, p. 119.

5. Winship, *GR*, pp. 120–33.

6. Bradford, *Bradford's History*, p. 250.

7. Douglas Bradburn, "The Eschatological Origins of the English Empire," in Douglas Bradburn and John C. Coombs (eds.), *Early Modern Virginia: Reconsidering the Old Dominion* (Charlottesville, VA, 2011), pp. 38–44; David L. Smith, "Fiennes, William, first Viscount Saye and Sele (1582–1662)," ODNB.

8. Nicholas Tyacke, *Anti-Calvinists: The Rise of English Arminianism, c. 1590–1640* (Oxford, 1987); Peter Lake, "Introduction: Puritanism, Arminianism and Nicholas Tyacke," in Kenneth Fincham and Peter Lake (eds.), *Religious Politics in Post-Reformation England: Essays in Honour of Nicholas Tyacke* (Woodbridge, Suffolk, 2006), pp. 1–15.

9. Giles Firmin, *The Real Christian* (1670), p. 26.

10. Dod, *Bright Star*, 1st fol., fol. 51r; William Prynne, *The Church of Englands Old Antithesis to New Arminianisme* (1629), p. 79.

11. Tim Harris, *Rebellion: Britain's First Stuart Kings, 1567–1642* (Oxford, 2014), chap. 7, for this and next paragraph. On the Church of England as a self-identifying member of the Reformed churches, see Anthony Milton, *Catholic and Reformed: The Roman and Protestant Churches in English Protestant Thought, 1600–1640* (Cambridge, 1995), chaps. 8 and 9.

12. Thomas Cogswell, *The Blessed Revolution: English Politics and the Coming of War, 1621–1624* (Cambridge, 1989), "Prologue;" Webster, *Godly Clergy*, p. 66. See also Harris, *Rebellion*, chap. 7, for this and next paragraph.

13. Winship, *GR*, pp. 166–7, for this and next paragraph.

14. Ibid., p. 167.

15. Richard Cust, *Charles I: A Political Life* (Harlow, Essex, 2005), pp. 89–91; Jonathan D. Moore, *English Hypothetical Universalism: John Preston and the Softening of Reformed Theology* (Grand Rapids, MI, 2007), chap. 6. On Preston's Puritanism, see ibid., pp. 12–24; Peter Lake. "The 'Court,' the 'Country' and the Northamptonshire Connection: Watching the 'Puritan Opposition' Think (Historically) about Politics on the Eve of the English Civil War," *Midland History* 35 (2010), pp. 28–70.

16. Winship, *GR*, pp. 189–92, for this and next paragraph.

17. Lake, "The 'Court,' the 'Country' and the Northamptonshire Connection," p. 49.

18. Winship, *GR*, pp. 67–8, 192–3.

19. *MR*, vol. 1, p. 387; Charles M. Andrews, *The Colonial Period of American History*, 4 vols. (New Haven, CT, 1934), vol. 1, pp. 336–74; Ronald Dale Karr, "The Missing Clause: Myth and the Massachusetts Bay Charter of 1629," *NEQ* 77 (2004), pp. 89–107.

20. Karr, "The Missing Clause," pp. 135–6, 193; Noah Millstone, *Manuscript Circulation and the Invention of Politics in Early Stuart England* (Cambridge, 2016), chap. 7.

21. Robert Charles Winthrop, *Life and Letters of John Winthrop*, 2 vols. (Boston, MA, 1869), vol. 1, pp. 309; vol. 2, p. 168; Bremer, *Winthrop*, pp. 125–35, 140–6; Heale and Holmes, *Gentry*, pp. 26–7.

22. Winship, *GR*, pp. 168–9.

23. Winthrop, *Life and Letters*, vol. 1, pp. 344–5.

24. Levy, "Early Puritanism," pp. 166–7.

25. Bradburn, "Eschatological Origins," p. 40; Levy, "Early Puritanism," pp. 167–79; Louise Timko, "Puritans in Bermuda, 1612–1650" (Ph.D. diss., Drew University, 1996), pp. 29, 84–6. The only minister who is known to have been a conformist on Bermuda and that only for a short length of time, Nathaniel White, had been put under £200 bond by the company, under pressure from Archbishop Laud "to follow the orders and discipline of the Church of England" before he could immigrate to Bermuda. In Bermuda, White did not require ceremonial conformity from the laity who attended his services. White had been put under that bond after preaching a sermon at Oxford arguing that bishops were the same order of clergy as ordinary ministers for which he had been suspended from his ministry. The point would not have been controversial in the sixteenth century, but it was dangerously offensive to the bishops in the 1630s; see Nathaniel White, *The Pastors Charge and Cure* (1645), sig. A2[ii]r–a2v; idem, *Truth Gloriously Appearing* (1645), pp. 80–1. There was brief experimenting with alternate Reformed liturgies on Bermuda around 1620, but that episode quickly ended. See John Henry Lefroy, *Memorials of the*

*Discovery and Early Settlement of Bermuda, 1515–1685*, 2 vols. (1879), vol. 1, p. 151; [Nathaniel Butler], *The Historye of the Bermudaes, or Summer Islands*, ed. J. Henry Lefroy, Hakluyt Society, *Works*, 1st ser., 6 (1882), pp. 171–3; Vernon A. Ives (ed.), *The Rich Papers: Letters from Bermuda, 1615–1646* (Toronto, 1984), pp. 100, 107, 337–46.

26. Lefroy, *Memorials*, vol. 1, pp. 131, 132, 164, 256, 319, 418, 419, 482, 498, 499. A.C. Hollis Hallett (ed.), *Bermuda under the Sommer Islands Company, 1612–1684: Civil Records*, 3 vols. (Bermuda, 2005), vol. 1, pp. 12, 45, 65, 66, 105, 122, 140–1, 148; Joan de Rivera, "Shipwrecked Spaniards 1639: Grievances against Bermudans," trans. L.D. Gurrin, *Bermuda Historical Quarterly* 18 (1961), p. 27; Freeman, "Demons," p. 62. For another case of demonic possession, see *WJ*, p. 119.

27. Polly Ha, "Godly Globalisation: Calvinism in Bermuda," *JEH* 66 (2015), p. 548, suggests that there was a "presbyterian model of government by ministers and overseers" in each parish. She does not explain what an entirely secular civic office like overseer has to do with Presbyterianism. Bermuda ministers presided over their parishes with the ordinary English lay parish officers. Ha further claims (p. 552) that ministers "relied on a form of suspension from the Lord's supper, in which they declared a person infamous." Her source, however, says it was the governor and council who declared a person infamous and does not mention suspension from the Lord's Supper. One minister tried to set up a Presbyterian government with lay elders for the colony in the late 1610s. It does not seem to have ever gotten off the ground; see Ives (ed.), *Rich Papers*, pp. 10–11, 110, 116; Hallett (ed.), *Bermuda*, vol. 1, p. 113.

28. Governor Philip Wood in 1634 thought that five ministers were the "least" the colony should have; it rarely had that many, and sometimes only one; see Hallett (ed.), *Bermuda*, vol. 1, p. 247; idem, *Chronicle of a Colonial Church* (Bermuda, 1993), chaps. 3, 4; Timko, "Puritans," pp. 57–64, 65; Lefroy, *Memorials*, vol. 1, p. 535; Rivera, "Shipwrecked Spaniards," pp. 26, 27; Alison Games, *Migration and the Origins of the English Atlantic World* (Cambridge, MA, 1999), pp. 48, 85, 91; Lefroy, *Memorials*, vol. 1, pp. 231, 595; Lewis Hughes, *To the Right Honourable, The Lords and Others of his Majesties most Honourable Privie Councell* (1625), sig. B4r–v; Michael J. Jarvis, " 'In the Eye of All Trade': Maritime Revolution and the Transformation of Bermudian Society, 1612–1800" (Ph.D. diss., College of William and Mary, 1998), pp. 143–62.

29. Bremer, *Winthrop*, p. 160; Winship, *GR*, p. 186.

30. Bremer, *Winthrop*, pp. 169, 162–4.

31. Richard M. Gamble, *In Search of the City on a Hill: The Making and Unmaking of an American Myth* (2012), pp. 28–30; John Winthrop, "A Modell of Christian Charity," *MHSC*, 3rd ser., 7 (1838), pp. 46, 47.

32. William Attersoll, *A Commentarie upon the Fourth Booke of Moses* (1618), p. 419; Nicholas Byfield, *A Commentary: Or, Sermons upon the Second Chapter of the First Epistle of Saint Peter* (1623), p. 187.

33. Winthrop, "Modell," p. 47; Winship, *GR*, p. 172.

34. Perry Miller, *Errand into the Wilderness* (Cambridge, MA, 1956), p. 12.

35. Theodore Dwight Bozeman, "The Puritan 'Errand into the Wilderness' Reconsidered," *NEQ* 59 (1986), pp. 231–5; Gamble, *In Search*, pp. 133–63, chap. 6; online at http://www.presidency.ucsb.edu/ws/?pid=85199 (accessed June 15, 2017). In the 1970s, Sacvan Bercovitch attracted a great deal of attention by embroidering Miller's claim with a further claim that Winthrop and subsequent puritans envisioned New England as the site of the millennium's New Jerusalem. The claim has been thoroughly discredited. For a review, see Michael P. Winship, "What Puritan Guarantee," *Early American Literature* 47 (2012), pp. 411–20.

36. Winship, *GR*, pp. 170–1.

## Chapter 8  John Cotton Comes to Massachusetts

1. *WJ*, p. 95; Darrett B. Rutman, *Winthrop's Boston: A Portrait of a Puritan Town, 1630–1649* (Chapel Hill, NC, 1965), p. 179; William Hubbard, *A General History of New England* (Boston, MA, 1848), pp. 134, 135, 158.

2. Winship, *GR*, pp. 134–45.
3. Ibid., pp. 145–6.
4. Ibid. pp. 147–8.
5. Ibid., p. 179; Mather, *MCA*, vol. 1, pp. 262–3.
6. Winship, p. 179; David Cressy, *Coming Over: Migration and Communication Between England and New England in the Seventeenth Century* (Cambridge, 1987), p. 87; Moore, *P*, p. 23.
7. Michael P. Winship, "Straining the Bonds of Puritanism: English Presbyterians and Massachusetts Congregationalists Debate Ecclesiology, 1636–1640," in Crawford Gribben and R. Scott Spurlock (eds.), *Puritans and Catholics in the Trans-Atlantic World, 1600–1800* (Basingstoke, 2015), pp. 93–4, 109n17; Winship, *GR*, pp. 153–4.
8. Mather, *MCA*, vol. 1, pp. 263–4, 340; John Norton, *Abel Being Dead yet Speaketh* (1658), pp. 28, 30; Richard S. Dunn, *Sugar and Slaves: The Rise of the Planter Class in the English West Indies, 1624–1713* (Chapel Hill, NC, 1972), p. 49.
9. *WJ*, pp. 95–6; Winship, "Straining," p. 93.
10. *MR*, vol. 1, pp. 101, 84, 92, 82; Everett H. Emerson (ed.), *Letters from New England: The Massachusetts Bay Colony, 1629–1638* (Amherst, MA, 1976), p. 97.
11. Winship, *GR*, pp. 184–94.
12. Baird Tipson, "Invisible Saints: The 'Judgment of Charity' in the Early New England Churches," *CH* 44 (1975), pp. 460–71.
13. Winship, *GR*, pp. 174–5.
14. Ibid., pp. 194, 195.
15. Ibid., pp. 196–7, 200–1.
16. Ibid., pp. 226–9.
17. Ibid., pp. 125–6.
18. "Memoirs of Roger Clap," *Dorchester Antiquarian and Historical Society* 1 (1844), p. 21; George Selement and Bruce C. Woolley (eds.), *Thomas Shepard's Confessions*, *CSMP* 58 (Boston, MA, 1981), p. 196; Winship, *GR*, p. 235.
19. Mather, *MCA*, vol. 1, p. 325; Winship, *MH*, pp. 61–2, 233.
20. Ibid., p. 233.

## Chapter 9 Protestant Reformation and Counter-Reformation in the 1630s

1. Richard Cust, "Charles I and Popularity," in Thomas Cogswell, Richard Cust and Peter Lake (eds.), *Politics, Religion and Popularity in Early Stuart Britain* (Cambridge, 2002), pp. 235–58; Kevin Sharpe, *The Personal Rule of Charles I* (New Haven, CT, 1992), pp. 212n22, 382.
2. Sharpe, *Personal Rule*, pp. 229–33; Mark Kishlansky, "A Whipper Whipped: The Sedition of William Prynne," *HJ* 56 (2013), pp. 603–27; William Prynne, *Histrio-mastix* (1633), pp. 848–58, sig. Rrrrr3[i]r.
3. Richard Cust, *Charles I and the Aristocracy* (Cambridge, 2013), chap. 2; Sharpe, *Personal Rule*, pp. 394, 399.
4. Alistair Dougall, *The Devil's Book: Charles I, the Book of Sports and Puritanism in Tudor and Early Stuart England* (Exeter, 2012), p. 138. The Book of Sports had been issued before in 1618, but the 1633 reissue was enforced much more vigorously.
5. Peter Lake, "Puritanism, Arminianism and a Shropshire Axe-Murder," *Midland History* 12 (1989), p. 46; Barbara Coulton, "Rivalry and Religion: The Borough of Shrewsbury in the Early Stuart Period," *Midland History* 28 (2003), pp. 32–6.
6. Lake, "Puritanism, Arminianism," p. 47; Coulton, "Rivalry," p. 35; Clarke, *Generall Martyrologie*, pp. 464–5, 471; Patricia Crawford, *Women and Religion in England: 1500–1720* (Abingdon, Oxon, 1993), p. 132.
7. Coulton, "Rivalry," p. 35; Nicholas Tyacke, *Aspects of English Protestantism, c. 1530–1700* (Manchester, 2001), pp. 121–3. Isabel MacBeath Calder (ed.), *Activities of the Puritan Faction of the Church of England, 1625–33* (1957), pp. xxii, 10.
8. Tyacke, *Aspects*, p. 121. Calder (ed.), *Activities*, pp. 61, 103.

9. Coulton, "Rivalry," p. 37; Darren Oldridge, *Religion and Society in Early Stuart England* (Aldershot, Hants, 1998), pp. 42–3.

10. Kenneth Fincham and Nicholas Tyacke, *Altars Restored: The Changing Face of English Religious Worship 1547–c.1700* (Oxford, 2007), chap. 5, p. 201; Kenneth Fincham, "The Restoration of Altars in the 1630s," *HJ* 44 (2001), pp. 935–9; Julian Davies, *The Caroline Captivity of the Church: Charles I and the Remoulding of Anglicanism 1625–1642* (Oxford, 1992), pp. 221, 225–6, 234; Webster, *Godly Clergy*, pp. 217–24.

11. Fincham and Tyacke, *Altars*, chap. 6; Sir William Brereton, *Travels in Holland, the United Provinces, England, Scotland, and Ireland, 1634–1635* (Manchester, 1844), p. 187.

12. Peter Studley, *The Looking-Glasse of Schisme* (1634), pp. 22–5, 29, 87.

13. Como, *Blown by the Spirit*, pp. 167–72; Christopher W. Marsh, *The Family of Love in English Society, 1550–1630* (Cambridge, 1994). Familist motifs circulated in what Como has preferred to call the perfectionist strain of antinomianism in *Blown by the Spirit*.

14. Studley, *Looking-Glasse*, pp. 104, 154, 158; Richard More, *A True Relation of the Murders Committed in the Parish of Clunne in the County of Salop by Enoch ap Evan* (1641), pp. 22, 77–8.

15. Studley, *Looking-Glasse*, pp. 25, 29.

16. Ibid., pp. 35–43.

17. Ibid., pp. 8–13, 23–4, 44, 153; More, *True Relation*, p. 77.

18. Lake, "Puritanism, Arminianism," pp. 50, 56; Clarke, *Generall Martyrologie*, p. 446.

19. Clarke, *Generall Martyrologie*, p. 468; John Gorham Palfrey, *History of New England during the Stuart Dynasty*, 3 vols. (Boston, MA, 1865–70), vol. 1, pp. 392–403; Winship, *GR*, p. 202.

20. Winship, *GR*, pp. 201–3.

21. *MR*, vol. 1, pp. 126, 128; Winship, *GR*, p. 317n18.

22. Winship, *GR*, pp. 208–9.

23. Ibid., pp. 212, 219.

24. *WJ*, p. 137.

25. ibid., p. 216.

26. *MR*, vol. 1, pp. 140, 139.

27. Winship, *GR*, p. 217.

28. *WJ*, p. 137.

29. Nathaniel Morton, *New-Englands Memorial* (Cambridge, MA, 1669), p. 82.

30. Winship, *GR*, pp. 220–2; Morton, *New-Englands Memorial*, pp. 79–80.

31. *WJ*, pp. 163–4; Glenn W. LaFantasie (ed.), *The Correspondence of Roger Williams*, 2 vols. (Hanover, NH, 1988), vol. 2, p. 610.

32. Bush, *CJC*, pp. 264–6 for this and next paragraph.

33. Clarke, *Generall Martyrologie*, p. 468.

34. More, *True Relation*, sig. A3v.

35. Henry Burton, *For God, and the King* (Amsterdam, 1637), pp. 19–20, 24, 31–2, 70, 83, 85, 87; idem, *A Narration of the Life of Mr. Henry Burton* (1643), pp. 10–11; Kenneth Gibson, "Burton, Henry (bap. 1578, d. 1647/8)," *ODNB*.

36. Samuel R. Gardiner, *History of England from the Accession of James I to the Outbreak of the Civil War, 1603–1642*, 10 vols. (1883–84), vol. 8, pp. 226–31; Sharpe, *Personal Rule*, pp. 758–63; Mark Kishlansky, "Martyrs' Tales," *JBS* 53 (2014), pp. 345–50; Samuel Rawson Gardiner (ed.), *Documents Relating to the Proceedings against William Prynne, in 1634 and 1637* (1877), p. 87.

37. Gardiner, *History of England*, vol. 8, pp. 231–5.

38. William Laud, *A Speech Delivered in the Starr-Chamber* (1637).

39. Karen Ordahl Kupperman, *Providence Island, 1630–1641: The Other Puritan Colony* (Cambridge, 1995), p. 301; Sharpe, *Personal Rule*, pp. 763–4.

40. Rutman, *Winthrop's Boston*, p. 179.

41. Bremer, *CC*, p. 108; John S. Morrill, "The Making of Oliver Cromwell," in J.S. Morrill (ed.), *Oliver Cromwell and the English Revolution* (New York, 1990), pp 34–6; Susanna Bell, *The Legacy of a Dying Mother to Her Mourning Children* (1673), p. 49.

42. Winship, *MH*, pp. 38–40, 41; Hall (ed.), *Antinomian*, pp. 317, 322, 339.
43. Martha Saxton, *Being Good: Women's Moral Values in Early America* (New York, 2003), p. 78; Winship, *MH*, pp. 42–3.
44. Winship, *MH*, pp. 178–80.
45. Hall (ed.), *Antinomian*, pp. 351–2
46. Ibid., p. 364.
47. Knewstubs, *A Confutation*, fols. 71v–74r; Caroline Walker Bynum, *The Resurrection of the Body in Western Christianity, 200–1336* (New York, 1995).
48. Winship, *MH*, pp. 52–3, 84, 87–9, 190–2.
49. Ibid., p. 1. Cf. Edmund Jessop or William Etherington, *A Discovery of the Errors of the English Anabaptists* (1623), p. 89. For the authorship, see Peter Lake, *The Boxmaker's Revenge: "Orthodoxy," "Heterodoxy," and the Politics of the Parish in Early Stuart London* (2001), p. 98.
50. Winship, *MH*, p. 197.
51. Ibid., pp. 50–1.
52. Ibid., pp. 50, 55; Hall (ed.), *Antinomian*, p. 314.
53. Winship, *MH*, pp. 55, 58–9, 76–7; Hall (ed.), *Antinomian*, pp. 206–7.
54. Winship, *MH*, pp. 52, 133–5, 144.
55. Ibid., pp. 90–4, 112–13.
56. Michael McGiffert (ed.), *God's Plot* (Amherst, MA, 1972), p. 74.
57. Hall (ed.), *Antinomian*, p. 371.
58. Winship, *MH*, pp. 21–4, 32–4.
59. Ibid., pp. 52, 96, 137, 146, 189–90; McGiffert (ed.), *God's Plot*, p. 65.
60. Winship, *MH*, pp. 22–4, 35–6, 68; David Como, "Puritans, Predestination and the Construction of Orthodoxy," in Lake and Questier (eds.), *Conformity and Orthodoxy*, pp. 64–87.
61. Winship, *MH*, pp. 108–9; Peter Lake and David Como, " 'Orthodoxy and Its Discontents': Dispute Settlement and the Production of 'Consensus' in the London (Puritan) Underground," *JBS* 39 (2000), pp. 34–70.
62. Winship, *MH*, 64–6, 94.
63. Ibid., pp. 86–92, 95–101, 107–19, 122–5, 131–3.
64. Ibid., pp. 53–4, 116, 143–4, 101–5.
65. Ibid., chap. 8.
66. Ibid., pp. 202, 203.
67. Ibid., pp. 58, 221–3; McGiffert (ed.), *God's Plot: The Paradoxes of Puritan Piety Being the Autobiography & Journal of Thomas Shepard*, p. 74; Hall (ed.), *Antinomian*, p. 373.
68. Winship, *MH*, pp. 68–9.
69. Ibid., pp. 243–6, 306n8, 309n38; Thomas Shepard, *De Gelykenis der Tien Maagden Verklaart en Toegepast*, 2 vols. (Leiden, 1743), vol. 1, sig. *2r; William K.B. Stoever, "The Godly Will's Discerning: Shepard, Edwards, and the Identification of True Godliness," in Stephen J. Stein (ed.), *Jonathan Edwards's Writings: Text, Context, Interpretation* (Bloomington, IN, 1996), pp. 85–99.
70. Sydney V. James, *John Clarke and His Legacies: Religion and Law in Colonial Rhode Island, 1638–1750* (University Park, PA, 1999), p. 12.
71. Winship, *MH*, pp. 220, 233–4; Charles H. Bell (ed.), *John Wheelwright* (Boston, MA, 1876), pp. 44, 54.
72. Matthew Reynold, *Godly Reformers and Their Opponents in Early Modern England: Religion in Norwich c. 1560–1643* (Woodbridge, Suffolk, 2005), p. 219; *WJ*, p. 275; John Ball, *A Tryall of the New-Church Way in New-England* (1644), p. 24; John Cotton Manuscript, Cotton Families Collection, Pilgrim Hall Museum Archives, Plymouth, Massachusetts; Bush, *CJC*, pp. 257–62; Richard Mather, *An Apologie of the Churches in New-England for Church-Covenant* (1643); Winship, "Straining," p. 96.
73. *WJ*, p. 275.
74. "Conference of the Elders of Massachusetts with the Rev. Robert Lenthal, of Weymouth, Held at Dorchester, Feb. 10, 1639," *Congregational Quarterly* 19 (1877), p. 240; *WJ*, pp. 275–6, 281–2; *MR*, vol. 1, p. 252.

75. Ball, *Tryall*, sig. A2[ii]v; Winship, "Straining," pp. 89–111.

76. Calamy, *ABH*, vol. 2, pp. 222–3; Ball, *Tryall*.

77. Keith L. Sprunger, *A History of English and Scottish Churches of the Netherlands in the Sixteenth and Seventeenth Centuries* (Leiden, 1982), pp. 329–35; Bremer, *CC*, p. 128.

78. Sprunger, *History*, pp. 300–6; Ford, "Church of Ireland", pp. 52–68.

79. D. Stevenson, *The Scottish Revolution 1637–1644: The Triumph of the Covenanters* (Newton Abbot, Devon, 1973), pp. 60–4; Joad Raymond, *Pamphlets and Pamphleteering in Early Modern Britain* (Cambridge, 2003), chap. 5.

80. John Ball, *A Friendly Triall of the Grounds Tending to Separation* (Cambridge, 1640), pp. 12, 157; Winship, "Straining," pp. 101–2.

81. Conrad Russell, *The Fall of the British Monarchies, 1637–1642* (Oxford, 1991), pp. 90–123.

82. Mark Charles Fissel, *The Bishops' Wars: Charles I's Campaigns against Scotland, 1638–1640* (Cambridge, 1994), pp. 264–72.

83. David R. Como, "Secret Printing, the Crisis of 1640, and the Origins of Civil War Radicalism," *Past and Present* 196 (2007), pp. 37–82; Anon., *Englands Complaint to Iesus Christ* (1640), sig. B2[i]r–v; N.E., *Information for the Ignorant* (1640), sig. B2[ii]v; Samuel How, *The Sufficiencie of the Spirits Teaching* (1640).

84. John Adamson, *The Noble Revolt: The Overthrow of Charles I* (2007), pp. 45–50; Russell, *Fall*, chap. 4.

## Chapter 10  A Miraculous Year Goes Bad

1. Christopher Love, *Mr. Love's Case* (1651), pp. 25–6, 28.

2. Robert Tichborne, *A Cluster of Canaans Grapes* (1649), sig. A2 1r; Halcomb, "SH," pp. 121–3; Love, *Love's Case*, p. 27.

3. Love, *Love's Case*, pp. 15–16.

4. Ibid., pp. 16, 25; F.W. Huisman, "Het Leven van Christopher Love (1618–1651)," in W.J. op 't Hof and F.W. Huisman (eds.), *Nederlandse Liefde voor Christopher Love (1618–1651)* (Amstelveen, 2013), p. 63.

5. Anthony Milton, "Unsettled Reformations, 1603–1662," in *OHA*, p. 76; Alan Ford, *James Ussher: Theology, History, and Politics in Early-Modern Ireland and England* (Oxford, 2007), pp. 240–51; Russell, *Fall*, pp. 249–72. Russell remains the standard account of the high politics of this period.

6. Mary Love, "The Life of Mr. Christopher Love," DWL, MS 28.57, pp. 27–9.

7. David Cressy, *England on Edge: Crisis and Revolution, 1640–1642* (Oxford, 2006), pp. 158–60, chap. 9.

8. Adamson, *Noble Revolt*, pp. 10–12.

9. *Memoirs of the Life of Mr. Ambrose Barnes* (1867), p. 128; Anon., *The Whole Triall of Mr Love* (1651), p. 68; Love, "Life," pp. 29–38.

10. Russell, *Fall*, chaps. 12, 13.

11. Anon., *Whole Triall*, p. 68; *CSPD, 1641–43*, p. 372; Christopher Love, *Englands Distemper, Having Division and Error, as Its Cause* (1645), pp. 16, 20, 29–30; George Laurence and Christopher Love, *The Debauched Cavalleer* (1642), p. 8; J. Morrill, "Charles I, Tyranny and the English Civil War," in J. Morrill (ed.), *The Nature of the English Revolution* (Harlow, Essex, 1993), pp. 285–306.

12. Anne Venn, *A Wise Virgins Lamp Burning* (1658), p. 5.

13. Chad Van Dixhoorn (ed.), *The Minutes and Papers of the Westminster Assembly, 1643–1652*, 5 vols. (Oxford, 2012), vol. 1, chap. 1; Robert S. Paul, *The Assembly of the Lord: Politics and Religion in the Westminster Assembly and the "Grand Debate"* (Edinburgh, 1985), pp. 105–10.

14. Michael Braddick, *God's Fury, England's Fire: A New History of the English Civil Wars* (2008), pp. 309–11; George Yule, *Puritans in Politics, 1640–1647* (Appleford, Oxon, 1981), pp. 120–2.

15. Tyacke, *Aspects*, chap. 4; Polly Ha, *English Presbyterianism, 1590–1640* (Stanford, CA, 2011); Paul, *Assembly*, p. 226; Rosemary D. Bradley, "The Failure of Accommodation: Religious Conflicts between Presbyterians and Independents in the Westminster Assembly, 1643–1646," *Journal of Religious History* 12 (1982), pp. 24–6.

16. George Wharton, *A Second Narrative of the Late Parliament* (1658), p. 15; Keith Lindley, "Tichborne, Robert (1610/11–1682)," ODNB; E.A. Wrigley, "A Simple Model of London's Importance in Changing English Society and Economy 1650–1750," *Past & Present* 37 (1967), p. 44; Reynolds, *Godly Reformers*, p. 21.

17. Keeble and Nuttall, *CCRB*, vol. 1, p. 268; John Morill, "The Church in England, 1642–9" in John Morrill (ed.), *Reactions to the English Civil War, 1642–9* (1982), pp. 106–7.

18. Halcomb, "SH," pp. 25–6, 31–2; Murray Tolmie, *Triumph of the Saints: Separate Churches of 1616–1649* (Cambridge, 1977), pp. 103–4.

19. Thomas Edwards, *Antapologia* (1644), p. 51; *A Letter of the Ministers of London* (1645), p. 3; Winship, *GR*, 323n4; Christopher Love, *A Modest and Clear Vindication* (1649), p. 6.

20. Winship, *GR*, pp. 83, 102; Anon., *A Glimpse of Sions Glory* (1641), sig. ¶r, p. 33; Henry Burton, *The Protestation Protested* (1641), pp. 11, 12, 13; Thomas Edwards, *Reasons Against the Independent Government of Particular Congregations* (1641), sig. *2v, pp. 7, 8, 24, 26; Richard Mather, *Church-Government and Church-Covenant Discussed* (1643), sig. ***v, p. 46; Thomas Goodwin, Philip Nye, Sidrach Simpson, Jeremiah Burroughs and William Bridge, *An Apologeticall Narration* (1644), p. 23. For the authorship of *Glimpse*, see Crawford Gribben, *The Puritan Millennium: Literature and Theology, 1550–1682* (rev. edn., Eugene, OR, 2008), p. 48; Ann Hughes, *Gangraena and the Struggle for the English Revolution* (Oxford, 2004), p. 127.

21. T.M. Lawrence, "Goodwin, Thomas (1600–1680)," ODNB; Tom Webster, "Burroughes, Jeremiah (bap. 1601?, d. 1646)," ODNB; Barbara Donagan, "Nye, Philip (bap. 1595, d. 1672)," ODNB; Tai Liu, "Simpson, Sidrach (c.1600–1655)," ODNB; Richard L. Greaves, "Bridge, William (1600/01–1671)," ODNB; A.S.P. Woodhouse, *Puritanism and Liberty: Being the Army Debates (1647–9 from the Clarke Manuscripts with Supplementary Documents)* (Chicago, 1965), p. 126.

22. Judith Maltby, "Extravagances and Impertinencies: Set Forms, Conceived and Extempore Prayer in Revolutionary England," in Natalie Mears and Alec Ryrie (eds.), *Worship and the Parish Church in Early Modern Britain* (Farnham, Surrey, 2013), pp. 221–33; Paul, *Assembly*, p. 518. The wording of one section of the Confession might have been left slightly vague to patch over disagreements: see Richard A. Mueller, "Diversity in the Reformed Tradition," in Michael A.G. Haykin and Mark Jones (eds.), *Drawn into Controversie: Reformed Theological Diversity and Debates Within Seventeenth-Century British Puritanism* (Göttingen, 2011), pp. 19–29; Alan D. Strange, "The Imputation of the Active Obedience of Christ at the Westminster Assembly," in Haykin and Jones (eds.), *Drawn into Controversie*, pp. 31–82; Isabel Rivers, *Reason, Grace, and Sentiment: A Study of the Language of Religion and Ethics in England, 1660–1780*, 2 vols. (Cambridge, 1991), vol. 1, pp. 13–14; Jan Stievermann, "Biblical Interpretation in Eighteenth-Century America," in Paul Gutjahr (ed.), *The Oxford Handbook of the Bible in America* (New York, 2017), p. 266.

23. Paul, *Assembly*, pp. 180–1; Bernard Capp, "The Religious Marketplace: Public Disputations in Civil War and Interregnum England," *English Historical Review* 129 (2014), pp. 47–78; Matthew C. Bingham, "English Baptists and the Struggle for Theological Authority, 1642–1646," *JEH* 68 (2017), pp. 563–4; Cressy, *England*, chap. 10; Michael R. Watts, *The Dissenters*, 2 vols. (Oxford, 1978), vol. 1, p. 82.

24. Watts, *Dissenters*, vol. 1, pp. 80–1, 97–8.

25. Paul, *Assembly*, pp. 186–8; *The Letters and Journals of Robert Baillie*, ed. David Lang, 3 vols. (Edinburgh, 1851), vol. 1, p. 122.

26. Goodwin, Nye, Simpson, Burroughs, Bridge, *Apologeticall Narration*, pp. 23, 31, 35.

27. John Lightfoot, *The Whole Works of The Rev. John Lightfoot*, ed. John Pitman, 13 vols. (1824), vol. 13, p. 46; John Coffey, *John Goodwin and the Puritan Revolution: Religion and*

*Intellectual Change in Seventeenth-Century England* (Harlow, Essex, 2006), pp. 104–7, 108–12; John Coffey, "The Toleration Controversy during the English Revolution," in Christopher Durston and Judith Maltby (eds.), *Religion in Revolutionary England* (Manchester, 2006), pp. 42–68.

28. Tolmie, *Triumph*, pp. 17–27; Stephen Marshall, *A Sermon of the Baptizing of Infants* (1644), p. 52.

29. W.T. Whitley (ed.), "Debate on Infant Baptism, 1643," *Transactions of the Baptist Historical Society* 1 (1908–9), pp. 243–4.

30. Daniel Featly, *Katabaptistai Kataptüstoi: The Dippers Dipt* (1645), p. 1; Halcomb, "SH," pp. 148–50; Geoffrey F. Nuttall, *Visible Saints: The Congregational Way, 1640–1660* (Oxford, 1957), pp. 117–21; *WJ*, p. 611.

31. Roger Pooley, "Crisp, Tobias (1600–1643)," ODNB; Tobias Crisp, *Christ Alone Exalted* (1690), 1st pag., pp. 206, 212.

32. Crisp, *Christ Alone*, 1st pag., pp. 9, 374, 573.

33. Ibid., 1st pag., pp. 317, 291; David Parnham, "The Covenantal Quietism of Tobias Crisp," *CH* 75 (2006), pp. 511–54; idem, "The Humbling of 'High Presumption': Tobias Crisp Dismantles the Puritan Ordo Salutis," *JEH* 56 (2005), pp. 50–74.

34. Como, *Blown by the Spirit*, chap. 5, pp. 401–2; Crisp, *Christ Alone*, 1st pag., p. 13, 2nd pag., p. 12.

35. Whitney Greer Gamble, "'If Christ fulfilled the law, we are not bound': The Westminster Assembly Against English Antinomian Soteriology, 1643–1647" (Ph.D. thesis, University of Edinburgh, 2014).

36. Seaver, *Wallington's World*, p. 107; Como, *Blown by the Spirit*, pp. 448–52; Gamble, "'If Christ,'" pp. 1,666–7. Of the eight ministers who wrote endorsements of Edward Fisher's *Marrow of Modern Divinity*, an attempt to mediate between orthodoxy and antinomianism, five are identifiable as Congregationalists and only one as a Presbyterian. I thank Elliot Vernon for a discussion.

37. *Hartlib*, 39/2/5B; *WJ*, p. 612; Richard Mather, *The Summe of Certain Sermons upon Genes. 15.6* (Cambridge, MA, 1652).

38. Edwards, *The First and Second Part of Gangraena* (1646), pt. 2, p.13; Nicholas Lockyer, *An Olive-Leaf, or, A Bud of the Spring* (1650), pp. 48–50; idem, *England Faithfully Watcht with, in her Wounds* (1646), p. 58; Samuel Richardson, *Divine Consolations* (1649), sig. q2[i]v.

39. Rosemary Bradley, "'Jacob and Esau Struggling in the Wombe': A Study of Presbyterian and Independent Religious Conflicts, 1640–48" (Ph.D. thesis, University of Kent, 1975), p. 254; Wharton, *Second Narrative*, p. 15; Tichborne, *Cluster*, pp. 39–45, 109, 192; idem, *The Rest of Faith* (1649), pp. 14, 28, 30.

40. Tai Liu, "Cokayn, George (bap. 1620, d. 1691)," ODNB.

41. Tichborne, *Cluster*, p. 2

42. Ibid, pp. 120, 167–8.

43. J.C. Davis, "Against Formality: One Aspect of the English Revolution," *Transactions of the Royal Historical Society*, 6th ser. (1992), vol. 3, pp. 265–88; Nuttall, *Holy Spirit*, p. 119; *Papers Given to the Honorable Committee of Lords and Commons and Assembly of Divines* (1648) [Wing P295], p. 91; Gribben, *Puritan Millennium*, pp. 253–8.

44. Thomas Blunt, *Glossographia* (1656), *s.v.* "Sectary."

45. John Coffey, "Puritanism and Liberty Revisited: The Case for Toleration in the English Revolution," *HJ* 41 (1998), pp. 961–85; Winship, *MH*, pp. 242–3; "Roger Williams (1604?–1683)," ODNB, archive article.

46. Thomas Parker, *The Copy of a Letter* (1650), p. 5.

47. Thomas Parker, *The Visions and Prophecies of Daniel Expounded* (1646); Robert Parker, *The Mystery of the Vialls Opened* (1651); Elizabeth Avery, *Scripture-Prophecies Opened* (1647), p. 46. For examples of Familist influence, see Avery, *Scripture-Prophecies*, pp. 3, 9, 36–7; Parker, *Copy*, pp. 7–8; see also Gribben, *Puritan Millennium*, pp. 193–9.

48. Parker, *Copy*, sig. A2r, pp. 11, 13; London Provincial Assembly, *A Testimony to the Truth of Jesus Christ* (1648), pp. 4, 5, 20–1; Hughes, Gangraena, pp. 374–8.

49. Rogers, *Ohel*, pp. 402–5; Crawford Gribben, *God's Irishmen: Theological Debates in Cromwellian Ireland* (New York, 2007), chap. 6; Claire Cross, "The Church in England 1640–1660," in G.E. Aylmer (ed.), *The Interregnum: The Quest for Settlement, 1646–1660* (1972), p. 117.

50. [Westminster Assembly], *Propositions Concerning Church-Government and Ordination* (Edinburgh, 1647) [Wing 1446a], p. 19; [Westminster Assembly], *The Answer of the Assembly of Divines* (1645), pp. 15–16; Hunter Powell, *The Crisis of British Protestantism: Church Power and the Puritan Revolution, 1638–44* (Manchester, 2015), pp. 203–6.

51. F.W. Huisman, "Leven," pp. 20, 23; Anon., *Love's Name Lives* (1651), pp. 13, 14; Elliot Vernon, "Love, Christopher (1618–1651)," ODNB; Love, "Life," p. 51; Chad Van Dixhoorn, *God's Ambassdors: The Westminster Assembly and the Reformation of the English Pulpit* (Grand Rapids, MI, 2017), chaps. 4, 6.

52. Bradley, " 'Jacob,' " p. 421.

53. Edwards, *Gangraena* (1646), pp. 109–10 [Thomason Tracts E.323[2]]; Lightfoot, *Whole Works*, p. 265.

54. Adam Martindale, *The Life of Adam Martindale, Written by Himself*, ed. Richard Parkinson (Manchester, 1845), pp. 61–9, quote from p. 61.

55. Bradley, " 'Jacob,' " p. viii.

### Chapter 11 The Wobbly Rise and Precipitous Collapse of Presbyterian England

1. Love, *Englands Distemper*, pp. 24, 5; idem, *Short and Plaine Animadversions on Some Passages in Mr. Dels Sermon* (1647), sig. A2r.

2. Wilbur Cortez Abbot, *The Writings and Speeches of Oliver Cromwell*, 4 vols. (Oxford, 1988), vol. 1, p. 287; Braddick, *God's Fury*, pp. 323–34; Austin Woolrych, *Britain in Revolution, 1625–1660* (Oxford, 2002), pp. 301–19.

3. J.C. Davis, *Oliver Cromwell* (2001), chap. 6; Baxter, *RB*, bk. i, p. 51; Woolrych, *Britain*, pp. 299, 301; Clive Holmes, *The Eastern Association in the English Civil War* (Cambridge, 1974), pp. 197–212.

4. Love, *Short and Plaine Animadversions*, sig. A2v: John Wilson, *Fairfax: A Life of Thomas, Lord Fairfax* (1985), p. 95.

5. Ian Gentles, *The New Model Army in England, Ireland and Scotland 1645–53* (Oxford, 1992), chap. 4; Davis, *Oliver Cromwell*, chap. 6; Baxter, *RB*, bk. i, p. 51; Abbot, *Writings and Speeches*, p. 377.

6. Love, *Short and Plaine Animadversions*, sig. A2v.

7. Ibid., sig. A2r-v; David Como, *Radical Parliamentarians and the English Civil War* (Oxford, 2018), pp. 294–5, 295n77. I thank Professor Como for sharing the page proofs before publication.

8. See Yule, *Puritans*, chap. 7 for a detailed account of the following episode.

9. *Report of the Royal Commission on Historical Manuscripts*, vol. 13 (1892), p. 297; Yule, *Puritans*, pp. 159–60.

10. Anne Hughes, *Gangraena and the Struggle for the English Revolution* (Oxford, 2004), chap. 5; Keith Lindley, *Popular Politics and Religion in Civil War London* (Aldershot, Hants, 1997), p. 287; Yule, *Puritans*, pp. 180–7.

11. Yule, *Puritans*, pp. 187–9; Vernon, "SCC," pp. 41–58.

12. Braddick, *God's Fury*, pp. 317–18, 389, 393.

13. Yule, *Puritans*, pp. 192–3; *The Journal of the House of Commons* (1803), vol. 4, pp. 562–3; Anon., *Certain Considerations and Cautions Agreed upon by the Ministers of London* (1646), pp. 6–8.

14. Shaw, *HEC*, vol. 2, pp. 6, 29–33; A.G. Matthews, *Calamy Revised: Being a Revision of Edmund Calamy's Account of the Ministers and Others Ejected and Silenced, 1660–2* (Oxford, 1934), pp. lxxii, 553; Tai Lui, *Puritan London: A Study of Religion and Society in the City Parishes* (Newark, DL, 1986), p. 70; Vernon, "SCC," p. 327.

15. Bradley, "'Jacob,'" pp. 602, 605–6; Hughes, *Gangraena*, pp. 326–7; Vernon, "SCC," pp. 84–8.
16. Humphrey Saunders, *An Anti-Diatribe* (1655), pp. 173–4.
17. Margaret M. Verney, *Memoirs of the Verney Family*, 2 vols. (1904), vol. 1, p. 356; Venn, *Wise Virgins*, p. 11; Lui, *Puritan London*, p. 164.
18. Vernon, "SCC," chap. 4; Christopher Love, *The Hearers Duty* (1653), pp. 17–18.
19. Morrill, "Church in England," passim.
20. Christopher Love, *Works of Darkness Brought to Light* (1647), p. 11; *An Ordinance Presented to the Honorable House of Commons, by Mr. Bacon, a Lawyer in Suffolk, and Mr Taet* (1646); Youngkwon Chung, "Parliament, the Heresy Ordinance of 1648, and Religious Toleration in Civil War England," *Journal of Church and State* 57 (2015), pp. 119– 52.
21. Edwards, *First and Second Part*, pt. 1, p. 15; pt. 2, pp. 29, 31, 113–19; Lawrence Clarkson, *The Lost Sheep Found* (1660), pp. 5–21; Stephen D. Snobelen, "Best, Paul (1590–1657)," ODNB; B.J. Gibbons, "Overton, Richard (fl. 1640–1663)," ODNB.
22. *An Ordinance . . . Mr Taet* (1646).
23. Love, *Works*, p. 9; Tolmie, *Triumph*, pp. 181–7; Richard Overton, *A Remonstrance of Many Thousand Citizens* (1646); Rachel Foxley, *The Levellers: Radical Political Thought in the English Revolution* (Manchester, 2013); Thomas Edwards, *The Third Part of Gangraena* (1646), p. 217; Love, *Works*, p. 9. See Como, *Radical Parliamentarians*, for the evolution of these political opinions among the sectaries in the early 1640s.
24. Love, *Works*, p. 9.
25. Ibid.
26. See Ian Gentles, "The Struggle for London in the Second Civil War," *HJ* 26 (1983), pp. 277–305; Mark Kishlansky, *The Rise of the New Model Army* (Cambridge, 1979), chap. 8; Valerie Pearl, "London's Counter-Revolution," in Aylmer (ed.), *Interregnum*, pp. 29–56 for this and the next two paragraphs. Woolrych, *Britain*, p. 355.
27. Alan Everitt, *The Community of Kent and the Great Rebellion: 1640–1660* (Leicester, 1966), pp. 230–40.
28. Woolrych, *Britain*, pp. 399–419; Laura Stewart, *Rethinking the Scottish Revolution: Covenanted Scotland 1637–1651* (Oxford, 2016), chap. 6.
29. William Allen, *A Faithful Memorial* (1659), pp. 4–5; Patricia Crawford, "'Charles Stuart, That Man of Blood!,'" *JBS* 16 (1977), pp. 41–61.
30. *A Declaration of the Committee of Estates of the Parliament of Scotland* (1648), p. 11; Shaw, *HEC*, vol. 2, pp. 18–21, 79; W.K. Jordan, *The Development of Religious Toleration in England from the Convention of the Long Parliament to the Restoration* (Cambridge, MA, 1938), pp. 111–15.
31. David Underdown, *Pride's Purge: Politics in the Puritan Revolution* (Oxford, 1971), chap. 5; Henry Ireton, *A Remonstrance of His Excellency Thomas Lord Fairfax* (1648), p. 64.
32. Underdown, *Pride's Purge*, chap. 6.
33. Blair Worden, *The Rump Parliament, 1648–1653* (Cambridge, 1974), pp. 191–2, 206–7; Cross, "Church in England," pp. 106–11; Shaw, *HEC*, vol. 2, pp. 137–51; Derek Hirst, "The Failure of Godly Rule in the English Republic," *Past and Present* 132 (1991), pp. 38–41; Vernon, "SCC," pp. 164–5.
34. Worden, *Rump*, p. 81, Underdown, *Pride's Purge*, pp. 176–8, 180; Leland H. Carlson, "A History of the Presbyterian Party from Pride's Purge to the Dissolution of the Long Parliament," *CH* 11 (1942), pp. 85–6; Cust, *Charles I: A Political Life*, pp. 449–59; Clive Homes, "The Trial and Execution of Charles I," *HJ* 53 (2010), pp. 289–316; Love, "Life," p. 85; Vernon, "SCC," chap. 6, pp. 202–24; Lindley, "Tichborne, Robert."
35. London Provincial Assembly, *A Vindication of the Presbyterial Government* (1649), pp. 11–12, 113; Vernon, "SCC," pp. 141–2, 215–16.
36. Carlson, "History," pp. 86–9; Mary Love, "The Life of Mr. Christopher Love," DWL, MS 28.57, pp. 88–9; Vernon, "SCC," p. 269.
37. Vernon, "SCC," pp. 277–8, 278n16.

38. Anon., *Whole Triall*, p. 35.
39. Christopher Love, *Mr. Love's Case* (1651), pp. 8–9; Anon., *Whole Triall*, p. 23.
40. Love, *Love's Case*, p. 30; Baxter, *RB*, bk. i, 66; Gentles, *New Model Army*, p. 398; Carlson, "History," p. 89; Worden, *Rump*, pp. 81–2; Francis J. Bremer, "In Defence of Regicide: John Cotton on the Execution of Charles I," *William and Mary Quarterly*, 3rd ser., 37 (1980), p. 122.
41. Anon., *Whole Triall*, p. 24; Love, *Love's Case*, pp. 9–13.
42. Anon., *Whole Triall*, pp. 51, 121; Love, "Life," p. 64.
43. Christopher Love, *A Cleare and Necessary Vindication* (1651), pp. 1–15, 39, 42; op 't Hof and Huisman (eds.), *Nederlandse Liefde*, pp. 422–3; Worden, *Rump*, pp. 246–8.
44. Love, *Love's Case*, p. 26; Edmund Calamy, *The Saints' Rest* (1651); Thomas Manton, *A Sermon Preached at the Funerall of M. Christopher Love* (1651).
45. Christopher Love, *The True Doctrine of Mortification and Sincerity* (1654), sig. A4r; J. van de Kamp, "De International Receptive van Loves Geschriften," in op 't Hof and Huisman (eds.), *Nederlandse Leifde*, pp. 403–16.
46. Love, *Cleare and Necessary Vindication*, p. 23.
47. C. Standford Terry (ed.), *The Cromwellian Union: Papers Relating to the Negotiations for an Incorporating Union Between England and Scotland* (Edinburgh, 1902), pp. xxiv–xxvii; Carla Gardina Pestana, *The English Atlantic in an Age of Revolution, 1640–1661* (Cambridge, MA, 2004), chap. 3; Worden, *Rump*, p. 85.

## Chapter 12  Shaking Out Antichrist in the 1650s

1. John Owen, *The Works of John Owen*, ed. William H. Goold, 21 vols. (1850–52), vol. 8, pp. 318, 326–7, 32.
2. Blair Worden, *God's Instruments: Political Conduct in the England of Oliver Cromwell* (Oxford, 2012), p. 72; Halcomb, "SH," pp. 38, 261–72.
3. H.G. Tibbutt (ed.), *The Minutes of the First Independent Church (Now Bunyan Meeting House) at Bedford, 1656–1766*, Bedfordshire Historical Record Society 55 (1976), pp. 15–17, 21; Richard L. Greaves, *Glimpses of Glory: John Bunyan and English Dissent* (Stanford, CA, 2002), p. 62; Halcomb, "SH," p. 104; John Brown, *John Bunyan: His Life, Times, and* Work (1885), p. 93.
4. Nuttall, *Visible Saints*, pp. 137–40; John Owen et al., *The Humble Proposals of Mr Owen, Mr Tho Goodwin, Mr Nye, Mr Simpson and Other Ministers* (1652), p. 5.
5. Morrill, "Church in England," p. 90.
6. Thomas Michael Lawrence, "Transmission and Transformation: Thomas Goodwin and the Puritan Project 1600–1704" (Ph.D. thesis, Cambridge University, 2002), chap. 4; Patrick Little and David L. Smith, *Parliament and Politics during the Cromwellian Protectorate* (Cambridge, 2007), pp. 209–10.
7. Carolyn Polizzotto, "The Campaign against The Humble Proposals of 1652," *JEH* 38 (1987), pp. 569–81; Barbara K. Lewalski, *The Life of John Milton: A Critical Biography* (Oxford, 2003), p. 328; John P. Rumrich, "Milton's Arianism: Why It Matters," in Stephen B. Dobranski and John P. Rumrich (eds.), *Milton and Heresy* (Cambridge, 1998), chap. 4; Worden, *God's Instruments*, pp. 80–2; Paul C.H. Lim, *Mystery Unveiled: The Crisis of the Trinity in Early Modern England* (Oxford, 2012), pp. 38–68; John Coffey, "John Owen and the Puritan Toleration Controversy, 1646–59," in Mark Jones and Kelly M. Kapic (eds.), *The Ashgate Research Companion to John Owen's Theology* (Farnham, Surrey, 2012), pp. 227–48.
8. Halcomb, "SH," pp. 98, 276; Claire Cross, " 'He-Goats Before the Flocks': A Note on the Part Played by Women in the Founding of Some Civil War Churches," *Studies in Church History* 8 (1972), pp. 195–202; Crawford, *Women and Religion*, pp. 129–39. E.B. Underhill (ed.), *The Records of a Church of Christ Meeting in Broadmead, Bristol, 1640–1687* (1848), p. 11. For the thinness of Milton's relationship to puritanism, see Martin, *Milton*.
9. Gentles, *New Model Army*, p. 33; Stachniewski and Pacheco (eds.), *Grace*, pp. 1–10.

10. Stachniewski and Pacheco (eds.), *Grace*, pp. 14–15.
11. Ibid., pp. 16–17; Lim, *Mystery*, pp. 109–15; Ariel Hessayon, "Abiezer Coppe and the Ranters," in Laura Lunger Knoppers (ed.), *The Oxford Handbook of Literature and the English Revolution* (Oxford, 2012), pp. 346–74; Worden, *God's Instruments*, pp. 80–1.
12. Stachniewski and Pacheco (eds.), *Grace*, pp. 18–24.
13. Ibid., pp. 25–75; Greaves, *Glimpses*, pp. 54, 54n54; Nuttall, *Visible Saints*, pp. 109–15.
14. Stachniewski and Pacheco (eds.), *Grace*, pp. 75–6; Brown, *John Bunyan*, p. 113.
15. Sally Bruyneel, *Margaret Fell and the End of Time: The Theology of the Mother of Quakerism* (Waco, TX, 2010), pp. 199–204; Barbour, *The Quakers*, pp. 99, 144, chap. 4; Moore, *Light*, pp. 130–1, 144–5, chaps. 4, 11; Peter Elmer, " 'Saints or Sorcerers': Quakerism, Demonology and the Decline of Witchcraft in Seventeenth-Century England," in Jonathan Barry, Marianne Hester, and Gareth Roberts (eds.), *Witchcraft in Early Modern Europe: Studies in Culture and Belief* (Cambridge, 1996), pp. 145–80; Kate Peters, *Print Culture and the Early Quakers* (Cambridge, 2005), pp. 101–7.
16. Norman Penney (ed.), *"The First Publishers of Truth": Being Early Records (Now First Printed) of the Introduction of Quakerism into the Counties of England and Wales* (1907), p. 259; Barry Reay, *The Quakers and the English Revolution* (1985), p. 58; Richard Baxter, *Quakers Catechism* (1655), sig. 3Ar; Peters, *Print Culture*, p. 155; Moore, *Light*, pp. 118–20, 126–7, chap. 5.
17. Watts, *Dissenters*, vol. 1, p. 199; Peters, *Print Culture*, pp. 196–8; Reay, *Quakers*, pp. 59–60; William C. Braithwaite, *The Beginnings of Quakerism* (1912), pp. 220, 179; William Sheils, "English Catholics at War and Peace," in Christopher Durston and Judith Maltby (eds.), *Religion in Revolutionary England* (Manchester, 2006), pp. 137–57; Albert J. Loomie, "Oliver Cromwell's Policy toward the English Catholics: The Appraisal by Diplomats, 1654–1658," *Catholic Historical Review* 90 (2004), pp. 29–44; Kenneth Fincham and Stephen Taylor, "Episcopal Identity, 1640–1662," in *OHA*, pp. 472–3; Ann Hughes, "The Cromwellian Church," in *OHA*, p. 454.
18. Nuttall, *Visible Saints*, pp. 123–4, Watts, *Dissenters*, vol. 1, pp. 200–2; W. Lewis, *History of the Congregational Church, Cockermouth* (Cockermouth, 1870), p. 19; Greaves, *Glimpses*, pp. 75–6.
19. John Bunyan, *Some Gospel-Truths Opened* (1656), p. 143; idem, *A Vindication of the Book Called, Some Gospel-Truths Opened* (1657); James Blackley, *A Lying Wonder Discovered* (1659).
20. Thomas Smith, *The Quaker Disarm'd* (1659), sig. C2[ii]r. Bunyan's Calvinism had a tincture of Martin Luther; see Greaves, *Glimpses*, pp. 105–8.
21. Smith, *Quaker*, sig. C2[ii]r.
22. Rogers, *Ohel*, p. 494.
23. Brown, *John Bunyan*, pp. 235–8; Halcomb, "SH," pp. 107–8; Tibbutt, *Minutes*, p. 120; Greaves, *Glimpses*, pp. 96–8; Anne Hughes, "The Pulpit Guarded: Confrontations between Orthodox and Radicals in Revolutionary England," in Anne Laurence, W.R. Owens and Stuart Sim (eds.), *John Bunyan and His England, 1628–88* (1990), pp. 31–50; Smith, *Quaker*, sigs. B3[i]v–C2[i]v, C2v; Bunyan, *Some Gospel-Truths*, p. 26.
24. Bunyan, *Some Gospel-Truths*, sig. A5[v]v.
25. Rachel Adcock, *Baptist Women's Writings in Revolutionary Culture, 1640–1680* (Farnham, Surrey, 2015), p. 69n4; Ferdinando Nicolls, *The Life and Death of Mr. Ignatius Jurdain* (1655), sig. a2r, p. 8.
26. Susanna Parr, *Susanna's Apologie Against the Elders* (Oxford, 1659), pp. 1, 8, 56; Bernard Capp, *England's Culture Wars: Puritan Reformation and Its Enemies in the Interregnum, 1649–1660* (Oxford, 2012), pp. 123–7; Hirst, "Failure," pp. 38–41.
27. Parr, *Susana's Apologie*, pp. 8, 34, 69, 80; Anon., *One Blow More at Babylon* (1650), p. 2; Toby Allein, *Truths Manifest Revived* (1659), pp. 24, 105.
28. Parr, *Susanna's Apologie*, p. 2; Calamy, *ABH*, vol. 2, p. 211; Allein, *Truths Manifest*, p. 67; Anon., *One Blow*, pp. 1–2; Capp, *England's Culture Wars*, pp. 241–2; Alan John Kittermaster, "Politics and Religion in Exeter, 1635–1660" (Ph.D. thesis, University of

Exeter, 1985), pp. 174–80, 203.

29. E.T., *Diotrephes Detected, Corrected, and Rejected* (1658), p. 5; Parr, *Susanna's Apologie*, pp. 4, 76–9.

30. Parr, *Susanna's Apologie*, pp. 7, 8, 12, 88.

31. Ibid., pp. 9–10, 13.

32. Ibid., pp. 7, 13, 14, 28–9, 56; Adcock, *Baptist Women's Writings*, p. 106n83.

33. Parr, *Susanna's Apologie*, p. 15; Allan Brockett, *Nonconformity in Exeter, 1650–1875* (Manchester, 1962), p. 11.

34. Calamy, *ABH*, vol. 2, pp. 211–12; Allein, *Truths Manifest*, p. 39; Capp, *England's Cultural Revolution*, pp. 243–51.

35. Hughes, "Cromwellian Church," in *OHA*, pp. 449–51; Anthony à Wood, *The History and Antiquities of the University of Oxford*, 3 vols. (1792–96), vol. 2, p. 661; J.T. Gillespie, "Presbyterianism in Devon and Cornwall in the Seventeenth Century" (M.A. diss., University of Durham, 1943), p. 13; Christopher Durston, "Policing the Cromwellian Church: The Activities of the County Ejection Committees, 1654–1659," in Patrick Little (ed.), *The Cromwellian Protectorate* (Woodbridge, Suffolk, 2007), pp. 188–206.

36. Thomas Ford, *Singing the Psalmes the Duty of Christians* (1653), pp. 45–6.

37. Parr, *Susanna's Apologie*, pp. 15–21, 32, 35–6, 53, 95–9. The Congregationalists give their account of this incident and the subsequent one involving Mary Allein (see p. 157) in Thomas Mall, *True Account of What Was Done by a Church of Christ in Exon* (1658), and Lewis Stuckeley, *Manifest Truth* (1658). These accounts do not contradict the gist of their opponents' versions, although they have different emphases and they engage in a great deal of hair-splitting.

38. Parr, *Susanna's Apologie*, pp. 39, 110.

39. Ibid., pp. 29, 32, 39–40, 110.

40. Ibid., p. 89; Allein, *Truths Manifest*, p. 14; Julie Spraggon, *Puritan Iconoclasm during the English Civil War* (Woodbridge, Suffolk, 2003), p. 196.

41. Calamy, *ABH*, vol. 2, p. 227; R.N. Worth, *Puritanism in Devon and the Exeter Assembly* (n.p., 1877), p. 31.

42. Paul C.H. Lim, *In Pursuit of Purity, Unity and Liberty: Richard Baxter's Puritan Ecclesiology in its Seventeenth-Century Context* (Leiden, 2004), pp. 117–43; Shaw, *HEC*, vol. 2, pp. 152–62; George R. Abernathy, "The English Presbyterians and the Stuart Restoration 1648–1663," *Transactions of the American Philosophical Society*, n.s., 55 (1965), pp. 8–17.

43. Worth, *Puritanism*, p. 33; Nuttall, *Visible Saints*, pp. 94–100, 122–3; John Humfrey, *A Plea for the Non-Conformists* (1674), pp. 53–5; *The Agreement of the Associated Ministers and Churches of the Counties of Cumberland, and Westmerland* (1656); *The Agreement of the Associated Ministers of the County of Essex* (1658); Allein, *Truths Manifest*, pp. 37, 72, 105; *English Historical Review* 10 (1895), pp. 744–73; Parr, *Susanna's Apologie*, p. 33.

44. Woolrych, *Britain*, pp. 531–6, 539–59; B.S. Capp, *The Fifth Monarchy Men: A Study in Seventeenth-Century Millenarianism* (1972), chap. 5.

45. See Little and Smith, *Parliament* for a recent account of these parliaments.

46. Allein, *Truths Manifest*, pp. 78–80; Charles Harding Firth, *The Last Years of the Protectorate, 1656–1658*, 2 vols. (1909), vol. 1, pp. 154–5; *MHSC*, 5th ser., 8 (1882), p. 181.

47. Abbott, *Writings and Speeches*, vol. 4, p. 473.

48. Allein, *Truths Manifest*, pp. 10–11.

49. Allein, *Truths Manifest*, pp. 13, 15.

50. Parr, *Susanna's Apologie*, pp. 43, 90; Allein, *Truths Manifest*, pp. 15, 42.

51. Ibid., pp. 25–6, 28, 36, 40, 64; Stuckeley, *Manifest Truth*, p. 23.

52. E.T., *Diotrephes*, p. 2; Allein, *Truths Manifest*, pp. 45, 48, 97, 100, 106.

53. Allein, *Truths Manifest*, pp. 10–13, 16–18, 101, 111.

54. Worth, *Puritanism*, pp. 38–9; Allein, *Truths Manifest*, pp. 39, 58–9; Brockett, *Nonconformity*, p. 27.

55. Edmund Calamy, *Memoirs of the Life of the Late Reverend Mr. John Howe* (1724),

pp. 14–15; London Provincial Assembly, *A Vindication of Presbyteriall-Government, and Ministry* (1649), p. 137; Halcomb, "SH," pp. 136–8; Bradley, "'Jacob,'" pp. 622–3; Parr, *Susanna's Apologie*, p. 11.

56. *Agreement . . . Essex*, sig. A2r–v.
57. Christopher Durston, "Godly Rule and the Failure of Cultural Revolution, 1645–1660," in idem and Eales (eds.), *Culture of English Puritanism*, pp. 211–14; J.S. Rutt (ed.), *The Diary of Thomas Burton*, 4 vols. (1828), vol. 2, pp. 264–5.
58. Hirst, "Failure," pp. 33–66; Durston, "Godly Rule," pp. 210–33; Bernard Capp, "Republican Reformation: Family, Community and the State in Interregnum Middlesex, 1649–60," in Helen Berry and Elizabeth Foyster (eds.), *The Family in Early Modern England* (Cambridge, 2007), pp. 40–66; Capp, *England's Cultural Revolution*, pp. 134–9; R.D. Dale, *The History of English Congregationalism* (1907), pp. 379–80.
59. Christopher Durston, *Cromwell's Major-Generals: Godly Government during the English Revolution* (Manchester, 2001).
60. Owen, *Works*, vol. 8, p. 467.
61. Woolrych, *Britain*, p. 718; Little and Smith, *Parliament*, pp. 217–19.
62. A.G. Matthews (ed.), *The Savoy Declaration of Faith and Order, 1658* (1659), "Introduction."
63. *A Declaration of the Faith and Order Owned and Practised in the Congregational Churches in England* (1659), sig. A2 [i]v, p. 27. For Goodwin and Nye's authorship, see BL, Add. Ms 23622, fol. 132r (penciled foliation).
64. Tim Cooper, *John Owen, Richard Baxter and the Formation of Nonconformity* (Farnham, Surrey, 2011), pp. 248–54; Woolrych, *Britain*, pp. 718–19, 721–2; Little and Smith, *Parliament*, pp. 152, 217–18; Peter Toon, *God's Statesman: The Life and Work of John Owen, Pastor, Educator, Theologian* (Grand Rapids, MI, 1973), pp. 109–14; Abernathy, "English Presbyterianism," pp. 26–30; William M. Lamont, *Richard Baxter and the Millennium: Protestant Imperialism and the English Revolution* (1979), pp. 197–8.
65. Barry Reay, "The Quakers, 1659, and the Restoration of the Monarchy," *History* 63 (1978), pp. 193–213.
66. Robert Halley, *Lancashire: Its Puritanism and Nonconformity*, 2 vols. (Manchester, 1889), vol. 2, pp. 76–90.
67. Martindale, *Life*, p. 131.
68. Halley, *Lancashire*, pp. 90–104; David Underdown, *Royalist Conspiracy in England, 1649–1660* (New Haven, CT, 1960), pp. 257, 273; Reay, *Quakers*, pp. 91–5; Richard Parkinson (ed.), *The Autobiography of Henry Newcome*, 2 vols. (Manchester, 1842), vol. 1, p. 108; Sean Kelsey, "Booth, George, first Baron Delamer [Delamere] (1622–1684)," ODNB.
69. Woolrych, *Britain*, pp. 737–65.
70. Ibid., pp. 763–70; *The Journal of the House of Commons* (1803), vol. 8, p. 862; "March, 1659/60: An Act for Approbation and Admission of Ministers of the Gospel to Benefices and Publick Lectures," *Acts and Ordinances of the Interregnum, 1642–1660*, ed. C.H. Firth and R.S. Rait (1911), pp. 1,459–62.
71. See Abernathy, "English Presbyterians," pp. 48–60, for this and next paragraph.

## Chapter 13　Consolidating Reformation in New England

1. Palfrey, *History*, vol. 2, p. 13; *WJ*, p. 432.
2. *Records of the Colony of New Plymouth, in New England: Acts of the Commissioners of the United Colonies of New England, 1643–1679*, vol. 1 (Boston, MA, 1859), pp. 3–4.
3. David D. Hall, *A Reforming People: Puritanism and the Transformation of Public Life in New England* (New York, 2011), p. 48; George D. Langdon, Jr., *Pilgrim Colony: A History of New Plymouth, 1620–1691* (New Haven, CT, 1966), pp. 94–5.
4. Mary Beth Norton, *Founding Fathers and Mothers: Gendered Power and the Forming of American Society* (New York, 1996), pp. 41–2, 51–2, 64–8, 101–2, 115–16, 337–9; Hall,

*WW*, pp. 36–9.

5. Edgar J. McManus, *Law and Liberty in Early New England: Criminal Justice and Due Process, 1620–1692* (Amherst, MA, 1993), pp. 46–52; Bradley Chapin, *Criminal Justice in Colonial America, 1606–1660* (Athens, GA, 1983), pp. 141–2.

6. McManus, *Law*, pp. 6–18, 36; Hall, *Reforming*, pp. 147–54; Peter Charles Hoffer, *Law and People in Colonial America* (Baltimore, MD, 1998), p. 108; Marshall, *Heretics and Believers*, p. 352; Benedict, *Christ's Churches*, p. 479.

7. George Francis Dow, *Records and Files of the Quarterly Courts of Essex County, Massachusetts*, vol. 1 (Salem, MA, 1911), p. 37; McManus, *Law*, p. 30.

8. McManus, *Law*, pp. 22–3; *WJ*, pp. 500–2.

9. McManus, *Law*, pp. 26–8, 35–6.

10. Ibid., pp. 187–9, appendix A; John Trusler, *A Concise View of the Common and Statute Law of England* (1781), pp. 323–4; Larry Dale Gragg, "The Troubled Voyage of the Rainbow," *History Today* 39 (1989), pp. 36–41; Lorenzo J. Greene, *The Negro in Colonial New England, 1620–1776* (New York, 1942), pp. 63–4.

11. John Murrin, "Trial by Jury in Seventeenth-Century New England," in David D. Hall, John Murrin and Thad Tate (eds.), *Saints and Revolutionaries: Essays on Early American History* (New York, 1984), pp. 190–2; Chapin, *Criminal Justice*, p. 129; McManus, *Law*, p. 41; *MR*, vol. 4, pt. 2, pp. 217–18; Jane Kamensky, *Governing the Tongue: The Politics of Speech in Early New England* (New York, 1997), pp. 103–11.

12. Moore, *P*, pp. 55–6; M. Michelle Jarrett Morris, *Under Household Government: Sex and Family in Puritan Massachusetts* (Cambridge, MA, 2013), p. 15; Deborah Colleen McNally, "To Secure Her Freedom: 'Dorcas ye Blackmore': Race, Redemption, and the Dorchester First Church," *NEQ* 89 (2016), pp. 533–55.

13. E. Jennifer Monaghan, *Learning to Read and Write in Colonial America* (Amherst, MA, 2005), pp. 31–4, 41–5; Howard Hotson, "'A Generall Reformation of Common Learning' and its Reception in the English-Speaking World," in Collinson and Ha (eds.), *Reception of Continental Reformation*, pp. 193–228; John Demos, *A Little Commonwealth: Family Life in Plymouth Colony* (New York, 1970), p. 143; Hall, *WW*, pp. 31–3.

14. Langdon, *Pilgrim Colony*, pp. 91–3.

15. Ibid., pp. 59–60, 135; J.M. Bumsted, "A Well-Bounded Toleration: Church and State in the Plymouth Colony," *Journal of Church and State*, 2nd ser., 10 (1968), pp. 267, 268; Monaghan, *Learning*, pp. 31–4; Demos, *Little Commonwealth*, p. 143.

16. Hall, *FS*, p. 147; H. Roger King, *Cape Cod and Plymouth Colony in the Seventeenth Century* (Lanham, MD, 1994), pp. 115–20.

17. Michael Leroy Oberg, *Uncas: First of the Mohegans* (Ithaca, NY, 2003), pp. 34–72; Margaret Ellen Newell, *Brethren by Nature: New England Indians, Colonists, and the Origins of American Slavery* (Ithaca, NY, 2015), pp. 32–42.

18. Francis J. Bremer, *Building a New Jerusalem: John Davenport, a Puritan in Three Worlds* (New Haven, CT, 2012), pp. 176–80, 212; Cornelia Hughes Dayton, *Women before the Bar: Gender, Law, and Society in Connecticut, 1639–1789* (Chapel Hill, NC, 1995), pp. 27–8; McManus, *Law*, p. 176; John Davenport, *The Power of Congregational Churches Asserted* (1672), pp. 16–17; *Hartlib*, 39/2/5A–6B; Mather, *MCA*, vol. 1, p. 328; Hubbard, *General History*, p. 320; Charles J. Hoadly (ed.), *Records of the Colony and Plantation of New Haven (Connecticut) from 1638–1649* (Hartford, CT, 1857), p. 262; William Wallace Tooker, *The Indian Place-Names on Long Island and Islands Adjacent with Their Probable Significations* (Stag Harbor, NY, 1911), pp. 118–19; Richard W. Cogley, *John Eliot's Mission to the Indians before King Philip's War* (Cambridge, MA, 1999), p. 42.

19. William MacDonald (ed.), *Select Charters and Other Documents Illustrative of American History, 1606–1775* (New York, 1914), p. 62; Maria Louise Greene, *The Development of Religious Liberty in Connecticut* (Boston, MA, 1905), p. 74; Thomas Hooker, *A Survey of the Summe of Church-Discipline* (1648), vol. 3, p. 5; idem, *The Covenant of Grace Opened* (1649), pp. 21–2; BL, Add. Ms 23622, fol. 171.

20. See Levy "Early Puritanism," pp. 69–348, for an overview.

21. Jon Butler (ed.), "Two 1642 Letters of Virginia Puritans," *Massachusetts Historical Society Proceedings* 84 (1972), pp. 99–109; Levy, "Early Puritanism," p. 128.

22. Levy, "Early Puritanism," pp. 90–113, 122–33; Pestana, *English Atlantic*, pp. 232, 152; Butler (ed.), "Two 1642 Letters," p. 100; Edward L. Bond, *Damned Souls in a Tobacco Colony: Religion in Seventeenth-Century Virginia* (Macon, GA, 2000), pp. 130, 130n74; James B. Bell, *Empire, Religion and Revolution in Early Virginia,1607–1786* (Basingstoke, Hants, 2013), p. 87. The impossibly precise population figures Bell cites have been rounded off.

23. Pestana, *English Atlantic*, p. 232; Timko, "Puritans," pp. 44–5, 99–122, 127; Nathaniel White, *Truth Gloriously Appearing* (1646), p. 53; Timko, "Puritans," p. 127; William Prynne, *A Fresh Discovery of Some Prodigious New Wandring-Blasing-Stars* (1645), 2nd pag., pp. 2–3, 6–7, 11; White, *Truth*, p. 44.

24. Lefroy, *Memorials*, vol. 1, p. 595; Timko, "Puritans," pp. 122–9; *WJ*, p. 635.

25. Hallett, *Chronicle*, pp. 51–2; Timko, "Puritans," pp. 135–9; *WP*, vol. 5, p. 72.

26. Michael P. Winship, "North America to 1662," in *OHA*, p. 266; Evan Haefeli, "Toleration and Empire: The Origins of American Religious Pluralism," in Steven Foster (ed.), *British North America in the Seventeenth and Eighteenth Centuries* (New York, 2013), p. 111; *WP*, vol. 5, pp. 83–4, 96–9, 183; Hallett, *Chronicle*, p. 52; *MR*, vol. 2, p. 167.

27. *Hartlib*, 39/2/6A. For this and the next paragraph, see Robert Emmet Wall, *Massachusetts Bay: The Crucial Decade, 1640–1650* (New Haven, CT, 1972), chaps. 5, 6, and George Lyman Kittredge, "Dr. Robert Child the Remonstrant," *CSMP* 21 (1920), pp. 1–146.

28. *Hartlib*, 39/2/6A; Andrews, *Colonial Period*, vol. 1, p. 232n2.

29. Robert Brenner, *Merchants and Revolution: Commercial Change, Political Conflict and London's Overseas Traders 1550–1653* (Cambridge, 1993), pp. 523–8.

30. *Articles and Orders, Made and Agreed upon the 9th. Day of July, 1647* (1647).

31. *WJ*, pp. 720–1. According to White, *Truth*, pp. 9–10, magistrates were to "restrain . . . atheism, polytheism, idolatry, blasphemy, etc." and "assist and preserve the Churches of Jesus Christ." If one of these churches fell into errors in doctrine or practice and failed to reform after being rebuked by neighboring churches, the magistrates were to step in. White's views on religious liberty are discussed in Polly Ha, "Religious Toleration and Ecclesiastical Independence in Revolutionary Britain, Bermuda, and the Bahamas," *JEH* 84 (2015), pp. 807–27, but without mentioning any of these magisterial powers. Lefroy, *Memorials*, vol. 1, pp. 652, 654–5.

32. Samuel Eliot Morison, *Harvard College in the Seventeenth Century*, 2 vols. (Cambridge, MA, 1935), vol. 2, pp. 41–2.

33. Levy, "Early Puritanism", pp. 292–4; Bond, *Damned Souls*, pp. 147–9; William DeLoss Love, *The Fast and Thanksgiving Days of New England* (Boston, MA, 1895), p. 156; Moore, *P*, pp. 55, 65–6; Bremer, *Lay Empowerment*, p. 111; Bremer, *CC*, pp. 131–74.

34. Bush, *CJC*, pp. 461–2, 469; Sewall, "Diary," p. 437; John Cotton, *The Powring Out of the Seven Vials, or an Exposition, of the 16. Chapter of the Revelation* (1642), "Sixth Vial," pp. 20–2. The consolation prize of the expedition was Jamaica: see Carla Gardina Pestana, *The English Conquest of Jamaica: Oliver Cromwell's Bid for Empire* (Cambridge, MA, 2017), chaps. 1–4.

35. Williston Walker, *The Creeds and Platforms of Congregationalism* (New York, 1893), p. 169.

36. Cooper, *TTL*, chap. 4, pp. 145–9; Thomas Lechford, *Plain Dealing; or, News from New England*, ed. J. Hammond Trumbull (Boston, MA, 1867); Edward Winslow, *Hypocrisie Unmasked* (1647), p. 101; John Cotton, *The Grounds and Ends of the Baptisme of the Children of the Faithfull* (1646), A3r; George Phillips, *A Reply to a Confutation of Some Grounds for Infants Baptisme* (1645), pp. 1–2; D. Roger Thompson, *Divided We Stand: Watertown, Massachusetts, 1630–1680* (Amherst, MA, 2003), p. 70; William G. McLoughlin, *New England Dissent, 1630–1833*, 2 vols. (Cambridge, MA, 1971), vol. 1, pp. 14–18; Walker, *Creeds*, p. 169.

37. *WJ*, p. 715; Mather, *MCA*, vol. 2, p. 211; Thomas Brightman, *A Revelation of the Revelation*,

*that is the Revelation of St. John* (Amsterdam, 1611), pp. 994–5.

38. Cooper, *TTL*, pp. 80–6; Bremer, *CC*, p. 173; Mather, *MCA*, vol. 2, p. 236.

39. *WJ*, pp. 635, 715; Cooper, *TTL*, pp. 81–4.

### Chapter 14  Old England's Corruptions Come to New England

1. Mather, *MCA*, vol. 1, pp. 271, 295, 301; Giles Firmin, *Of Schism* (1658), p. 59; John Norton, *Responsio ad totam quaestionum syllogen à clarissimo viro domino Guilielmo Apollonio* (1648); idem, *A Discussion of that Great Point in Divinity, the Sufferings of Christ* (1653); *WJ*, p. 654.

2. Mather, *MCA*, vol. 1, pp. 295–6.

3. John Norton, "The Negative Vote, 1643," *Massachusetts Historical Society Proceedings* 46 (1913), pp. 276–85; idem, *Discussion*, sig. A4v–A4[i]r; Hamilton Andrews Hill, *History of the Old South Church (Third Church) Boston, MA, 1669–1884*, 2 vols. (Boston, MA, 1890), vol. 1, p. 66; Timothy J. Sehr, *Colony and Commonwealth: Massachusetts Bay, 1649–1660* (New York, 1989), p. 132.

4. Mark Valeri, *Heavenly Merchandize: How Religion Shaped Commerce in Puritan America* (Princeton, NJ, 2010), chap. 3; John Hull, "The Diaries of John Hull," *Archaeologia Americana* 3 (1857), p. 151; Meredith Marie Neuman, *Jeremiah's Scribes Creating Sermon Literature in Puritan New England* (Philadelphia, PA, 2013), chap. 2.

5. John Hull, "Sermon Notes, 1657–1660," Historical Society of Pennsylvania, Gratz Collection, Box 1, "9 of 2d. 1656. Mr. Powell."

6. *MR*, vol. 1, p. 336; vol. 2, p. 238; Robert Charles Anderson, "Michael Powell of Dedham and Boston," *New England Historical and Genealogical Register* 131 (1977), pp. 173–4; Chandler Robbins, *A History of the Second Church, Or Old North, in Boston* (Boston, MA, 1852), pp. 7, 210.

7. Moore, *P*, p. 55; Robbins, *History*, pp. 7–8; MA, vol. 10, p. 88.

8. William Pynchon, *The Meritorious Price of Our Redemption* (1650), t.p.; Michael P. Winship, "Contesting Control of Orthodoxy among the Godly: William Pynchon Reexamined," *William and Mary Quarterly* 54 (1997), pp. 795–822; *MR*, vol. 4, pt. 1 (1854), p. 29.

9. Winship, "Contesting Control," pp. 814, 815; *MR*, vol. 4, pt. 1 (1854), p. 48; Sehr, *Colony*, pp. 98–9.

10. Bush, *CJC*, pp. 454–8, 496–504; *MHSC*, 3rd ser., 1 (1825, reprint 1846), pp. 35–7; Sehr, *Colony*, pp. 47–8, 131–4; Winship, "Contesting Control," p. 815n54.

11. *MR*, vol. 4, pt. 1, pp. 114, 177.

12. Sehr, *Colony*, pp. 134–6, 141–3; MA, vol. 10, p. 86; Richard Baxter, *A Defence of the Principles of Love* (1671), 2nd pag., pp. 124, 175.

13. *MR*, vol. 4, pt. 1, p. 210. More sweeping, proactive efforts by the General Court to supervise lay preaching provoked fierce push-back from the churches, and the General Court had to back down. See Sehr, *Colony*, pp. 136–41.

14. David D. Hall (ed.), *Witch-Hunting in Seventeenth-Century New England: A Documentary History 1638–1693* (Boston, MA, 1991), pp. 89–91; Norton, *Founding Fathers*, pp. 81–3, 161–4.

15. Larry Dale Gragg, *The Quaker Community on Barbados: Challenging the Culture of the Planter Class* (Columbia, MO, 2009), p. 41; Stefano Villani, "Fisher, Mary (c. 1623–1698)," ODNB; Adrian Chastain Weimer, *Martyrs' Mirror: Persecution and Holiness in Early New England* (New York, 2011), pp. 101–5.

16. Humphrey Norton, *New-England's Ensigne* (1659), pp. 6–8.

17. Richard D. Pierce (ed.), *The Records of the First Church in Boston, MA, 1630–1868*, CSMP 39 (1961), pp. 52–4; Moore, *P*, p. 78; King, *Cape Cod*, p. 91; William Sewel, *The History of the Rise, Increase, and Progress, of the Christian People Called Quakers* (1722), p. 160; James Bowden, *The History of the Society of Friends in America*, 2 vols. (1850), vol. 1, p. 55; Barbour, *The Quakers*, p. 45.

18. Norton, *New-England's Ensigne*, pp. 23–23; *Records of the Colony of New Plymouth in*

*New England, Court Orders*, vol. 3 (Boston, MA, 1855), pp. 111, 113.

19. George Bishop, *New England Judged* (1661), p. 38; Bell (ed.), *Wheelwright*, p. 70; Rufus Jones, *The Quakers in the American Colonies* (2nd edn., New York, 1966), pp. 51, 53; Norton, *New-England's Ensigne*, pp. 98–9; William Coddington, *A Demonstration of True Love unto You the Rulers of the Colony of the Massachusetts* (n.p., 1674), pp. 17, 20; S.G., *A Glass for the People of New England* (1676), pp. 4–5, 9.

20. Bowden, *History*, vol. 1, pp. 103–4, 105–6; Bishop, *New England*, pp. 40, 42, 172–3; Norton, *New England's Ensigne*, 50–2.

21. Carla Gardina Pestana, *Quakers and Baptists in Colonial Massachusetts* (Cambridge, 1991), p. 25; Norton, *New-England's Ensigne*, p. 78; John Norton, *The Orthodox Evangelist* (1654), "To the Church, and Inhabitants, of Ipswich in New-England."

22. Norton, *New-England's Ensigne*, pp. 56, 70–3; Bishop, *New England*, p. 57.

23. Langdon, *Pilgrim Colony*, pp. 72–5; King, *Cape Cod*, pp. 92–100.

24. Jones, *Quakers*, p. 72.

25. Bishop, *New England*, pp. 79–80; Norton, *New-England's Ensigne*, p. 98.

26. *MR*, vol. 4, pt. 1, pp. 348, 381; John Norton, *The Heart of N-England Rent* (Cambridge, MA, 1658), pp. 39, 45, 50; Hull, "Diaries," p. 202; George Bishop, *New England Judged. The Second Part* (1667), pp. 246–7; Peters, *Print Culture*, p. 230n146.

27. Bishop, *New England*, pp. 95, 108; MA, vol. 10, pp. 254; *MR*, vol. 4, pt. 1, p. 383.

28. Bishop, *New England*, pp. 119–20; Coddington, *Demonstration*, pp. 9–10; MA, vol. 10, p. 254.

29. Michael Joseph Canavan, "Where Were the Quakers Hanged in Boston?" (Boston, MA, 1911), pp. 5–10; Bishop, *New England*, pp. 109, 195.

30. Arthur J. Worrall, *Quakers in the Colonial Northeast* (Hanover, NH, 1980), p. 14; George Ellis, *The Puritan Age and Rule in the Colony of the Massachusetts Bay, 1629–1685* (Boston, MA, 1888), p. 469; Edward Burrough, *A Declaration of the Sad and Great Persecution and Martyrdom of the People of God* (1661), pp. 29, 30; Bishop, *New England . . . Second Part*, pp. 11, 22.

31. Foster, *LA*, p. 182; Sehr, *Colony*, pp. 239–41.

32. Mather, *Church-Government*, p. 21; idem, *A Disputation Concerning Church Members* (1658), p. 14.

33. Richard Mather and Jonathan Mitchel, *Defence of the Answer* (Cambridge, MA, 1662), pp. 31, 45.

34. Pope, *HWC*, pp. 13–25; Mather, *MCA*, vol. 1, p. 291.

35. The Ipswich church resolved to expand its membership before Chelmsford, but it is not known if it put its resolution into practice; Pope, *HWC*, p. 24; Joseph B. Felt, *The Ecclesiastical History of New England*, 2 vols. (Boston, MA, 1855), vol. 2, p. 141.

36. Robert G. Pope (ed.), *The Notebook of the Reverend John Fiske, 1644–1675*, CSMP 47 (Boston, MA, 1961), p. 110; Wilson Waters, *History of Chelmsford, Massachusetts* (Lowell, MA, 1917), pp. 35–6, 754.

37. Pope (ed.), *Notebook*, pp. 121, 130.

38. Mather, *Disputation*; Walker, *Creeds*, pp. 257–62.

39. Pope, *HWC*, pp. 17–21; Increase Mather, *The First Principles of New-England, Concerning the Subject of Baptisme & Communion of Churches* (Cambridge, MA, 1675), pp. 9, 13, 24; Mather, *MCA*, vol. 2, p. 99; *Records of the First Church at Dorchester* (Boston, MA, 1891), pp. 1, 168.

40. Pierce (ed.), *Records*, pp. 56–7.

41. John Norton, *Three Choice and Profitable Sermons upon Severall Texts of Scripture* (Cambridge, MA, 1664), p. 13.

42. Sehr, *Colony*, p. 276.

43. Hutchinson, *HC*, vol. 1, p. 180; Norton, *Responsio*, pp. 119–20; idem, *Three . . . Sermons*, p. 11; Jenny Hale Pulsipher, *"Subjects unto the Same King": Indians, English, and the Contest for Authority in Colonial New England* (Philadelphia, PA, 2005), p. 45.

44. Braithwaite, *Beginnings of Quakerism*, pp. 477–8; Langdon, *Pilgrim Colony*, p. 76.

45. *HP*, vol. 2, pp. 26, 65, 68, 69.
46. Sewel, *History*, p. 288.
47. Ibid.; Bishop, *New England . . . Second Part*, p. 43; *HP*, vol. 2, pp. 102–3; "Mather Papers," p. 198; Hutchinson, *HC*, vol. 1, p. 189.
48. Palfrey, *History*, vol. 2, pp. 528–31; "Mather Papers," p. 204.
49. Douglas L. Winiarski, *Darkness Falls on the Land of Light: Experiencing Religious Awakenings in Eighteenth-Century New England* (Chapel Hill, NC, 2017), p. 383; "Mather Papers," p. 204; Charles Chauncy, *Antisynodalia Scripta Americana* (1662), pp. 5, 6.
50. "Mather Papers," pp. 193, 204; Norton, *Three . . . Sermons*, pp. 16–28; Mather, *MCA*, pp. 297–8.

## Chapter 15  Waban's Reformation

1. Daniel Gookin, "Historical Collections of the Indians in New England," *MHSC*, 1st ser., 1 (1792), p. 184; John Eliot and Thomas Mayhew, *Tears of Repentance* (1653), p. 7; John Eliot, *A Further Account of the Progress of the Gospel* (1660), p. 71; Kathleen J. Bragdon, *Native People of Southern New England, 1500–1650* (Norman, OK, 1996), pp. 141, 200–8; Cogley, *John Eliot's Mission*, pp. 54, 58; John Eliot, *The Day-Breaking, If Not the Sun-Rising* (1647), p. 21.
2. James L. Axtell, *The Invasion Within: The Contest of Cultures in Colonial North America* (New York, 1986), p. 252; William Cronon, *Changes in the Land: Indians, Colonists, and the Ecology of New England* (New York, 1983), pp. 87–8; Cogley, *John Eliot's Mission*, p. 132; Eliot and Mayhew, *Tears*, p. 7.
3. Eliot, *Further Account*, p. 72. All of the Waban quotations are from seventeenth-century English translations of lost transcriptions of his native-tongue speeches.
4. Ibid., pp. 31, 34, 71, 72; idem, *Day-Breaking*, p. 1; Cogley, *John Eliot's Mission*, p. 42; cf., Roger Williams, *A Key into the Language of America* (1643), p. 129.
5. Bragdon, *Native People*, pp. 126, 178–9, 180–1, 190; William Scranton Simmons, *Spirit of the New England Tribes: Indian History and Folklore, 1620–1984* (Hanover, NH, 1986), p. 44.
6. Eliot and Mayhew, *Tears*, sig. Bv; Cogley, *John Eliot's Mission*, pp. 15–16.
7. *MR*, vol. 2, pp. 5, 56, 84, 134.
8. *WJ*, p. 682; Eliot, *Day-Breaking*, pp. 1–7.
9. Eliot, *Day-Breaking*, pp. 6–7, 23, 33; idem, *Further Account*, p. 32.
10. Bragdon, *Native People*, p. 171 Thomas Shepard, *The Clear Sun-Shine of the Gospel* (1648), p. 19; Edward Winslow, *The Glorious Progress of the Gospel* (1649), pp. 11–14, 19–21, 28–9, 32; Eliot and Mayhew, *Tears*, p. 7; Eliot, *Further Account*, p. 32; idem, *Day-Breaking*, pp. 20, 22.
11. Winslow, *Glorious Progress*, sig. B2[ii]v, p. 14; William Kellaway, *The New England Company, 1649–1776: Missionary Society to the American Indians* (1961); Jean M. O'Brien, *Dispossession by Degrees: Indian Land and Identity in Natick, Massachusetts, 1650–1790* (Lincoln, NE, 1997), pp. 32–42.
12. William Gouge, *Strength out of Weakness* (1652), pp. 17–18; Cogley, *John Eliot's Mission*, pp. 83–90.
13. Cogley, *John Eliot's Mission*, pp. 207–8; Eliot and Mayhew, *Tears*, p. 2; Gouge, *Strength*, sig. ar, pp. 13–14, 18–19, 33–4; Andrew Crome, "Politics and Eschatology: Reassessing the Appeal of the 'Jewish Indian' Theory in England and New England in the 1650s," *Journal of Religious History* 40 (2015), pp. 326–46.
14. Eliot and Mayhew, *Tears*, pp. 3, 24.
15. Shepard, *Clear Sun-Shine*, p. 10; Eliot and Mayhew, *Tears*, pp. 8, 11, 17, 19, 20, 25, 34.
16. Eliot, *Further Account*, p. 31.
17. Ibid., pp. 30–4; Cogley, *John Eliot's Mission*, pp. 44–97, 105–8, 119–24, 140–3; Shepard, *Clear Sun-Shine*, pp. 6–7; Matthew Mayhew, *The Conquests and Triumphs of Grace* (1695), p. 64; David J. Silverman, *Faith and Boundaries: Colonists, Christianity, and Community among the Wampanoag Indians of Martha's Vineyard, 1600–1871* (New York,

2005), chap. 1.
18. Shepard, *Clear Sun-Shine*, pp. 10, 33; Henry Whitfield, *The Light Appearing More and More towards the Perfect Day* (1651), p. 7.
19. John Eliot, "Eliot's Account of Indian Churches in New-England, 1673," *MHSC*, 1st. ser., 10 (1809), pp. 126–7.

## Chapter 16  English Puritanism under Persecution

1. Theodosia Alleine et al., *The Life and Death of Mr. Joseph Alleine* (1672), 1st pag., pp. 43, 46–7, 94.
2. Ibid., p. 95.
3. Ibid., pp. 63, 96 (mispaginated as 69).
4. N.H. Keeble, *The Restoration: England in the 1660s* (Oxford, 2002), pp. 42–5, 113–15; J. Horsfall Turner (ed.), *The Rev. Oliver Heywood B.A., 1630–1702; His Autobiography, Diaries, Anecdote and Event Books*, 4 vols. (Brighouse, Yorkshire, 1882–85), vol. 1, p. 180; Fincham and Taylor, "Episcopal Identity," pp. 457–82.
5. Barry Till, "The Worcester House Declaration and the Restoration of the Church of England," *Historical Research* 70 (1997), pp. 213–18.
6. Douglas R. Lacey, *Dissent and Parliamentary Politics in England, 1661–1689* (New Brunswick, NJ, 1969), pp. 13, 269n41; Baxter, *RB*, bk. ii, p. 277; Frank Bate, *The Declaration of Indulgence, 1672: A Study in the Rise of Organised Dissent* (1908), p. 14, 14n65; Samuel Clarke, *A Discourse against Toleration* (1660); John Humfrey, *A Proposition for the Safety and Happiness of the King and Kingdom* (1667), p. 56; John Corbet, *A Discourse of the Religion of England* (1667), p. 39; Keeble, *Restoration*, pp. 63–4.
7. Till, "Worcester House Declaration," pp. 225–7.
8. Keeble and Nuttall, *CCRB*, pp. 116–18.
9. Haefeli, "Toleration and Empire," pp. 121–8.
10. Baxter, *RB*, bk. i, pp. 48–9.
11. Alleine, *Life*, 1st pag., p. 63; A.B., *A Letter from a Minister to a Person of Quality* (1662), p. 1.
12. Winship, *Seers*, p. 37; David J. Appleby, *Black Bartholomew's Day: Preaching, Polemic and Restoration Nonconformity* (Manchester, 2007), chaps. 2, 3.
13. John Spurr, *The Restoration Church of England, 1646–1660* (New Haven, CT, 1991), pp. 188–90, 205–7; Norman Sykes, *From Sheldon to Secker: Aspects of English Church History, 1660–1768* (Cambridge, 1958), pp. 25–6; Thomas Lathbury, *A History of the Book of Common Prayer* (Oxford 1858), pp. 390–3; John Ramsbottom, "Presbyterians and 'Partial Conformity' in the Restoration Church of England," *JEH* 43 (1992), pp. 249–70; J.T. Cliffe, *The Puritan Gentry Besieged, 1650–1700* (1993), chap. 8.
14. John Spurr, " 'Latitudinarianism' and the Restoration Church," *HJ* 31 (1988), pp. 61–82; John Parkin, "John Wilkins and Latitudinarianism," in William Poole (ed.), *John Wilkins (161–1672): New Essays* (Leiden, 2017), pp. 108–9; Fincham and Tyacke, *Altars*, pp. 306–7; Roger Thomas, "Comprehension and Indulgence," in Geoffrey Nuttall and Owen Chadwick (eds.), *From Uniformity to Unity 1662–1962* (1962), pp. 189–253.
15. Cory Cotter, "Going Dutch: Beyond Bartholomew's Day," in N.H. Keeble (ed.), *"Settling the Peace of the Church": 1662 Revised* (Oxford, 2014), pp. 175–6; Alleine, *Life*, 1st pag., pp. 63–4.
16. Richard L. Greaves, *Deliver Us from Evil: The Radical Underground in Britain, 1660–1663* (New York, 1986).
17. Charles Stanford, *Joseph Alleine: His Companions & Times, a Memorial of "Black Bartholomew,"* 1662 (1861), p. 227; Alleine, *Life*, 1st pag., pp. 111–12; Joseph Alleine, *A Call to Archippus* (1664), p. 8; Joseph Alleine, *An Alarme to Unconverted Sinners* (1672), pp. 8, 10.
18. Alleine, *Life*, 1st pag., p. 66; Alleine, *Alarme*, p. 97.
19. Alleine, *Life*, 2nd pag., p. 141; Alex Walsham, "Phanaticus: Hugh Peter, Antipuritanism and the Afterlife of the English Revolution," *Parergon* 32 (2015), pp. 77–8.
20. Stanford, *Joseph Alleine*, pp. 227, 242; Alleine, *Life*, 1st pag., p. 67, 71.

21. Alleine, *A Call*, pp. 11–12; Alleine, *Life*, 2nd pag., p. 126.
22. Keeble, *Restoration*, pp. 120–1, 159–60; Spurr, *Restoration Church*, pp. 52–3; Richard Alleine, *The Best of Remedies for the Worst of Maladies* (1667), passim; Matthew Mead, *Solomon's Prescription for the Removal of the Pestilence* (1665), pp. 61–73; Thomas Blake, *Eben-ezer, or, Profitable Truths after Pestilential Times* (1666), p. 91; Thomas Vincent, *Gods Terrible Voice in the City* (1667), pp. 21–4.
23. Keeble, *Restoration*, p. 121; Baxter, *RB*, bk. iii, p. 13.
24. George Trosse, *The Life of the Reverend Mr. Geo. Trosse* (Exeter, 1714), p. 84; Brockett, *Nonconformity*, pp. 27–9.
25. Trosse, *Life*, pp. 85–6.
26. Ibid., pp. 87, 89–90.
27. Keeble and Nuttall, *CCRB*, vol. 2, p. 189.
28. Henry, *Account*, p. 90.
29. Turner (ed.), *Oliver Heywood*, vol. 1, p. 195; Alleine, *Life*, 1st pag., pp. 66, 79; John Whitlock, *A Short Account of the Life of the Reverend Mr. William Reynolds* (1698), p. 43.
30. Trosse, *Life*, pp. 89–91; Alleine, *Life*, 1st pag., p. 66.
31. William Bradshaw, *Unreasonablenesse of the Separation* (1614), sig. Ir, I2r; William Rathband (ed.), *A Most Grave, and Modest Confutation of the Errors of the Sect, Commonly Called Brownists* (1644), pp. 40–1.
32. Appleby, *Black Bartholomew's Day*, p. 21.
33. Mark Goldie et al. (eds.), *The Entring Book of Roger Morrice*, 6 vols. (Woodbridge, Suffolk, 2007), vol. 5, p. 142; David Wykes, "The Minister's Calling: The Preparation and Qualification of Candidates for the Presbyterian Ministry in England, 1660–1689," *Nederlands Archief voor Kerkgeschiedenis* 82 (2004), pp. 271–80; Henry, *Account*, pp. 116–17; John Flavel, *The Whole Works*, 2 vols. (1701), vol. 1, sig. a[1]r; Giles Firmin, *The Questions between the Conformist and the Nonconformist, Truly Stated* (1681), sig. B2v–r; Henry Fishwick (ed.), *The Notebook of the Rev. Thomas Jolly* (Manchester, 1895), p. 41.
34. Alleine, *Life*, 1st pag., p. 41; Bremer, *CC*, p. 235; Keeble, *Restoration*, pp. 162–8.
35. Spurr, *Restoration Church*, p. 104; Bate, *Declaration*, p. 57, Baxter, *RB*, bk. iii, p. 19.
36. Keeble, *Restoration*, pp. 168–70.
37. Donald A. Spaeth, *The Church in an Age of Danger: Parsons and Parishioners, 1660–1740* (Cambridge, 2000), chap. 7; Richard L. Greaves, *Enemies under His Feet: Radicals and Nonconformists in Britain, 1664–1677* (Stanford, CA, 1990), p. 160; Baxter, *RB*, bk. iii, p. 19; Alleine, *Life*, 1st pag., pp. 79–93.
38. Dewey D. Wallace, *Shapers of English Calvinism, 1660–1714: Variety, Persistence, and Transformation* (New York, 2011), chap. 4.
39. John Spurr, *English Puritanism, 1603–1689* (New York, 1998), pp. 134–5; Spaeth, *Church in an Age of Danger*, p. 156; William Harris, *Some Memoirs of the Life and Character of the Reverend and Learned Thomas Manton* (1725), p. 73; Tim Harris, *Restoration: Charles II and His Kingdoms, 1660–1685* (2005), pp. 28–9; N.H. Keeble, *The Literary Culture of Nonconformity* (Athens, GA, 1987), pp. 137–8.
40. R. Tudor Jones, *Congregationalism in England, 1662–1962* (1962), p. 42; Phillip Nye, *A Case of Great and Present Use* (1677), p. 17; Bremer, *CC*, p. 222; Baxter, *RB*, bk. iii, p. 19; Lacey, *Dissent*, pp. 16–18: John Owen, *Truth and Innocence Vindicated* (1669), pp. 396–7.
41. Keeble, *Restoration*, pp. 140–1; Greaves, *Glimpses*, pp. 135–40; Michael Davies, "The Silencing of God's Dear Ministers: John Bunyan and His Church in 1662," in Keeble (ed.), *"Settling,"* p. 105.
42. Richard Greaves, *John Bunyan and English Nonconformity* (1992), chap. 9; idem, *Glimpses*, p. 612.
43. John Bunyan, *The Pilgrim's Progress*, ed. Cynthia Wall (New York, 2009), pp. 13, 19, 34–6, 70, 75–6, 78, 88–92.
44. Ibid., pp. 96, 111–15, 125, quotation from p. 114.
45. Rivers, *Reason, Grace, and Sentiment*, vol. 1, pp. 53–88; Neil Lettinga, "Covenant Theology Turned Upside Down: Henry Hammond and Caroline Anglican Moralism: 1643–1660,"

*Sixteenth Century Journal* 24 (1993), pp. 653–69.

46. Stephen Hampton, *Anti-Arminians: The Anglican Reformed Tradition from Charles II to George I* (Oxford, 2008); Tyacke, *Aspects*, chap. 12; Michael P. Winship, "Defining Puritanism in Restoration England: Richard Baxter and Others Respond to a Friendly Debate," *HJ* 54 (2011), pp. 689–715; Christopher Haigh, " 'Theological Wars': 'Socinians' v. 'Antinomians' in Restoration England," *JEH* 67 (2016), pp. 325–50.

47. Thomas, "Comprehension," pp. 196–206.

48. Keeble, *Restoration*, pp. 121–2.

49. Gary S. De Krey, *London and the Restoration, 1659–1683* (New York, 2005), pp. 111, 119–21; Greaves, *Enemies*, pp. 155–64; *CSPD, 1671*, p. 496; *CSPD, 1671–2*, pp. 27–9.

50. Keeble, *Restoration*, p. 170.

51. Bate, *Declaration*, pp. 71–82.

52. Spurr, *Restoration Church*, pp. 161–2; Harris, *Restoration*, pp. 28, 63–4; Keeble, *Literary Culture*, p. 59; John Miller, *Popery and Politics in England 1660–1688* (Cambridge, 1973), chap. 3.

53. Miller, *Popery and Politics*, p. 59; Greaves, *Glimpses*, pp. 250, 275, 291, 315; Crawford Gribben, *John Owen and English Puritanism: Experiences of Defeat* (Oxford, 2016), p. 250; Cliffe, *Puritan Gentry Besieged*, pp. 115–16; Bate, *Declaration*, appendix vii; Kinda Skea, "The Ecclesiastical Identities of Puritan and Nonconformist Clergy, 1640–1672" (Ph.D. thesis, University of Leicester, 2015).

## Chapter 17  English Puritanism Goes Public Again

1. Fishwick (ed.), *Notebook*, pp. xvii, 131–2; Turner (ed.), *Oliver Heywood*, vol. 1, p. 181.

2. Fishwick (ed.), *Notebook*, pp. 44, 127, 138; BL, Stowe Ms 745, fol. 79v.

3. Fishwick (ed.), *Notebook*, pp. xix, xx, xxi, 31, 51, 98; Matthews, *Calamy Revised*, p. ix.

4. Fishwick (ed.), *Notebook*, pp. 7, 15.

5. Winship, "Defining Puritanism," p. 696; Fishwick (ed.), *Notebook*, pp. 7, 11; John Addey, *Sin and Society in the Seventeenth Century* (1989), p. 65.

6. Heywood, *Autobiography*, vol. 1, p. 232; Watts, *Dissenters*, vol. 1, p. 280.

7. W.J. Sheils, "Oliver Heywood and his Congregation," *Studies in Church History* 23 (1986), pp. 263–5; Calamy, *ABH*, vol. 2, pp. 395, 791–2; Heywood, *Autobiography*, vol. 1, pp. 231, 232, 234.

8. Samuel S. Thomas, *Creating Communities in Restoration England: Parish and Congregation in Oliver Heywood's Halifax* (Leiden, 2013), pp. 53, 54, 57–8, 60–1, 64–9, 75, 80–1.

9. Heywood, *Autobiography*, vol. 1, p. 277; vol. 2, p. 20.

10. Ibid., vol. 2, pp. 20, 22; vol. 3, p. 109.

11. Thomas, *Creating Communities*, p. 135, Heywood, *Autobiography*, vol. 4, p. 65.

12. Thomas, *Creating Communities*, pp. 133–4, chap. 5; Heywood, *Autobiography*, vol. 4, pp. 65–6.

13. Heywood, *Autobiography*, vol. 4, p. 66.

14. Thomas, *Creating Communities*, pp. 69–78; Baxter, *RB*, bk. iii, p. 100; idem, *Richard Baxters Answer to Dr. Edward Stillingfleet's Charge of Separation* (1680), pp. 51, 53, 58; John Barret, *The Rector of Sutton Committed with the Dean of St. Paul's* (1680) pp. 21, 25–6; John Troughton, *An Apology for the Non-Conformists* (1681), pp. 65, 70; John Howe, *An Answer to Dr. Stillingfleet's Mischief of Separation* (1680), pp. 5, 25, 46.

15. Heywood, *Autobiography*, vol. 3, p. 109.

16. Ibid., pp. 109, 152; vol. 2, pp. 31–2.

17. Jacqueline Rose, *Godly Kingship in Restoration England: The Politics of the Royal Supremacy, 1660–1688* (Cambridge, 2011), pp. 93–104; Gary S. De Krey, *Restoration and Revolution in Britain: A Political History of the Era of Charles II and the Glorious Revolution* (Basingstoke, Hants, 2007), p. 105.

18. Rose, *Godly Kingship*, pp. 93–104; Thomas, "Comprehension," pp. 211–13.

19. Fishwick (ed.), *Notebook*, p. 18; BL, Stowe Ms 745, fols. 79r–80r; Bremer, *CC*, pp. 223–5.

20. Fishwick (ed.), *Notebook*, pp. xxv, 22–4, 33, 49, 96, 99, 137, 138; Bremer, *CC*, pp. 233–44.
21. Bremer, *CC*, pp. 216–18; Martindale, *Life*, p. 128; Fishwick (ed.), *Notebook*, pp. 216–22; Thomas, "Comprehension," pp. 219–22.
22. Richard Baxter, *A Second True Defence of the Meer Nonconformists* (1681), p. 55; Fishwick (ed.), *Notebook*, p. 26.
23. Andrew Marvell, *The Rehearsal Transpros'd*, ed. Martin Dzelzainis and Annabel M. Patterson, in idem (eds.), *The Prose Works of Andrew Marvell*, 2 vols. (New Haven, CT, 2003), vol. 1, pp. 183–95. In 1678, Marvell intervened in an intra-puritan debate about predestination with a tract endorsing the arguments of the moderate Calvinist John Howe (see p. 271) for putting predestination "within the due limits of Scripture and Saving Knowledge"; see Andrew Marvell, *Remarks upon a Late Disingenuous Discourse*, ed. N.H. Keeble, in Dzelzainis and Patterson (eds.), *Prose Works*, vol. 2, p. 417. On Marvell's religion, see William Lamont, "The Religion of Andrew Marvell: Locating the 'Bloody Horse,'" in Conal Condren and A.D. Cousins (eds.), *The Political Identity of Andrew Marvell* (Aldershot, Hants, 1990), pp. 188–212. Some scholars, conceiving of Marvell as more of a freethinker than a puritan, insist that he could not really have meant what he said about Howe; see, for example, Nicholas von Maltzahn, "Milton, Marvell, and Toleration," in Sharon Achinstein and Elizabeth Sauer (eds.), *Milton and Toleration* (Oxford, 2007), p. 92; Nigel Smith, *Andrew Marvell: The Chameleon* (New Haven, CT, 2010), p. 331; H.C. Foxcroft (ed.), *A Supplement to Burnet's History of My Own Time* (Oxford, 1902), p. 216.
24. Andrew Marvell, *An Account of the Growth of Popery and Arbitrary Government in England*, ed. Nicholas von Maltzahn, in Dzelzainis and Patterson (eds.), *Prose Works*, vol. 2, pp. 279, 280.
25. Goldie, *RM*, pp. 149–50, 154.
26. J. P. Kenyon, *The Popish Plot* (1972), p. 52.
27. Ibid., pp. 183, 198, 203, 204.
28. Harris, *Restoration*, pp. 146–63.
29. Henry G. Horwitz, "Protestant Reconciliation in the Exclusion Crisis," *JEH* 15 (1964), pp. 201–17. John Faldo, *Quakerism, No Christianity* (1675), sig. A4(ii)v, A4(v)r, has an endorsement by twenty-five leading Presbyterian and Congregational ministers.
30. Edward Polhill, *The Samaritan* (1682), p. 118; Gilbert Burnett, *History of His Own Times*, 2 vols. (1724), vol. 1, p. 495.
31. David Hey, *The Fiery Blades of Hallamshire: Sheffield and Its Neighbourhood, 1660–1740* (Leicester, 1991), p. 266; James G. Miall, *Congregationalism in Yorkshire: A Chapter of Modern Church History* (1868), p. 350; Heywood, *Autobiography*, vol. 2, pp. 199–201; David L. Wykes, "The Contribution of the Dissenting Academy to the Emergence of Rational Dissent," in Knud Haakonssen (ed.), *Enlightenment and Religion: Rational Dissent in Eighteenth-Century Britain* (Cambridge, 1996), pp. 99–139.
32. Heywood, *Autobiography*, vol. 2, pp. 24–5, 194–8, 20; vol. 3, 115–16; Fishwick (ed.), *Notebook*, p. 44.
33. Heywood, *Autobiography*, vol. 3, p. 214.
34. Nathaniel Bisbie, *Prosecution no Persecution* (1682), p. 13; Harris, *Restoration*, pp. 237–62.
35. Heywood, *Autobiography*, vol. 2, pp. 217, 218.
36. Ibid., p. 219; Warren Johnston, *Revelation Restored: The Apocalypse in Later Seventeenth-Century England* (Woodbridge, Suffolk, 2011), pp. 32–3, 215, 222.
37. Johnston, *Revelation Restored*, pp. 261–309.
38. Joseph Hunter, *Rise of the Old Dissent Exemplified in the Life of Oliver Heywood* (1842), pp. 328–33; Heywood, *Autobiography*, vol. 2, p. 221.
39. Hunter, *Rise*, pp. 328–33; William Gibson, *Religion and the Enlightenment, 1600–1800: Conflict and the Rise of Civic Humanism in Taunton* (Bern, 2005), pp. 118, 126–7.
40. Gibson, *Religion*, pp. 109–10, 130, 133–4; Harris, *Restoration*, pp. 311–17.
41. Tim Harris, *Revolution: The Great Crisis of the British Monarchy, 1685–1720* (2006), pp. 46–57, 73–94.
42. Steve Pincus, *1688: The First Modern Revolution* (New Haven, CT, 2009), p. 110; Harris,

*Revolution*, pp. 73–94; Richard Greaves, *Secrets of the Kingdom: British Radicals from the Popish Plot to the Revolution of 1688-9* (Stanford, CA, 1992), p. 19; Gibson, *Religion*, pp. 137–9, 145.

43. Harris, *Revolution*, chap. 5.
44. Pincus, *1688*, pp. 200–9; Lacey, *Dissent*, pp. 177–85, 202–8.
45. Brent S. Sirota, *The Christian Monitors: The Church of England and the Age of Benevolence, 1680-1730* (New Haven, CT, 2014), pp. 56–7; Gary S. De Krey, "Rethinking the Restoration: Dissenting Cases for Conscience, 1667–1672," *HJ* 38(1995), pp. 53–83; John Marshall, *John Locke, Toleration, and Early Enlightenment Culture* (Cambridge, 2006).
46. Harris, *Revolution*, p. 263; Sirota, *Christian Monitors*, pp. 77–87; Sykes, *From Sheldon to Secker*, pp. 83–5.
47. Harris, *Revolution*, chap. 8
48. Richard Baxter, *Catholick Communion Defended against Both Extreams* (1684), p. 6.

## Chapter 18  Religious Pluralism Comes to Puritan New England

1. "Danforth Papers," *MHSC*, 2nd ser., 8 (1826), p. 98.
2. Palfrey, *History*, vol. 2, chap. 15 for next three paragraphs, except where noted.
3. *MR*, vol. 4, pt. 2, pp. 167, 201, 200, 205.
4. Hutchinson, *HC*, vol. 1, pp. 216–17; vol. 2, pp. 453–4; *HP*, vol. 2, pp. 145–6.
5. "Danforth Papers," pp. 99–101.
6. Ibid, pp. 103–5; Ken MacMillan, " 'Bound by Our Regal Office': Empire, Sovereignty, and the American Colonies in the Seventeenth Century," in Foster (ed.), *British North America*, pp. 93–4.
7. Bernard Bailyn, *The New England Merchants in the Seventeenth Century* (New York, 1964), pp. 110–11, 115–17, 128; "Mather Papers," p. 192; *Documents Relative to the Colonial History of the State of New York*, vol. 3 (Albany, NY, 1853), pp. 18, 16–19, 83; "Danforth Papers," p. 83.
8. "Danforth Papers," pp. 108–9, 110; Percy Lewis Kaye, *English Colonial Administration under Lord Clarendon, 1660-1667* (Baltimore, MD 1905), pp. 36–7.
9. Cronon, *Changes*, pp. 154–5.
10. Bremer, *New Jerusalem*, pp. 197, 202–4, 208–11, 290–301.
11. Isabel MacBeath Calder (ed.), *Letters of John Davenport, Puritan Divine* (New Haven, CT, 1937), pp. 256–7; Benjamin Trumbull, *A Complete History of Connecticut*, 2 vols. (New Haven, CT, 1818), vol. 1, 468.
12. *HP*, vol. 2, p. 120.
13. George Andrews Hill, *History of the Old South Church (Third Church) Boston, MA, 1669-1884*, 2 vols. (Cambridge,1890), vol. 1, pp. 63. Ibid., pp. 1–112, for this and next two paragraphs.
14. Cooper, *TTL*, p. 96; Hill, *History*, vol. 1, pp. 25–6; Hall, *WW*, p. 17.
15. Michael P. Winship, "Cotton Mather, Astrologer," *NEQ* 63 (1990), pp. 308–14; Hill, *History*, vol. 1, pp. 54–80; Deborah Colleen McNally, "Within Patriarchy: Gender and Power in Massachusetts's Congregational Churches, 1630–1730" (Ph.D. diss., University of Washington, 2013), chap. 4.
16. John Oxenbridge, *New-England Freemen Warned and Warmed, to Be Free Indeed* (Cambridge, MA, 1673), p. 44; Calder (ed.), *Letters*, p. 282; John Davenport, *A Sermon Preach'd at the Election of the Governour, at Boston in New-England, May 19th 1669* (Cambridge, MA, 1670), pp. 12–16.
17. Hill, *History*, p. 102
18. *MA*, vol. 10, p. 289; Hill, *History*, pp. 102, 110.
19. *MR*, vol. 4, pt. 2, pp. 491, 492.
20. Ibid., pp. 493, 494; Pope, *HWC*, p. 185.
21. Nathan Eusebius Wood, *The History of the First Baptist Church of Boston (1665-1899)* (Philadelphia, PA, 1899), p. 80.
22. David A. Weir, *Early New England: A Covenanted Society* (Grand Rapids, MI, 2005), pp. 117–22; McLoughlin, *New England Dissent*, vol. 1, pp. 49–90; Wood, *History*,

pp. 99–108; Foster, *LA*, pp. 204–5; Bremer, *CC*, p. 241.
23. *The Public Records of the Colony of Connecticut from 1666 to 1678* (Hartford, 1852), p. 109; Pope, *HWC*, pp. 127–30, chap. 4; Hall, *FS*, pp. 214–17.
24. Jonathan M. Chu, *Neighbors, Friends, or Madmen: The Puritan Adjustment to Quakerism in Seventeenth-Century Massachusetts Bay* (Westport, CT, 1985), chap. 7; Moore, *Light*, chap. 17.
25. Samuel Willard, *The Child's Portion* (Boston, MA, 1684), pp. 191–2; Increase Mather, *The Necessity of Reformation* (Boston, MA, 1679), pp. 3, 12; idem, *A Call from Heaven* (Boston, MA, 1685), pp. 104–8; Hall, *FS*, p. 231.

## Chapter 19  New England's Reformations Come of Age

1. Abijah Perkins Marvin, *History of the Town of Lancaster, Massachusetts* (Lancaster, MA, 1879), pp. 37, 44, 48, 49.
2. Hall, *FS*, pp. 95, 181–2; Marvin, *History*, pp. 91–3.
3. Marvin, *History*, p. 90; Daniel W. Wells and Reuben F. Wells, *A History of Hatfield, Massachusetts* (Springfield, IL, 1910), pp. 60.
4. Marvin, *History*, p. 93; Cooper, *TTL*, pp. 124–32, 135, 137–8; Gerald F. Moran and Maris A. Vinovskis, *Religion, Family, and the Life Course* (Ann Arbor, MI, 1992), p. 189; Hall, *FS*, p. 95.
5. Marvin, *History*, pp. 41, 7; Robert J. Dinkin, "Seating the Meeting House in Early Massachusetts," *New England Quarterly* 43 (1970), pp. 450–64; Hall, *FS*, p. 183.
6. Almira Larkin White, *Genealogy of the Descendants of John White of Wenham and Lancaster*, 2 vols. (Haverhill, MA, 1900), vol. 1, pp. 12, 15; Hall, *WW*, p. 248; Hugh Amory, "'A Bible and Other Books': Enumerating the Copies in Seventeenth-Century Essex County," in R.C. Alston (ed.), *Order and Connexion* (Cambridge, 1997), p. 27; Pope (ed.), *Notebook*, pp. 13, 48.
7. Mary Rowlandson, *The Sovereignty & Goodness of God* (Boston, MA, 1682), p. 40; *MHSC*, 5th ser., 5 (1878), p. 453.
8. Rowlandson, *Soveraignty*, p. 72.
9. James D. Drake, *King Philip's War: Civil War in New England, 1675–1676* (Amherst, MA, 1999), pp. 65–71; Daniel Gookin, "An Historical Account of the Doings and Sufferings of the Christian Indians," *American Antiquarian Society Transactions and Collections* 20 (1836), p. 436; Pulsipher, "*Subjects*," pp. 113–17, 147.
10. Drake, *King Philip's War*, p. 221n3.
11. Gookin, "Historical Account," p. 487; Thomas Wheeler, *A Thankefull Remembrance of Gods Mercy* (Boston, MA, 1676), pp. 6, 7; Pulsipher, "*Subjects*," pp. 191–2; Rowlandson, *Soveraignty*, sig. A2v, pp. 3–4.
12. Ibid., pp. 9, 24, 40.
13. Ibid., pp. 11–14, 15, 17, 23, 28, 31, 35, 38.
14. Ibid., pp. 72–3; Kathryn Zabelle Derounian, "The Publication, Promotion, and Distribution of Mary Rowlandson's Indian Captivity Narrative in the Seventeenth Century," *Early American Literature* 23:3 (1988), pp. 239–61.
15. Gookin, "Historical Account," pp. 512, 552; Pulsipher, "*Subjects*," pp. 138–41.
16. Pulsipher, "*Subjects*", p. 241; Daniel R. Mandell, *Behind the Frontier: Indians in Eighteenth-Century Eastern Massachusetts* (Lincoln, NE, 1996), p. 33; Erik R. Seeman, *Death in the New World: Cross-Cultural Encounters, 1492–1800* (Philadelphia, PA, 2010), p. 174.
17. Laura Arnold Leibman (ed.), *Experience Mayhew's Indian Converts: A Cultural Edition* (Amherst, MA, 2008), p. 110; John Eliot, *A Brief Narrative of the Progress of the Gospel Amongst the Indians* (1671), p. 4; Mather, *MCA*, vol. 1, p. 567; Gookin, "Historical Account," p. 205; Delores Bird Carpenter, *Early Encounters: Native Americans and Europeans in New England—From the Papers of W. Sears Nickerson* (East Lansing, MI, 1994), pp. 173–85; Douglas L. Winiarski, "A Question of Plain Dealing: Josiah Cotton, Native Christians, and the Quest for Security in Eighteenth-Century Plymouth County," *NEQ* 77 (2004), pp. 368–413;

Kellaway, *New England Company*, chap. 9; Mandell, *Behind the Frontier*, pp. 48–57, 59.

18. Leibman (ed.), *Experience*, pp. 113, 115, 118, 120–2, 122, 124, 131, 133, 134–5, 141, 144, 145, 155, 158, 160, 163, 184, 188, 195, 199, 212, 217, 233, 258, 274, 287, 298, 299, 300, 323–5, 328; Ives Goddard and Kathleen J. Bragdon, *Native Writings in Massachusetts*, 2 vols. (Philadelphia, PA, 1988), vol. 1, pp. 375–471; Douglas L. Winiarski, "Native American Popular Religion in New England's Old Colony, 1670–1770," *Religion and American Culture* 15 (2005), pp. 161–2; Cotton Mather, Increase Mather and Nehemiah Walter, *A Letter about the Present State of Christianity, among the Christianized Indians of New England* (Boston, MA, 1705), pp. 7, 8; Silverman, *Faith*, p. 55; Mayhew, *Indian Converts*, p. 145; Mather, *MCA*, vol. 2, pp. 432–3; Isaac Backus, *A History of New England with Particular Reference to the Baptists*, 2 vols. (Newton, MA, 1871), pp. 346–7.

19. Leibman (ed.), *Experience*, pp. 78, 134, 135, 154, 187, 192, 208; Kellaway, *New England Company*, p. 241; Mandell, *Behind the Frontier*, pp. 108–9; Obed Macy, *The History of Nantucket* (Boston, MA, 1835), pp. 268–9.

20. Leibman (ed.), *Experience*, p. 142; Silverman, *Faith*, p. 285.

21. Increase Mather, *A Brief History of the War with the Indians in New-England* (1676), pp. 3, 16, 17, 19, 27, 29, 36, 39; Hambrick-Stowe, *Practice of Piety*, pp. 129–32.

22. *Plymouth Church Records 1620–1859*, 2 vols. (New York, 1920–23), vol. 1, pp. 149–50.

23. Ibid., vol. 1, pp. 151–3.

24. Ibid., vol. 1, p. 152; Daniel R. Mandell, *King Philip's War: The Conflict Over New England* (New York, 2007), p. 109.

25. T.H. Breen, *Puritans and Adventurers: Change and Persistence in Early America* (New York, 1980), p. 87; Pulsipher, "*Subjects*," chap. 9.

26. Pope, *HWC*, chap. 7.

27. Ibid.

28. Cotton Mather, *Ratio Disciplina Fratrum Nov-Anglorum* (Boston, MA, 1724), p. 80; E. Brooks Holifield, *The Covenant Sealed: The Development of Puritan Sacramental Theology in Old and New England, 1570–1720* (New Haven, CT, 2002), p. 183; Mather, *MCA*, vol. 2, pp. 203, 237–8.

29. Hall, *WW*, pp. 152–61.

30. Paul R. Lucas, *Valley of Discord: Church and Society along the Connecticut River, 1636–1725* (Hanover, NH, 1976), p. 139; Moran and Vinovskis, *Religion*, pp. 85–101; Amanda Porterfield, *Female Piety in Puritan New England: The Emergence of Religious Humanism* (New York, 1992), pp. 130–1.

31. Increase Mather, *A Discourse Concerning the Subject of Baptisme* (Cambridge, 1675), p. 51; Pope, *HWC*, chap. 8.

## Chapter 20  New England's Puritan Autonomy Ends

1. Robert Toppan (ed.), *Edward Randolph, Including His Letters and Official Papers from the New England, Middle and Southern Colonies in America . . . 1676–1703*, 7 vols. (Boston, MA, 1898–1909), vol. 2, pp. 217, 219.

2. Ibid., p. 224.

3. Palfrey, *History*, vol. 3, pp. 289–370; Toppan, *Edward Randolph*, vol. 3, pp. 267, 277; "Mather Papers," passim.

4. Toppan, *Edward Randolph*, vol. 3, pp. 276–7; Palfrey, *History*, vol. 3, pp. 376–7; Hall, *LAP*, p. 191.

5. Palfrey, *History*, vol. 3, p. 385n3; Toppan, *Edward Randolph*, vol. 3, pp. 276–7; *MHSC*, 3rd ser., vol. 1 (1825), pp. 77–8, 81.

6. Jeremy Belknap, *The History of New-Hampshire: History, 1614–1715*, 3 vols. (2nd edn., Boston, MA, 1813), vol. 1, p. 319; *CSPC, 1681–1685*, p. 563.

7. Belknap, *History*, vol. 1, pp. 165, 319–21, 329, 330; *CSPC, 1681–1685*, p. 576.

8. Thomas Maule, *New-England Persecutors Mauled with Their Own Weapons* (New York, 1697), pp. 50–1; *CSPC, 1685–1688*, p. 62; Anon., *A Vindication of New-England* (Boston, MA, n.d.), p. 8.

9. Palfrey, *History*, vol. 3, p. 391; Sewall, "Diary," p. 114.

10. Palfrey, *History*, vol. 3, pp. 484–7; Sewall, "Diary," p. 140.

11. Sewall, *Diary*, p. 165.

12. *HP*, vol. 2, pp. 293, 295; Newton E. Key, "Annesley, Samuel (bap. 1620, d. 1696)," ODNB; *John Dunton's Letters from New-England* (Boston, MA, 1867), p. 137.

13. Increase Mather, *A Briefe Discourse Concerning the Unlawfulness of the Common Prayer Worship* (Cambridge, MA, 1686); Thomas James Holmes, *Increase Mather, A Bibliography of His Works*, 2 vols. (Cleveland, OH, 1931), vol. 1, pp. 51–63.

14. Palfrey, *History*, vol. 3, p. 517.

15. Viola Barnes, *The Dominion of New England* (New Haven, CT, 1923), pp. 124–6; "Letter from Rev. John Higginson to His Son Nathaniel Higginson, August 31, 1698," *Essex Institute Historical Collections* 43 (1907), p. 183; "Mather Papers," pp. 370, 571; DWL, MS 12.78, p. 205; Fishwick (ed.), *Notebook*, p. 11; Hutchinson, *HC*, vol. 1, p. 302; Hill, *History*, vol. 1, pp. 266–8; Sewall, "Diary," pp. 142, 202, 208; Henry Wilder Foote, *Annals of King's Chapel*, 2 vols. (Boston, MA, 1882), vol. 1, p. 82; Nicholas Byfield, *An Account of the Late Revolution in New-England* (1689), p. 13.

16. John Tulley, *An Almanack for the Year of Our Lord, MDCLXXXVIII* (Boston, MA, 1687), pp. 16, 17; Thomas Ken, *An Exposition on the Church-Catechism* (Boston, MA, 1688); Sewall, "Diary," pp. 150–1, 152, 178; Increase Mather, *Testimony against Several Prophane and Superstitious Customs* (1687), sig. A2r; Sewall, "Diary," p. 178.

17. Johnson, *AE*, pp. 78–83; Palfrey, *History*, vol. 3, p. 523; Barnes, *Dominion*, pp. 69–70, 85–90, 110–11, 115–16; Hall, *LAP*, pp. 207–11.

18. Cotton Mather, *Memorable Providences, Relating to Witchcrafts and Possessions* (Boston, MA, 1689), p. 46.

19. Ibid., pp. 2, 14, 15, 16, 17.

20. Ibid., pp. 3, 46; John Langdon Sibley, *Biographical Sketches of Graduates of Harvard University*, vol. 2 (Boston, MA, 1881), pp. 130–2.

21. Mather, *Memorable Providences*, p. 48.

22. Ibid., pp. 48, 49; "Mather Papers," p. 368; Richard Godbeer, *The Devil's Dominion: Magic and Religion in Early New England* (New York, 1992), pp. 43–7, 69–84.

23. Mather, *Memorable Providences*, pp. 2–3; Richard Weisman, *Witchcraft, Magic, and Religion in 17th-Century Massachusetts* (Amherst, MA, 1984), p. 76.

24. Sharpe, *Witchcraft*, p. 26; Godbeer, *Devil's Dominion*, chap. 5; Mather, *Memorable Providences*, p. 9; "Mather Papers," p. 368.

25. Robert Calef, "More Wonders of the Invisible World," in Samuel G. Drake (ed.), *The Witchcraft Delusion in New England*, 3 vols. (Boston, MA, 1866), vol. 3, p. 153; Mather, *Memorable Providences*, pp. 7–9; Obadiah Gill, *Some Few Remarks upon a Scandalous Book* (Boston, MA, 1700), p. 63; John Demos, *Entertaining Satan: Witchcraft and the Culture of Early New England* (New York, 1982), p. 12; Peter Elmer, *Witchcraft, Witch-Hunting, and Politics in Early Modern England* (Oxford, 2016), pp. 246, 246n50.

26. Sewall, "Diary," p. 236; Mather, *Memorable Providences*, pp. 12, 13, 31.

27. Mather, *Memorable Providences*, pp. 31–2, 43, 44, 50, 51.

28. Ibid., pp. 52–3.

29. Gill, *Some Few Remarks*, p. 63.

30. Elmer, *Witchcraft*, chap. 5; Allison P. Coudert, *Religion, Magic, and Science in Early Modern Europe and America* (Santa Barbara, CA, 2011), p. 54; Mather, *Memorable Providences*, pp. 23–4, 38–9.

31. Elmer, *Witchcraft*, pp. 185–8, 210–24; Michael Hunter, *Science and the Shape of Orthodoxy: Intellectual Change in Late Seventeenth-Century Britain* (Woodbridge, Suffolk, 1995), chap. 12.

32. Ronald A. Bosco (ed.), *Paterna: The Autobiography of Cotton Mather* (Delmar, NY, 1976), p. 96; Anon., *New-England's Faction Discovered* (1690), p. 4.

33. Palfrey, *History*, pp. 570–7; Samuel Mather, *The Life of the Very Reverend and Learned*

*Cotton Mather* (Boston, MA, 1729), p. 43.
34. Morison, *Harvard College*, vol. 2, pp. 475–6; Dewey D. Wallace, Jr., "Morton, Charles (bap. 1627, d. 1698)," ODNB.
35. Johnson, *AE*, pp. 95, 96–7; *CSPC, 1699* and *Addenda, 1621–1698*, p. 164.
36. *CSPC, 1699* and *Addenda, 1624–1698*, p. 164; Johnson, *AE*, pp. 95, 96–7.
37. Anon., *New-England's Faction*, p. 4; Maule, *New-England Persecutors*, p. 51; Charles McLean Andrews (ed.), *Narratives of the Insurrections, 1675–1690* (New York, 1915), p. 207; Foote, *Annals*, vol. 1, p. 107.

### Chapter 21  Hopes Raised and Dashed

1. Thomas, "Comprehension," p. 244.
2. Bremer, *CC*, p. 234; Fishwick (ed.), *Notebook*, pp. 33, 49; Hall, *LAP*, pp. 46, 124, 240; Increase Mather, "Diary", June 20, 1688, Mather Family Papers, Box 3, Folder 4, American Antiquarian Society; Johnson, *AE*, pp. 145–6.
3. Thomas, "Comprehension," p. 245; Harris, *Revolution*, pp. 376–8, 400.
4. Henry Horwitz, *Parliament, Policy and Politics in the Reign of William III* (Manchester, 1977), pp. 21–6.
5. Calamy, *ABH*, vol. 1, p. 448; Sirota, *Christian Monitors*, pp. 79–86; Timothy John Fawcett, *The Liturgy of Comprehension, 1689: An Abortive Attempt to Revise the Book of Common Prayer* (Southwold on Sea, Suffolk, 1973); Goldie, *RM*, p. 245. Henry Horwitz, "Comprehension in the Later Seventeenth Century: A Postscript," *CH* 34 (1965), pp. 342–8.
6. Johnson, *AE*, pp. 168–9.

### Chapter 22  The Final Parting of the Ways for English Puritans

1. Crisp, *Christ Alone*, sig. A2[i]v; Matthew Mead, *The Vision of the Wheels Seen by the Prophet Ezekiel* (1689), sig. A2r; Baxter, *RB*, bk. iii, p. 103.
2. Crisp, *Christ Alone*, sig. A2v, A2[i]r; Keeble and Nuttall, *CCRB*, vol. 2, pp. 301–2; Francis J. Bremer, "Mather, Nathaniel (1630–1697)," ODNB.
3. Frederick James Powicke, *The Reverend Richard Baxter under the Cross (1662–1691)* (1927), p. 174; John Flavel, *Planelogia* (1691), sig. [a4]v.
4. Richard Baxter, *An Unsavoury Volume of J. Crandon's Anatomized* (1654), p. 5; Worldcat. org search for au:Richard Baxter, title:Saints Everlasting Rest, February 14, 2017; Frederick J. Powicke, "Story and Significance of the Rev. Richard Baxter's 'Saints' Everlasting Rest,'" *Bulletin of the John Rylands Library* 5 (1920), pp. 473–4.
5. William K.B. Stoever, *"A Faire and Easie Way to Heaven": Covenant Theology and Antinomianism in Early Massachusetts* (Middletown, CT, 1978), pp. 93–6.
6. Baxter, *Unsavoury Volume*, p. 5; idem, *The Life of Faith* (1670), p. 196.
7. J.V. Fesko, *Beyond Calvin: Union with Christ and Justification in Early Modern Reformed Theology (1517–1700)* (Göttingen, 2012), pp. 306, 307–8, 309–11, 311–12, 313–14, 314–16.
8. John Humfrey, *The Middle Way of Predetermination Asserted* (1679). For an extended discussion of Baxter's theology, see Hans Boersma, *A Hot Pepper Corn: Richard Baxter's Doctrine of Justification in Its Seventeenth-Century Context of Controversy* (Zoetermeer, NL, 1993).
9. Edmund Calamy, *An Historical Account of My Own Life*, 2 vols. (1829), vol. 1, p. 308; Increase Mather, *A Dissertation Concerning the Future Conversion of the Jewish Nation* (Boston, MA, 1709), pp. 1, 2; Mather, *MCA*, vol. 1, pp. 291–2.
10. Mather, *MCA*, vol. 1, pp. 291–2.
11. David P. Field, *"Rigide Calvinisme in a Softer Dresse": The Moderate Presbyterianism of John Howe, 1630–1705* (Edinburgh, 2007), pp. 144, 166–79; Carl R. Trueman, *John Owen: Reformed Catholic, Renaissance Man* (Aldershot, Hants, 2007), pp. 29–31;

Dewey D. Wallace, Jr., *Puritans and Predestination: Grace in English Protestant Theology, 1525–1695* (Chapel Hill, NC, 1982), pp. 142–4; John Howe, *The Reconcileableness of God's Prescience of the Sins of Men, with the Wisdom and Sincerity of His Counsels* (1677), pp. 38, 40. For a pre-Civil War precedent, see Moore, *English Hypothetical Universalism*.

12. Jonathan D. Moore, "The Extent of the Atonement: English Hypothetical Universalism versus Particular Redemption," in Haykin and Jones (eds.), *Drawn into Controversie*, pp. 132–4; Lim, *Mystery Unveiled*, pp. 200–13; Wallace, *Puritans*, pp. 144–57; Fesko, *Beyond Calvin*, pp. 313–14.

13. Crisp, *Christ Alone*, sig. A2[i]v–b2[i]v; Wallace, *Puritans*, pp. 180–1.

14. Powicke, *The Reverend Richard Baxter*, pp. 174–5; [John Howe], *Some Considerations of a Certificate Prefixed to Dr. Crisp's Works* (1691), p. 1. The attribution of *Some Considerations* to Howe is by Roger Thomas, *The Baxter Treatises*, DWL, Occasional Paper 8 (1959), p. 23, without explanation, but it seems sound. Richard Baxter identified *Some Consideration's* author on the basis of its "style" as one of the twelve signers of the Crisp attestation whom he "greatly esteeme[d]." See DWL, MS 59.11, fol. 24r. The "style" of *Some Considerations* is calm and reasonable, like Howe's. Its substance is also Howe's: what the godly agree upon is much more important than their disagreements; they should interpret each other's arguments charitably and not get bogged down in rigidly defining and disputing terms. A long section from *Some Considerations* with these arguments is in the later explanation of their signatures that seven signers gave, and Howe's is the first name on the list of signers. See Flavel, *Planelogia*, sigs. a4r–a4[iv]v. The substance of *Some Consideration's* arguments was repeated in sermons Howe gave while trying to calm the dispute that grew out of this one (see below). See John Howe, *The Carnality of Religious Contention* (1693), pp. 39–57.

15. Michael G. Hall (ed.), "The Autobiography of Increase Mather," *American Antiquarian Society, Proceedings* 71 (1961), p. 338; Hall, *LAP*, pp. 238–9.

16. *Heads of Agreement Assented to by the United Ministers in and about London* (1691); Bremer, *CC*, pp. 249–50.

17. Alexander Gordon (ed.), *Freedom After Ejection: A Review (1690–1692) of Presbyterian and Congregational Nonconformity in England and Wales* (Manchester, 1917), p. 160; Daniel Williams, *The Answer to the Report* (1698), pp. 2, 3.

18. "Mather Papers," pp. 7–8, 31, 35–6; Nathaniel Mather, *A Discussion of the Lawfulness of a Pastor's Acting as an Officer in Other Churches* (1698); DWL, MS 12.78 1, 243; Roger Thompson, "The Break-up of Nonconformity," in Geoffrey Nutall (ed.), *The Beginnings of Nonconformity* (1962), p. 38.

19. Matthew Mead, *Two Sticks Made One* (1692), pp. 23, 27–8.

20. Samuel Palmer, *The Nonconformist's Memorial*, 3 vols. (1802), vol. 3, p. 400; Andrew Clark (ed.), *The Life and Times of Anthony Wood*, 3 vols. (Oxford, 1894), vol. 3, p. 378.

21. Goldie, *RM*, pp. 195–6; Cliffe, *Puritan Gentry Besieged*, chap. 15.

22. Isaac Chauncy, *Neonomianism Unmask'd* (1692), pt. 1, p. 10; David L. Wykes, "Religious Leadership and English Dissent after the Glorious Revolution: The Role of the Rev. Dr. Daniel Williams (ca. 1643–1715/16)," in Jan Wim Buisman, Marjet Derks and Peter Raedts (eds.), *Episcopacy, Authority, and Gender: Aspects of Religious Leadership in Europe, 1100–2000* (Leiden, 2015), p. 131; Fesko, *Beyond Calvin*, pp. 360–7; Daniel Williams, *An Answer to Mr. J. Humphrey's Second Printed Letter* (1695), p. 1.

23. Ebenezer Turell, *The Life and Character of the Reverend Benjamin Colman* (Boston, MA, 1749), p. 21; Thomas Young, *An Apology for the Congregational Ministers* (1698), p. 189; idem, *A Censure of Three Scandalous Pamphlets* (1699), p. 40; John Humfrey, *Animadversions* (1699), p. 1, passim.

24. Daniel Williams, *Practical Discourses on Several Important Subjects*, 2 vols. (1738), vol. 1, p. xv; Stephen Lobb, *A Defence of the Report, Concerning the Present State of the Differences in Doctrinals* (1698), pp. 8–9; Richard Taylor, *A History of the Union between the Presbyterian and Congregational Ministers in and about London* (1698), pp. 13–17;

Isaac Chauncy, *Examen confectionis pacificae* (1692), p. 2.

25. The disagreement was about when repentance appeared in the process of justification. John Humfrey, *Peace at Pinners-Hall Wish'd* (1692), "To the Reader"; Daniel Williams, *Gospel Truth* (1st edn., 1692), p. 119; idem, *A Defence of Gospel-Truth* (1693), sig. Av; Thomas Cole, *A Discourse of Christian Religion* (1692), pp. 239–40, 244, 247, 248, 288–9, 385–6; Daniel Williams, *Gospel Truth* (3rd edn., 1698), pp. 310, 314–15.

26. Taylor, *History*, p. 10.

27. Chauncy, *Neonomianism*, pt. 3, p. 98.

28. Taylor, *History*, pp. 7–8.

29. Williams claimed that the righteousness referred to in Philippians 3:9 was primarily a justified human's righteousness, not, as was conventionally thought, Christ's; Williams, *Gospel Truth* (1st edn., 1692), sig. A4iir, pp. 41–2; Williams, *Defence*, sig. A2r; Calamy, *ABH*, vol. 1, p. 515; Isaac Chauncy, *A Rejoynder to Mr. Daniel Williams* (1693), pp. 13–14; Fesko, *Beyond Calvin*, pp. 361–2; cf. Richard Baxter, *A Treatise of Justifying Righteousness* (1676), 2nd pag., pp. 256–7.

30. Taylor, *History*, pp. 9, 16; Williams, *Defence*, sig. A2r; Chauncy, *Neonomianism*, pt. 3, pp. 96, 101–2.

31. Taylor, *History*, pp. 9–21, 22; Vincent Alsop, *A Faithful Rebuke to a False Report* (1697), p. 21; Chauncy, *Neonomianism*; Fesko, *Beyond Calvin*, chap. 18.

32. Daniel Williams, *Man Made Righteous by Christ's Obedience* (1694), sigs. A3v–A4r; idem, *Gospel Truth*, 3rd edn., pp. 310–13; Nathaniel Mather, *The Righteousness of God through Faith* (1694), "To the Reader".

33. Wykes, "Religious Leadership," pp. 129–31; Young, *Censure*, p. 19.

34. Young, *Apology*, p. 187; Mather, *Righteousness*, p. 44.

35. Mather, *Righteousness*, p. 44; Williams, *Defence*, p. 25; idem, *Man*, sig. A2v; Richard Baxter, *Richard Baxter's Catholick Theologie* (1675), 2nd pag., p. 13, 3rd pag., pp. 227–30; Joseph Truman, *The Great Propitiation* (1672), pp. 221, cf. pp. 87–91.

36. Mather, *Righteousness*, pp. 45–6, 72; Williams, *Defence*, p. 47.

37. Williams, *Man*, pp. 11–12, 84, 92, 96, 99, 107, 135–6; Carl Trueman, *The Claims of Truth: John Owen's Trinitarian Theology* (Carlisle, Cumbria, 1998), pp. 214–20; Fesko, *Beyond Calvin*, pp. 310–11.

38. Williams, *Gospel Truth*, 3rd edn., p. 310; idem, *Answer to the Report*, p. 9; Wykes, "Religious Leadership," p. 132; Taylor, *History*, p. 25; John Howe, *Works*, 2 vols. (1724), vol. 1, p. 64; T.G. Crippen (ed.), "Origin of the Congregational Fund Board," *Transactions of the Congregational Historical Society* 5 (1911–12), pp. 134–48.

39. Timothy Stanton, "The Reception of Locke in England in the Early Eighteenth Century: Metaphysics, Religion and the State," in S.-J. Savonius-Wroth, Paul Schuurman, and Jonathan Walmsley (eds.), *The Continuum Companion to Locke* (2010), p. 297; John Seed, *Dissenting Histories: Religious Division and the Politics of Memory in Eighteenth-Century England* (Edinburgh, 2008), pp. 20–9, 58; David Wykes, "After the Happy Union: Presbyterians and Independents in the Provinces," *Studies in Church History* 32 (1996), pp. 283–95; Watts, *Dissenters*, vol. 1, p. 270.

40. DWL, MS 38.18, pp. 89, 91–3.

41. D. Bruce Hindmarsh, *The Spirit of Early Evangelicalism: True Religion in a Modern World* (New York, 2018), pp. 27–32, 77–9, 97–8, 180–7; Isabel Rivers, *Vanity Fair and the Celestial City: Dissenting, Methodist, and Evangelical Literary Culture in England, 1720–1800* (Oxford, 2018), chap. 4.

### Chapter 23  A Godly Massacre of the Innocents in Post-Puritan Massachusetts

1. Increase Mather, *A Sermon Concerning Obedience* (Boston, MA, 1714), pp. ii–iii; Foster, *LA*, p. 251.

2. Hall, *LAP*, pp. 249–51, 254; Johnson, *AE*, p. 229.

3. Mary Beth Norton, *In the Devil's Snare: The Salem Witchcraft Crisis of 1692* (New York,

2002), pp. 102–11, quotation from p. 108.

4. Godbeer, *Devil's Dominion*, pp. 192–3; Mather, *MCA*, vol. 2, p. 620; Cotton Mather, *Little Flocks Guarded against Grievous Wolves* (Boston, MA, 1691), "To the Reader," pp. 3, 103, 108; James Allen, Joshua Moodey, Samuel Willard and Cotton Mather, *The Principles of the Protestant Religion Maintained* (Boston, MA, 1690), sig. *r.

5. Mather, *Little Flocks*, pp. 3, 103; idem, *The Serviceable Man* (Boston, MA, 1690), pp. 35–7; David S. Lovejoy, *The Glorious Revolution in America* (New York, 1974), p. 346.

6. George Lincoln Burr, *Narratives of the Witchcraft Cases 1648 to 1706* (New York, 1914), pp. 160–1; Bernard Rosenthal (ed.), *Records of the Salem Witch-Hunt* (New York, 2009), pp. 173, 198, 199, 220; Deodat Lawson, *Christs Fidelity the Only Shield Against Satans Malignity* (Boston, MA, 1693), p. 54; Norton, *Devil's Snare*, p. 169.

7. Wendy Warren, *New England Bound: Slavery and Colonization in Early America* (New York, 2016), pp. 67–8; Jasper Danckaerts, *Journal of a Voyage to New York in 1679–80* (Brooklyn, 1867), p. 378; Lorenzo Johnston Greene, *The Negro in Colonial New England, 1620–1776* (New York, 1942), p. 73.

8. Burr, *Narratives*, pp. 155–6.

9. John Hale, *A Modest Enquiry into the Nature of Witchcraft* (Boston, MA, 1702), pp. 21–2.

10. See Bernard Rosenthal, "General Introduction," in Rosenthal (ed.), *Records*, pp. 33–6 for the English witchcraft authorities with which the New Englanders would have been familiar and pp. 34–5 specifically for the difference between the Salem magistrates' use of evidence and the most relevant English case, the 1662 Lowestoft witch trial; Norton, *Devil's Snare*, pp. 299–300; W. Baker, *A Storm of Witchcraft. The Salem Trials and the American Experience* (New York, 2015), chap. 6. For an extended discussion of recent historians' interpretations of the magistrates' motives, see Tony Fels, *Switching Sides: How a Generation of Historians Lost Sympathy for the Victims of the Salem Witch Hunt* (Baltimore, MD, 2018), p. 219n17.

11. Emerson W. Baker and John G. Reid, *The New England Knight: Sir William Phips, 1651–1695* (Toronto, 1998), chaps. 1–6.

12. Burr, *Narratives*, pp. 184, 199, 200; Norton, *Devil's Snare*, pp. 197–8.

13. Baker, *Storm*, p. 186; Burr, *Narratives*, p. 184. The analogous English incident, the East Anglian witch-hunt of 1645–47, which saw up to two hundred people executed, was also facilitated by the breakdown of the regional judicial system; see Malcolm Gaskill, *Witchfinders: A Seventeenth-Century English Tragedy* (Cambridge, MA, 2005), pp. 224–5; Jim Sharpe, *Instruments of Darkness: Witchcraft in Early Modern England* (Philadelphia, PA, 1996), pp. 129, 140–2.

14. Increase Mather, *Cases of Conscience Concerning Evil Spirits Personating Men* (Boston, MA, 1693), sig. G2[2]r–v.

15. Burr, *Narratives*, pp. 183–4.

16. Bernard Rosenthal, *Salem Story: Reading the Witch Trials of 1692* (Cambridge, 1993), chap. 4.

17. Wendel Craker, "Spectral Evidence, Non-Spectral Acts of Witchcraft and Confessions at Salem in 1692," in Brian P. Levack (ed.), *New Perspectives on Witchcraft, Magic, and Demonology*, vol. 3 (New York, 2013), p. 344; Baker, *Storm*, p. 158.

18. Rosenthal (ed.), *Records*, pp. 467, 481, 482.

19. Clive Holmes, "The Opinion of the Cambridge Association, 1 August 1692: A Neglected Text of the Salem Witch Trials," *NEQ* 89 (2016), pp. 643–67; Cotton Mather, *Wonders of the Invisible World* (Boston, MA, 1693), sig. A2[v]r–v, B2[i]v–B2[ii]r; idem, *A Midnight Cry* (Boston, MA, 1692), p. 63.

20. Mather, *Wonders*, sig. A2[i]v–A2[ii]r.

21. Hall, *WW*, pp. 178–82.

22. Norton, *Devil's Snare*, pp. 216–17.

23. Sewall, "Diary," p. 363; Samuel G. Drake (ed.), *The Witchcraft Delusion in New England*, 3 vols. (Boston, MA, 1866), vol. 3, p. 38.

24. Burr, *Narratives*, p. 177.
25. Norton, *Devil's Snare*, pp. 257–62; Hale, *Modest Enquiry*, p. 38; Rosenthal (ed.), *Records*, pp. 690–1.
26. Burr, *Narratives*, p. 369n1; Norton, *Devil's Snare*, p. 271; Drake (ed.), *Witchcraft Delusion*, vol. 3, pp. 46–8.
27. Drake (ed.), *Witchcraft Delusion*, vol. 3, p. 46.
28. Ibid., p. 48; Burr, *Narratives*, p. 369n1.
29. Burr, *Narratives*, p. 189; Drake (ed.), *Witchcraft Delusion*, vol. 3, p. 47; Samuel Willard, *Some Miscellany Observations on Our Present Debates* (Philadelphia, PA, 1692), p. 6; Rosenthal (ed.), *Records*, pp. 690–1, 693–5.
30. "To John Cotton Holmes/BPL October 20, 1692," Salem Witch Trials Documentary Archive and Transcription Project, University of Virginia; online at http://salem.lib. virginia.edu/letters/to_cotton2.html (accessed May 16, 2018); Norton, *Devil's Snare*, pp. 280–4; Baker, *Storm*, p. 197; Willard, *Miscellany Observations*, pp. 8–9; Burr, *Narratives*, pp. 184, 188; Foster, *LA*, 262–3, 264.
31. Norton, *Devil's Snare*, p. 262; George H. Moore, *Notes on the History of Witchcraft in Massachusetts* (Worcester, MA, 1883), p. 70; Sewall, "Diary," p. 367; Drake (ed.), *Witchcraft Delusion*, vol. 3, p. 54.
32. Drake (ed.), *Witchcraft Delusion*, p. 197; Norton, *Devil's Snare*, pp. 286–8.
33. Burr, *Narratives*, p. 197; Everett Kimball, *The Public Life of Joseph Dudley: A Study of the Colonial Policy of the Stuarts in New England, 1660–1715* (New York, 1911), pp. 64–6; Evan Haefeli, "Dutch New York and the Salem Witch Trials: Some New Evidence," *Proceedings of the American Antiquarian Society* 110, pt. 2 (2000), pp. 296, 298; Norton, *Devil's Snare*, p. 382n7.
34. Burr, *Narratives*, pp. 200–1; Drake (ed.), *Witchcraft Delusion*, vol. 3, pp. 126, 127; Norton, *Devil's Snare*, pp. 290–2; Richard Godbeer, *Escaping Salem: The Other Witch Hunt of 1692* (New York, 2005).
35. William Perkins, *A Discourse of the Damned Art of Witchcraft* (Cambridge, 1610), pp. 184, 199–200, 218; Stuart Clark, *Thinking with Demons: The Idea of Witchcraft in Early Modern Europe* (Oxford, 1997), chap. 37, p. 545; Elmer, *Witchcraft*, p. 298; Gary K. Waite, *Heresy, Magic and Witchcraft in Early Modern Europe* (Basingstoke, Hants, 2003), chap. 6; Godbeer, *Devil's Dominion*, pp. 155–7, 235–7; Weisman, *Witchcraft, Magic, and Religion*, pp. 78–105.
36. Hall (ed.), *Witch-Hunting*, pp. 32–3, 51–2; Burr, *Narratives*, p. 385n2.
37. Demos, *Entertaining Satan*, pp. 387–94; Thomas Hutchinson, *The Witchcraft Delusion of 1692*, ed. William Frederick Poole (Boston, MA, 1870), p. 18; James Kendall Hosmer, *The Life of Thomas Hutchinson* (Boston, MA, 1896), p. 86; James Sullivan, *The History of the District of Maine* (Boston, MA, 1795), p. 212.
38. *The Acts and Resolves, Public and Private, of the Province of the Massachusetts Bay . . .*, vol. 1 (Boston, MA, 1869), pp. 55–6, 58, 62–3; Jere R. Daniell, *Colonial New Hampshire: A History* (Millwood, NY, 1981), p. 171.
39. Willard, *Child's Portion*, p. 192.
40. A.G. Dorland, *The Royal Disallowance in Massachusetts* (Kingston, ON, 1917), p. 14; William G. McLoughlin, *New England Dissent, 1630–1833: The Baptists and the Separation of Church and State*, 2 vols. (Cambridge, MA, 1971), vol. 1, pp. 128–246; William Stevens Perry, *Historical Collections Relating to the American Colonial Church*, 5 vols. (Hartford, CT, 1870–78), vol. 3, pp. 189–90. Connecticut retained self-government and, unlike Massachusetts, it enshrined its version of Congregationalism in law. But there was a general awareness that if it tried to assert the privileges of its religious establishment too vigorously, it risked losing its charter. See McLoughlin, *New England Dissent*, vol. 1, pp. 263–77; Foster, *LA*, 269–70. For Congregational hegemony in New Hampshire, see Daniell, *Colonial New Hampshire*, pp. 171, 173–6.

# INDEX

Abbott, George 68
Abel (biblical) 14
Act of Uniformity 28, 205–7, 209, 220–1, 226, 253, 260
Adam (biblical) 14, 54, 166, 176
Adams, Thomas 188
adultery 51, 87–8, 92, 123
  death penalty for 160, 167–8
Allein, Mary 157–8
Allein, Tobie 157–9
Alleine, Joseph 203–13, 229
  *An Alarm to the Unconverted* 213
Alleine, Theodosia 203–4, 205, 213
Allen, John 176, 177
altars 12, 94
Amsterdam separatist church 62
Anabaptists 95–6, 293
Andros, Edmund 255–7, 260–1, 266, 289
Anglicanism, Anglicans
  Act of Uniformity and 207, 209
  Congregationalism and 255–6, 262, 279
  definition of 207
  intolerance and 216, 279
  James II and 230–1
  in Massachusetts 234, 254–6, 262
  Presbyterianism and 207, 209–10, 222, 265–7, 279
animal cruelty law, Massachusetts 52
Anne, Queen of Great Britain 231
anti-Calvinism 73–5
  *see also* Arminianism

Antichrist
  Catholic Church and 14, 74, 77, 110, 171, 274, 280, 286
  Church of England and 14, 15, 26–9, 39, 67, 274
  Cromwell as 156
  defined 293
  pope as 22, 74
  Presbyterianism and 47, 175
  Quakers and 149
anti-formalism 125–6, 127
antinomianism 123–5, 131, 173, 268–72, 274, 276–9, 293
Antinomian Controversy 104
anti-puritanism 40–1, 43, 47, 48, 51, 54, 60, 61, 74, 92–6, 141, 204, 213, 216–17
ap Evan, Edward 94
ap Evan, Enoch 94–6, 103
ap Evan, Joan 94–6
ap Evan, John 94–6
aristocracy 92
Arminianism 73, 76, 100, 215–16, 269–71, 274, 279, 293
Arminius, Jacob 73
*Articles and Orders* 174
Arundell, Thomas 9
Ashe, Simeon 111
association movement 155
  *see also* Devonshire Association; Worcestershire Association
assurance of salvation 2, 55–8, 63, 104, 106, 122–3, 150, 243
  Cotton on 106

Dod on 55–8
Shepard on 106
*see also* conversion narratives
astrology 237
Attaway, Mrs. 136
Austin, Ann 182
Avery, Elizabeth 126–7

Baily, John 255
Bale, John 20
Ball, John 110–12
baptism
    Congregationalists and tensions over 87,
        122, 176, 186–9, 236–40
    *see also* Baptists
Baptists
    England 122, 124–6, 131, 136, 139, 150–1,
        153, 156, 183, 213, 217, 223, 230, 269, 292
    New England 122, 176, 181, 183, 239–40,
        247, 254, 290, 292
Barbados 173, 182
Barlow, William 65
Barrington, Francis 76
Barrow, Henry 46–8
Bartlett, John 26
Bastwick, John 100
Bates, William 265–6
Baxter, Richard 211, 213, 232, 261, 265–6
    association movement and 155
    theology of 269–72, 274–9
    *The Saints' Everlasting Rest* 270
Bedford, Bedfordshire 146–51
Bell, Susanna 102
Bellingham, Richard 234
Bercovitch, Sacvan 315n36
Berkeley, William 171
Bermuda 78–9, 171, 172–4, 308n25, 309n27,
    309n28, 323n21
Bermuda Company 79, 172–3
Bermuda Congregational Church 172–4
Bernard, Richard 284
Best, Paul 136
Bible
    Geneva 22–4
    King James 23–4, 60
    reading strategies and 13, 22–3, 35, 57,
        63, 244–5
    sermon attendance and 31, 34, 52, 246
    prophecies 14, 67, 127, 145, 175, 228, 229,
        273–4, 285
    swearing on 255–6
bishops
    Puritan objections to 14–15, 41, 44, 48,
        60, 108, 224

Puritan proposed reform of 44–5, 118,
    205, 265
Black Bartholomew's Day 206–8, 212,
    218, 227
blasphemy act 148
blasphemy and heresy bill 135–6, 139
Book of Common Prayer
    in 1549 12–13
    in 1552 16
    in 1559 27–8
    in 1650s 150
    abolished 120
    clerical subscription and 43–4, 60, 206
    demons and 260
    Frankfurt church and 19–20
    Massachusetts and 191, 253–6, 262
    New Hampshire and 253
    puritan use of 28, 43, 60, 61, 63, 65,
        206–7
    reforming legislation and 38–9, 44–5,
        205, 223, 226, 266
    in the Restoration 204
Book of Sports 92, 310n4
Booth, George 163
Booth's Rising 163
Boston, Lincolnshire 65–8, 76, 79, 86
Boston, Mass. 85, 107, 165, 171, 173, 234,
    244, 251, 282
    Dominion of New England and 254–6,
        255, 256, 261–2
    Quakers and 178, 181–2, 184, 185,
        186, 281
Boston First Church 85, 90, 102–8, 168,
    177, 178–9, 183–4, 189, 237–8, 254
Boston Second Church 179–82, 283
Boston Third Church 237
Bowes, Isabella 61–2, 64
Bownde, Nicholas 53–4
Boyle, Robert 260
Bradford, William 62, 72–3, 169–70,
    173, 191
Bradstreet, Anne 2
Bradstreet, Simon 190, 234–5, 282, 284
Brattle, Thomas 287
Breedon, Thomas 235
Brend, William 184
Brewster, William 62, 72
Bridge, William 214
Brightman, Thomas 67
Britten, James 167
Brocklesby, Edward 28
Brown, Robert 46
Brownists 46
Bullinger Heinrich 13

Bunyan, John 2, 147–8, 150–1, 156,
    214–17
    *The Pilgrim's Progress from This World, to*
    *That Which Is to Come* 214–16
Burroughs, George 282, 286
Burroughs, Jeremiah 129
Burton, Henry 100–1

Cain (biblical) 14
Calvin, John 2, 21–4, 98
Calvinism 2, 23, 73–5, 207, 216, 269–72,
    274, 293
    *see also* predestination
Cambridge Platform 175–9, 187
Cambridge University 17, 30, 40, 66, 67, 73,
    218, 227, 267
Campion, Edmund 42
card playing 64, 87
Carleton, George 30–1, 33–4
Cartwright, Thomas 40–1, 43, 48
Caryl, Joseph 134
Catholicism
    Charles II's reign and 205, 216–17, 223–6
    Edward VI's reign and 11–12
    Elizabeth I's reign and 42
    Ireland 116
    James I's reign and 74
    James II's reign and 229–30
    Mary I's reign and 17
Cecil, William 27
Chaderton, Laurence 50
charity, judgment of 88–9
Charles I 74–7, 88, 97, 100–1, 104, 157, 164,
    165, 171, 213
    Civil War and 116–17 130, 133, 137–9
    counter-reformation of 91–3, 111–13
    execution of 139–40, 144
    puritanism and 77, 81, 141
    religion of 75
Charles II 144, 163–4, 191, 203–4, 207, 210,
    212, 219–20, 233
    Catholicism and 205, 216–17, 223, 224,
    229
    Exclusion Crisis and 224–8
    Massachusetts and 189–91, 233–5, 251–3,
    256
    Presbyterians and 141–2, 205
    religious toleration and 164, 205–6, 217,
    223
Charles V 20
Charles IX 39
chastity 91–2
Chauncy, Isaac 275–6
Chelmsford, Mass. 187–9, 191

Child, Robert 173
    petition 174
children
    bewitched 257–61
    Congregationalist baptism of 86, 186–9,
    191, 236, 249
    Congregational church membership of
    186–9
    Congregational covenant renewal and
    248–9
    Congregational discipline and 186–8
    education of, in New England 166, 169,
    242
Christian warfare 56–7
Christmas 78, 160, 254
Christmas riots 138
Church of England
    Arminianism 73, 76, 100, 215–16,
    269–71, 274, 279
    ceremonialism 70, 74, 94, 204
    Congregationalists and 85–6, 214, 272
    continental Reformed churches and 73,
    308n11
    Convocation 60, 266–7
    Elizabeth I's reign 37–49
    fasts 35
    James I reign 59–60
    James II reign 230
    predestination and 23, 73, 215, 269
    Presbyterianism in 39–41, 45–9, 131–5,
    212, 266–7, 271–2
    reform of, in 1640s, 117–20, 127–8,
    131–5, 139–40, 145
    *see also* nonconformity; puritanism,
    puritans; Presbyterianism
Church of Ireland 66, 111
Church of Scotland 20, 25, 111, 120, 142
Civil War 116–17, 130–1, 133, 142,
    205
Clarendon Code 210
Clarke, John 181
Clarke, Katherine 57–8
Clarke, Samuel 57–8
Clarkson, Lawrence 136
Cleeve Abbey 9
Cokayn, George 125
Cole, Thomas 275, 277
Commission for Regulating Colonies 96
communion tables 12, 94
comprehension 216, 226, 231, 266
Congregationalism, general
    origins of 47, 62–3
    puritan criticisms of 86, 97, 99–100, 119,
    121–5, 128, 219

Congregationalism, Congregationalists,
  American
  admission requirements 89–90, 109,
    170–1, 197–8, 242
  Anglicans and 255–6, 262, 279
  baptismal tensions and 87, 122, 176,
    186–9, 191–2, 236–40, 249
  beginnings of 85–86, 99
  Bermuda and 172–5, 323n21
  Cambridge Platform 175–9
  Charles II and 205, 219–20
  covenant renewal 247–50
  defined 293
  large 191, 236–40, 249–50
  lay preachers and 134, 148–51
  Lord's Supper, participation in 86, 109,
    122, 154–6, 163, 186–8, 222–3, 246,
    250, 253
  ministers' powers in 87, 249
  ordination in 99, 182, 227, 246
  Native American 198–9, 246, 247
  Presbyterianism and 176, 177, 240
  Providence Island and 102
  Quakers and 150, 182–6, 226, 240, 281
  religious toleration and 172–4, 234, 240,
    249, 280–1, 291–2
  strict 236–9, 240, 249–50
  synods of 175–7, 191–2, 236
  women and 126–7, 147–8, 151–9,
Congregationalism, Congregationalists,
  England
  in 1670s 218–20, 224, 226–7
  admission requirements 127, 148, 152
  Bedford, Bedfordshire, in 146–51
  church membership figures 213–14, 250,
    279
  Exeter, Devon, in 151–9
  expansion of 111, 119, 145
  indulgence (toleration) for 216, 226
  lay preachers and 134
  Lord's Supper, participation in 122,
    154–6, 163, 222–3
  Presbyterianism and 119–24, 127–9,
    132–4, 140–1, 143, 150–9, 161–3,
    204–5, 222–4, 268–9, 272–9
  Quakers and 149–51, 162, 240
  religious toleration and 121–4, 146–7,
    226, 239, 279
  Savoy Declaration 161
  Westminster Assembly and 120–2, 124,
    127–9
  see also Independency, Independents
Connecticut
  baptism 240,

Charles II 233
  education 168–9
  founding 109
  government 165–6
  laws 166–8, 170–1
  Quakers 183
  reformation 170–1
  religious pluralism 240
  witchcraft 290
consistory 18, 21, 32
Conventicle Act (1664) 209
Conventicle Act (1670) 216
Convention Parliament 164
conversion 54–5, 89, 114, 123, 148, 150, 195,
    197, 221–2
conversion narratives 89–90, 109, 127, 148
    170–1, 197–8, 242
Convocation 60, 266–7
Cooke, Briget 2
Cope, Anthony 50, 54, 60–1
Copeland, John 183
Cotton, Elizabeth 67, 87, 104
Cotton, John
  biblical prophecies and 67, 90, 175
  in England 65–8, 76, 79
  immigration of 85–7
  in Massachusetts 90, 102–3, 104–10, 142,
    173, 175, 178, 180, 183, 187
  monarchy and 89
Cotton, John, Jr. 248
Cotton, Seaborn 87, 253
Court of High Commission 44, 115
Covenant of Grace 54, 57, 105–6, 270, 293
Covenant of Works 54, 105–7, 123, 270, 293
covenant renewal 247–50
Craddock, Matthew 76
Crane, Elizabeth 48
Cranfield, Lionel 253
Cranmer, Thomas 15–16
Crisp, Samuel 268–9, 272
Crisp, Tobias 122–3, 124–5, 268–9, 272
Cromwell, Oliver 142–5, 147, 149, 153–4,
    156–7, 160–2, 175, 208, 224, 265, 266
  as Antichrist 156
  army prayer meeting and 138–9
  immigration to New England and 102
  religion of 130–1, 153–4
  religious toleration and 130–1, 147
Cromwell, Richard 161–2
Cushman, Thomas 248

dame schools 169
dancing 51, 54, 92, 160, 166, 204
Danforth, Thomas 284

Danvers, John 54
Davenport, John 109, 170–1, 236–8, 236–9
Declaration of Breda 164
Declaration of Indulgence (1672) 217,
    218–20, 223
Declaration of Indulgence (1687) 230–1
Dedham conference 43–4, 48
devil 2, 56, 58, 96, 158, 176, 194, 209, 260,
    286
    and Catholic Church 13–14, 21, 286
    learned culture and 260–1
    Native Americans and 194, 196, 280
    possession by 64–65, 78, 96
    sighting of 158, 196, 220
    as tempter 96, 244
    witchcraft and 257–60, 283–90
Devonshire Association 155
Directory for Public Worship 120
Disborough, Mercy 290
discipline, church
    in Bermuda 78
    Church of England and 3, 16, 29, 45, 119,
        205
    Congregationalist 98, 122, 187–8, 219,
        242
    Frankfurt church and 18–19
    in Geneva 21
    Millennial church and 67
    Presbyterian 39, 42 46, 222
    Westminster Assembly and 132–3
divorce 16, 167, 194
Dod, John 50–61, 63–4, 68, 73, 76, 80, 99,
    109–11
Dorcas 168
Dorchester, England 68–70
Dorchester church, Mass. 168
Dorchester Company 69, 76
drinking, 88, 160, 166, 256
Dryden, Erasmus 63
Dudley, Joseph 289
Dudley, Thomas 103
Dyer, Mary 183, 185–6
Dyke, Jeremiah 71

Easty, Mary 287–8
education
    of children 69, 166, 169
    for ministers 168–9
    religious 70, 153, 166, 168–9, 242
Edward VI 11, 14, 17, 27
Edwardian Reformation 13–17
Edwards, Jonathan
    A Treatise Concerning Religious
        Affections 108

Ejectors 154
elders
    Congregational 47, 103, 104, 125, 157,
        176, 179, 242
    Presbyterian 18–19, 39–40, 134–5, 140
Eleutheria 174–5
Eliot, John 194–7, 199, 246
Eliot Bibles 243–6
Elizabeth I 17, 21, 26, 30, 36, 48, 59, 135, 228
    puritanism and 24, 28, 37, 38, 41, 43–5,
        48, 74, 141
    religion of 27–8, 39, 41–2
Emmanuel College 50, 65
Endicott, John 190
Engagement oath 141
episcopacy 40, 294
Esau (biblical) 129
Essex, earl of (Robert Devereux) 116–17
Eve (biblical) 54, 166, 176
Exclusion Crisis 252
excommunication 19, 38, 62, 107–8, 158–9,
    188, 214
executions
    for adultery 87, 167–8
    Catholic 42, 150
    Quaker 185–6, 190
    separatist 48
    for treason 42, 114–15, 140–1, 143
    for witchcraft 182, 259, 285–7, 289–90
Exeter, Devon 151–9
exorcisms 64–5

Fairfax, Thomas 130–2
Family of Love, Familism 95, 99, 127,
    311n13
    New England and 99, 103–8, 127
fasting 24, 43, 59–60, 66, 78, 88, 97, 117, 119,
    135, 140, 142, 173, 175, 186, 220, 227,
    247, 258–9, 280
    Church of England 3, 35
    puritan 34–5
Feake, Christopher 157
Feoffees for Impropriations 93
Field, John 39–40, 42–3, 45–6
    An Admonition to Parliament (Field and
        Wilcox) 39–40, 42
Fiennes, William 73
Fifth Monarchists 156–7, 208
First Bishops' War 111
Fisher, Mary 182
Fiske, John 188, 242
Five Mile Act 210–12, 219, 220
Ford, Thomas 153–5, 159
Forme of Prayers 20, 22

Fourth Commandment 53–4
Fox, George 183
Fox, John 64–5
Foxe, John 21
  *Actes and Monuments of these Latter and Perillous Days* 21
Frederick V 73–4

gambling 166
games 54, 64, 92–3, 160, 166
Gardiner, Stephen 10
Geneva Bible 22–4
Geneva church 21–5, 29, 32, 40
Gerrish, Joseph 288
Gifford, George 46–7
Gifford, John 146–7
Glover, accused witch 258–60, 282–3
Golding, William 173
Goodman, Christopher 24
Goodwin, John 121, 257–8
Goodwin, Martha 257–60
Goodwin, Thomas 162
  *An Apologeticall Narration* (Goodwin et al.) 121, 162
Gouge, William 166
Great Awakening 108
Griffith, John 16
Grindal, Edmund 26–8, 41–2

Haffield, Widow 167
Hale, John 288
Hale, Sarah 288
Halfway Covenant 192
Hampton Court conference 59–60
Hannit, Japeth 247
Harrington, John 56
Harvard College 169, 176, 180, 241, 253, 261, 266, 291
Hathorne, William 234
Heads of Agreement 273
Henrietta Maria of France 92
Henry, Phillip 211
Henry VIII 9–10, 11, 16
heresy 17, 95, 99, 103–9, 118, 122, 135, 139, 147–8, 177, 178, 180
  definition of 294
Herrick, Mary 287–8
Herring, Julines 93, 96, 99–100
heterodoxy, defined 294
Heylin, Rowland 93
Heywood, Oliver 218, 220–3, 226–8
Hibbens, Anne 182
Hickman, Henry 210–11
Holder, Christopher 183

Hooker, Thomas 85, 87, 109, 170–1
Hooper, Anna 13
Hooper, John 9–10, 13–17, 21, 70
Howe, John 265–6, 269, 271, 272, 278
  as author of *Some Considerations of a Certificate Prefixed to Dr. Crisp's Works* 336n14
Howen (accuser of witchcraft) 258
Hughes, George 155
Hull, John 179
Humfrey, John 275
humiliation, day of 247
hunting 52
Hutchinson, Anne 33, 102–10, 123, 183
Hutchinson, Thomas 291
hymns 19

idleness 51, 196
idolatry 11, 14, 27–8, 66, 94, 126, 255–6
Independency, Independents 119, 121, 126, 128, 131–2, 138, 140, 294
  *see also* Congregationalism; sectaries
indulgence 216, 226
Isham, Elizabeth 63–4
Isham, John 63–4
Isham, Judith 63

Jacob (biblical) 129,
James II and VII 229–31, 233, 254, 256–7, 265–6
  Catholicism and 223, 261
  Exclusion Crisis and 225–8, 252
  Puritans and 230–1
James VI and I 91
  Calvinism and 73–5
  Presbyterianism and 59–60
  puritanism and 23–4, 60, 62–3, 66, 68, 71, 141
Jeremiah (biblical), 248
Job (biblical) 257
John the Baptist 28
Jollie, Thomas 218–19, 218–20, 224, 227, 255
Jollie, Timothy 227
Jurdain, Ignatius 151–2
justice of the peace, duties of 30
justification 55
  definition 294
  Richard Baxter and 270
  Tobias Crisp and 123
  Daniel Williams and 274–5

Keith, George 281
kidnapping 167–8, 244–5

King James Bible 23–4, 60
King Philip's War 243–8
King William's War 281
Knightley family 68
Knox, John 18–22, 24–6, 29
　　*The First Blast of the Trumpet Against the*
　　　*Monstrous Regiment of Women* 24

Lambe, Thomas 136
Lancaster, Mass. 241–4
Laud, William 81, 86, 91, 93–4, 96, 100–2,
　　104, 111–13, 115–16, 171, 207
Lee, John 167
Lenthall, Robert 110
Letham, Mary 167
Levellers, Levellerism 136–7
Leverett, John 175, 236, 239, 251
Leverett, Thomas 65
liberty of conscience 126, 172–4, 255, 281
Lincoln, earl of (Theophilus Clinton) 76
Locke, Anne 21–2, 26
Lockyer, Nicholas 121, 124–5
Long Parliament 163–4
Lord's Prayer 258
Lord's Supper
　　access in Church of England to 69, 119
　　in Bermuda 309n27
　　Christ's presence at 10, 12
　　comprehension bill and 226
　　Congregationalists and 86, 109–10, 122,
　　　154, 156, 163, 186, 222–3, 250
　　kneeling during, opposition to 13–14, 50,
　　　61, 95, 116, 211
　　Lutherans and 10
　　Native Americans and 199, 246
　　New Hampshire conflict over 253–4
　　office holding requirement 267
　　Presbyterians and 132, 134–5, 140, 152–6,
　　　161, 163, 211–12, 221–3, 250
　　Satanic version of 282
Louis XIV 216, 223, 228
Love, Christopher 114–19, 126–8, 130–2,
　　135, 137, 140–4, 152
Love, Mary 142–3
Luther, Martin 10
Lutherans 10–11, 59

Maine 109, 251–2, 280–1
Mall, Thomas 155
Marbury, Francis 33
Marley, John 116
Marprelate, Martin 48
marriage 51, 63, 166–7, 194, 250, 254
Marshall, Stephen 122

Martindale, Adam 129
martyrdom 24, 143, 186
Marvell, Andrew 224–5
　　*An Account of the Growth of Popery and*
　　　*Arbitrary Government in England* 225
Mary, mother of Jesus 9, 11, 27–8
Mary I 17–18, 24, 28–9, 38, 44
Mary II 231, 265
Maryland 172
Mary of Modena 256
Massachusett (language) 195, 198
Massachusetts, colony
　　Edmund Andros and 255–7, 260–1
　　Anglicans in 191, 234, 254–7, 262
　　Baptists in 176, 239–40
　　beginnings of 76–81, 85–90
　　and Bermuda 173–5
　　education in 168–9
　　government of 88, 165–6
　　laws of 166–9
　　provisional government of 261–2, 280–1
　　Quakers in 182–6, 240, 281
　　royal charters of 76, 96–8, 267, 280
　　and Virginia 171–2
　　William II 262
　　witchcraft in 182, 257–61, 281–92
Massachusetts Bay Company 76–80, 88
　　seal 195
Massachusetts General Court 88–9, 175–7,
　　233, 237–8, 291–2
　　Charles II and 190–2, 233–7, 251–3, 256
　　Edward Randolph and 251–2
　　religious dissenters and 97–9, 103, 105,
　　　110, 122, 173–6, 180–1, 183–6, 190–1,
　　　234, 239–40
　　town settlement and 241
Massasoit 72
Mather, Cotton 258–62, 271–2, 281, 283–8
Mather, Increase 254–6, 258, 265–9, 271–2,
　　275, 280–4, 288
Mather, Maria 280
Mather, Nathaniel 269, 273, 276–8
Mather, Richard 188–9
Mather, Samuel 180, 265
maypoles 54, 160, 204, 256
Mead, Matthew 273–4
melancholy 56
Metacomet (King Philip) 243–9
millennialism 67, 90, 110–11, 126, 294,
　　315n36
Miller, Perry 80–1
Milton, John, 147
ministers, New England 85, 180, 207
　　education 169–70 179, 181–2

maintenance of 169–170, 181–2, 241, 255, 291
Native American 247
second generation, 241–2
ministers, non-puritan 28–9, 60–5, 65–6, 68–9
ministers, puritan, England
  attempts to purge Church of England of 43–4, 60–1, 205–7, 209–10, 306n4
  conforming 60–1, 68–70
  education 55, 65–7, 73, 121, 210, 218, 227
  see also nonconformity
Minot, John 188–9
Minot, Lydia 188–9
Minot, Martha 189
missionaries 199
monarchy
  abolished 140–1
  power of, and puritans 40, 44, 45, 48, 60, 76, 89, 100, 108, 117, 225, 228, 231
  women in the 24
monasteries 9–10
Monck, George 163
Monmouth, duke of (James Scott) 229–30
Monmouth's Rebellion 254
Moodey, Joshua 253–4
Morton, Charles 261
Morton, Thomas 75
Moses (biblical) 51
murder 94–6, 123, 167

Nashaways 241
Nataôus 198
Natick 197–9, 245
Native Americans 72, 170, 193, 243,
  Martha's Vineyard Christianity 246–7
  population 243, 246, 247
  Praying Indians 194–9, 243–6
  war with 170, 243–8, 261, 280–1
navigation acts 251, 257
Neonomian Controversy 274–8
Netherlands 62–3, 71–2, 111
Newbury church, Mass. 176
New England
  declension 236, 248
  education 168–9
  governments 165–6, 169
  legal reforms 165–8
  maintenance of ministers 169–70
New England Company 76, 196, 246–7
New Hampshire 105, 109, 251–3
New Haven (colony)
  decline 236

education 168–9
founding 109
government 165–6, 170
laws 166–8 170
Quakers and 183
reformation 170
New Haven (town) church 170
New Model Army 130–2, 137–9, 174
Newton, George 203
New York 233
Nine Years' War 281
Noah (biblical) 166
Nominated Assembly 156–7
Nonantum 193–7
nonconformity
  clerical 13–15, 25–30, 35, 40–1, 43, 45, 60, 62–8, 71, 73, 78, 93, 100, 206–7, 216, 226, 231, 266
  lay 61, 64, 86, 109, 146, 210–11
Northampton, Northamptonshire 30–3, 36–7
Norton, John 178–86, 189–92, 237, 281
Notamun 199
Nova Scotia 185
Nye, Philip 162, 214

Oakes, Thomas 257
Oates, Titus 225
Oliver, Mary 109–10
Orders and Dealings of the Church of Northampton 32–3
Overton, Richard 136
Owen, John 145–7, 161–2
Oxenbridge John 238
Oxford University 9, 17, 151, 210, 227, 267

Pacification of Berwick 111
Parker, Abraham 188
Parker, Matthew 26, 28–30, 38, 41
Parker, Thomas 126–7
Parliament, puritans and
  pre-1640s 38–9, 44–5, 60, 75–7, 111–13
  1640s and 1650s 15–20, 126, 128, 132–4, 137–40, 142, 147, 148, 156–7, 160–4, 172–4, 181
  1660–89 205–6, 209–10, 216, 223–9, 266–7
Parr, Susanna 151–5, 158–9
  Susanna's Apologie against the Elders 158
Parris, Samuel 282
patronage 50
Paul III, pope 9

Paul (apostle) 69
Pawquash 170
Pennington, Isaac 102
Pequot tribe 170
Perkins, William 2, 284, 290
Persons, Robert 42
Petition of Right 76
Philip, King (Metacomet) 243–9
Philpott, John 27
Phips, William 283–4, 289
pilgrims 72
Pius V, pope 38
plague 209–10
plain-style preaching 50
plays 51, 69, 92–3, 160, 166, 204
Plymouth
  Baptists 239
  covenant renewal 247–9
  education 166, 169
  government 165, 169
  laws 166–8
  liberty of conscience bill 173
  maintenance of ministers 170
  Quakers and 183–4, 190
  royal charter 233
  settlement of 72
Plymouth Plantation 62, 72
polygamy 194
popery, defined 294
Popish Plot 225
popularity 41, 45, 74
possession, demonic 64–5, 78
Powell, Michael 179–82
powwows 193, 194
prayer 3, 24, 35, 52, 74, 94, 140, 142, 157,
    175, 246, 258, 94
  women leading 34
Praying Indians 194–9, 245–6
predestination 2, 10, 23, 34, 50, 73–5, 123,
    149–50, 268–71, 279
  double 23, 271, 294
  single 23, 271–2
prelacy, defined 294
Presbyterianism
  Anglicans and 265–7
  bishops and 205, 265
  Charles II and 141–2,
  Charles II reign, during 203–6, 220–3,
    226–7
  church membership figures 213, 279
  comprehension for 216, 226, 231, 265–6
  Congregationalism and 119–24, 127–9,
    132–4, 140–1, 143, 150–9, 161–3,
    204–5, 222–4, 268–9, 272–9

Declaration of Indulgence (1672) 217
Declaration of Indulgence (1687) 223–4
  discipline 18–19
  Elizabethan 39–48
  Frankfurt Church and 18–20
  Glorious Revolution and 232
  governing bodies of 18–19, 21–2, 134–5,
    140
  in James I reign 59–60
  in James II reign 231
  lay elders 134
  lay preaching and 150–1
  Lord's Supper and 132, 134–5, 140, 152,
    155–6, 163, 211–12, 221–3
  in New England 110, 176, 240
  ordination 116, 128, 140, 203, 211–12,
    226–7, 255
  reformed Church of England and 131–5,
    139–40, 145
  repression of 228–9
  revival 118
  Worcester House Declaration and 205
presbytery 18
Preston, John 75, 308n15
Pride, Thomas 139, 140
Pride's Purge 140, 163
Proctor, John 286–7
Proctor, John, Jr. 168
prophesying 30–1, 41–2, 67
proto-puritans 17–25
Providence Island 102
Prynne, William 92, 101
  *Histrio-mastix*, 92
psalm singing 19, 34
purgatory 11
puritanism, puritans
  end of 232, 267–9
  and monarchs 24, 40–1, 44–5, 48, 59–60,
    74, 77, 89, 117, 164, 190, 197, 219,
    223–5, 228, 231
  objections to bishops 14–15, 41, 44, 48,
    60, 108, 224
  proposed reforms of episcopacy 44–5,
    118, 205, 265
  scholarly use of the term 298n4
  culture of 30–1, 33–6, 51–8, 60–1, 63–5,
    95, 103, 106
Pynchon, William 180, 181

Quakers, England 149–51, 153, 159, 160,
    162, 163, 205, 213, 217, 223, 226, 240
Quakers, New England 182–6, 190–2, 254,
    281, 290
Quanapohit, James 244

Randolph, Edward 251–2, 254
Ranters 148, 160
Ratcliffe, Robert 254, 262
Reagan, Ronald 81
Reformed Churches, continental 10–11, 23, 73, 265, 267, 308n11
Rhode Island 99, 109, 112, 124, 126, 181, 183
Richardson, Samuel 124–5
Robinson, John 62–3, 71–2
Robinson, William 185
Rogers, John 2
Rogers, Samuel 102
Rothwell, Richard 64–5
Rowlandson, Joseph 241–5
Rowlandson, Mary White 242–5, 259
Roxbury church 198
Rump Parliament 139, 148, 156–7, 162–3, 180–1
Rye House Plot 229

Sabbath 53–4, 78, 87, 92, 98, 135, 269 256
    laws 160, 166, 291
sachem 193, 194, 195
saints 88–9, 186, 188
Salem, Mass. 97–9
    separatist Congregationalists 85–6
    settlement 76–7
    witchcraft trials 281–2
salvation
    antinomians on 123–4, 268
    Arminians on 73, 216, 271
    Richard Baxter on 269–71
    despair about 55–8, 63
    John Howe on 271–2
    Hutchinson circle on 104
    puritans on 54–5, 215, 272, 277–8
    Quakers on 149
    Daniel Williams on 274–5, 278, 337n25, 337n29
    see also assurance of salvation; conversion; justification; sanctification
Sancroft, William 231
sanctification 295
Sandwich, Plymouth (colony) 183
Sandys, Edwin 40
Satan see devil
Savoy Declaration 161–2
Saye and Sele, viscount (William Fiennes) 75
Sayle William 172, 173, 174
Scott, Katherine 183
Scott, Richard 183
Scotland, Church of 25, 111, 142

Scambler, Edward 31–2
Second Reformation, Netherlands 59
sectaries, sectarianism 126, 128, 131–2, 134, 137, 147–8, 295
Seekers 182–3
separatists 46–8, 62, 71–81, 85–7, 97–100, 110, 169, 210–11, 295
    and Congregationalism 47, 85–6
sermons
    gadding 33
    note-taking at 57, 171, 179, 221, 246
    puritan plain style 34 50
    repetition 34, 93, 105, 196, 243
Seventh Commandment 51–2
Sewall, Samuel 254
sex 51, 78, 160, 166, 194, 196
Shaumauw 241
Shepard, Thomas 103–9, 194–5
    The Parable of the Ten Virgins Opened and Applied 108
Shipley, Nathaniel 188
ship money case 101
Shrewsbury, earl of 62
Shrimpton, Samuel 256
Sibbes, Richard 2
sin
    antinomianism and 104, 123
    and conversion 2–3, 54–5, 122–3, 266–7, 270
    God's punishments for 18, 34, 97, 138, 244
    puritanism and 51–5
Skelton, Samuel 86
slavery 78, 102, 168, 170, 174, 282
Smith, James 168
smoking 87, 166
    see also tobacco, use
Smyth, John 62
Solemn League and Covenant 114–15, 118, 140–3, 164, 203, 206
Somers Islands 78
    see also Bermuda
sports and recreation 51–2, 53–4, 64, 78, 92–3, 160
St. Anne and St. Agnes, Aldergate church 116, 128
St. Antholin church 27
St. Bartholomew's Day Massacre 39
Stephenson, Marmaduke 185
St. Lawrence Jewry church 140
Stone, Mary 128
Stoughton, William 283–6, 290
stranger church 15
Strickland, William 38

Stuckeley, Lewis 152–9
    *Manifest Truth* 158
Studley, Peter 93–4, 96, 100
suicide 56
Sullivan, James 291
Sunday *see* Sabbath
*Susanna's Apologie against the Elders*
    (Parr) 158
swearing 52–3, 88, 160, 255–6
Swiss Reformation 10
Swiss Reformed churches 10–11, 14–15, 29
synod, Mass. 175–7, 191–2, 236

Tallents, Francis 272
*Te Deum* 19–20
Teellinck, Willem 59
Ten Commandments 50–5, 70, 123
theater 51, 92–3, 160, 166, 204
Third Commandment 52–3, 73
Thirty Years' War 74, 106
Throkmorton, Job 47–8
Tichborne, Robert 114–15, 118–21, 124–5,
    129, 136–7, 140, 144
    *A Cluster of Canaan's Grapes*, 125
Timewell, Stephen 229
tithes, defined 295
tobacco, use 97, 195, 244
    *see also* smoking
Toleration Act 266
Toney 174
Tories 227–9, 252, 266
Tory Reaction 228–9
transubstantiation 12
treason 114–15, 117, 143
Tregonwell, John 9
Triers 153–4
Trosse, George 210–12
Truman, Joseph 277
Turner, Thomas 173

United Brethren 273, 275–9
United Colonies of New England 165, 171
Upshall, Nicholas 182–3

Vane, Henry 104–5, 107–9, 191
Vassall, William 173
Venn, John 117, 128
Verney, Mary 134
Vestarian Controversy 29
vestments 11, 13–16, 26–9, 30, 50, 60–1,
    226
Virginia 171–2
Virginia Company 71
visible saints 88–9, 186, 188

Waban 193–9, 243, 245, 245–6
Wales 111
Wallington, Nehemiah 56–7, 119, 124
Wampanoag tribe 72, 243, 247
Warner, John 115, 128
Warwick, earl of (Robert Rich), 73, 75,
    101, 112
Welde, Thomas 88
Wentworth, Peter 38
Westminster Assembly 118, 120–4, 127–9,
    131, 133, 175, 207, 314n22
    Longer and Shorter catechisms 120
Westminster Confession 120, 162, 164
Weymouth church, Mass. 110
Whately, William 61, 68
Wheelwright, John 102, 105, 109, 183
Whigs 225–30, 252, 279
whippings 182, 183–4, 190–1
White, Joan 242
White, John 68–70, 76, 242
White, Mary 242
Whitgift, John 40–1, 43–5, 48, 60
*Whole Book of Psalmes* 19
Wilburn, Perceval 1, 29–33, 41
Wilcox, Thomas 39–40
    *An Admonition to Parliament* (Field and
    Wilcox) 39–40, 42
Willard, John 286–7
Willard, Samuel 261
William III (William of Orange) 231,
    261–2, 265–7, 281
Williams, Daniel 274–8
    *Gospel Truth* 276
Williams, John 66
Williams, Roger 97–9, 103, 108–9, 112,
    126
    *The Bloudy Tenent of Persecution* 126
Wilson, John 110, 189, 237
Winthrop, John 77, 79–81, 86, 88, 110,
    172–3, 176–7
Winthrop, John, Jr. 235
Winthrop, Margaret 79
Wiswall, John 189
witchcraft 182, 257–61, 281–92
women
    activism of 26–7, 62, 64, 103–6, 147–8,
    151–9
    actors 92
    church membership 242, 250
    Congregationalist 147–8
    conversion narratives 109, 127
    critique of, as monarchs 24
    death in childbirth 103
    leading prayer 34, 103

speaking in Congregational churches
127, 152, 154
and witchcraft 257–61, 281–92
Wood, Joseph 221–2
Worcester House Declaration 205
Worcestershire Association 155
Wright, Robert 94

Wrightwick, Henry 210
Wyeth, Nicholas 89

Yelverton, Christopher 38
York House conference 75

Zwingli, Huldrych 10